SUPERMAN BATMAN

# FINEST WORLDS

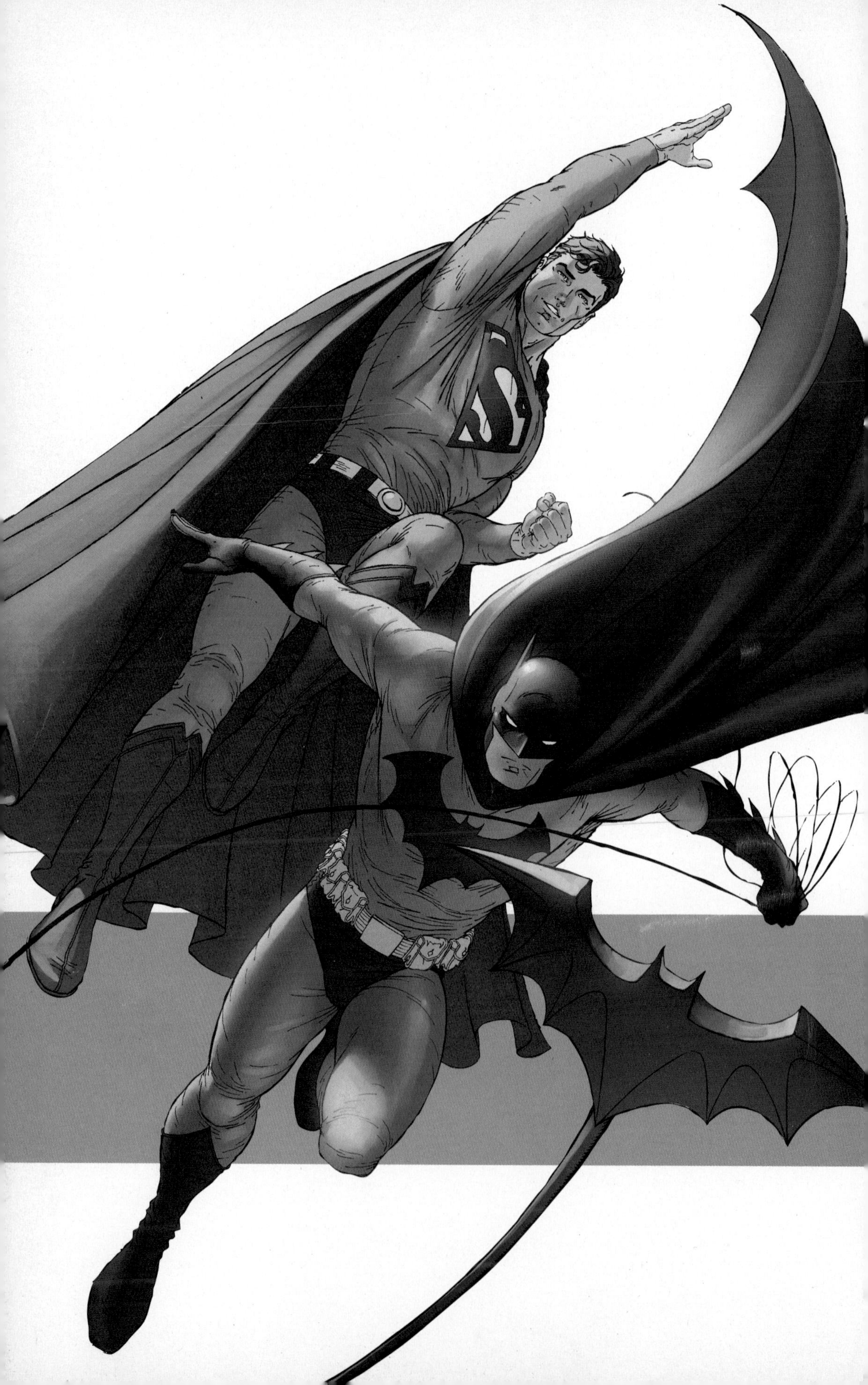

## THE FATHERS

**Michael Green** and **Mike Johnson**
Writers

**Ed Benes** / **Matthew Clark**
**Alan Goldman** / **Ian Churchill**
Pencillers

**Matt "Batt" Banning** / **Norm Rapmund**
**Marlo Alquiza** / **Rob Hunter**
Inkers

**John Rauch**
Colorist

**Ethan Van Sciver** and **Moose Baumann**
Cover

## LIL' LEAGUERS

**Michael Green** and **Mike Johnson**
Writers

**Rafael Albuquerque**
Artist

**Chris Peter**
Colorist

**Ryan Sook**
Covers

## SUPERBAT

**Michael Green** and **Mike Johnson**
Plot

**Mike Johnson**
Dialogue

**Rags Morales**
Penciller

**John Dell** with **Drew Geraci**
**Derek Fridolfs**
Inkers

**Nei Ruffino**
Colorist

**Rags Morales** with **Nei Ruffino**
Covers

All stories lettered by **Rob Leigh**

Batman created by Bob Kane

Superman created by Jerry Siegel and Joe Shuster

SUPERMAN BATMAN
# FINEST WORLDS

DAN DIDIO Senior VP-Executive Editor    EDDIE BERGANZA Editor-original series    ADAM SCHLAGMAN Associate Editor-original series    BOB JOY Editor-collected edition
ROBBIN BROSTERMAN Senior Art Director    PAUL LEVITZ President & Publisher    GEORG BREWER VP-Design & DC Direct Creative    RICHARD BRUNING Senior VP-Creative Director
PATRICK CALDON Executive VP-Finance & Operations    CHRIS CARAMALIS VP-Finance    JOHN CUNNINGHAM VP-Marketing    TERRI CUNNINGHAM VP-Managing Editor
AMY GENKINS Senior VP-Business & Legal Affairs    ALISON GILL VP-Manufacturing    DAVID HYDE VP-Publicity    HANK KANALZ VP-General Manager, WildStorm    JIM LEE Editorial Director-WildStorm
GREGORY NOVECK Senior VP-Creative Affairs    SUE POHJA VP-Book Trade Sales    STEVE ROTTERDAM Senior VP-Sales & Marketing    CHERYL RUBIN Senior VP-Brand Management
ALYSSE SOLL VP-Advertising & Custom Publishing    JEFF TROJAN VP-Business Development, DC Direct    BOB WAYNE VP-Sales

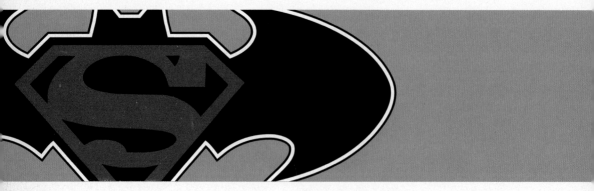

Cover art by ETHAN VAN SCIVER with MOOSE BAUMANN

SUPERMAN/BATMAN: FINEST WORLDS

Published by DC Comics. Cover and compilation Copyright © 2009 DC Comics. All Rights Reserved.

Originally published in single magazine form as SUPERMAN/BATMAN 50-56 Copyright © 2008, 2009 DC Comics. All Rights Reserved. All characters, their distinctive likenesses and related elements featured in this publication are trademarks of DC Comics. The stories, characters and incidents featured in this publication are entirely fictional. DC Comics does not read or accept unsolicited submissions of ideas, stories or artwork.

DC Comics, 1700 Broadway, New York, NY 10019. A Warner Bros. Entertainment Company. Printed in the USA. First Printing.
ISBN: 978-1-4012-2331-1    Softcover ISBN: 978-1-4012-2332-8

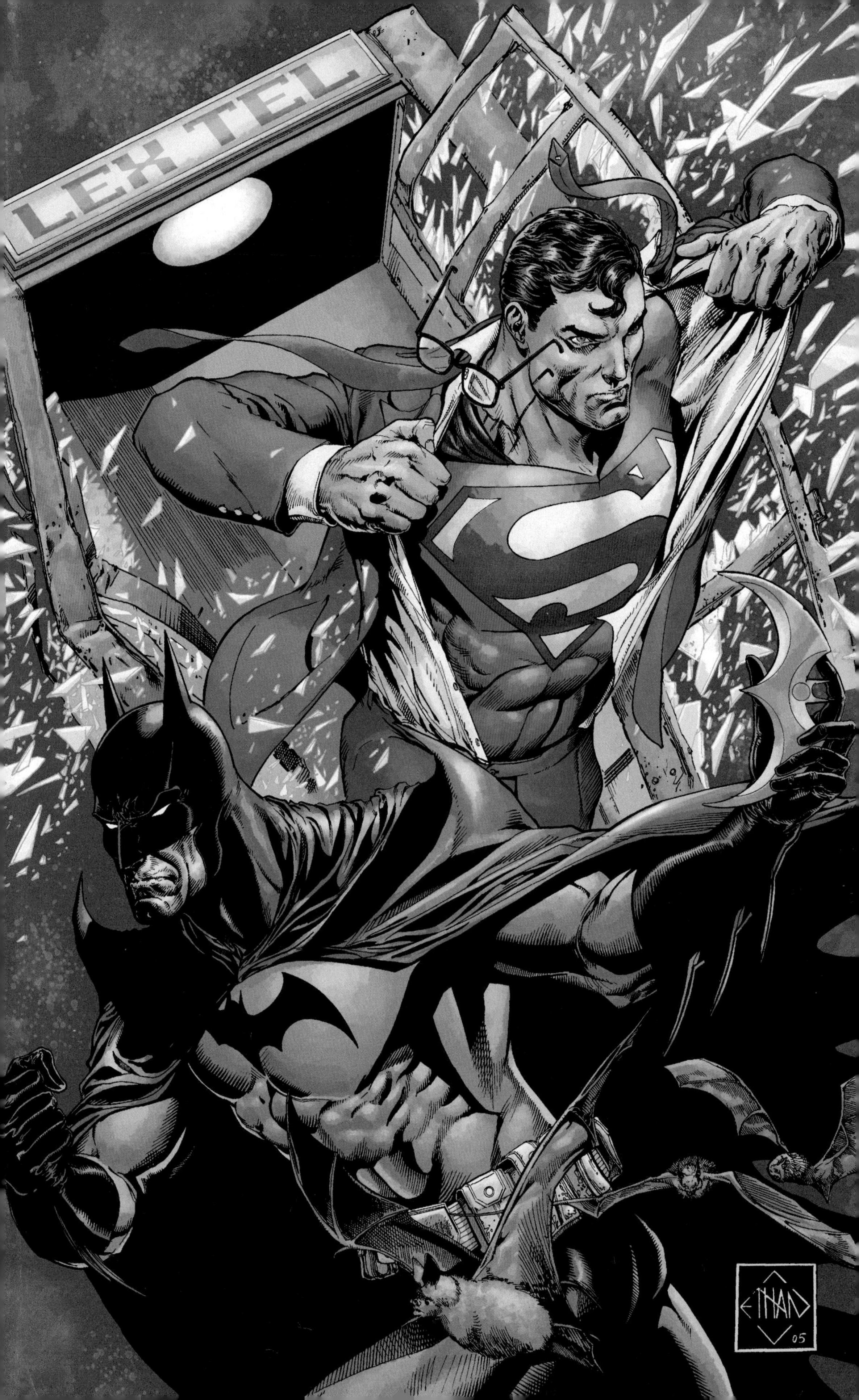
LEX TEL
ETHAN
05

SUPERMAN/BATMAN 50

THE FATHERS

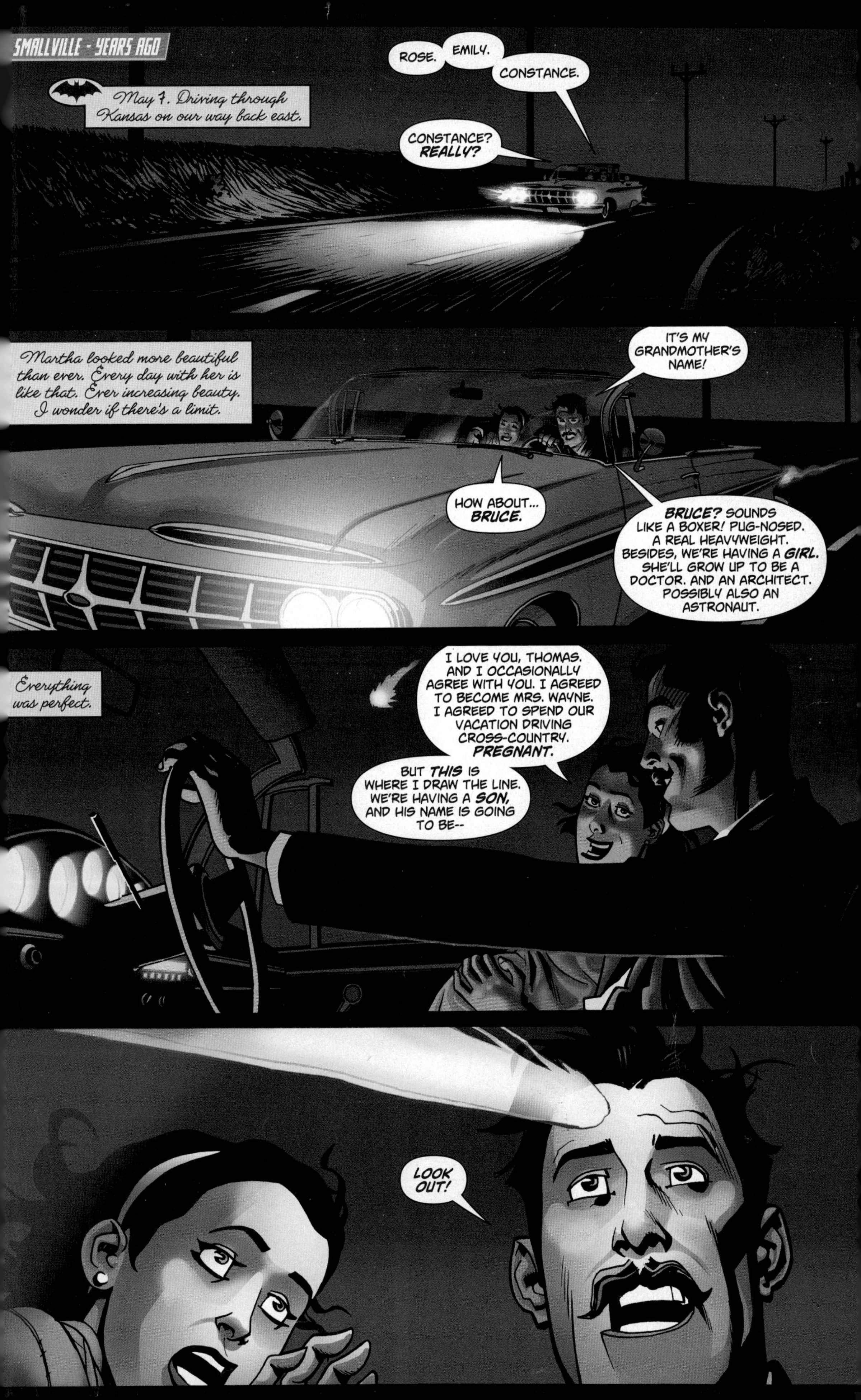
SMALLVILLE - YEARS AGO
May 7. Driving through Kansas on our way back east.
ROSE.
EMILY.
CONSTANCE.
CONSTANCE? REALLY?
Martha looked more beautiful than ever. Every day with her is like that. Ever increasing beauty. I wonder if there's a limit.
IT'S MY GRANDMOTHER'S NAME!
HOW ABOUT... BRUCE.
BRUCE? SOUNDS LIKE A BOXER! PUG-NOSED. A REAL HEAVYWEIGHT. BESIDES, WE'RE HAVING A GIRL. SHE'LL GROW UP TO BE A DOCTOR. AND AN ARCHITECT. POSSIBLY ALSO AN ASTRONAUT.
Everything was perfect.
I LOVE YOU, THOMAS. AND I OCCASIONALLY AGREE WITH YOU. I AGREED TO BECOME MRS. WAYNE. I AGREED TO SPEND OUR VACATION DRIVING CROSS-COUNTRY. PREGNANT.
BUT THIS IS WHERE I DRAW THE LINE. WE'RE HAVING A SON, AND HIS NAME IS GOING TO BE--
LOOK OUT!

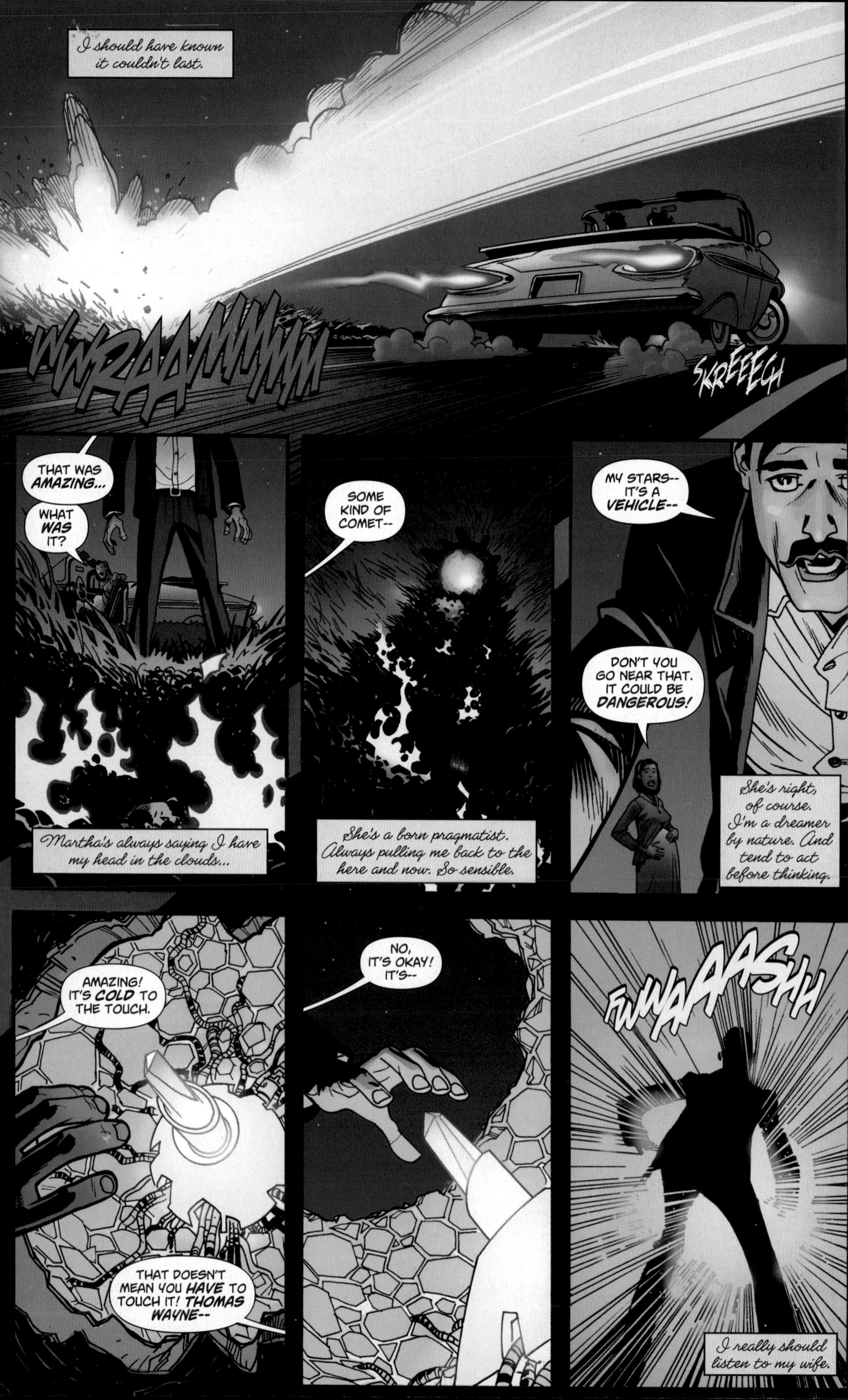

I should have known it couldn't last.
WWRAAMMMMM
SKREEECH
THAT WAS AMAZING...
WHAT WAS IT?
Martha's always saying I have my head in the clouds...
SOME KIND OF COMET--
She's a born pragmatist. Always pulling me back to the here and now. So sensible.
MY STARS-- IT'S A VEHICLE--
DON'T YOU GO NEAR THAT. IT COULD BE DANGEROUS!
She's right, of course. I'm a dreamer by nature. And tend to act before thinking.
AMAZING! IT'S COLD TO THE TOUCH.
THAT DOESN'T MEAN YOU HAVE TO TOUCH IT! THOMAS WAYNE--
NO, IT'S OKAY! IT'S--
FWWAAASHH
I really should listen to my wife.

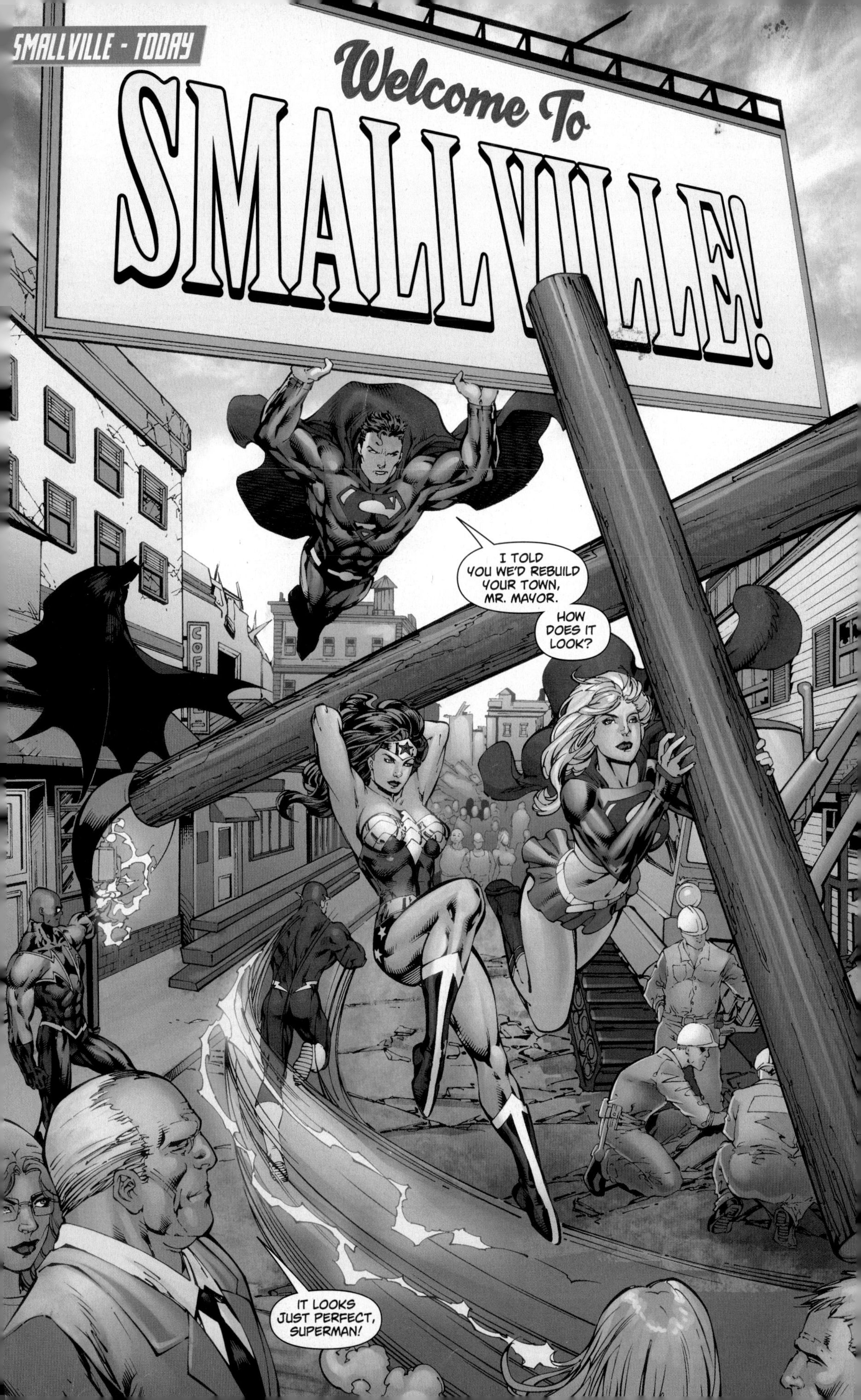
SMALLVILLE - TODAY
Welcome To SMALLVILLE!
I TOLD YOU WE'D REBUILD YOUR TOWN, MR. MAYOR.
HOW DOES IT LOOK?
IT LOOKS JUST PERFECT, SUPERMAN!

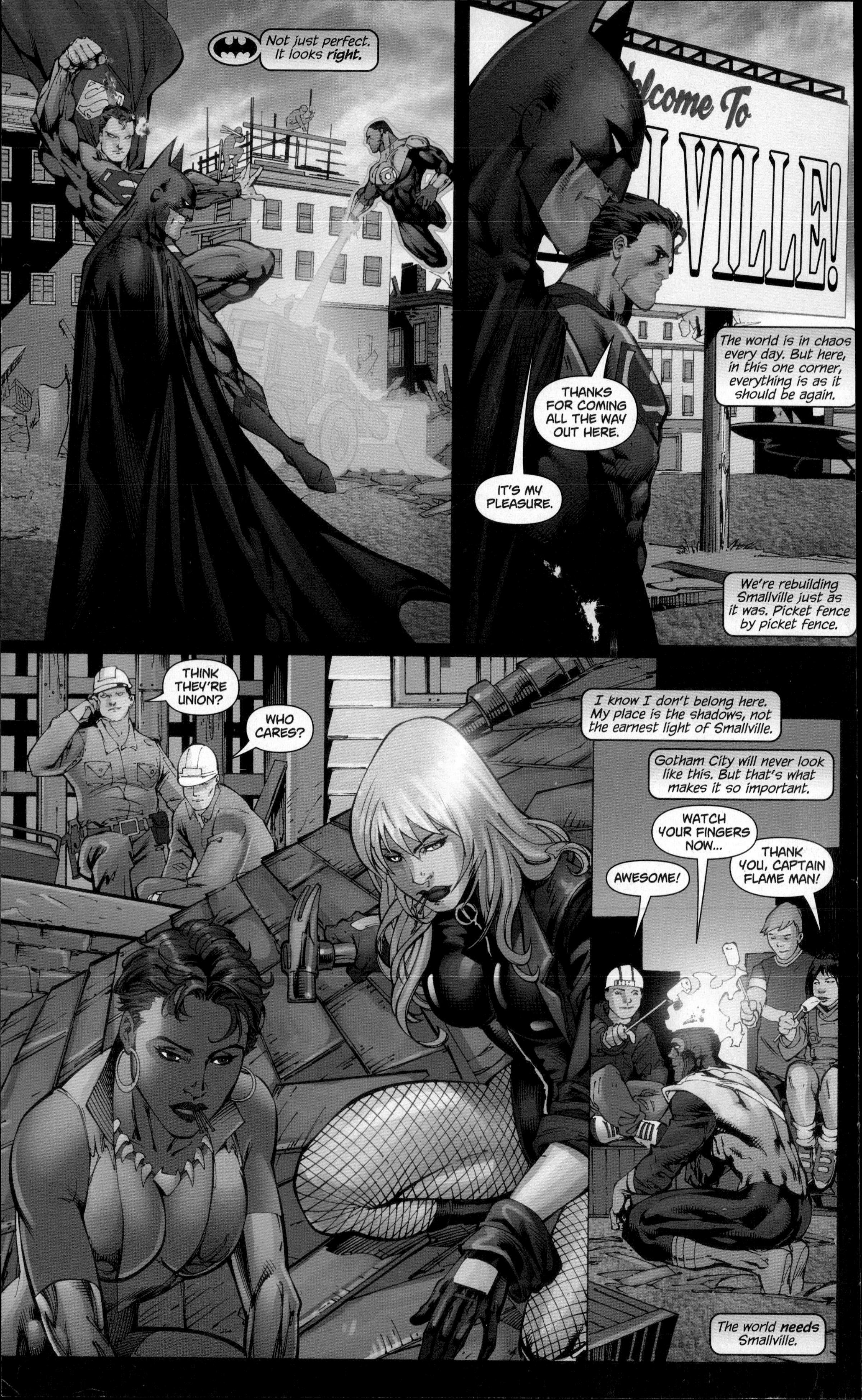
Not just perfect. It looks **right.**
Welcome To
...LLVILLE!
The world is in chaos every day. But here, in this one corner, everything is as it should be again.
THANKS FOR COMING ALL THE WAY OUT HERE.
IT'S MY PLEASURE.
We're rebuilding Smallville just as it was. Picket fence by picket fence.
THINK THEY'RE UNION?
WHO CARES?
I know I don't belong here. My place is the shadows, not the earnest light of Smallville.
Gotham City will never look like this. But that's what makes it so important.
WATCH YOUR FINGERS NOW...
AWESOME!
THANK YOU, CAPTAIN FLAME MAN!
The world **needs** Smallville.

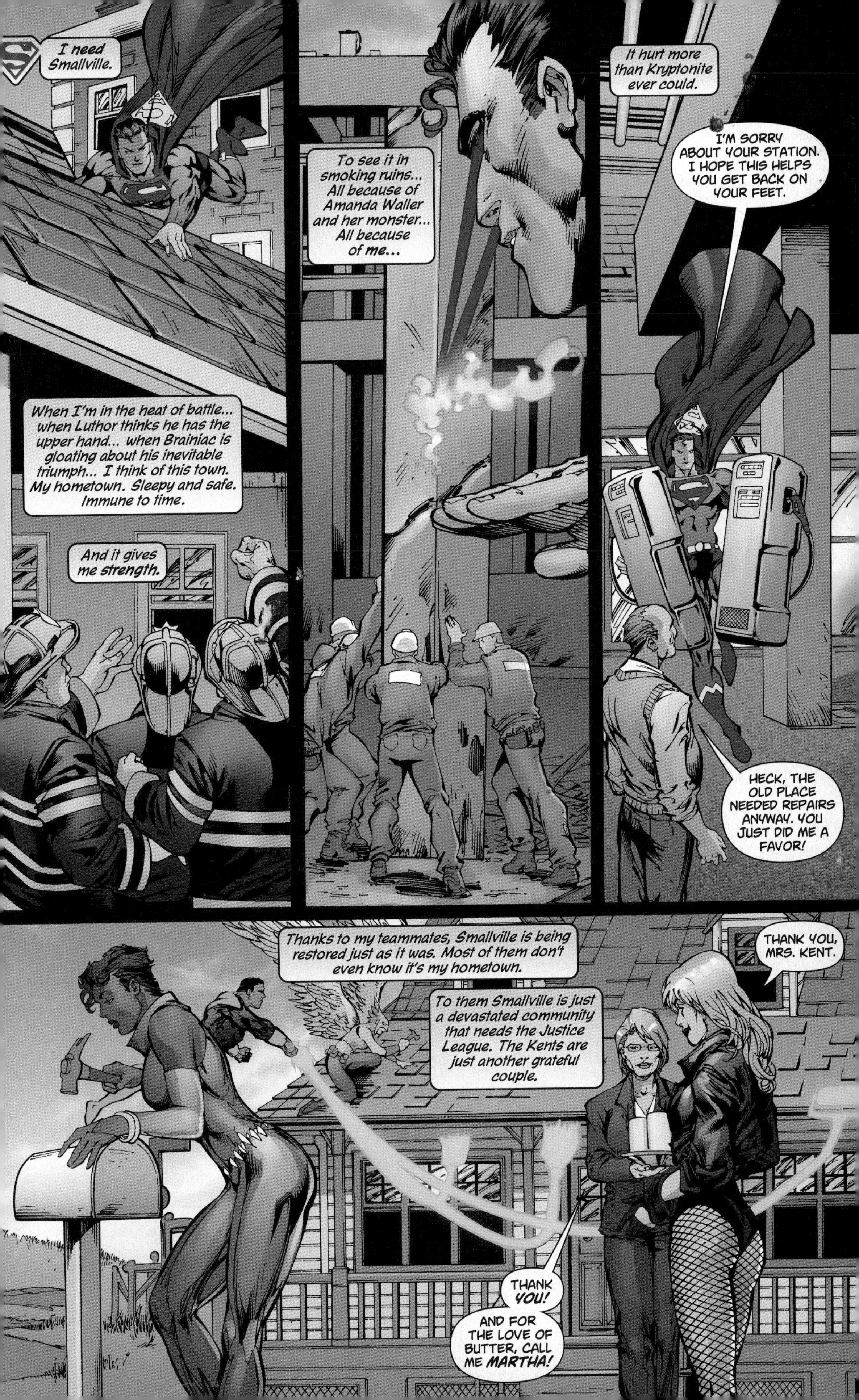
I need Smallville.
When I'm in the heat of battle... when Luthor thinks he has the upper hand... when Brainiac is gloating about his inevitable triumph... I think of this town. My hometown. Sleepy and safe. Immune to time.
And it gives me strength.
To see it in smoking ruins... All because of Amanda Waller and her monster... All because of me...
It hurt more than Kryptonite ever could.
I'M SORRY ABOUT YOUR STATION. I HOPE THIS HELPS YOU GET BACK ON YOUR FEET.
HECK, THE OLD PLACE NEEDED REPAIRS ANYWAY. YOU JUST DID ME A FAVOR!
Thanks to my teammates, Smallville is being restored just as it was. Most of them don't even know it's my hometown.
To them Smallville is just a devastated community that needs the Justice League. The Kents are just another grateful couple.
THANK YOU, MRS. KENT.
THANK YOU! AND FOR THE LOVE OF BUTTER, CALL ME MARTHA!

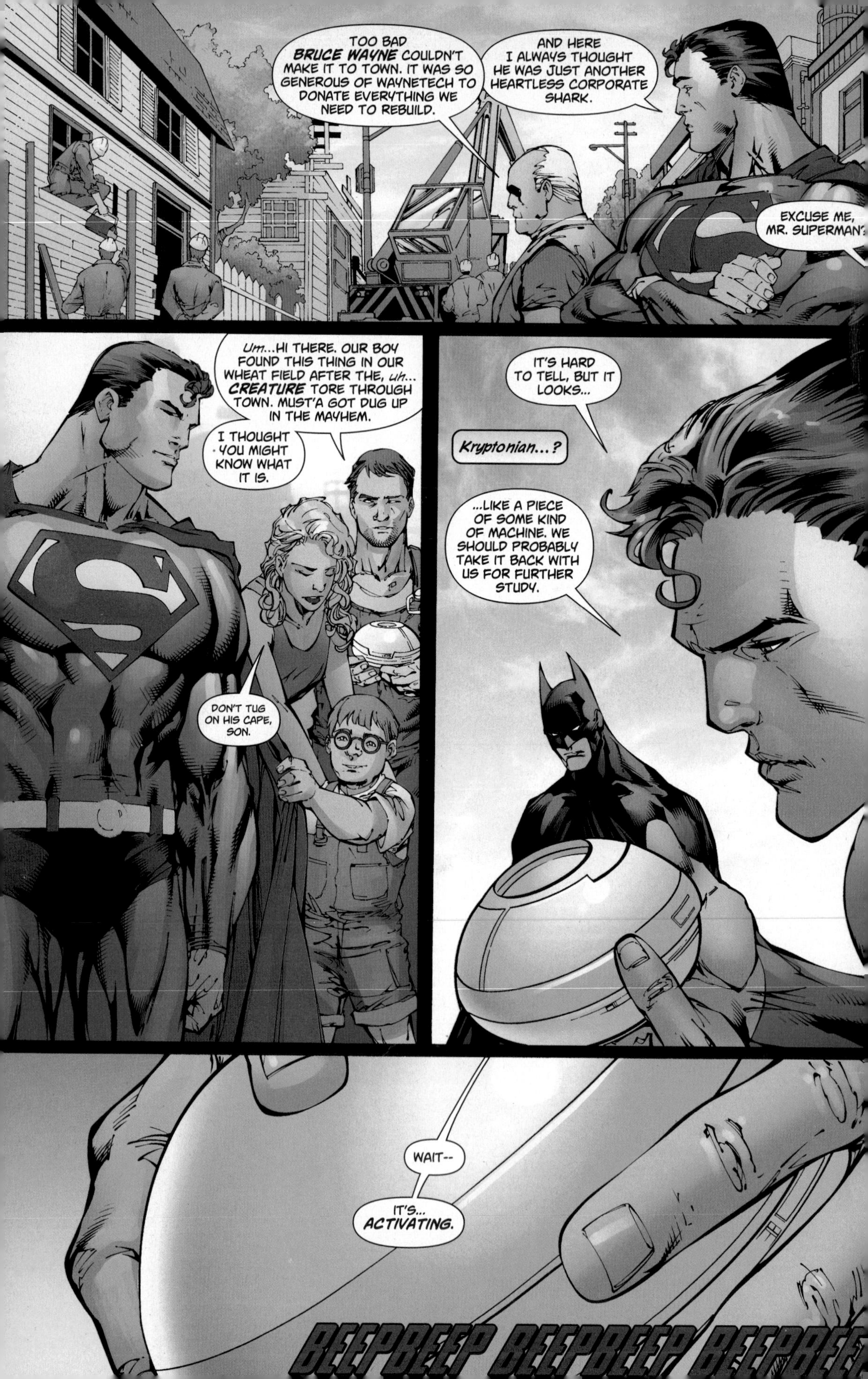

TOO BAD BRUCE WAYNE COULDN'T MAKE IT TO TOWN. IT WAS SO GENEROUS OF WAYNETECH TO DONATE EVERYTHING WE NEED TO REBUILD.
AND HERE I ALWAYS THOUGHT HE WAS JUST ANOTHER HEARTLESS CORPORATE SHARK.
EXCUSE ME, MR. SUPERMAN?
Um...HI THERE. OUR BOY FOUND THIS THING IN OUR WHEAT FIELD AFTER THE, uh... CREATURE TORE THROUGH TOWN. MUST'A GOT DUG UP IN THE MAYHEM.
I THOUGHT YOU MIGHT KNOW WHAT IT IS.
DON'T TUG ON HIS CAPE, SON.
IT'S HARD TO TELL, BUT IT LOOKS...
Kryptonian...?
...LIKE A PIECE OF SOME KIND OF MACHINE. WE SHOULD PROBABLY TAKE IT BACK WITH US FOR FURTHER STUDY.
WAIT--
IT'S... ACTIVATING.
BEEPBEEP BEEPBEEP BEEPBEE

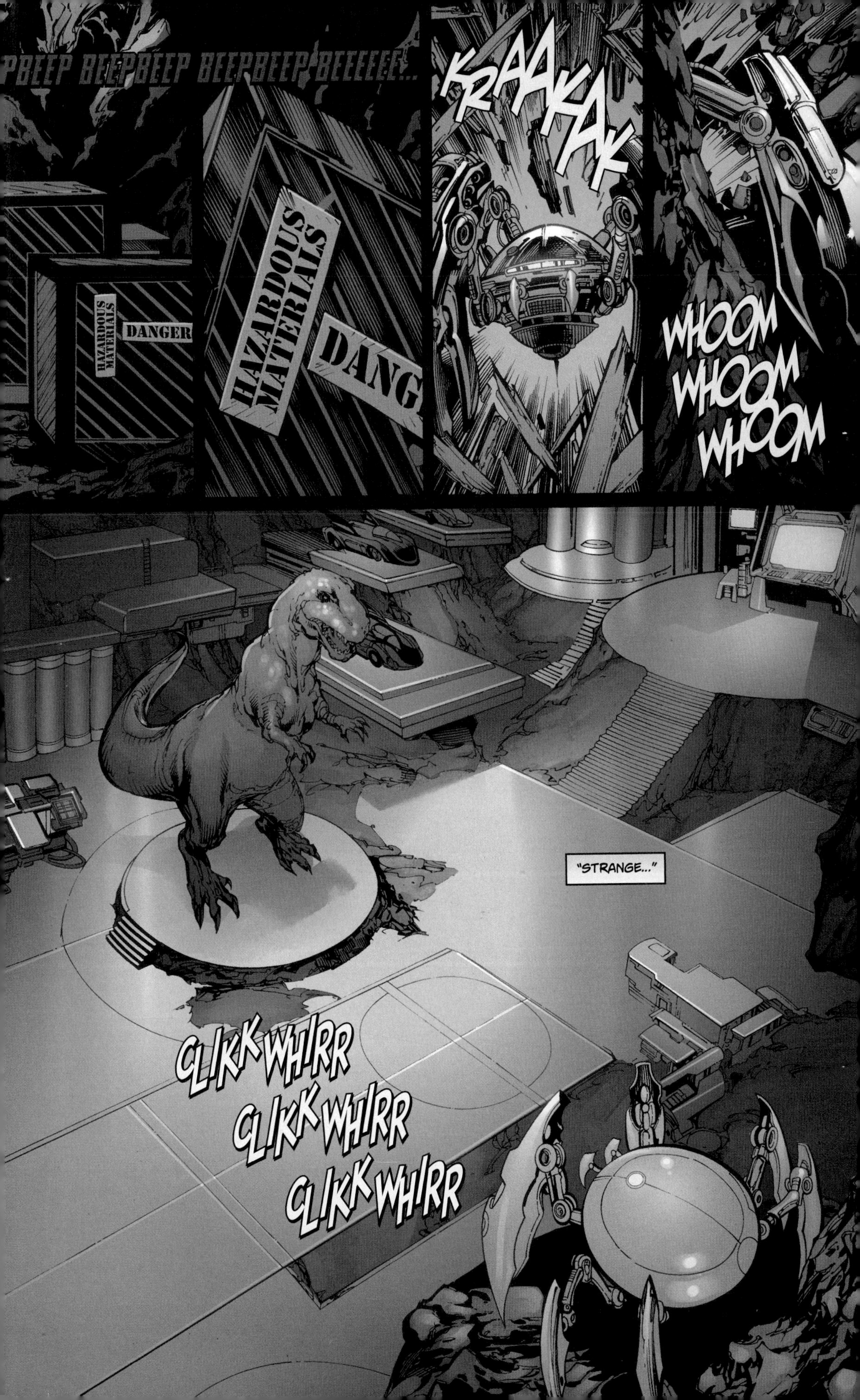
PBEEP BEEPBEEP BEEPBEEP BEEEEEE...
HAZARDOUS MATERIALS
DANGER
HAZARDOUS MATERIALS
DANG
KRAAKAK
WHOOM WHOOM WHOOM
"STRANGE..."
CLIKK WHIRR
CLIKK WHIRR
CLIKK WHIRR

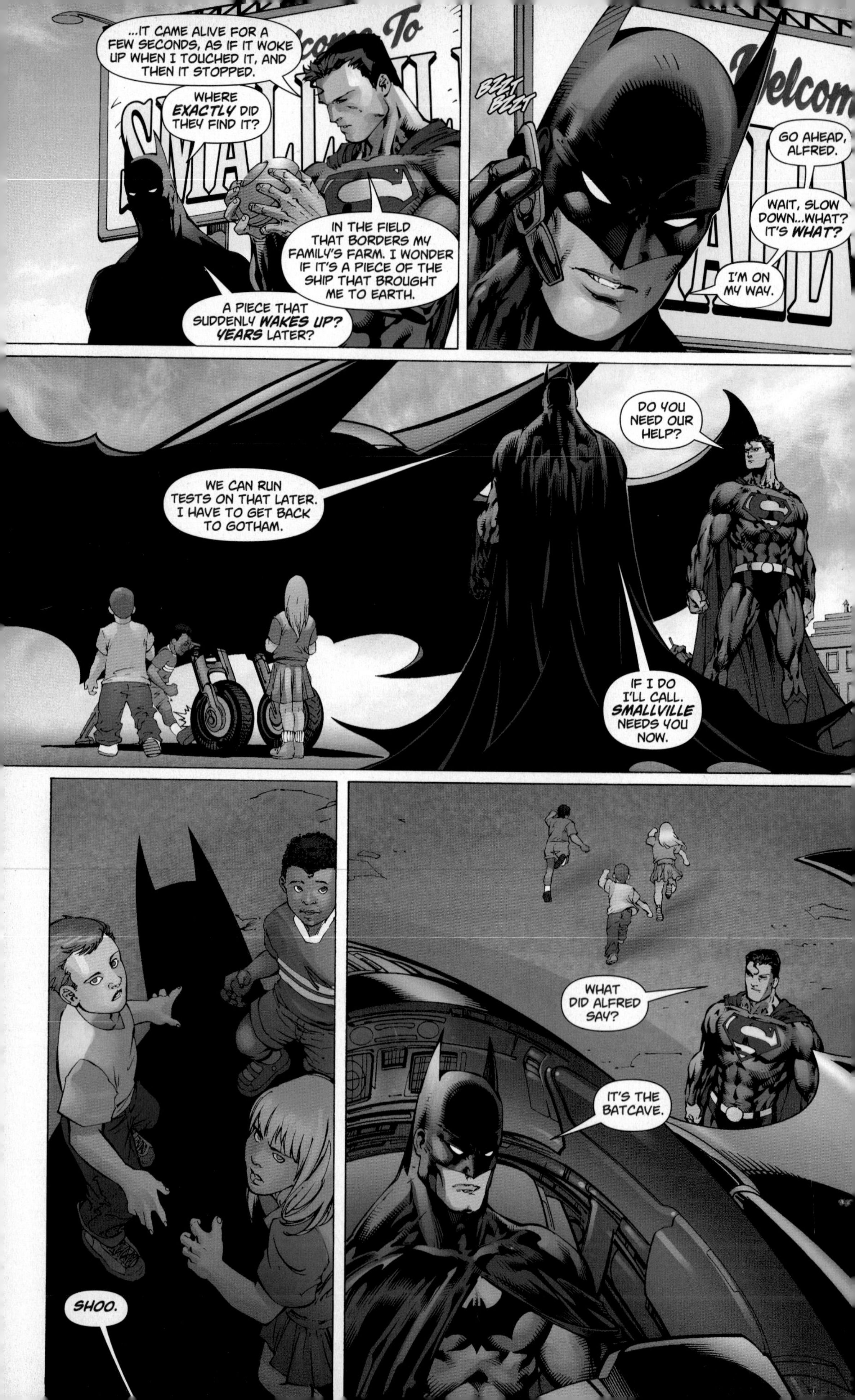
...IT CAME ALIVE FOR A FEW SECONDS, AS IF IT WOKE UP WHEN I TOUCHED IT, AND THEN IT STOPPED.
WHERE EXACTLY DID THEY FIND IT?
IN THE FIELD THAT BORDERS MY FAMILY'S FARM. I WONDER IF IT'S A PIECE OF THE SHIP THAT BROUGHT ME TO EARTH.
A PIECE THAT SUDDENLY WAKES UP? YEARS LATER?
BZZT BZZT
GO AHEAD, ALFRED.
WAIT, SLOW DOWN...WHAT? IT'S WHAT?
I'M ON MY WAY.
DO YOU NEED OUR HELP?
WE CAN RUN TESTS ON THAT LATER. I HAVE TO GET BACK TO GOTHAM.
IF I DO I'LL CALL. SMALLVILLE NEEDS YOU NOW.
SHOO.
WHAT DID ALFRED SAY?
IT'S THE BATCAVE.

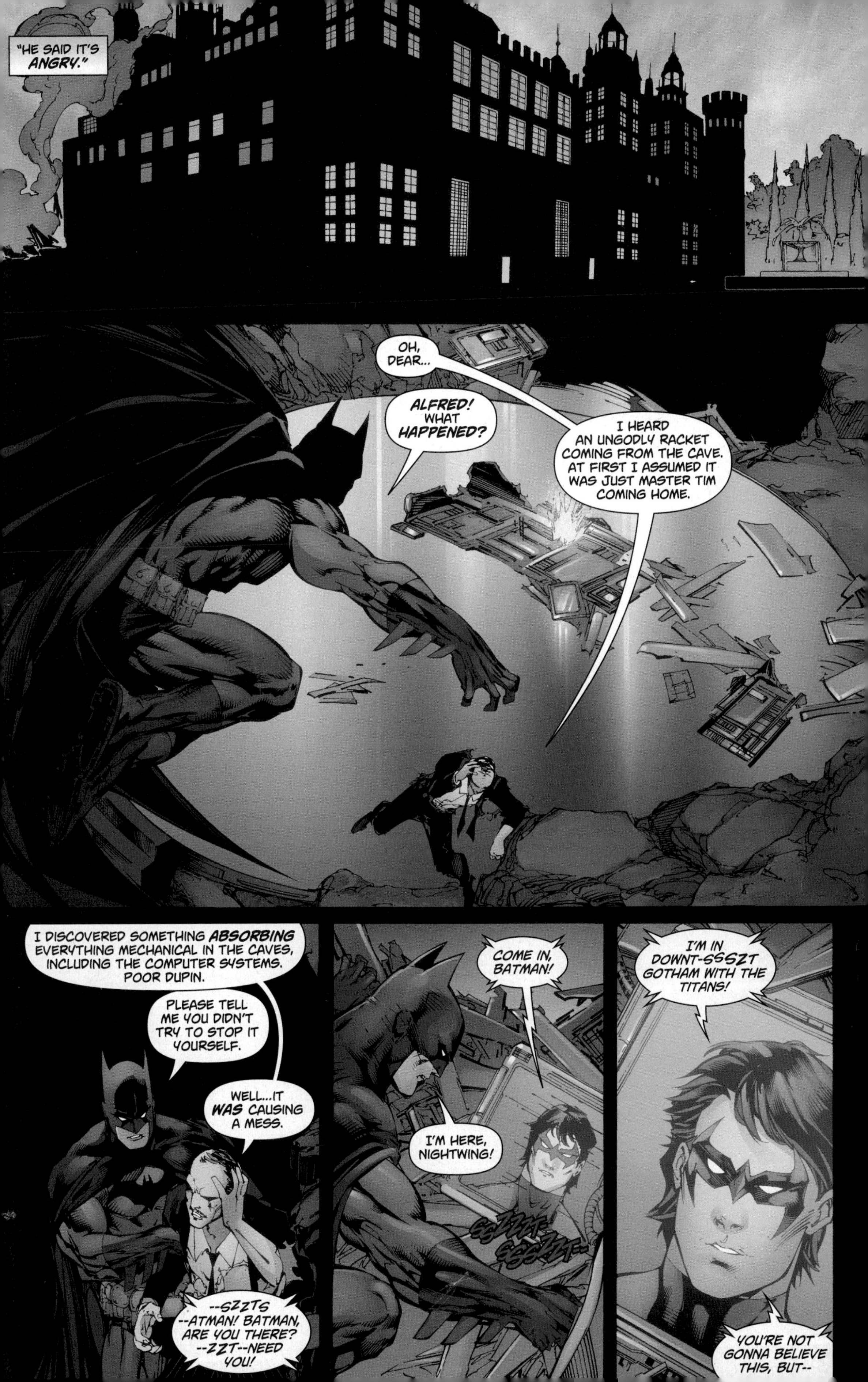
"HE SAID IT'S ANGRY."
OH, DEAR...
ALFRED! WHAT HAPPENED?
I HEARD AN UNGODLY RACKET COMING FROM THE CAVE. AT FIRST I ASSUMED IT WAS JUST MASTER TIM COMING HOME.
I DISCOVERED SOMETHING ABSORBING EVERYTHING MECHANICAL IN THE CAVES, INCLUDING THE COMPUTER SYSTEMS. POOR DUPIN.
PLEASE TELL ME YOU DIDN'T TRY TO STOP IT YOURSELF.
WELL...IT WAS CAUSING A MESS.
--SZZTS --ATMAN! BATMAN, ARE YOU THERE? --ZZT--NEED YOU!
COME IN, BATMAN!
I'M HERE, NIGHTWING!
I'M IN DOWNT-SSSZT GOTHAM WITH THE TITANS!
YOU'RE NOT GONNA BELIEVE THIS, BUT--

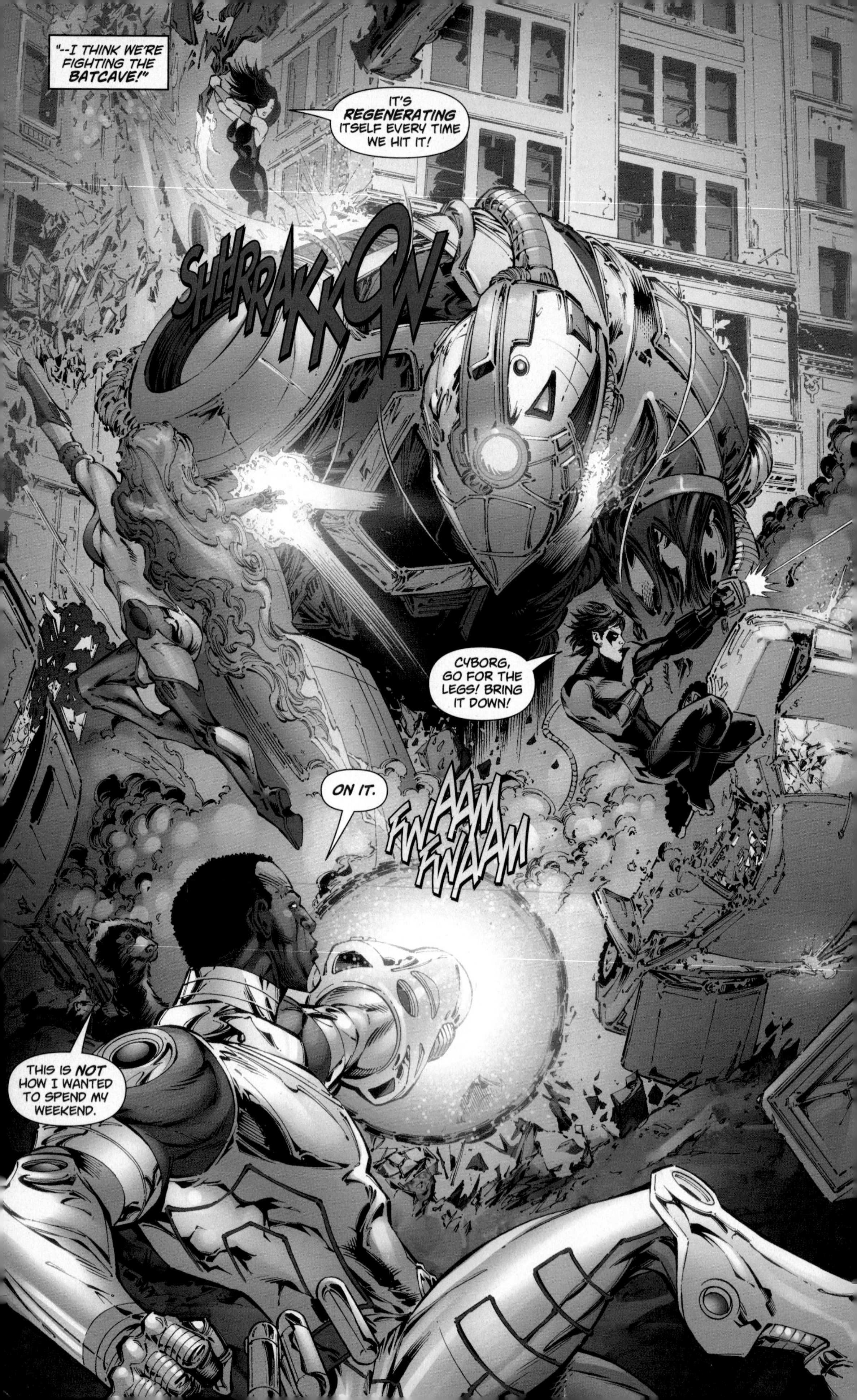
"--I THINK WE'RE FIGHTING THE BATCAVE!"
IT'S REGENERATING ITSELF EVERY TIME WE HIT IT!
SHHRRAKKKOW
CYBORG, GO FOR THE LEGS! BRING IT DOWN!
ON IT.
FWAAM FWAAM
THIS IS NOT HOW I WANTED TO SPEND MY WEEKEND.

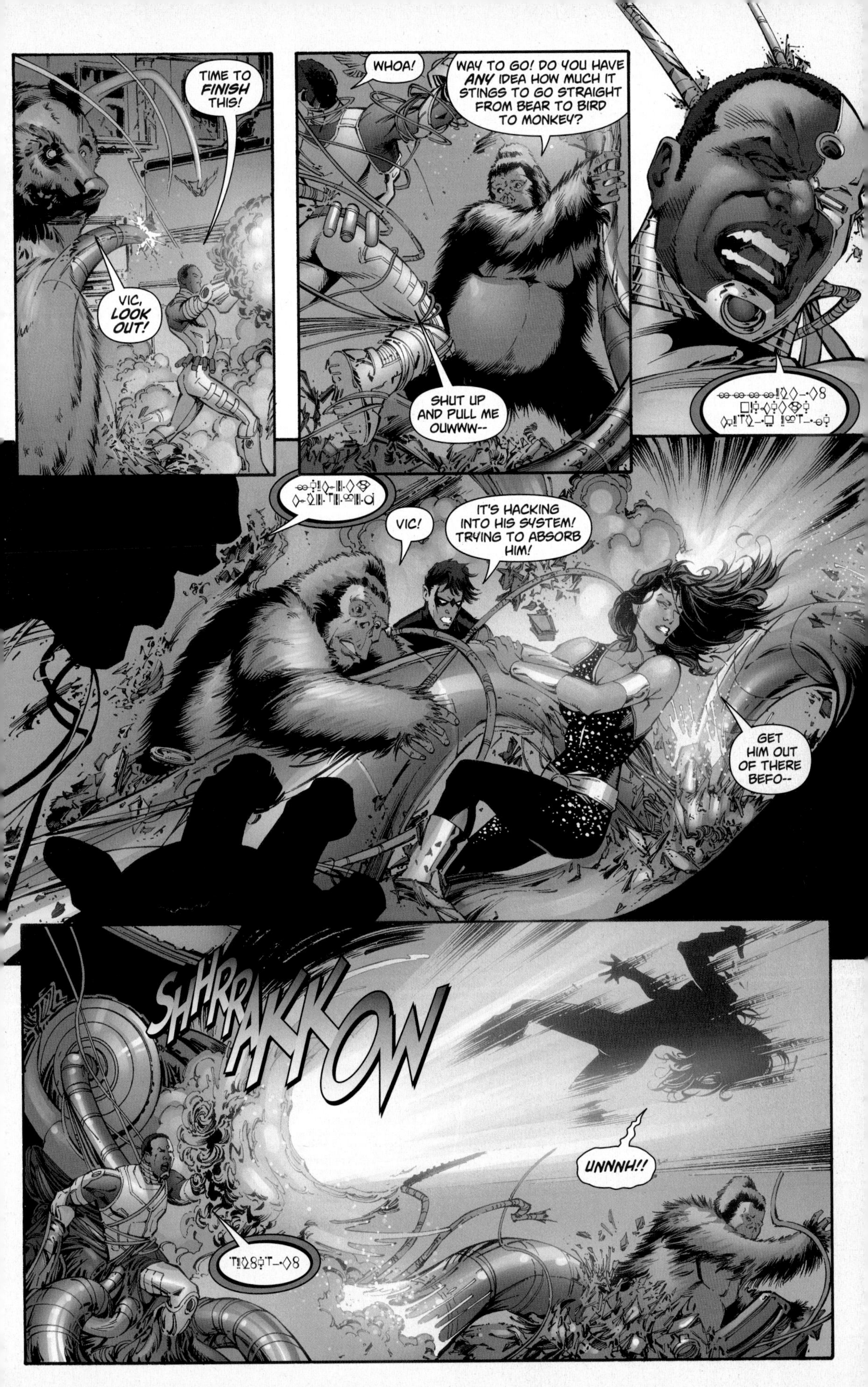
TIME TO FINISH THIS!
VIC, LOOK OUT!
WHOA!
WAY TO GO! DO YOU HAVE ANY IDEA HOW MUCH IT STINGS TO GO STRAIGHT FROM BEAR TO BIRD TO MONKEY?
SHUT UP AND PULL ME OUWWW--
VIC!
IT'S HACKING INTO HIS SYSTEM! TRYING TO ABSORB HIM!
GET HIM OUT OF THERE BEFO--
SHRRAKKOW
UNNNH!!

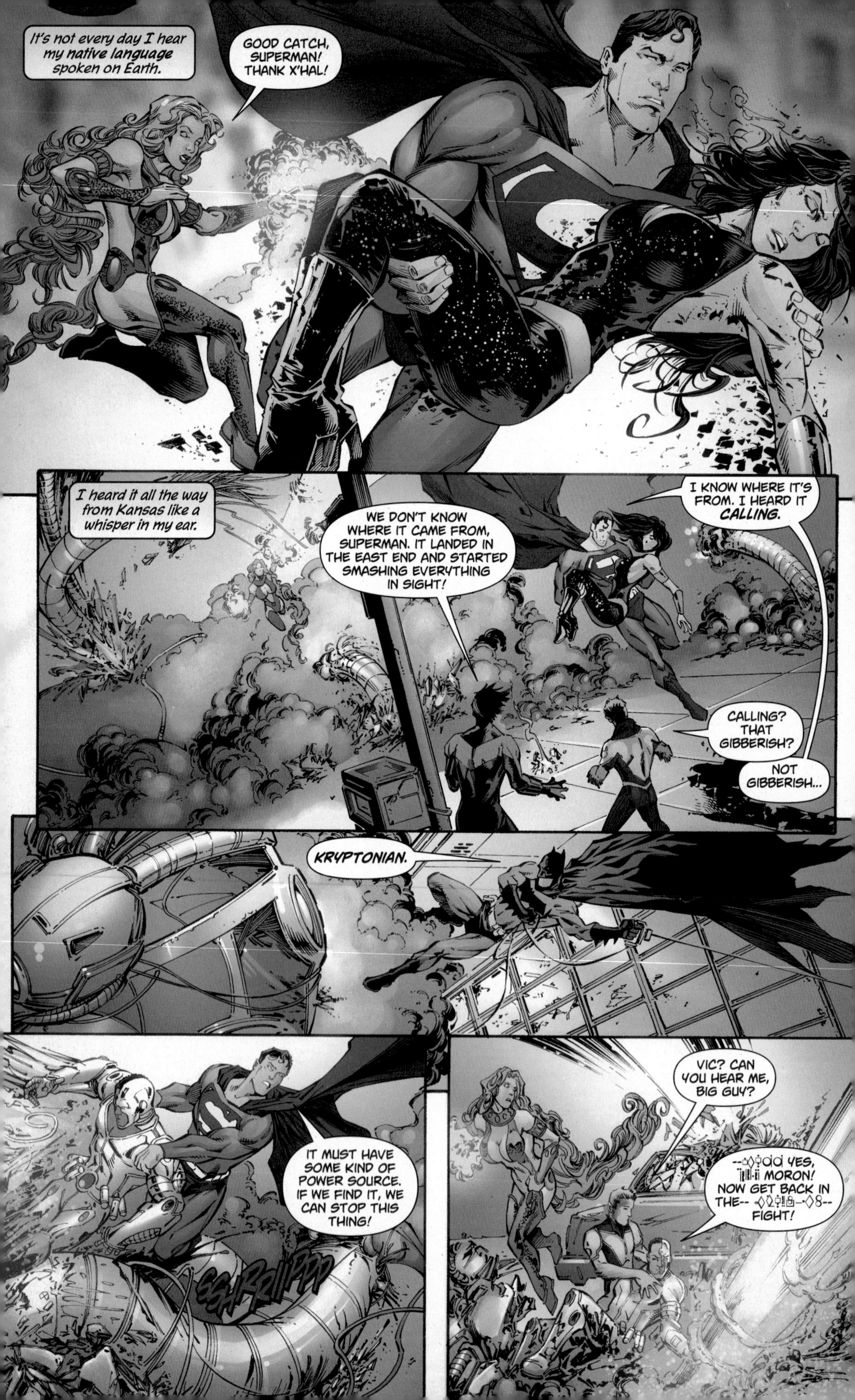

It's not every day I hear my native language spoken on Earth.
GOOD CATCH, SUPERMAN! THANK X'HAL!
I heard it all the way from Kansas like a whisper in my ear.
WE DON'T KNOW WHERE IT CAME FROM, SUPERMAN. IT LANDED IN THE EAST END AND STARTED SMASHING EVERYTHING IN SIGHT!
I KNOW WHERE IT'S FROM. I HEARD IT CALLING.
CALLING? THAT GIBBERISH?
NOT GIBBERISH...
KRYPTONIAN.
IT MUST HAVE SOME KIND OF POWER SOURCE. IF WE FIND IT, WE CAN STOP THIS THING!
SSHRRIIPPP
VIC? CAN YOU HEAR ME, BIG GUY?
YES, MORON! NOW GET BACK IN THE-- FIGHT!

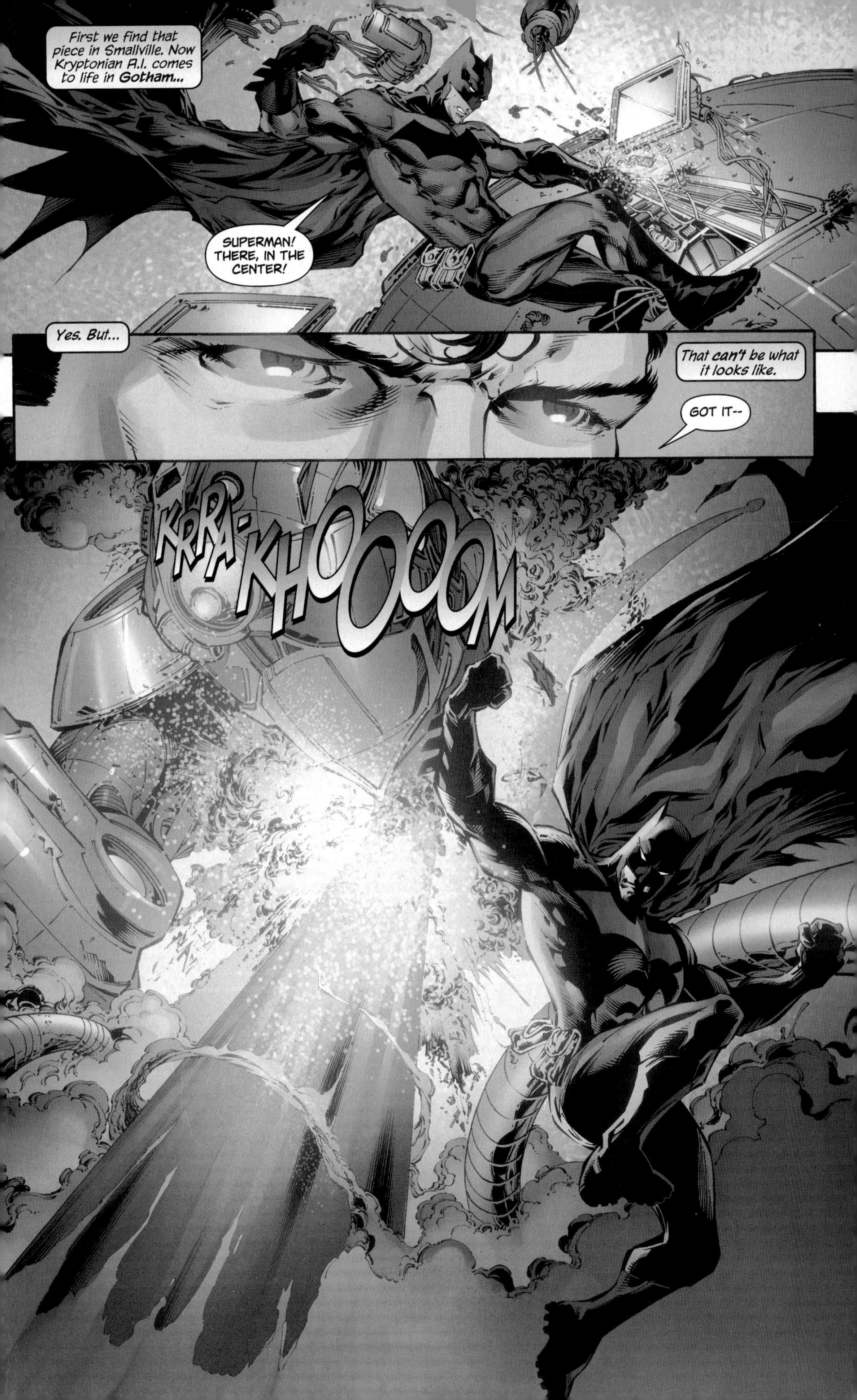
First we find that piece in Smallville. Now Kryptonian A.I. comes to life in Gotham...
SUPERMAN! THERE, IN THE CENTER!
Yes. But...
That can't be what it looks like.
GOT IT--
KRRA-KHOOOOM

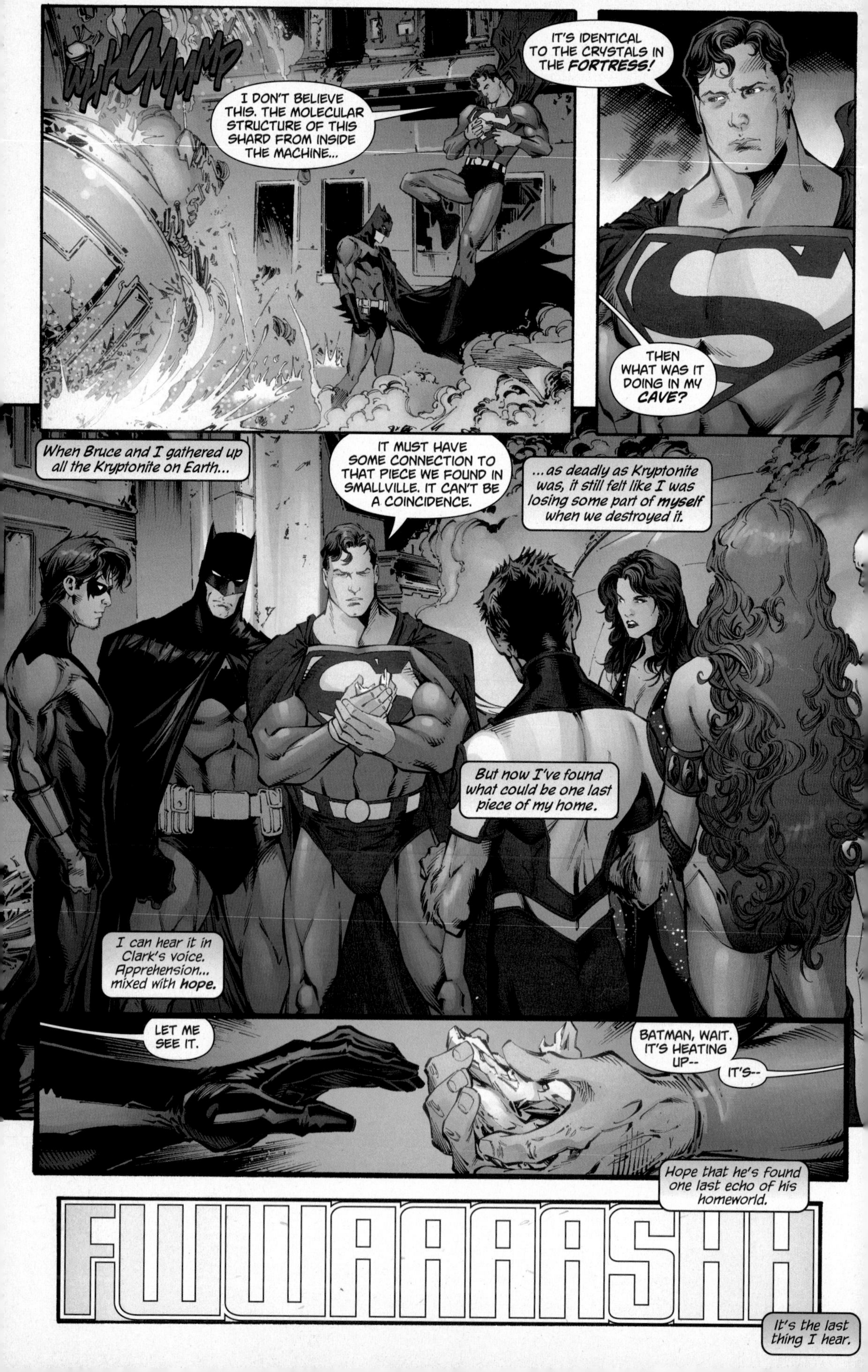
WHHOMMMMP
I DON'T BELIEVE THIS. THE MOLECULAR STRUCTURE OF THIS SHARD FROM INSIDE THE MACHINE...
IT'S IDENTICAL TO THE CRYSTALS IN THE FORTRESS!
THEN WHAT WAS IT DOING IN MY CAVE?
When Bruce and I gathered up all the Kryptonite on Earth...
IT MUST HAVE SOME CONNECTION TO THAT PIECE WE FOUND IN SMALLVILLE. IT CAN'T BE A COINCIDENCE.
...as deadly as Kryptonite was, it still felt like I was losing some part of myself when we destroyed it.
But now I've found what could be one last piece of my home.
I can hear it in Clark's voice. Apprehension... mixed with hope.
LET ME SEE IT.
BATMAN, WAIT. IT'S HEATING UP--
IT'S--
Hope that he's found one last echo of his homeworld.
FWWAAAASHH
It's the last thing I hear.

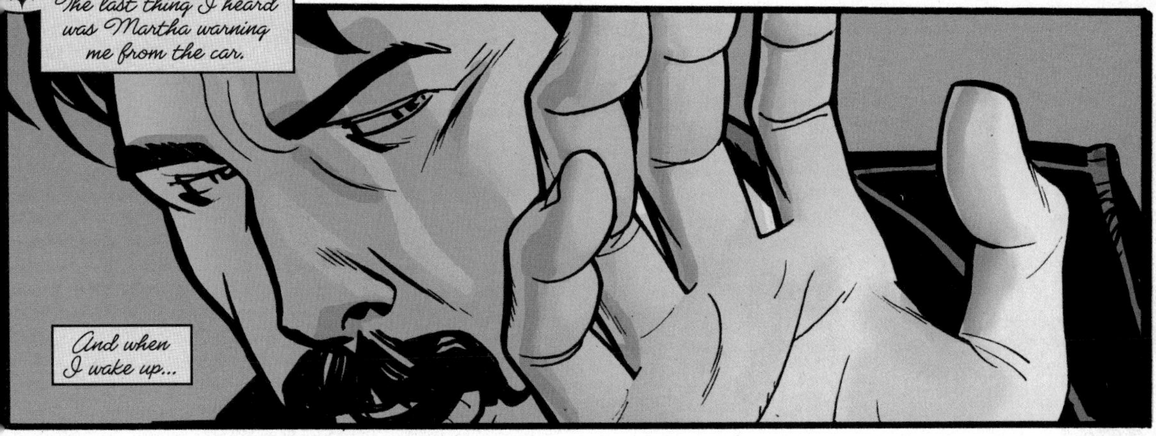
The last thing I heard was Martha warning me from the car.
And when I wake up...

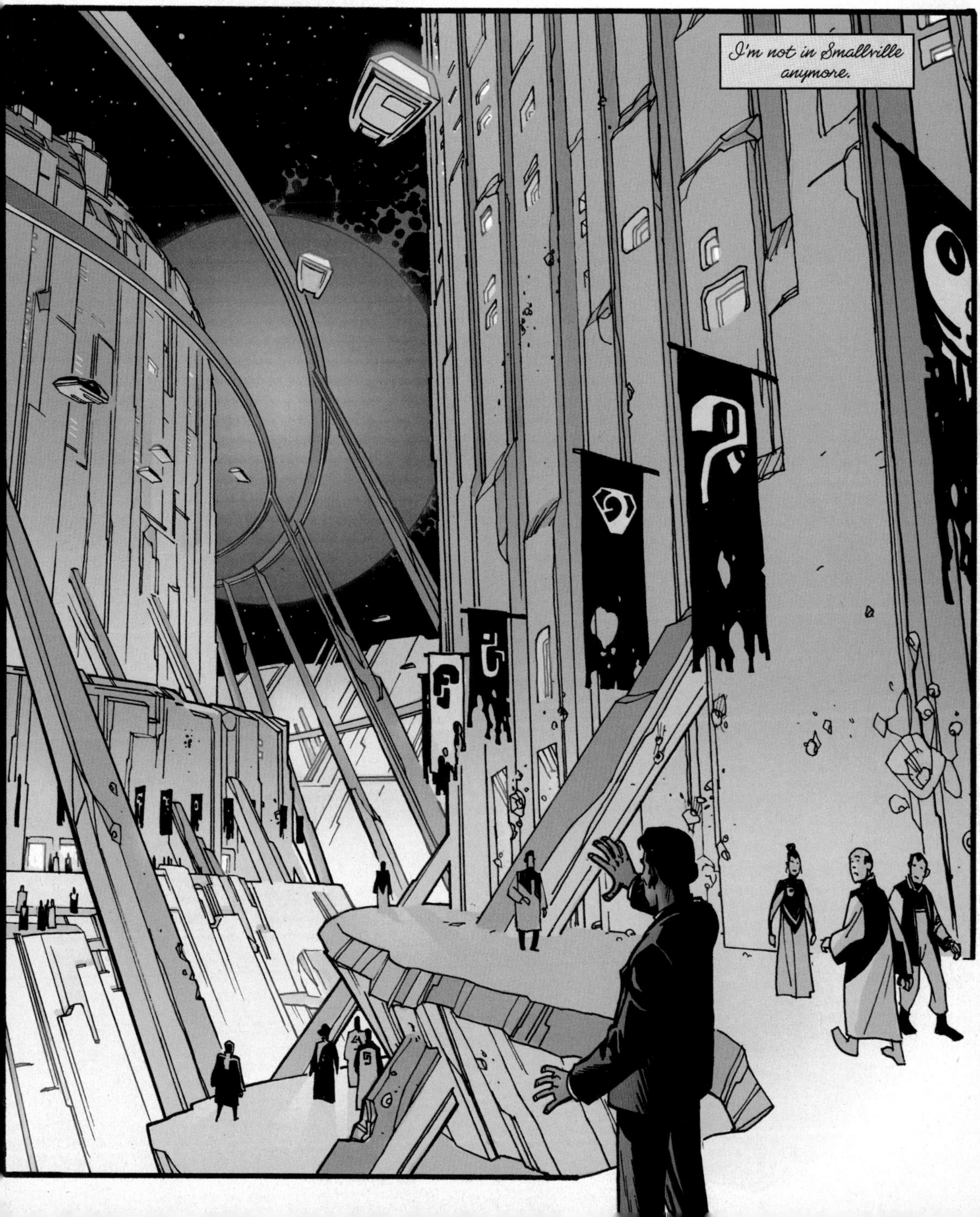
I'm not in Smallville anymore.

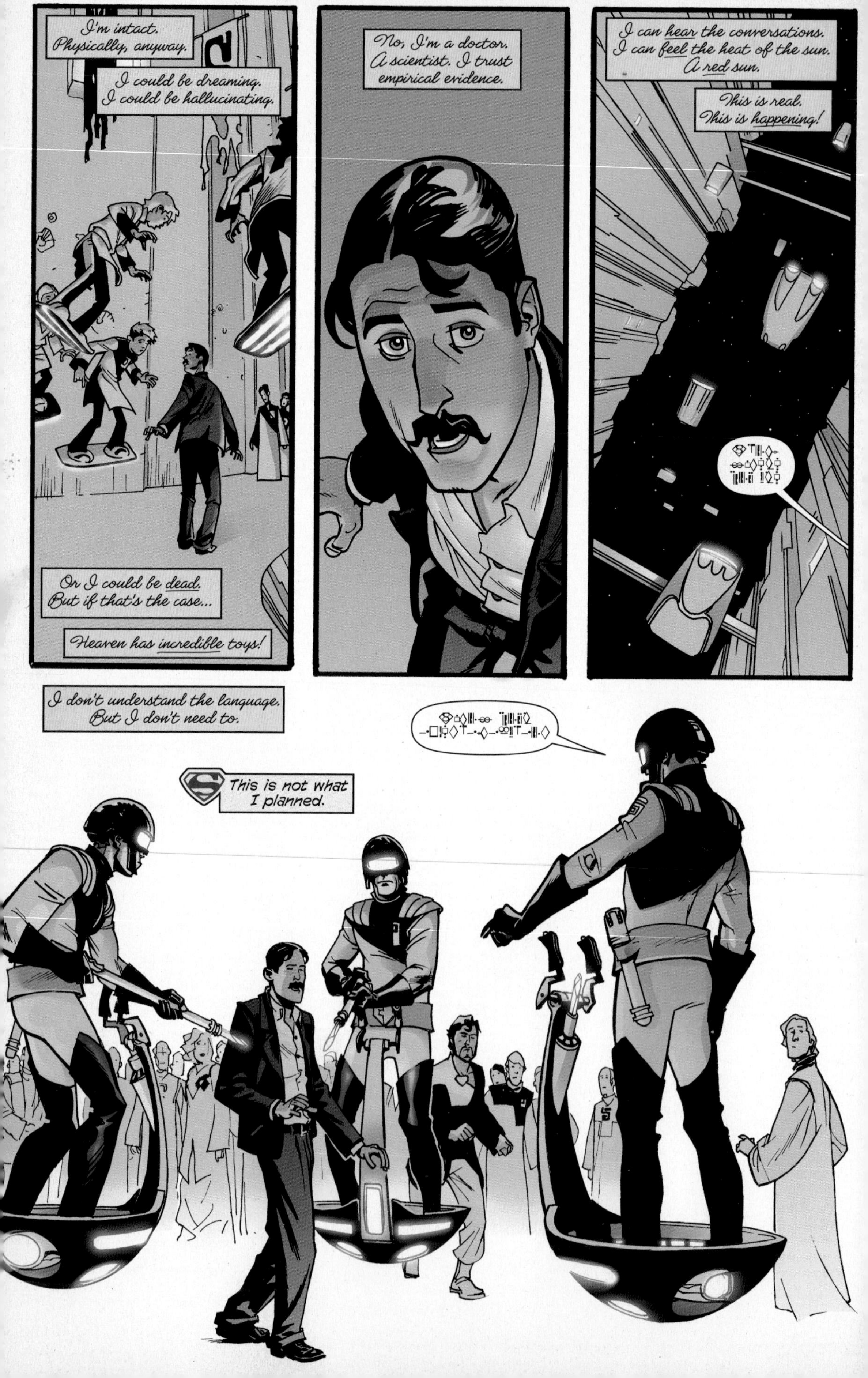

I'm intact. Physically, anyway.
I could be dreaming. I could be hallucinating.
Or I could be dead. But if that's the case...
Heaven has incredible toys!
No, I'm a doctor. A scientist. I trust empirical evidence.
I can hear the conversations. I can feel the heat of the sun. A red sun.
This is real. This is happening!
I don't understand the language. But I don't need to.
This is not what I planned.

But the stranger isn't backing down from the threat. He stands his ground. I like him already.

I just hope my family's name still matters in this city.

◇–ii'T □Ⅱ–∞–◇
Ⅶ◲–ii◲ ∞–◆ii–Ⅱ–◇◲ �◯ T'△–◇ⅠⅠ
◇◲–◇Ⅱ–◇Ⅱ'Ⅱ△◯T◯–ⅡⅠ◆

Someone comes to my rescue.

•◲ⅠⅠ–◲⑇◲
T◆◲–Ⅱ–◆
◲◲–◇Ⅶ◲Ⅱ ‼
◯ⅢⅡ◲ⅠⅡ◯◲T–◇Ⅶ◲

T△–◆Ⅶ
◇Ⅶ◆–◇Ⅰ‼

There's something about him. I can hear it in his voice. A natural authority. I like him already.

Ⅱ–ii◇–◆
•◲ⅠⅠ◲◇–Ⅱ–◯Ⅱ–8–◇Ⓡ◲
□Ⅱ–◇8 Ⅱ–◇◲◆ □Ⅱ'ii◇Ⅶ

WELCOME, MY FRIEND. MY NAME IS *JOR-EL.*

*THOMAS WAYNE.*

WAIT-- YOU SPEAK *ENGLISH?!*

COME. IT'S NOT SAFE TO SPEAK HERE. PARANOIA RUNS HIGH IN THESE DIFFICULT TIMES.

He doesn't look the least bit surprised to see me.

He should have arrived in the lab. I'll have to check my calculations.

WHERE AM I?!

YOUR BODY REMAINS SAFELY ON YOUR PLANET. BUT YOUR MIND...

...IS GIVEN FORM ON THE PLANET *KRYPTON.* THOUSANDS OF LIGHT-YEARS FROM YOUR HOME.

VWWRRRRRNNNN

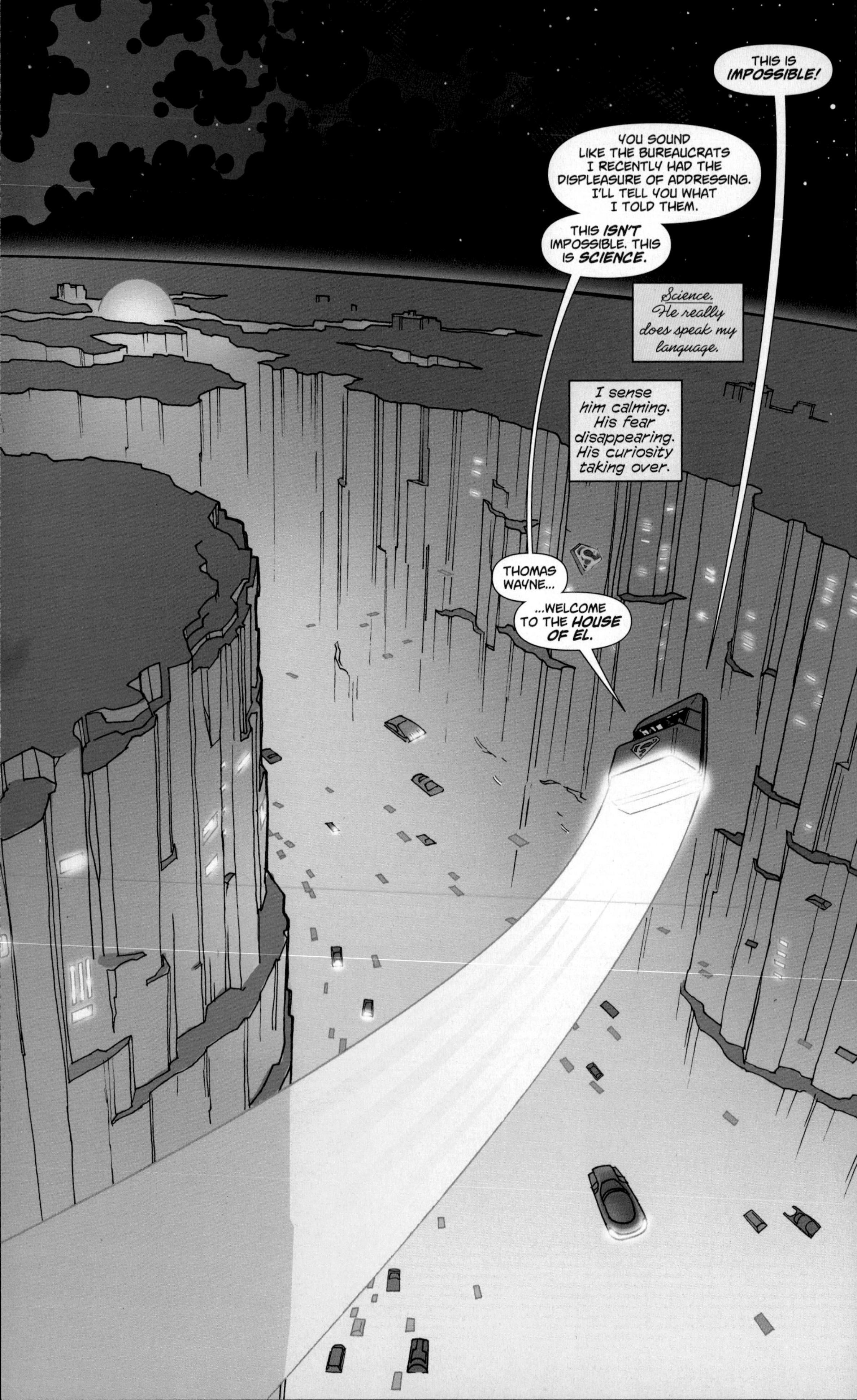
THIS IS IMPOSSIBLE!
YOU SOUND LIKE THE BUREAUCRATS I RECENTLY HAD THE DISPLEASURE OF ADDRESSING. I'LL TELL YOU WHAT I TOLD THEM.
THIS ISN'T IMPOSSIBLE. THIS IS SCIENCE.
Science. He really does speak my language.
I sense him calming. His fear disappearing. His curiosity taking over.
THOMAS WAYNE...
...WELCOME TO THE HOUSE OF EL.

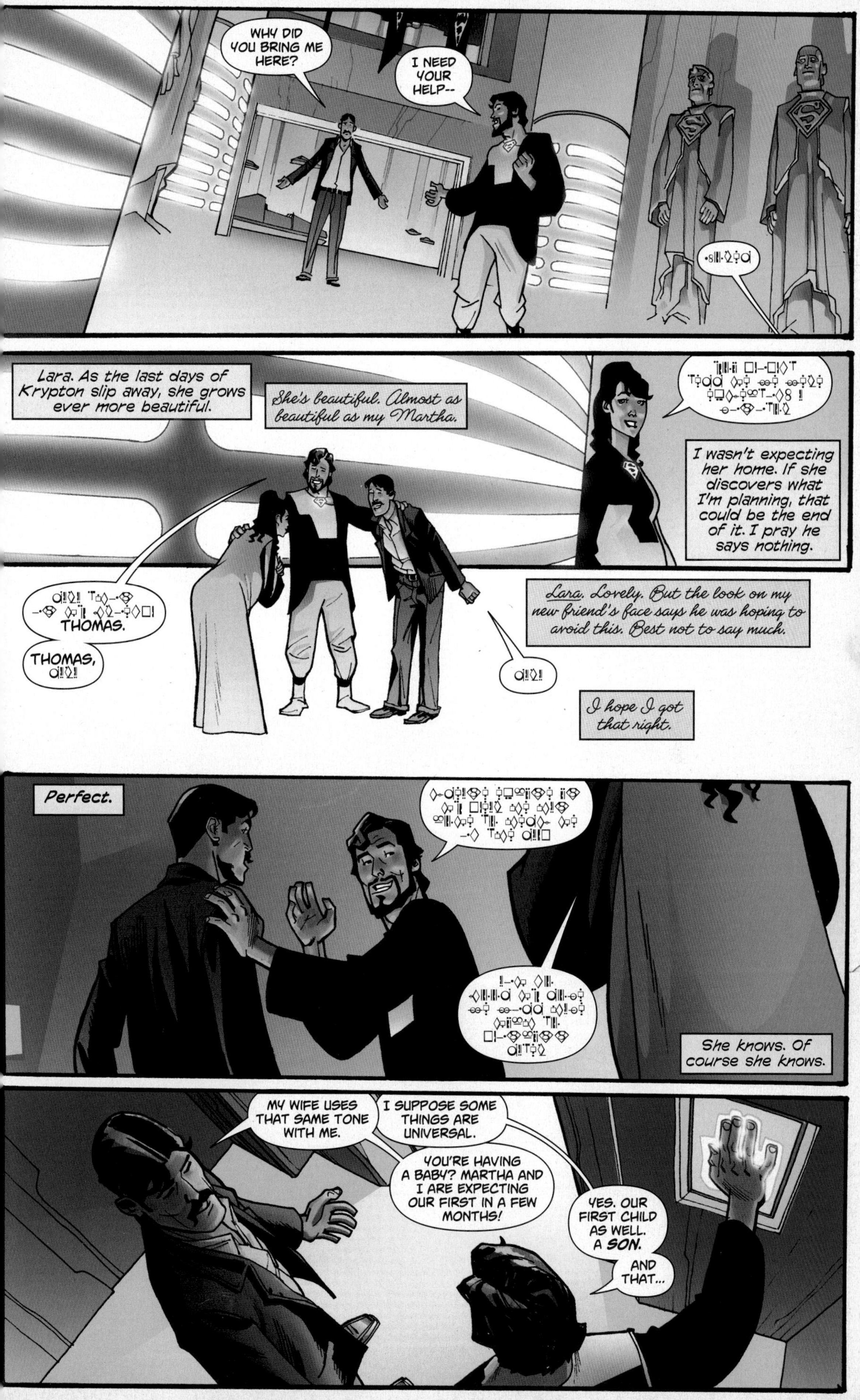
WHY DID YOU BRING ME HERE?
I NEED YOUR HELP--
Lara. As the last days of Krypton slip away, she grows ever more beautiful.
She's beautiful. Almost as beautiful as my Martha.
I wasn't expecting her home. If she discovers what I'm planning, that could be the end of it. I pray he says nothing.
THOMAS.
THOMAS,
Lara. Lovely. But the look on my new friend's face says he was hoping to avoid this. Best not to say much.
I hope I got that right.
Perfect.
She knows. Of course she knows.
MY WIFE USES THAT SAME TONE WITH ME.
I SUPPOSE SOME THINGS ARE UNIVERSAL.
YOU'RE HAVING A BABY? MARTHA AND I ARE EXPECTING OUR FIRST IN A FEW MONTHS!
YES. OUR FIRST CHILD AS WELL. A SON.
AND THAT...

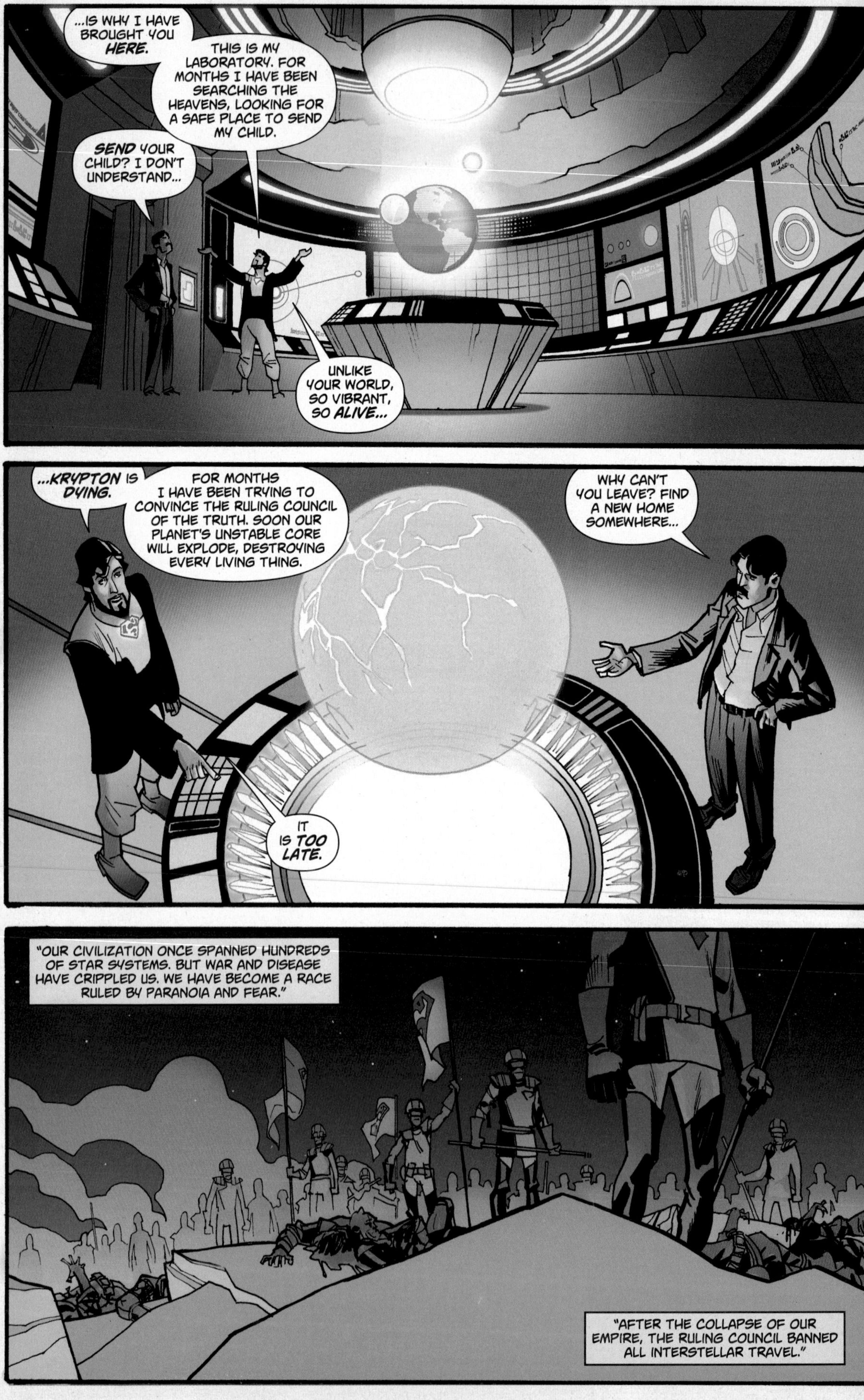
...IS WHY I HAVE BROUGHT YOU HERE.
THIS IS MY LABORATORY. FOR MONTHS I HAVE BEEN SEARCHING THE HEAVENS, LOOKING FOR A SAFE PLACE TO SEND MY CHILD.
SEND YOUR CHILD? I DON'T UNDERSTAND...
UNLIKE YOUR WORLD, SO VIBRANT, SO ALIVE...
...KRYPTON IS DYING.
FOR MONTHS I HAVE BEEN TRYING TO CONVINCE THE RULING COUNCIL OF THE TRUTH. SOON OUR PLANET'S UNSTABLE CORE WILL EXPLODE, DESTROYING EVERY LIVING THING.
WHY CAN'T YOU LEAVE? FIND A NEW HOME SOMEWHERE...
IT IS TOO LATE.
"OUR CIVILIZATION ONCE SPANNED HUNDREDS OF STAR SYSTEMS. BUT WAR AND DISEASE HAVE CRIPPLED US. WE HAVE BECOME A RACE RULED BY PARANOIA AND FEAR."
"AFTER THE COLLAPSE OF OUR EMPIRE, THE RULING COUNCIL BANNED ALL INTERSTELLAR TRAVEL."

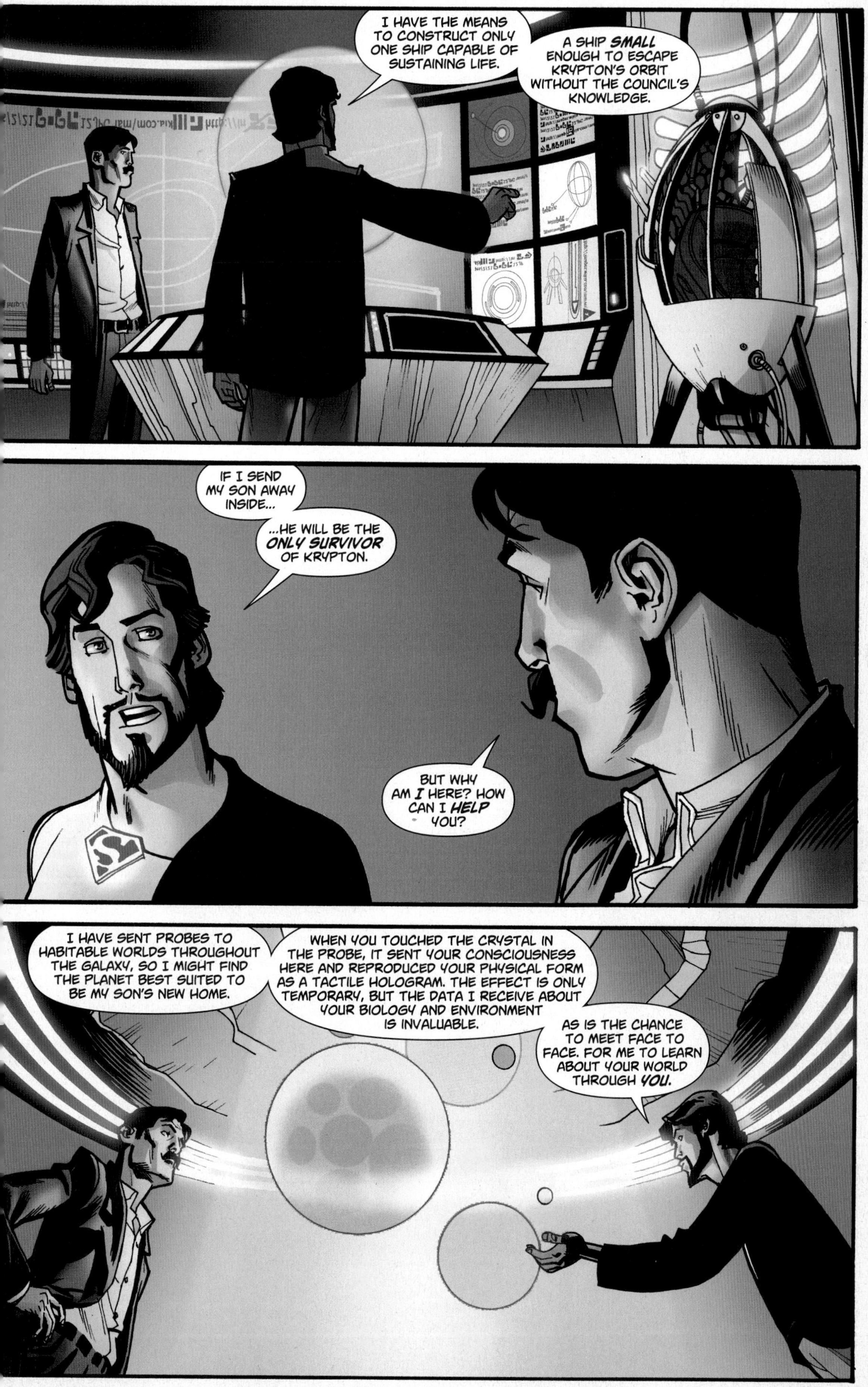
I HAVE THE MEANS TO CONSTRUCT ONLY ONE SHIP CAPABLE OF SUSTAINING LIFE.
A SHIP SMALL ENOUGH TO ESCAPE KRYPTON'S ORBIT WITHOUT THE COUNCIL'S KNOWLEDGE.
IF I SEND MY SON AWAY INSIDE...
...HE WILL BE THE ONLY SURVIVOR OF KRYPTON.
BUT WHY AM I HERE? HOW CAN I HELP YOU?
I HAVE SENT PROBES TO HABITABLE WORLDS THROUGHOUT THE GALAXY, SO I MIGHT FIND THE PLANET BEST SUITED TO BE MY SON'S NEW HOME.
WHEN YOU TOUCHED THE CRYSTAL IN THE PROBE, IT SENT YOUR CONSCIOUSNESS HERE AND REPRODUCED YOUR PHYSICAL FORM AS A TACTILE HOLOGRAM. THE EFFECT IS ONLY TEMPORARY, BUT THE DATA I RECEIVE ABOUT YOUR BIOLOGY AND ENVIRONMENT IS INVALUABLE.
AS IS THE CHANCE TO MEET FACE TO FACE. FOR ME TO LEARN ABOUT YOUR WORLD THROUGH YOU.

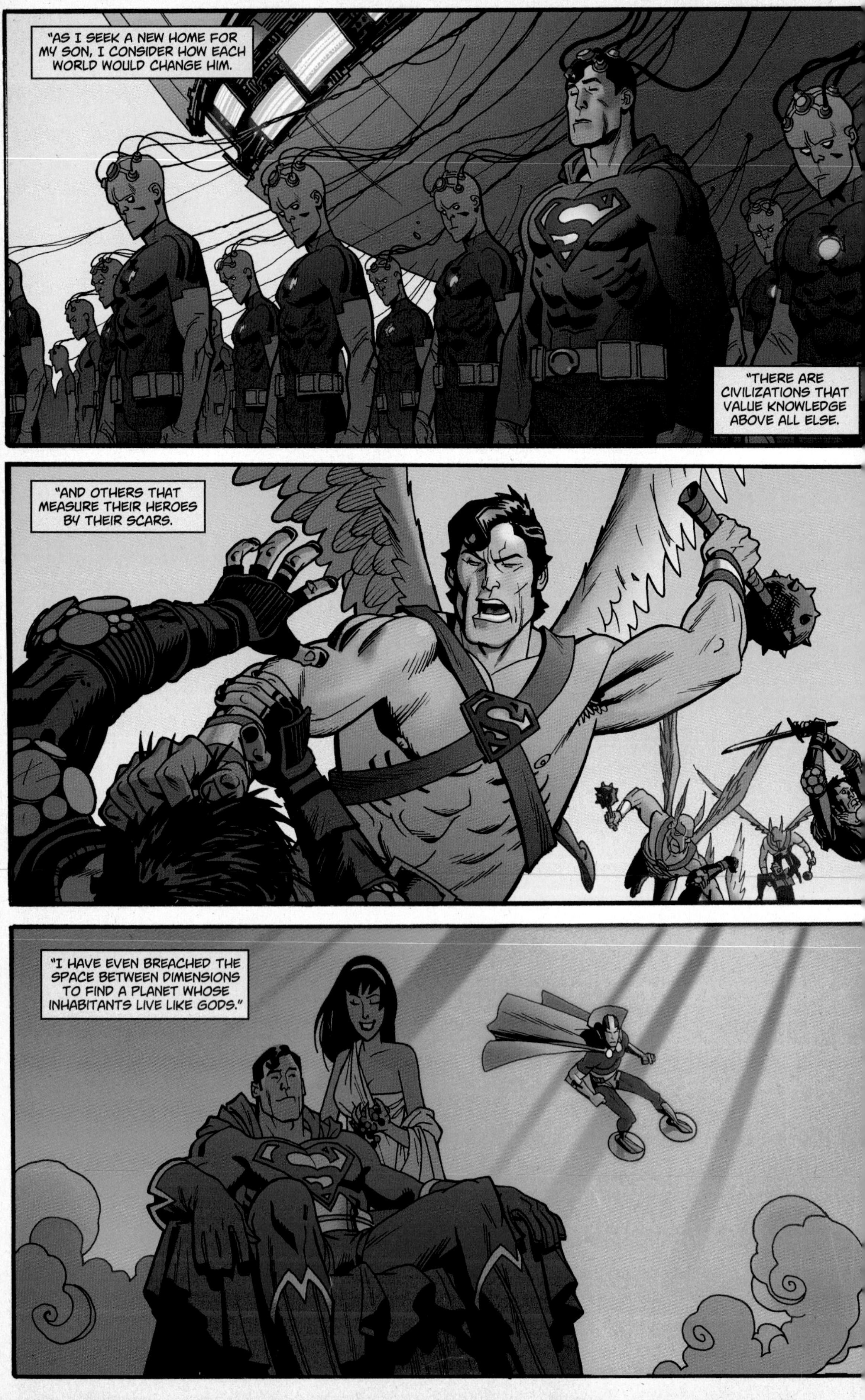
"AS I SEEK A NEW HOME FOR MY SON, I CONSIDER HOW EACH WORLD WOULD CHANGE HIM.
"THERE ARE CIVILIZATIONS THAT VALUE KNOWLEDGE ABOVE ALL ELSE.
"AND OTHERS THAT MEASURE THEIR HEROES BY THEIR SCARS.
"I HAVE EVEN BREACHED THE SPACE BETWEEN DIMENSIONS TO FIND A PLANET WHOSE INHABITANTS LIVE LIKE GODS."

AND THEN WE HAVE *YOUR* PLANET. ITS UNIQUE CHARACTERISTICS MAKE IT A SUITABLE HABITAT FOR KRYPTONIAN LIFE.

*I want to tell him its yellow sun will give my son powers that will make him invincible. But should I? Would he return home only to stoke fears of a coming threat?*

*What do I tell him? Do I say that Earth is where he should send his only child?*

I CAN'T LIE TO YOU, JOR-EL. WE'RE PROBABLY NOT THE MOST PEACEFUL CORNER OF THE GALAXY. WE HAVE A SPECIAL TALENT FOR EMBRACING THE WORST ASPECTS OF OUR NATURE.

BUT I BELIEVE THAT HUMANITY IS FUNDAMENTALLY *DECENT.*

"I COME FROM A TROUBLED PLACE CALLED GOTHAM.

"BUT IT'S MY HOME. AND I WILL DO EVERYTHING I CAN TO SAVE IT.

"I THINK MOST PEOPLE ON EARTH FEEL THAT WAY ABOUT THEIR HOMES.

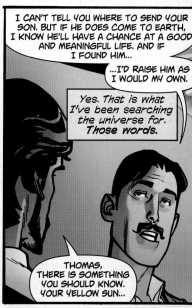

I CAN'T TELL YOU WHERE TO SEND YOUR SON. BUT IF HE DOES COME TO EARTH, I KNOW HE'LL HAVE A CHANCE AT A GOOD AND MEANINGFUL LIFE. AND IF I FOUND HIM...

...I'D RAISE HIM AS I WOULD MY OWN.

YES. *That is what I've been searching the universe for. Those words.*

THOMAS, THERE IS SOMETHING YOU SHOULD KNOW. YOUR YELLOW SUN...

WAIT--WHAT'S HAPPENING...?

THE PROBE'S EFFECT IS WEARING OFF. YOU WILL SOON AWAKEN ON YOUR PLANET.

WAIT. DO YOU KNOW YOUR CHILD'S NAME YET? IF WE EVER GET TO MEET...

*KAL.* YES. IF WE HAVE A BOY, MARTHA WANTS TO CALL HIM BRUCE...

KAL. HIS NAME WILL BE *KAL.*

*BRUCE.* IT IS A GOOD NAME.

*Farewell, Thomas Wayne.*

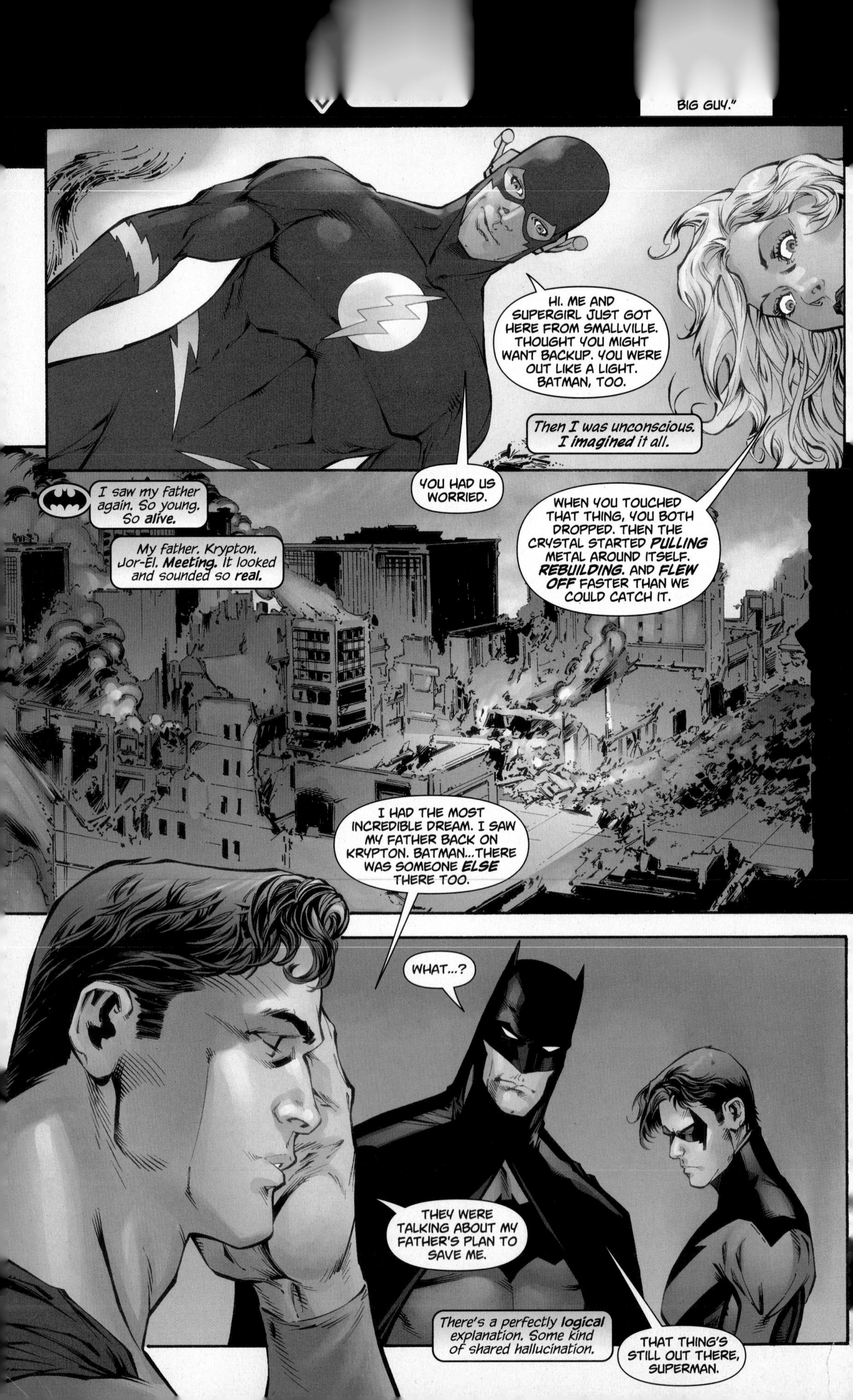
BIG GUY."
HI. ME AND SUPERGIRL JUST GOT HERE FROM SMALLVILLE. THOUGHT YOU MIGHT WANT BACKUP. YOU WERE OUT LIKE A LIGHT. BATMAN, TOO.
Then I was unconscious. I imagined it all.
YOU HAD US WORRIED.
I saw my father again. So young. So alive.
My father. Krypton. Jor-El. Meeting. It looked and sounded so real.
WHEN YOU TOUCHED THAT THING, YOU BOTH DROPPED. THEN THE CRYSTAL STARTED PULLING METAL AROUND ITSELF. REBUILDING. AND FLEW OFF FASTER THAN WE COULD CATCH IT.
I HAD THE MOST INCREDIBLE DREAM. I SAW MY FATHER BACK ON KRYPTON. BATMAN...THERE WAS SOMEONE ELSE THERE TOO.
WHAT...?
THEY WERE TALKING ABOUT MY FATHER'S PLAN TO SAVE ME.
There's a perfectly logical explanation. Some kind of shared hallucination.
THAT THING'S STILL OUT THERE, SUPERMAN.

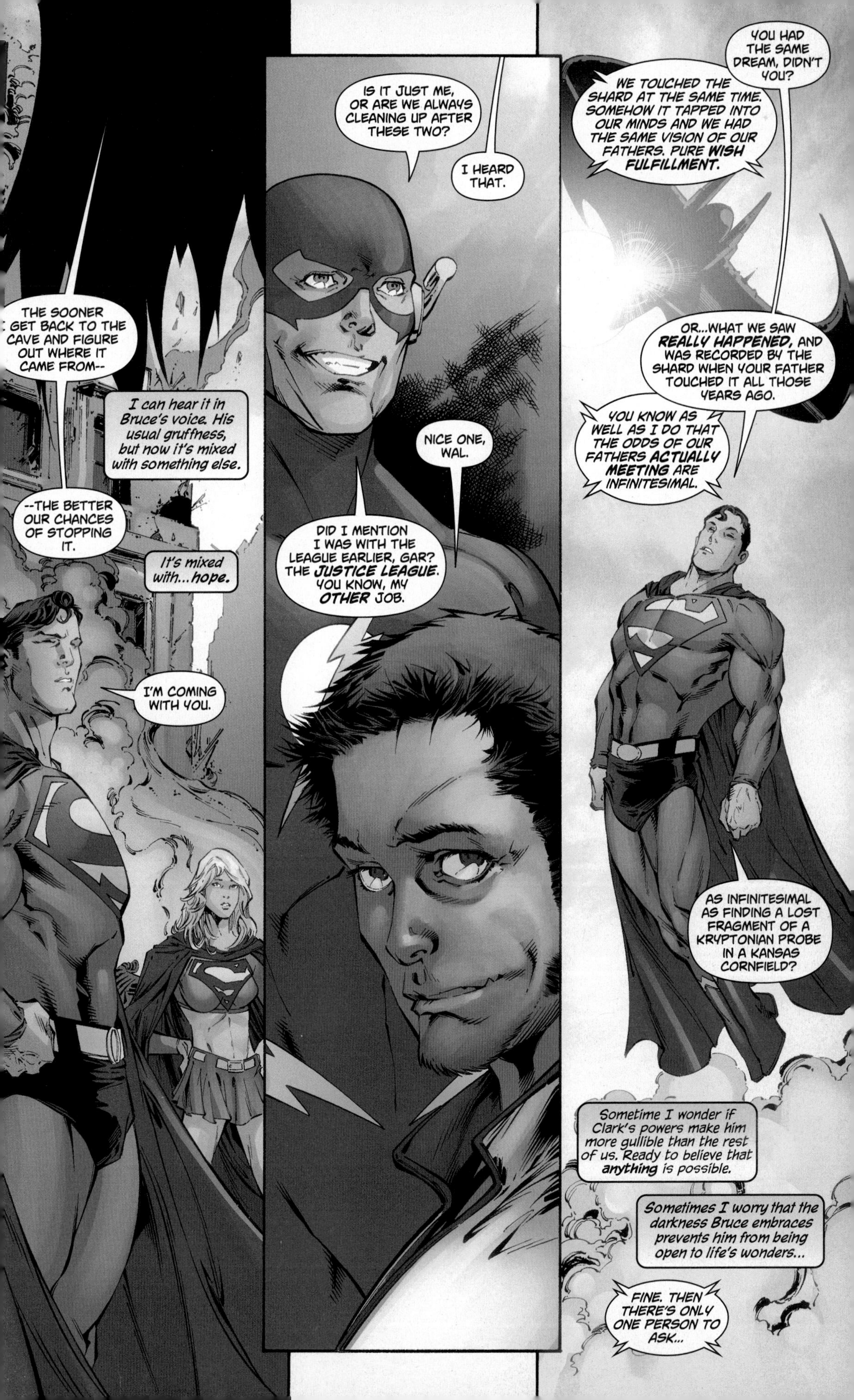
THE SOONER WE GET BACK TO THE CAVE AND FIGURE OUT WHERE IT CAME FROM--
I can hear it in Bruce's voice. His usual gruffness, but now it's mixed with something else.
--THE BETTER OUR CHANCES OF STOPPING IT.
It's mixed with... hope.
I'M COMING WITH YOU.
IS IT JUST ME, OR ARE WE ALWAYS CLEANING UP AFTER THESE TWO?
I HEARD THAT.
NICE ONE, WAL.
DID I MENTION I WAS WITH THE LEAGUE EARLIER, GAR? THE JUSTICE LEAGUE. YOU KNOW, MY OTHER JOB.
YOU HAD THE SAME DREAM, DIDN'T YOU?
WE TOUCHED THE SHARD AT THE SAME TIME. SOMEHOW IT TAPPED INTO OUR MINDS AND WE HAD THE SAME VISION OF OUR FATHERS. PURE WISH FULFILLMENT.
OR...WHAT WE SAW REALLY HAPPENED, AND WAS RECORDED BY THE SHARD WHEN YOUR FATHER TOUCHED IT ALL THOSE YEARS AGO.
YOU KNOW AS WELL AS I DO THAT THE ODDS OF OUR FATHERS ACTUALLY MEETING ARE INFINITESIMAL.
AS INFINITESIMAL AS FINDING A LOST FRAGMENT OF A KRYPTONIAN PROBE IN A KANSAS CORNFIELD?
Sometime I wonder if Clark's powers make him more gullible than the rest of us. Ready to believe that anything is possible.
Sometimes I worry that the darkness Bruce embraces prevents him from being open to life's wonders...
FINE. THEN THERE'S ONLY ONE PERSON TO ASK...

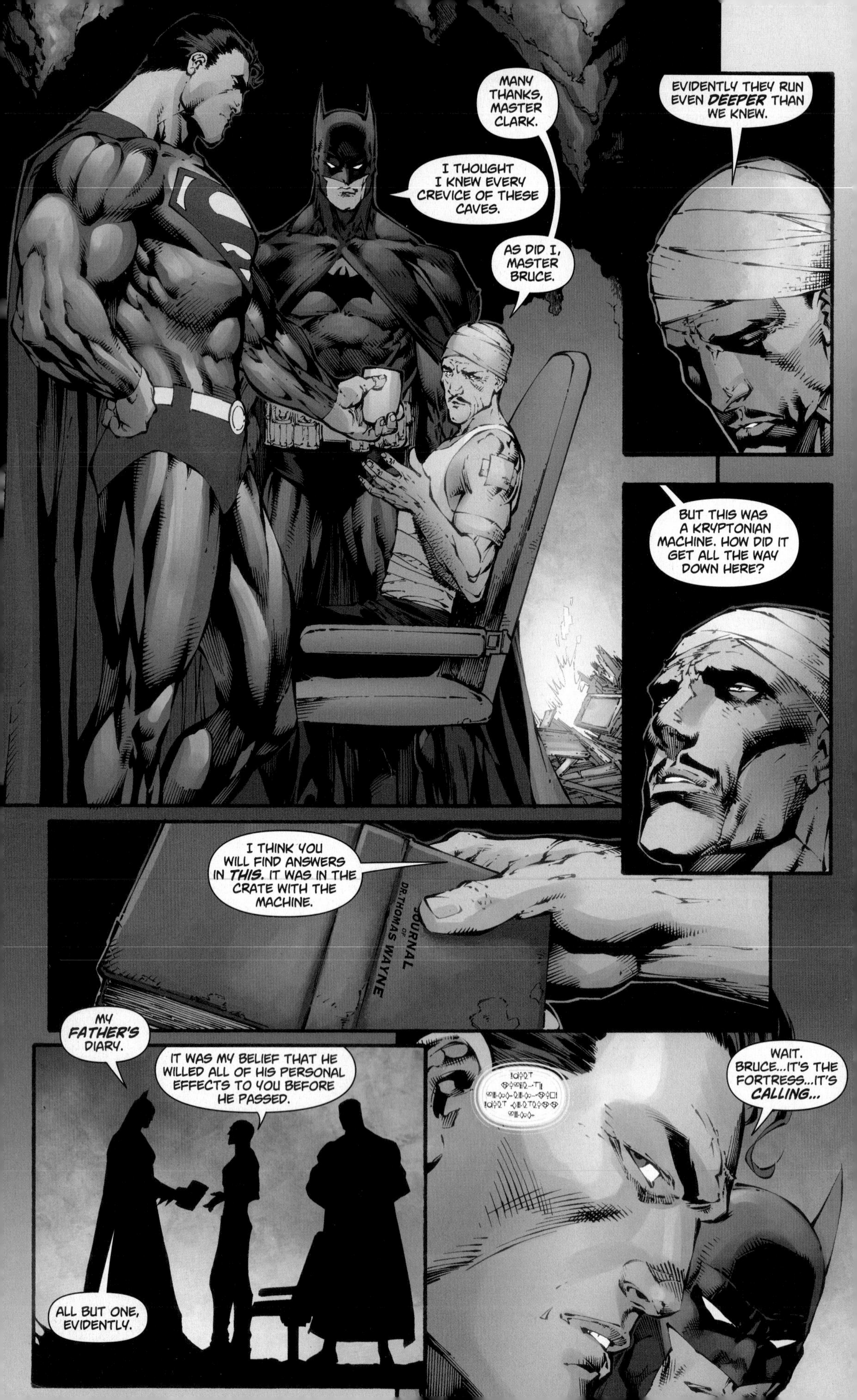
MANY THANKS, MASTER CLARK.
I THOUGHT I KNEW EVERY CREVICE OF THESE CAVES.
AS DID I, MASTER BRUCE.
EVIDENTLY THEY RUN EVEN DEEPER THAN WE KNEW.
BUT THIS WAS A KRYPTONIAN MACHINE. HOW DID IT GET ALL THE WAY DOWN HERE?
I THINK YOU WILL FIND ANSWERS IN THIS. IT WAS IN THE CRATE WITH THE MACHINE.
JOURNAL OF DR. THOMAS WAYNE
MY FATHER'S DIARY.
IT WAS MY BELIEF THAT HE WILLED ALL OF HIS PERSONAL EFFECTS TO YOU BEFORE HE PASSED.
ALL BUT ONE, EVIDENTLY.
WAIT. BRUCE...IT'S THE FORTRESS...IT'S CALLING...

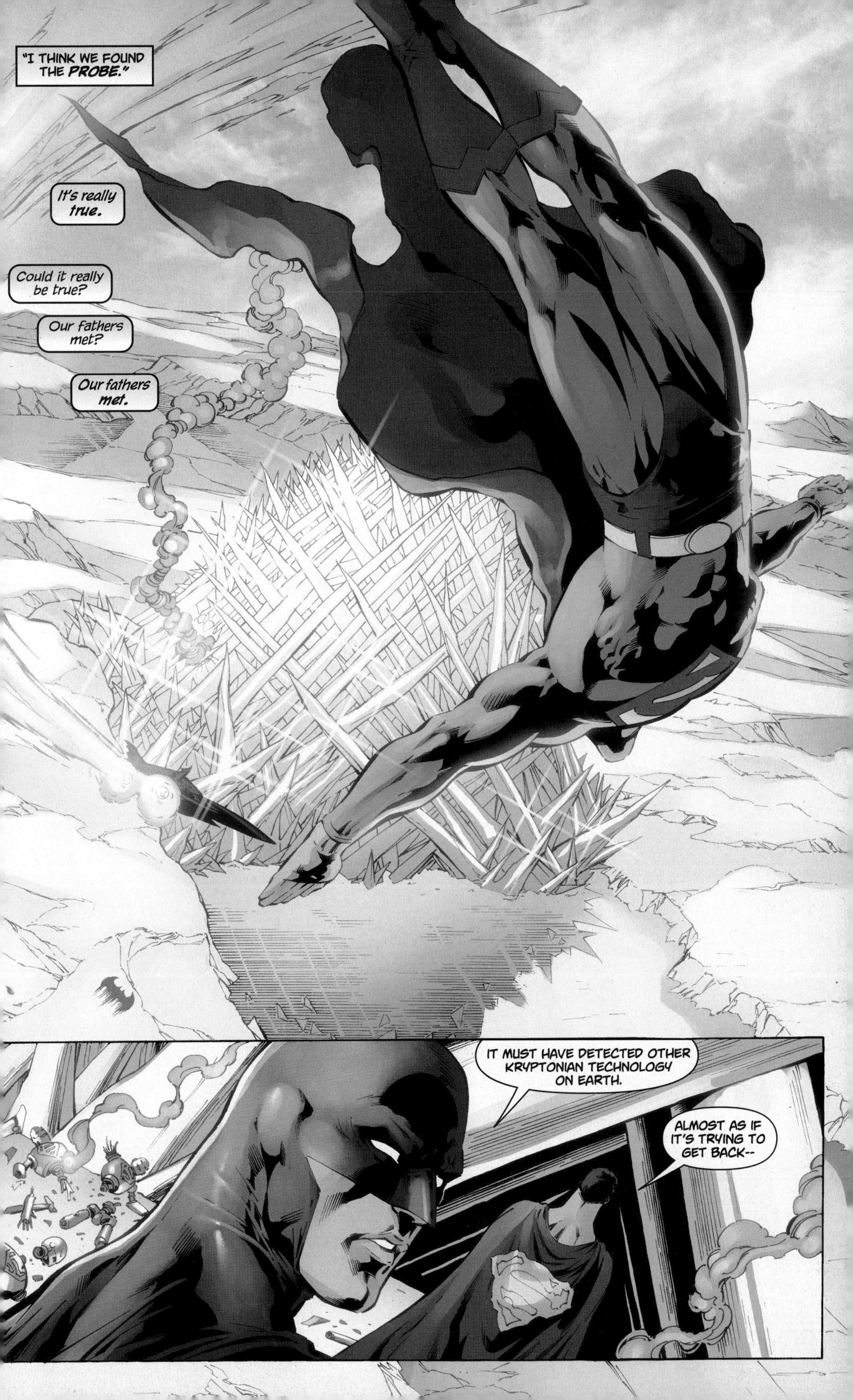
"I THINK WE FOUND THE PROBE."
It's really true.
Could it really be true?
Our fathers met?
Our fathers met.
IT MUST HAVE DETECTED OTHER KRYPTONIAN TECHNOLOGY ON EARTH.
ALMOST AS IF IT'S TRYING TO GET BACK--

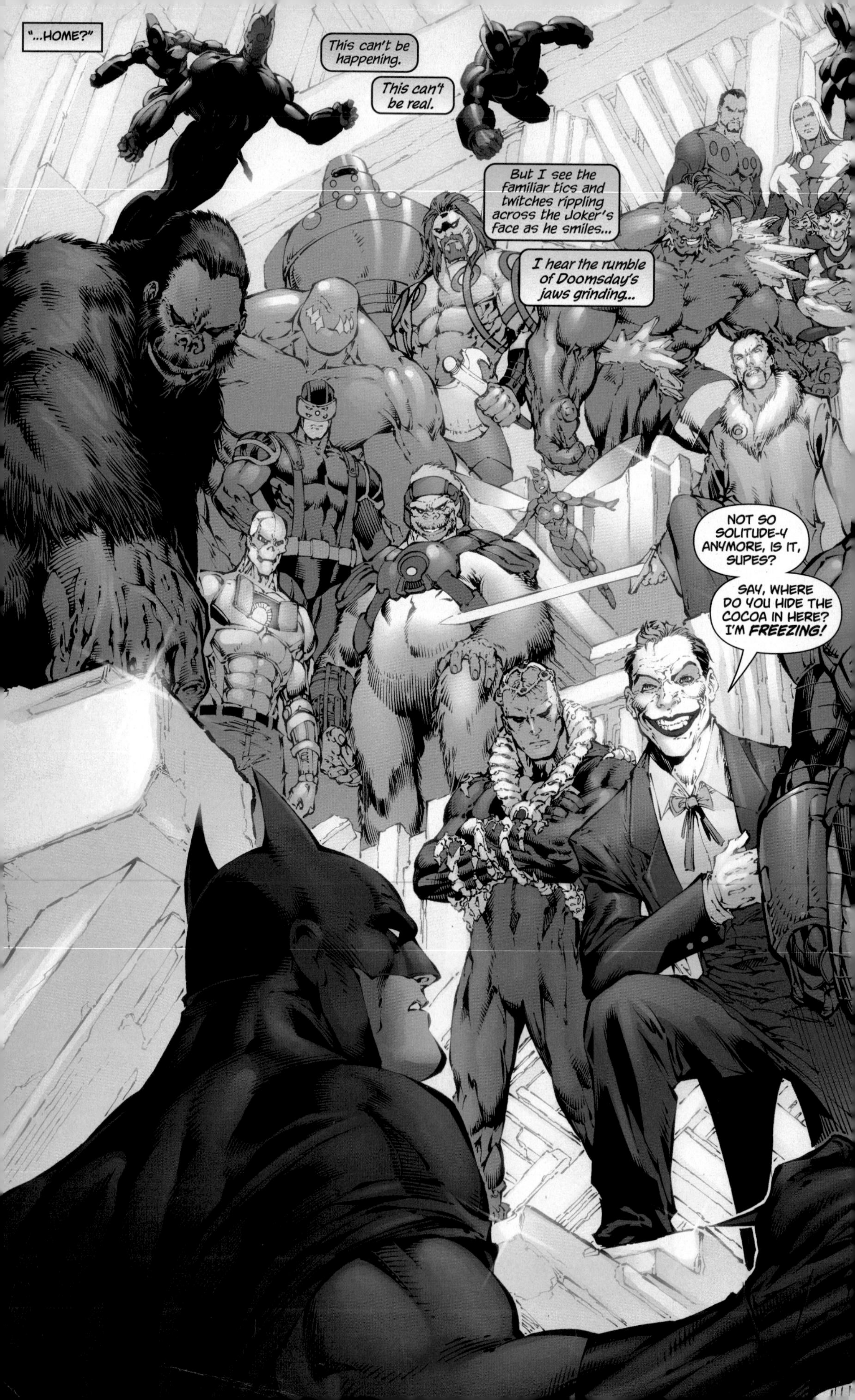
"...HOME?"
This can't be happening.
This can't be real.
But I see the familiar tics and twitches rippling across the Joker's face as he smiles...
I hear the rumble of Doomsday's jaws grinding...
NOT SO SOLITUDE-Y ANYMORE, IS IT, SUPES?
SAY, WHERE DO YOU HIDE THE COCOA IN HERE? I'M FREEZING!

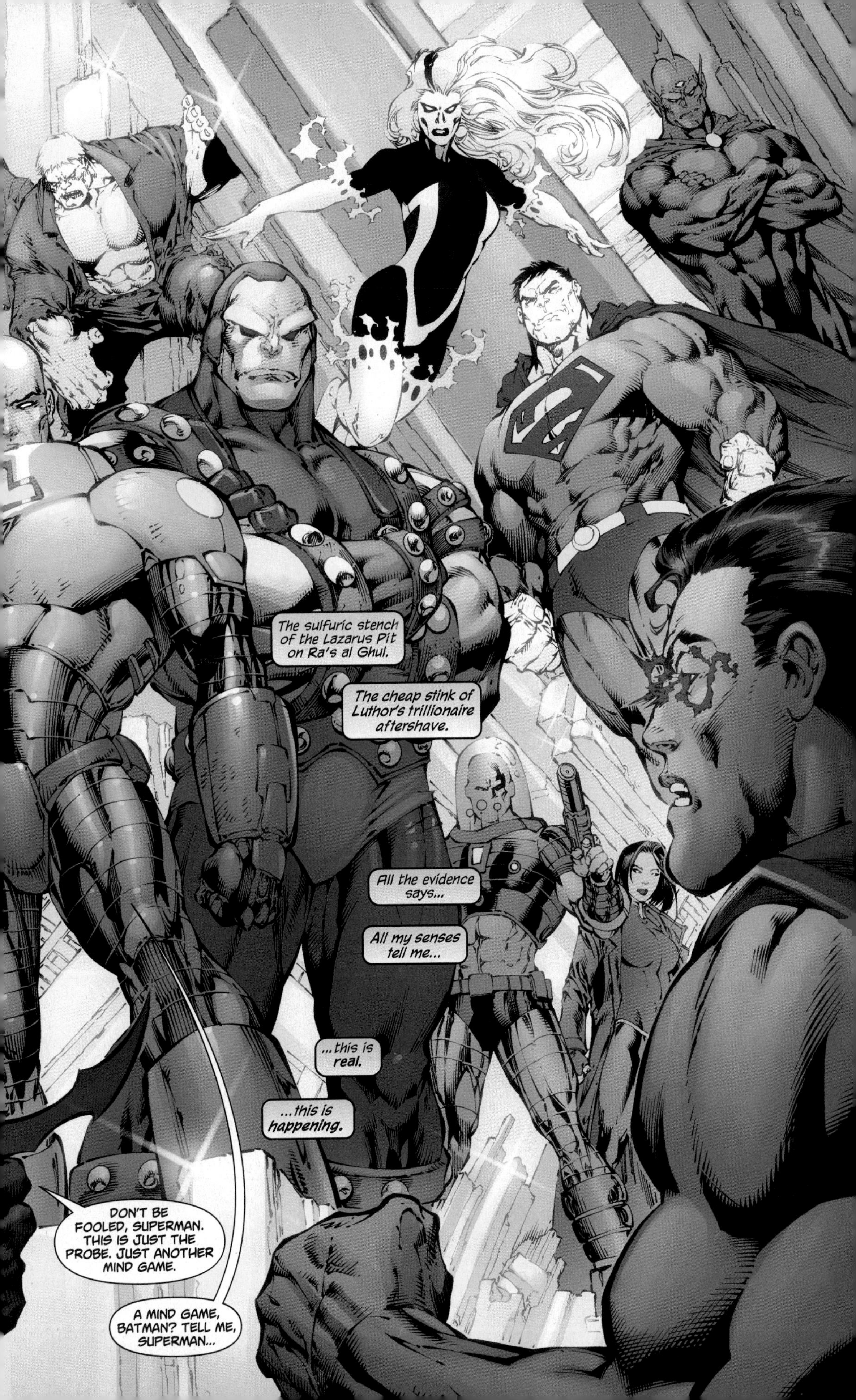

The sulfuric stench of the Lazarus Pit on Ra's al Ghul.
The cheap stink of Luthor's trillionaire aftershave.
All the evidence says...
All my senses tell me...
...this is real.
...this is happening.
DON'T BE FOOLED, SUPERMAN. THIS IS JUST THE PROBE. JUST ANOTHER MIND GAME.
A MIND GAME, BATMAN? TELL ME, SUPERMAN...

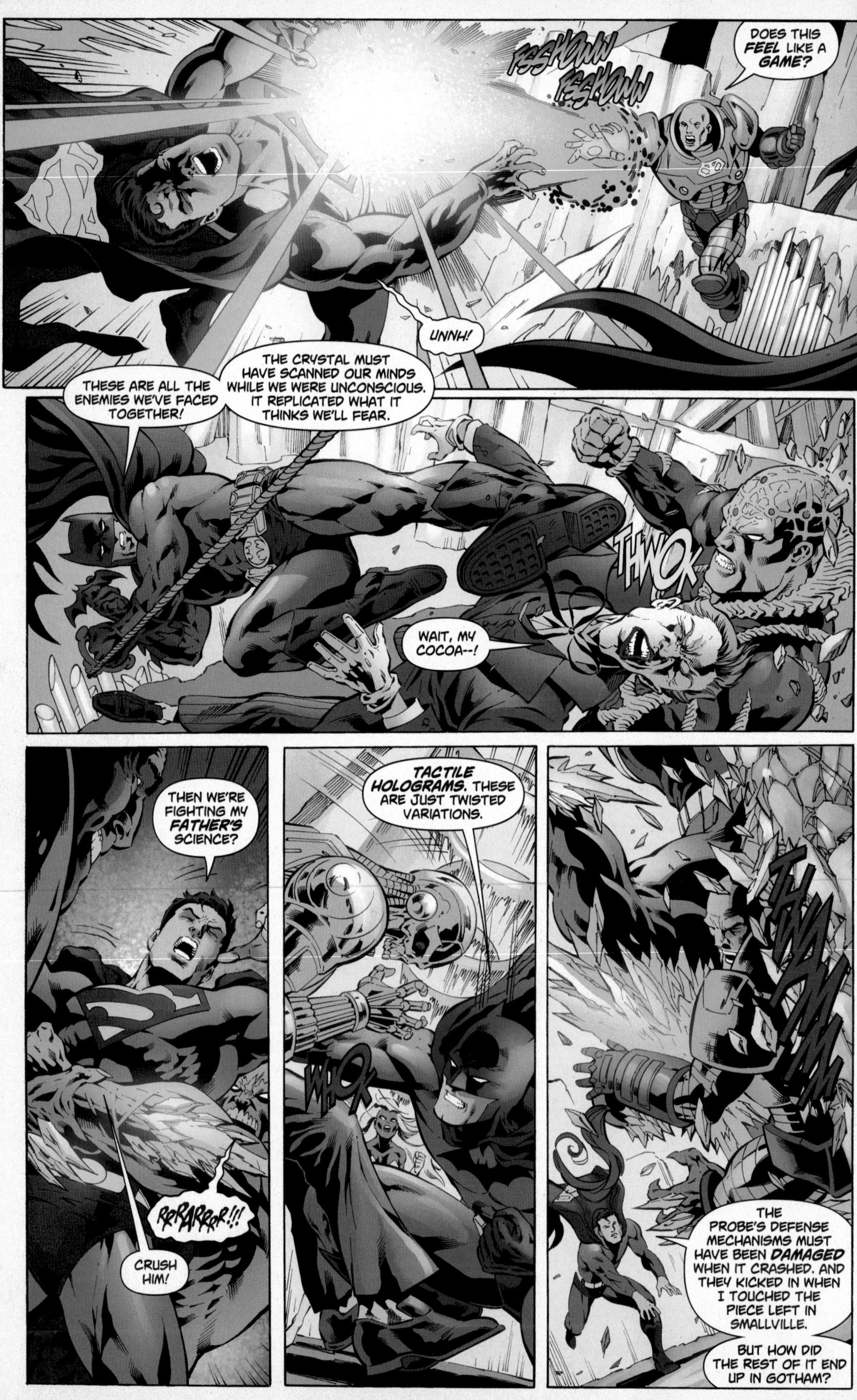

FSSHOWW FSSHOWW
DOES THIS FEEL LIKE A GAME?
UNNH!
THESE ARE ALL THE ENEMIES WE'VE FACED TOGETHER!
THE CRYSTAL MUST HAVE SCANNED OUR MINDS WHILE WE WERE UNCONSCIOUS. IT REPLICATED WHAT IT THINKS WE'LL FEAR.
THWOK
WAIT, MY COCOA--!
THEN WE'RE FIGHTING MY FATHER'S SCIENCE?
RRRARRRR!!!
CRUSH HIM!
TACTILE HOLOGRAMS. THESE ARE JUST TWISTED VARIATIONS.
WHOK
THWAMM
THE PROBE'S DEFENSE MECHANISMS MUST HAVE BEEN DAMAGED WHEN IT CRASHED. AND THEY KICKED IN WHEN I TOUCHED THE PIECE LEFT IN SMALLVILLE.
BUT HOW DID THE REST OF IT END UP IN GOTHAM?

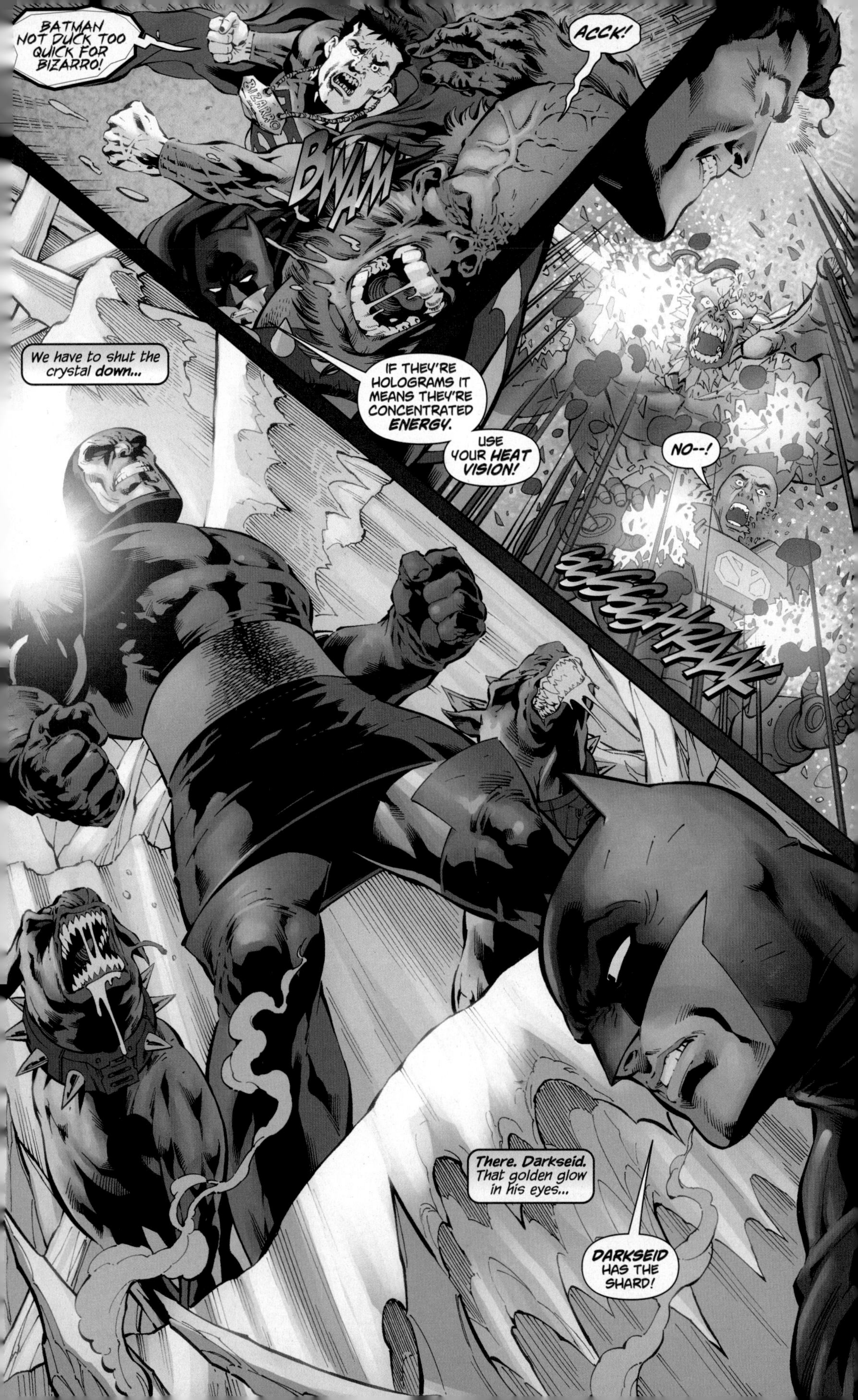
BATMAN NOT DUCK TOO QUICK FOR BIZARRO!
ACCK!
BIZARRO
BWAM
We have to shut the crystal **down...**
IF THEY'RE HOLOGRAMS IT MEANS THEY'RE CONCENTRATED **ENERGY.**
USE YOUR **HEAT VISION!**
NO--!
SSSSHRAAK
*There. Darkseid. That golden glow in his eyes...*
**DARKSEID** HAS THE SHARD!

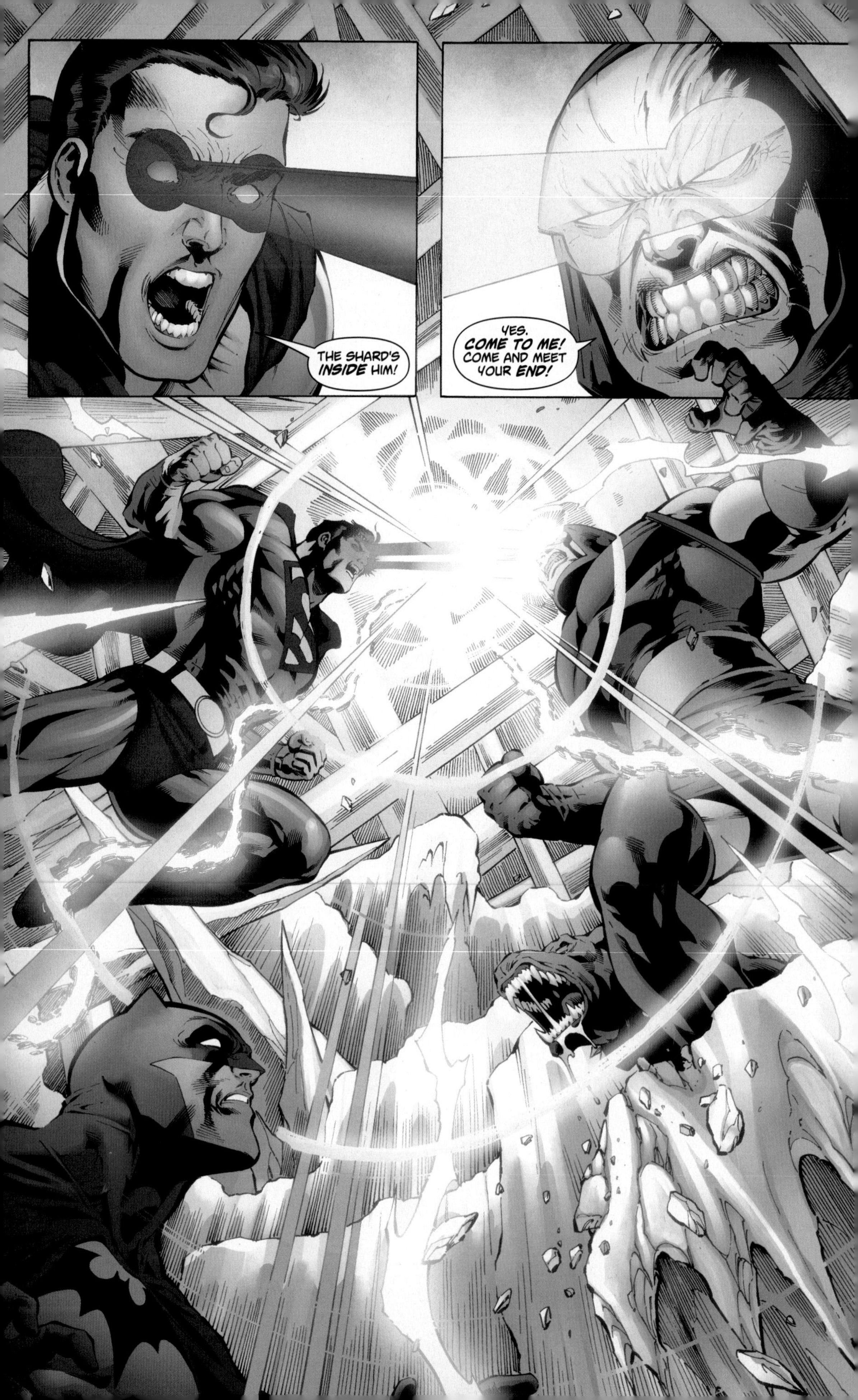
THE SHARD'S INSIDE HIM!
YES. COME TO ME! COME AND MEET YOUR END!

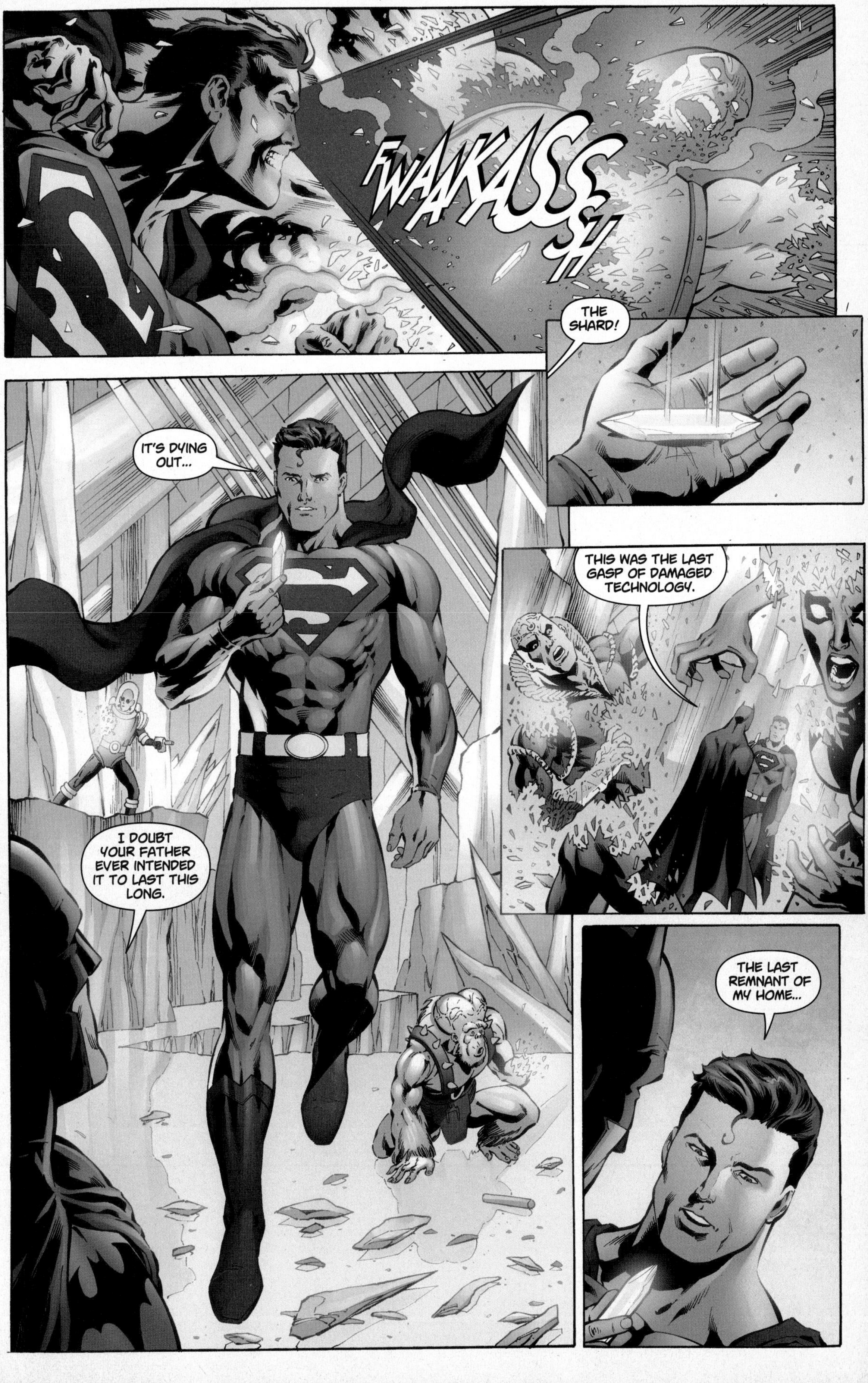
FWAKASSSSH
THE SHARD!
IT'S DYING OUT...
I DOUBT YOUR FATHER EVER INTENDED IT TO LAST THIS LONG.
THIS WAS THE LAST GASP OF DAMAGED TECHNOLOGY.
THE LAST REMNANT OF MY HOME...

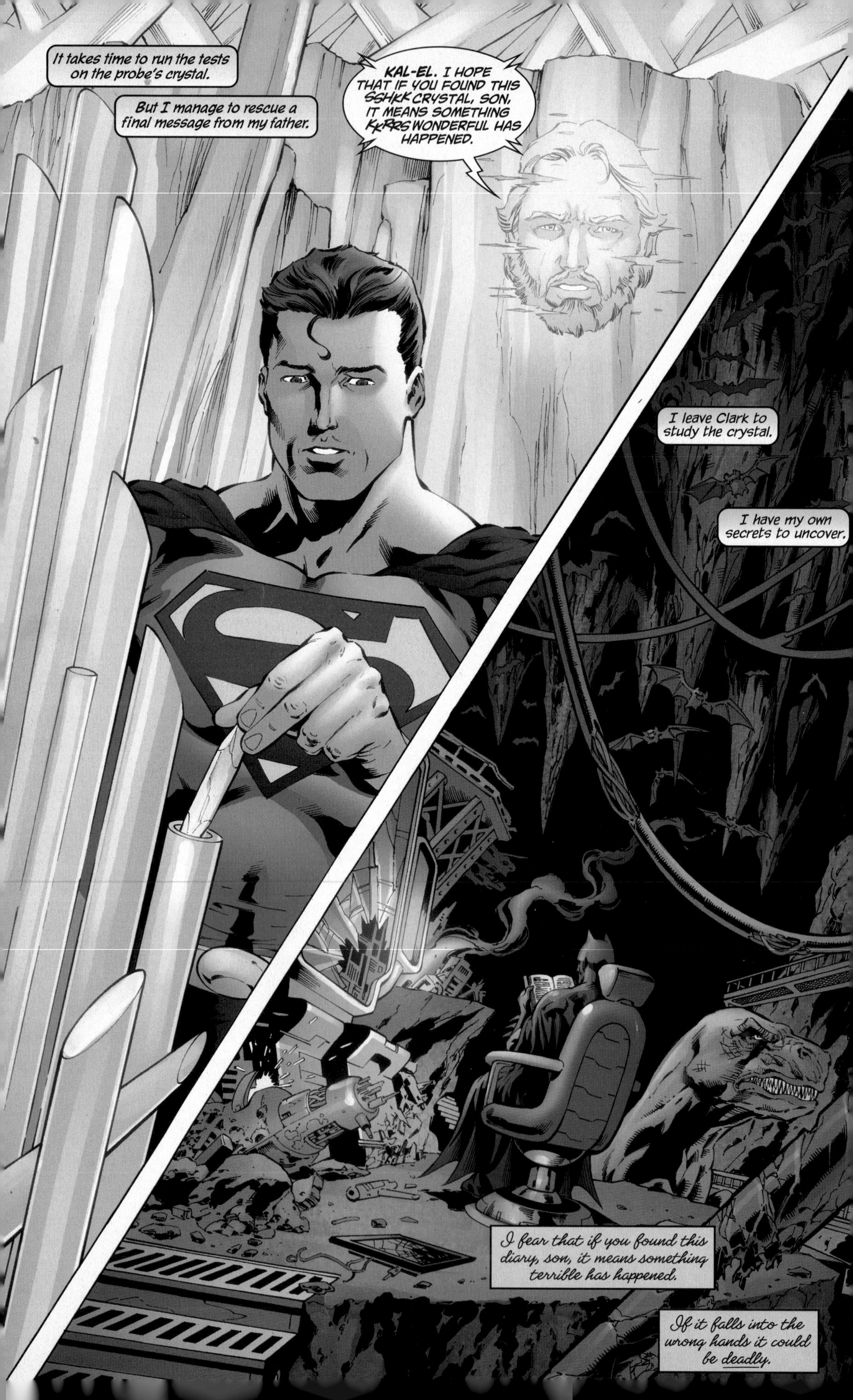

It takes time to run the tests on the probe's crystal.
But I manage to rescue a final message from my father.
KAL-EL. I HOPE THAT IF YOU FOUND THIS SSHKK CRYSTAL, SON, IT MEANS SOMETHING KKRRS WONDERFUL HAS HAPPENED.
I leave Clark to study the crystal.
I have my own secrets to uncover.
I fear that if you found this diary, son, it means something terrible has happened.
If it falls into the wrong hands it could be deadly.

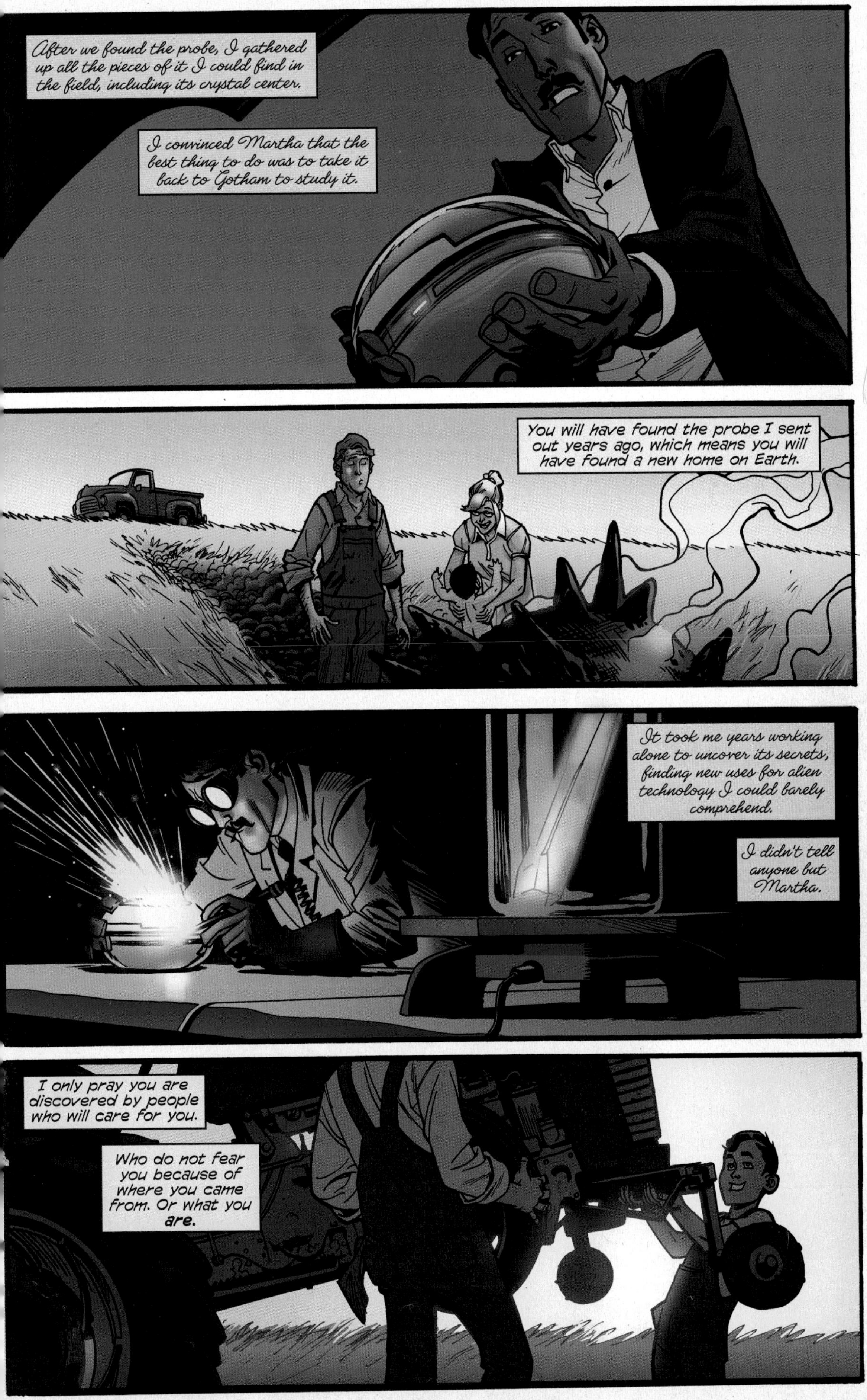
After we found the probe, I gathered up all the pieces of it I could find in the field, including its crystal center.
I convinced Martha that the best thing to do was to take it back to Gotham to study it.
You will have found the probe I sent out years ago, which means you will have found a new home on Earth.
It took me years working alone to uncover its secrets, finding new uses for alien technology I could barely comprehend.
I didn't tell anyone but Martha.
I only pray you are discovered by people who will care for you.
Who do not fear you because of where you came from. Or what you **are**.

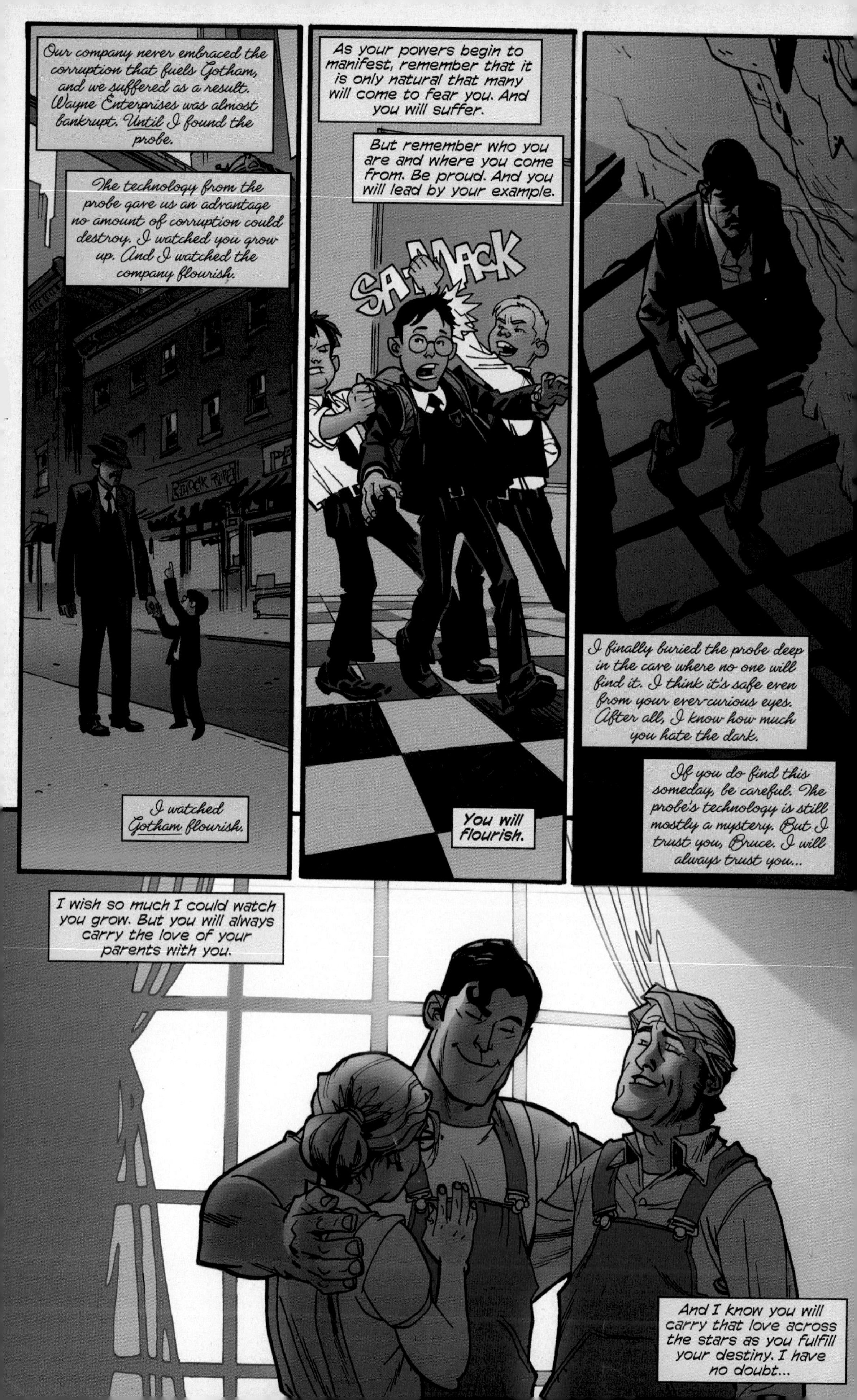
Our company never embraced the corruption that fuels Gotham, and we suffered as a result. Wayne Enterprises was almost bankrupt. Until I found the probe.
The technology from the probe gave us an advantage no amount of corruption could destroy. I watched you grow up. And I watched the company flourish.
I watched Gotham flourish.
As your powers begin to manifest, remember that it is only natural that many will come to fear you. And you will suffer.
But remember who you are and where you come from. Be proud. And you will lead by your example.
SA-MACK
You will flourish.
I finally buried the probe deep in the cave where no one will find it. I think it's safe even from your ever-curious eyes. After all, I know how much you hate the dark.
If you do find this someday, be careful. The probe's technology is still mostly a mystery. But I trust you, Bruce. I will always trust you...
I wish so much I could watch you grow. But you will always carry the love of your parents with you.
And I know you will carry that love across the stars as you fulfill your destiny. I have no doubt...

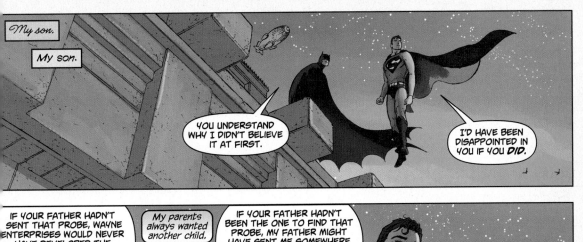

*My son.*

*My son.*

YOU UNDERSTAND WHY I DIDN'T BELIEVE IT AT FIRST.

I'D HAVE BEEN DISAPPOINTED IN YOU IF YOU *DID*.

IF YOUR FATHER HADN'T SENT THAT PROBE, WAYNE ENTERPRISES WOULD NEVER HAVE DEVELOPED THE TECHNOLOGY IT NEEDED TO SURVIVE. AND I WOULDN'T HAVE THE MEANS I NEED TO BE BATMAN *TODAY*.

*My parents always wanted another child.*

IF YOUR FATHER HADN'T BEEN THE ONE TO FIND THAT PROBE, MY FATHER MIGHT HAVE SENT ME SOMEWHERE ELSE. I WOULD HAVE BEEN RAISED ON ANOTHER WORLD, AND EARTH WOULD NEVER HAVE HEARD OF SUPERMAN.

*I'm so lucky to have the family I have. Lois, Kara, Ma & Pa.*

HE USED TO TALK ABOUT HIS *VISION* FOR GOTHAM. THAT WAS THE WORD HE USED. HIS *VISION* FOR THE CITY GOTHAM *COULD BECOME* SOMEDAY. NOW I KNOW WHERE THAT VISION CAME FROM.

*But Bruce is the closest thing I have...*

AND I ALWAYS WONDERED WHY MY FATHER CHOSE EARTH. THERE ARE HUNDREDS OF PLANETS CIRCLING *YELLOW SUNS*. HE COULD HAVE SENT ME TO ANY ONE OF THEM. NOW I KNOW WHY HE CHOSE *THIS ONE*.

*I've never had the luxury of family. But Clark has almost come to be...*

*...to a brother.*

*...the brother I never had.*

*Clark and I are so different. I question everything, while he is always ready to believe. But I take some comfort in knowing...*

*Bruce and I have so little in common. Sunlight gives me my strength, while he thrives in the shadows. But no matter how different we are...*

SUN'S UP NOW. I SHOULD GET BACK TO THE CAVE. DINNER'S GETTING COLD.

I JUST HEARD LOIS'S ALARM CLOCK. I'LL BE HOME JUST IN TIME TO MAKE HER BREAKFAST.

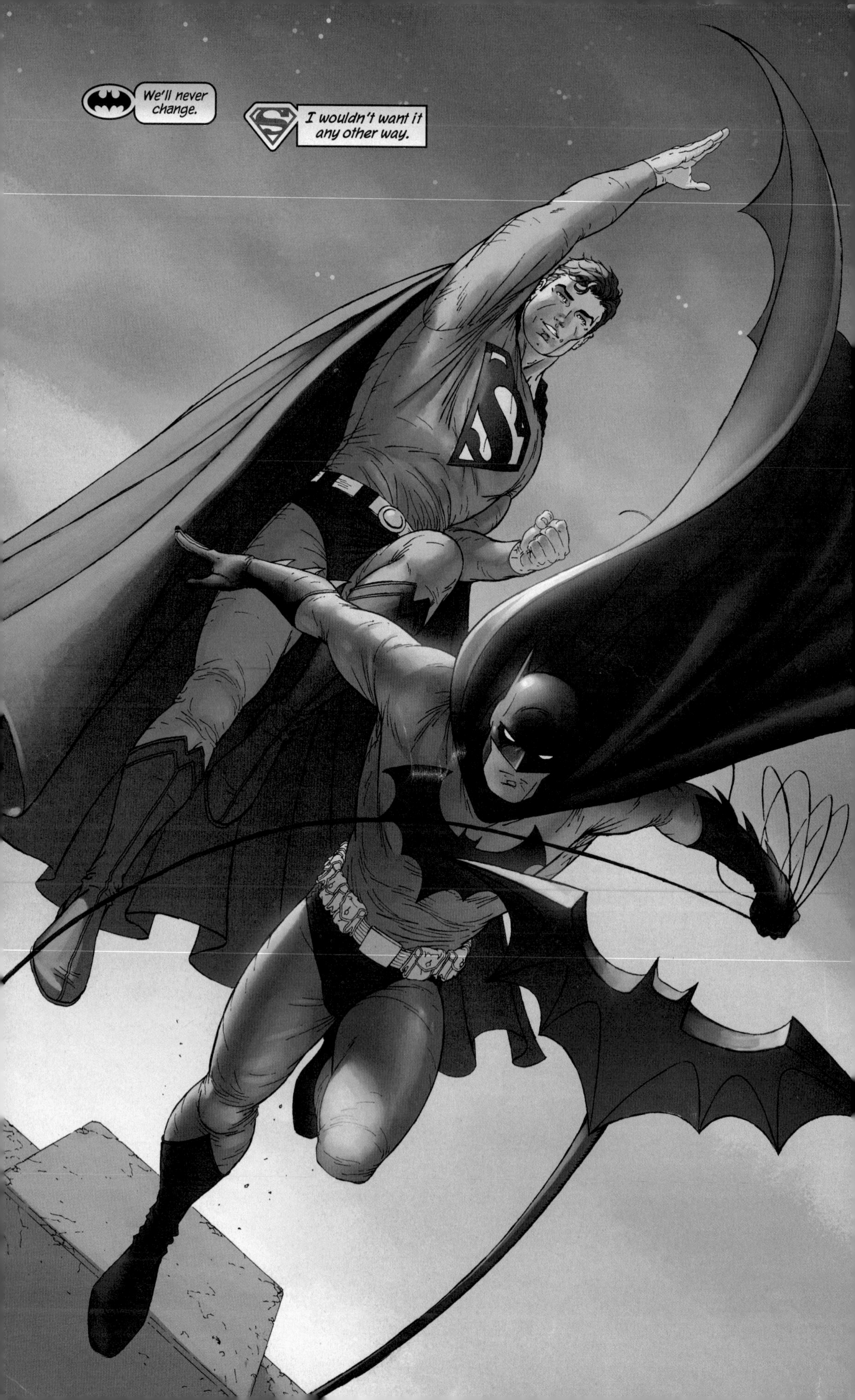
We'll never change.
I wouldn't want it any other way.

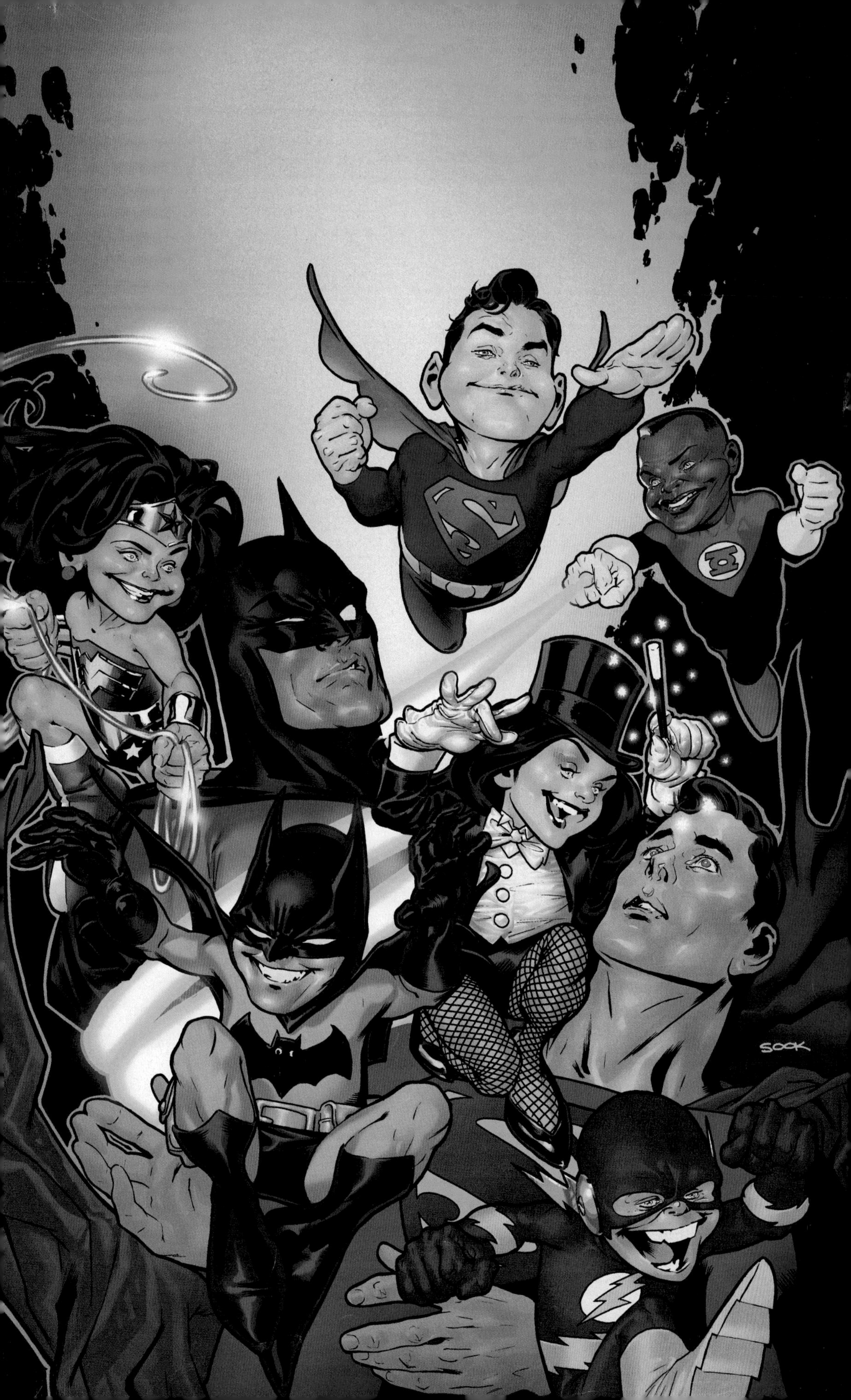
SOOK

SUPERMAN/BATMAN 51

LIL' LEAGUERS
part one

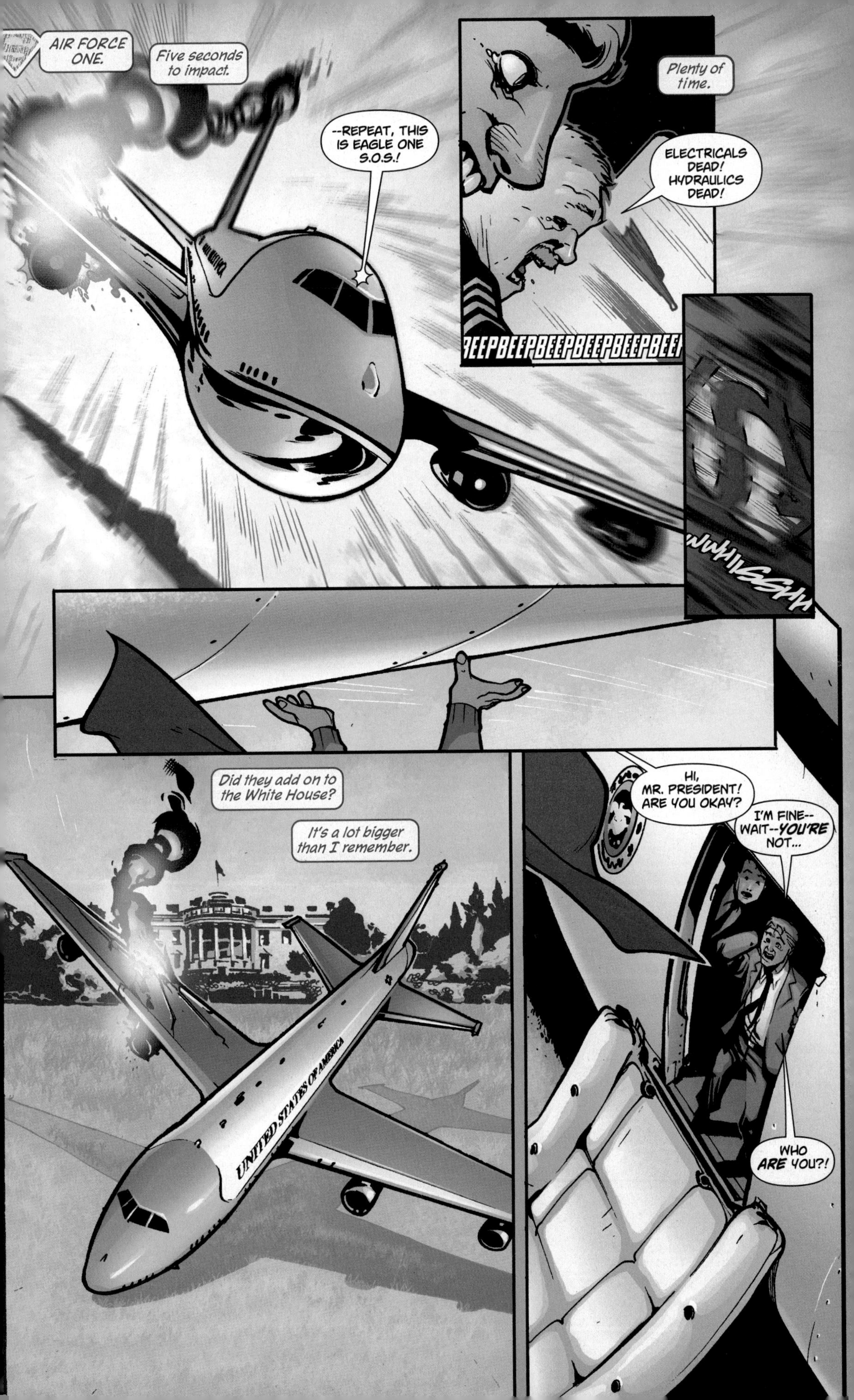

AIR FORCE ONE.
Five seconds to impact.
--REPEAT, THIS IS EAGLE ONE S.O.S.!
Plenty of time.
ELECTRICALS DEAD! HYDRAULICS DEAD!
BEEPBEEPBEEPBEEPBEEPBEE
WHHISSSH
Did they add on to the White House?
It's a lot bigger than I remember.
UNITED STATES OF AMERICA
HI, MR. PRESIDENT! ARE YOU OKAY?
I'M FINE-- WAIT--YOU'RE NOT...
WHO ARE YOU?!

Gotham.

Five seconds to **midnight**.

Something's **changed**.

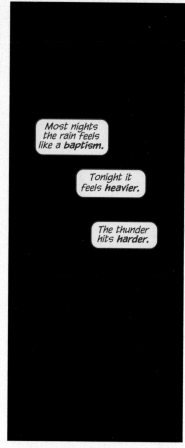

Most nights the rain feels like a **baptism**.

Tonight it feels **heavier**.

The thunder hits **harder**.

But the **vermin** never change.

Ever **superstitious**.

Ever **cowardly**.

HEY, YOU'RE NOT--

POK

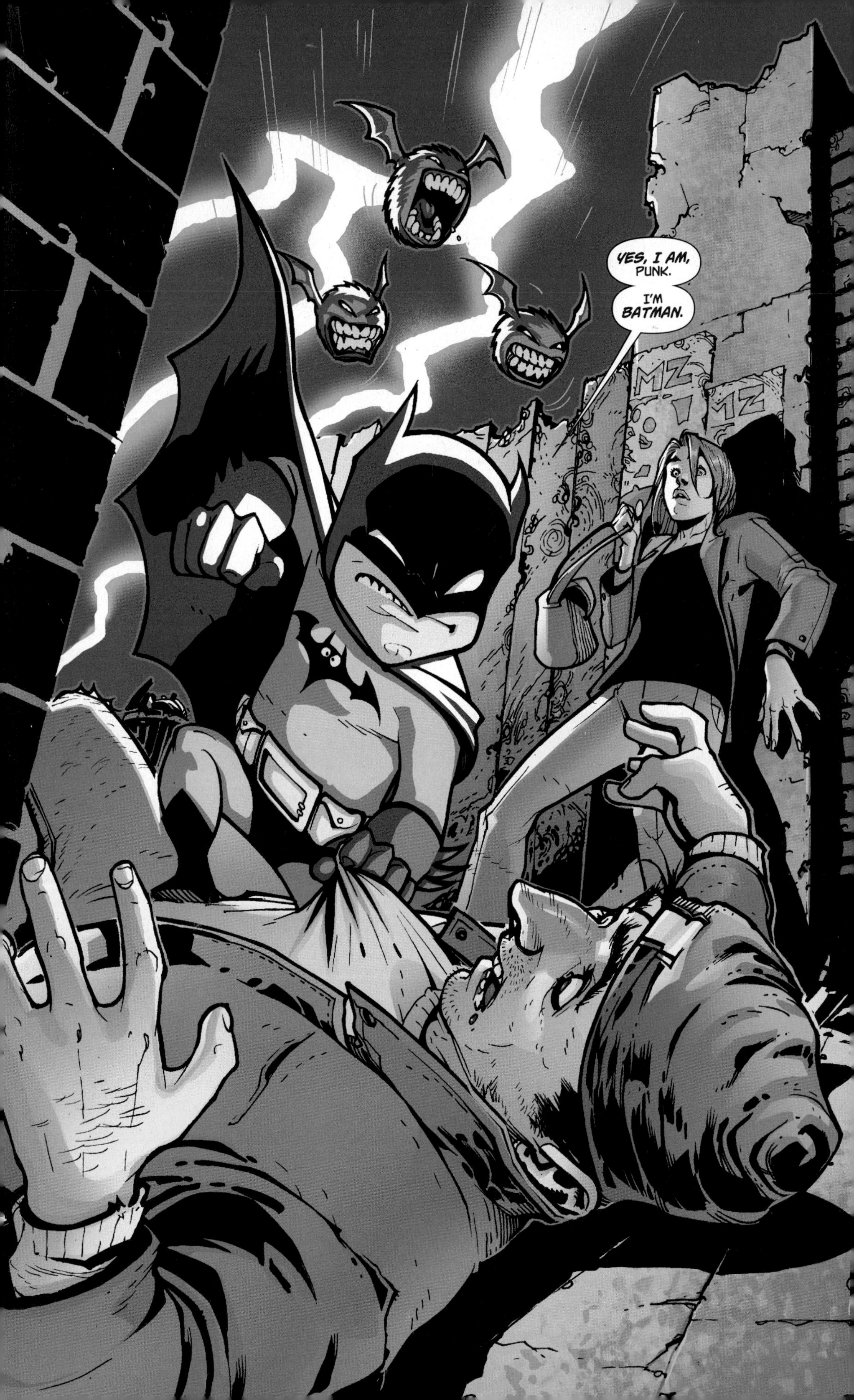
YES, I AM, PUNK.
I'M BATMAN.

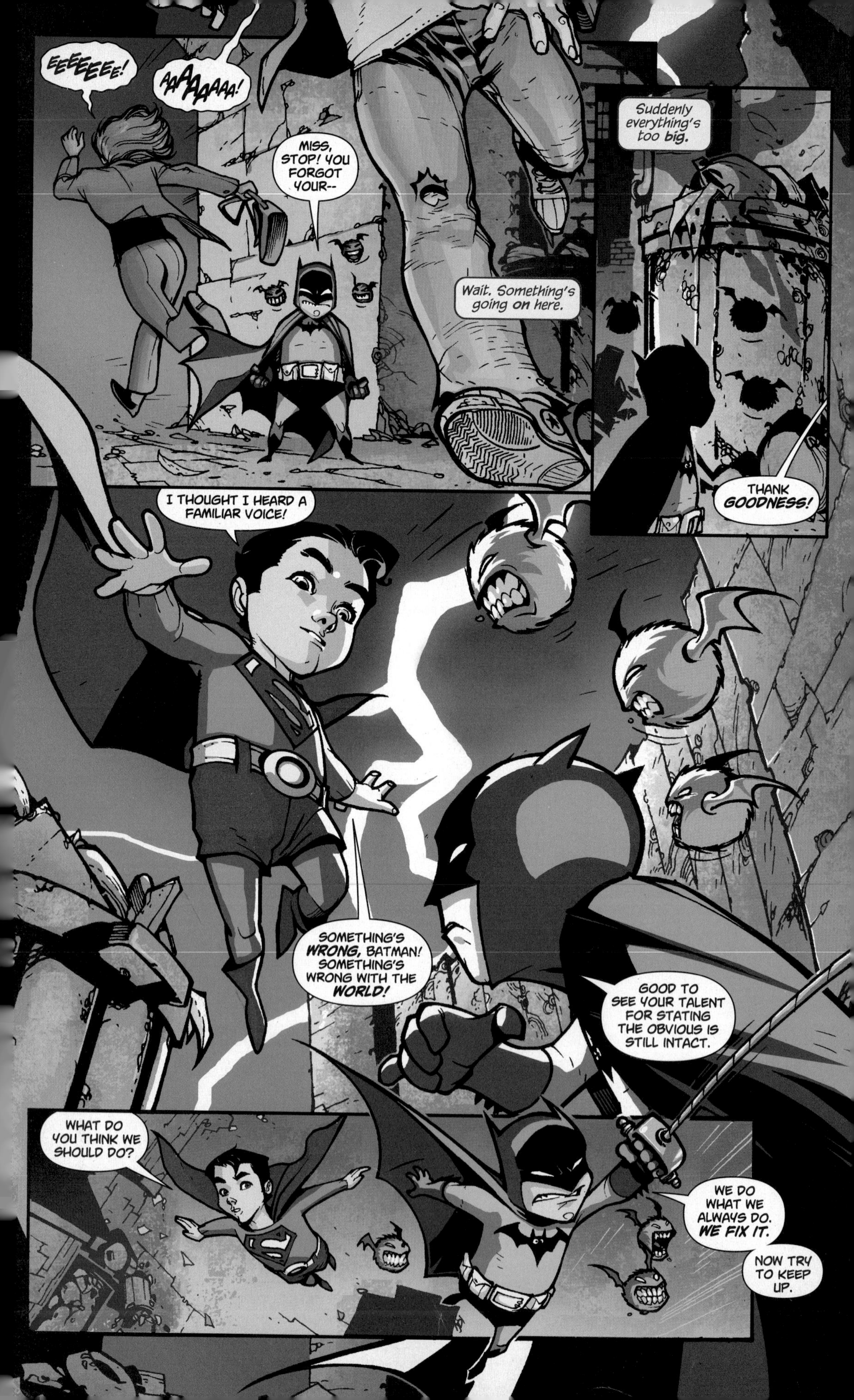
EEEEEEE!
AAAAAAAA!
MISS, STOP! YOU FORGOT YOUR--
Wait. Something's going on here.
Suddenly everything's too big.
THANK GOODNESS!
I THOUGHT I HEARD A FAMILIAR VOICE!
SOMETHING'S WRONG, BATMAN! SOMETHING'S WRONG WITH THE WORLD!
GOOD TO SEE YOUR TALENT FOR STATING THE OBVIOUS IS STILL INTACT.
WHAT DO YOU THINK WE SHOULD DO?
WE DO WHAT WE ALWAYS DO. WE FIX IT.
NOW TRY TO KEEP UP.

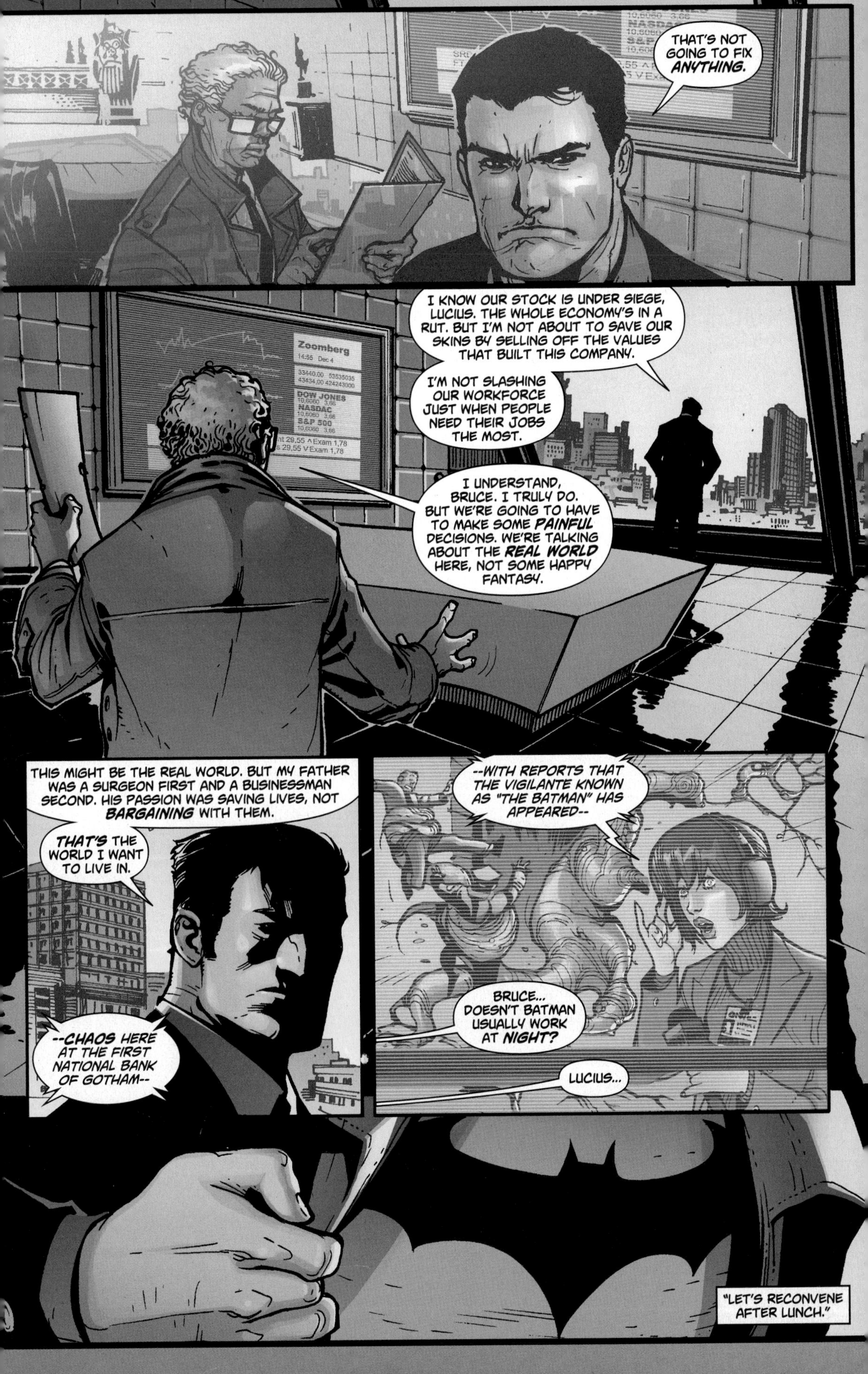
THAT'S NOT GOING TO FIX ANYTHING.
Zoomberg
14:55 Dec 4
DOW JONES
NASDAQ
S&P 500
I KNOW OUR STOCK IS UNDER SIEGE, LUCIUS. THE WHOLE ECONOMY'S IN A RUT. BUT I'M NOT ABOUT TO SAVE OUR SKINS BY SELLING OFF THE VALUES THAT BUILT THIS COMPANY.
I'M NOT SLASHING OUR WORKFORCE JUST WHEN PEOPLE NEED THEIR JOBS THE MOST.
I UNDERSTAND, BRUCE. I TRULY DO. BUT WE'RE GOING TO HAVE TO MAKE SOME PAINFUL DECISIONS. WE'RE TALKING ABOUT THE REAL WORLD HERE, NOT SOME HAPPY FANTASY.
THIS MIGHT BE THE REAL WORLD. BUT MY FATHER WAS A SURGEON FIRST AND A BUSINESSMAN SECOND. HIS PASSION WAS SAVING LIVES, NOT BARGAINING WITH THEM.
THAT'S THE WORLD I WANT TO LIVE IN.
--CHAOS HERE AT THE FIRST NATIONAL BANK OF GOTHAM--
--WITH REPORTS THAT THE VIGILANTE KNOWN AS "THE BATMAN" HAS APPEARED--
BRUCE... DOESN'T BATMAN USUALLY WORK AT NIGHT?
LUCIUS...
"LET'S RECONVENE AFTER LUNCH."

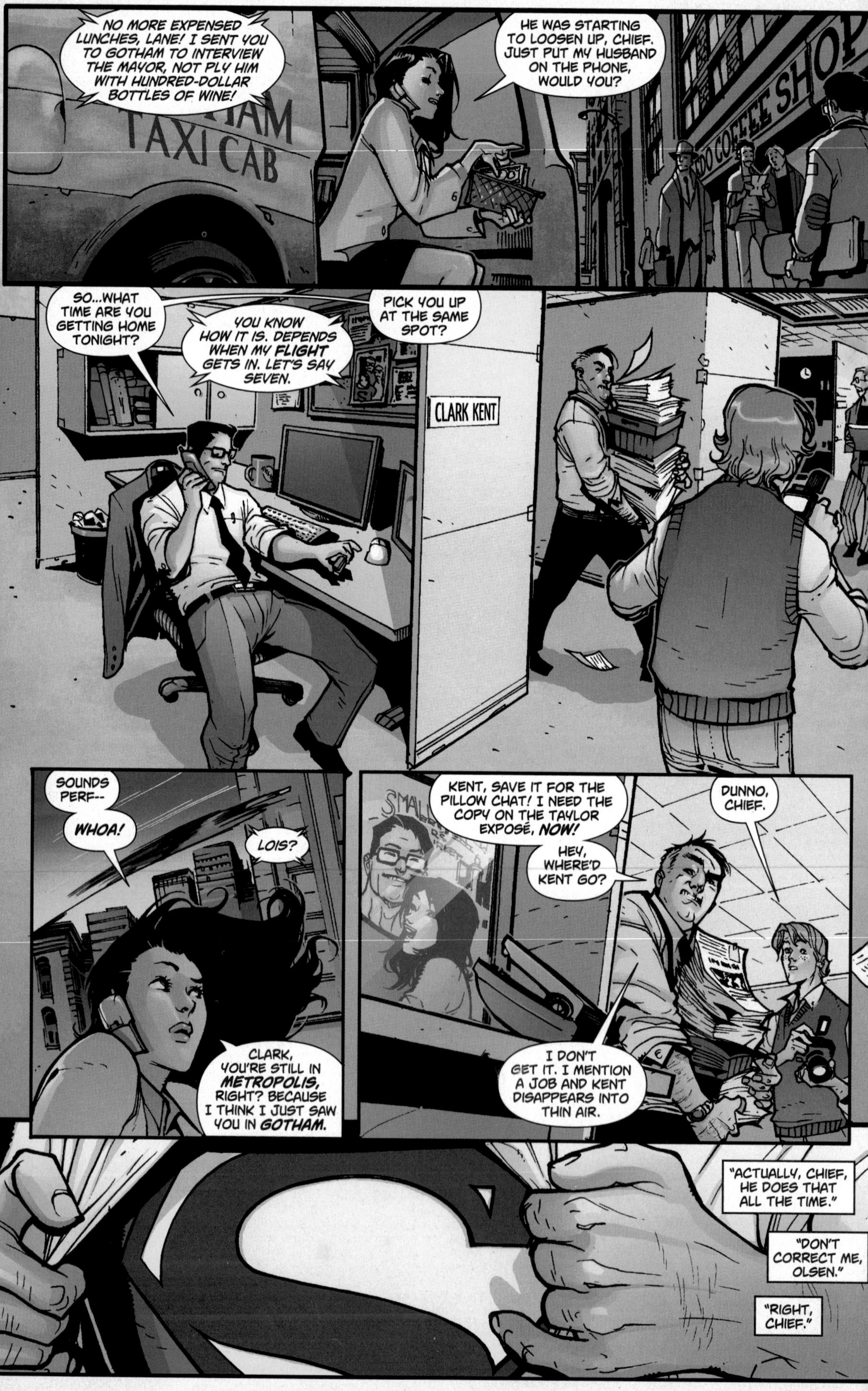
NO MORE EXPENSED LUNCHES, LANE! I SENT YOU TO GOTHAM TO INTERVIEW THE MAYOR, NOT PLY HIM WITH HUNDRED-DOLLAR BOTTLES OF WINE!
HE WAS STARTING TO LOOSEN UP, CHIEF. JUST PUT MY HUSBAND ON THE PHONE, WOULD YOU?
TAXI CAB
COFFEE SHOP
SO...WHAT TIME ARE YOU GETTING HOME TONIGHT?
YOU KNOW HOW IT IS. DEPENDS WHEN MY FLIGHT GETS IN. LET'S SAY SEVEN.
PICK YOU UP AT THE SAME SPOT?
CLARK KENT
SOUNDS PERF--
WHOA!
LOIS?
CLARK, YOU'RE STILL IN METROPOLIS, RIGHT? BECAUSE I THINK I JUST SAW YOU IN GOTHAM.
KENT, SAVE IT FOR THE PILLOW CHAT! I NEED THE COPY ON THE TAYLOR EXPOSÉ, NOW!
HEY, WHERE'D KENT GO?
DUNNO, CHIEF.
I DON'T GET IT. I MENTION A JOB AND KENT DISAPPEARS INTO THIN AIR.
"ACTUALLY, CHIEF, HE DOES THAT ALL THE TIME."
"DON'T CORRECT ME, OLSEN."
"RIGHT, CHIEF."

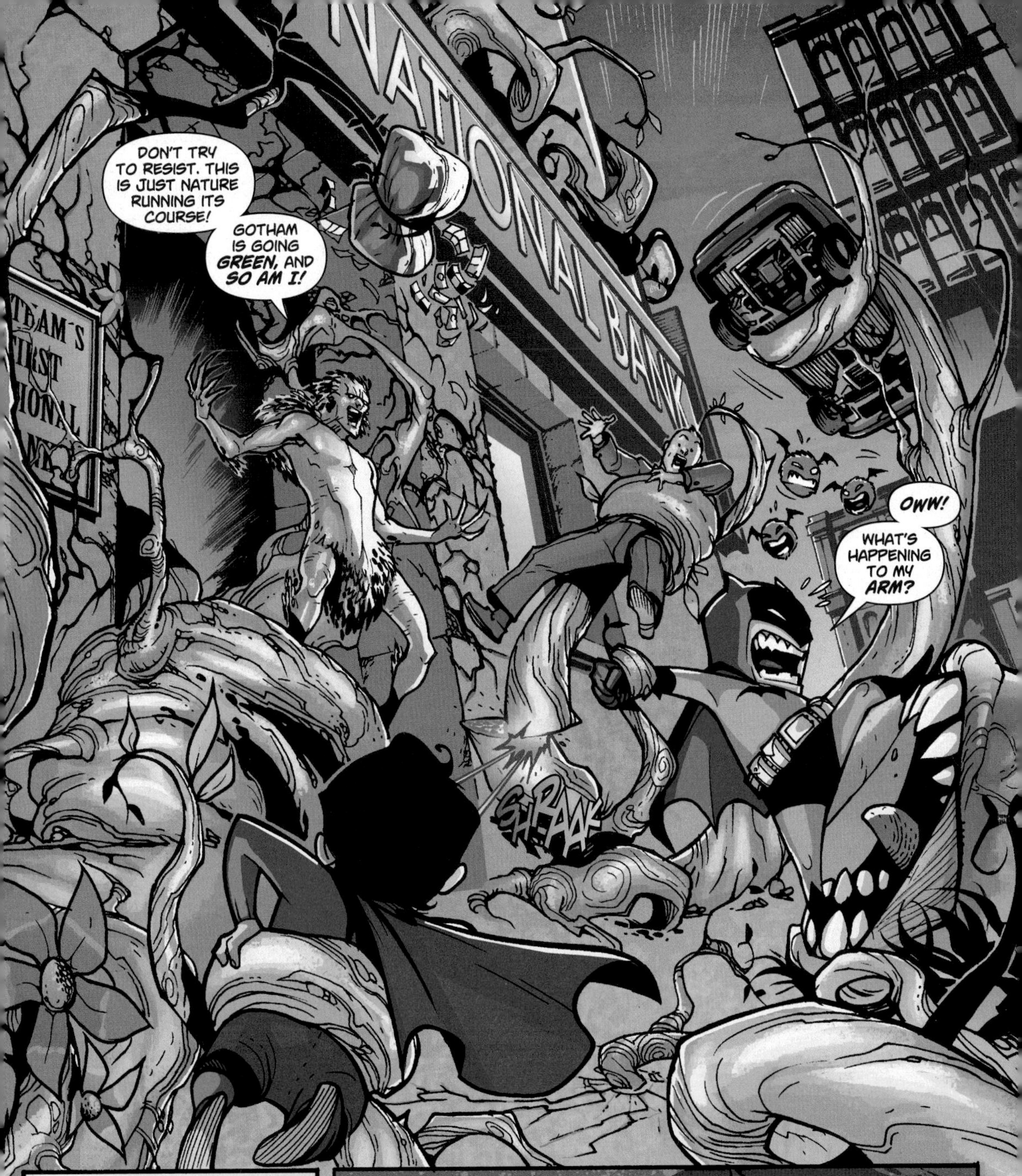
NATIONAL BANK
DON'T TRY TO RESIST. THIS IS JUST NATURE RUNNING ITS COURSE!
GOTHAM IS GOING GREEN, AND SO AM I!
SHRAAK
OWW!
WHAT'S HAPPENING TO MY ARM?

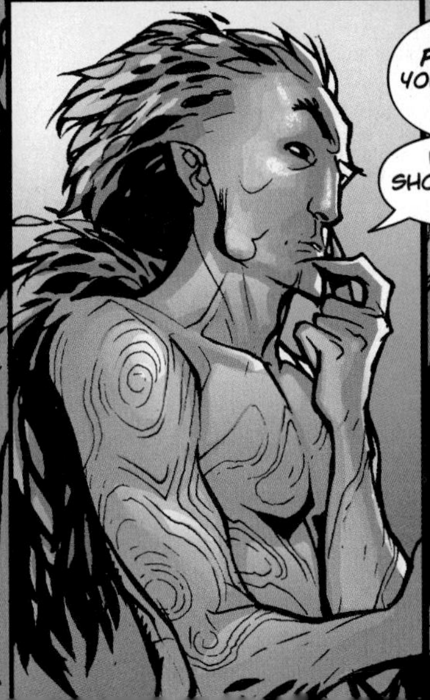
IT'S CALLED PAIN, YOU FOOL! YOU ACT LIKE YOU'VE NEVER FELT IT BEFORE.
WAITAMINUTE. SHOULDN'T YOU TWO BE TALLER?

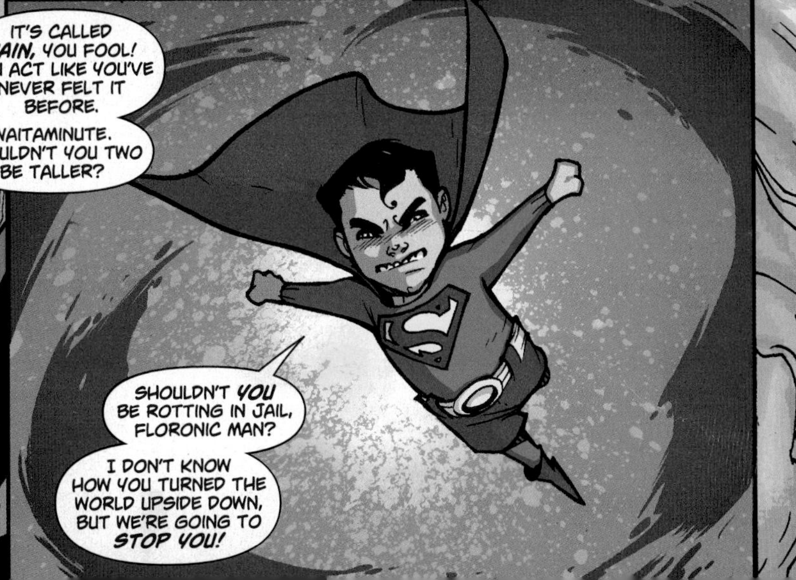
SHOULDN'T YOU BE ROTTING IN JAIL, FLORONIC MAN?
I DON'T KNOW HOW YOU TURNED THE WORLD UPSIDE DOWN, BUT WE'RE GOING TO STOP YOU!

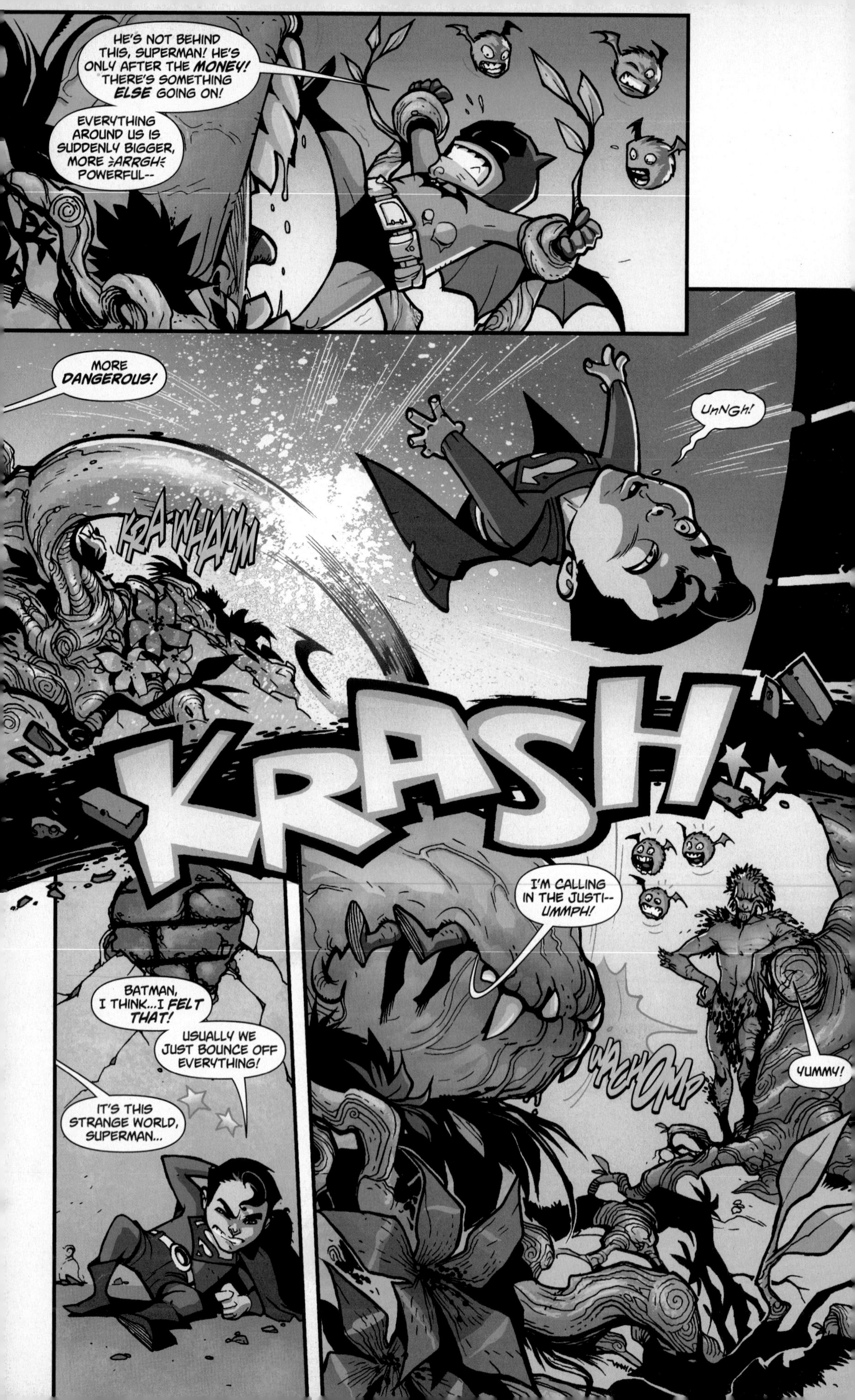
HE'S NOT BEHIND THIS, SUPERMAN! HE'S ONLY AFTER THE MONEY! THERE'S SOMETHING ELSE GOING ON!
EVERYTHING AROUND US IS SUDDENLY BIGGER, MORE ARRGH POWERFUL--
MORE DANGEROUS!
UnNGh!
KRA-WHAMM
KRASH
I'M CALLING IN THE JUSTI-- UMMPH!
BATMAN, I THINK...I FELT THAT!
USUALLY WE JUST BOUNCE OFF EVERYTHING!
IT'S THIS STRANGE WORLD, SUPERMAN...
WHOMP
YUMMY!

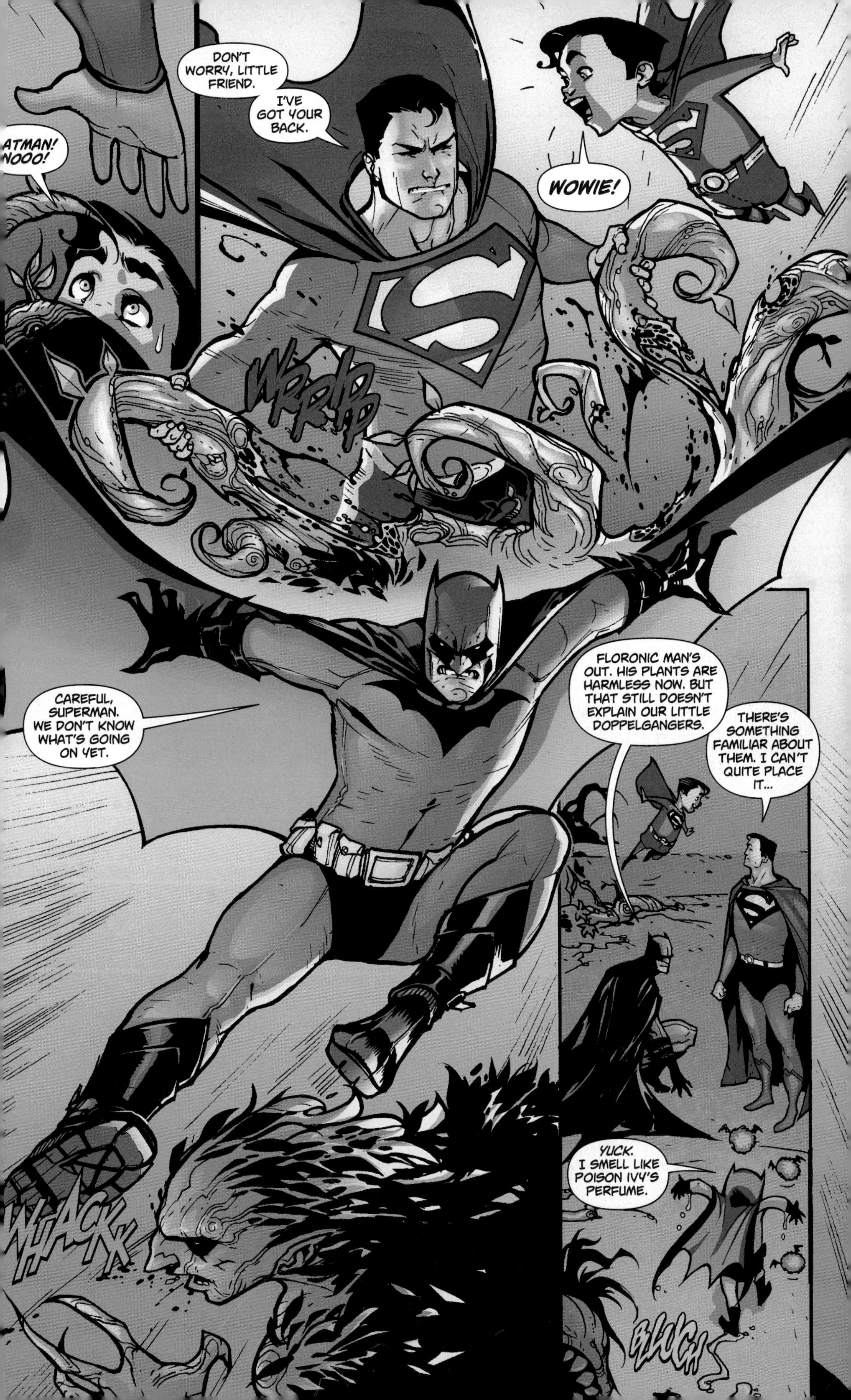
ATMAN! NOOO!
DON'T WORRY, LITTLE FRIEND.
I'VE GOT YOUR BACK.
WOWIE!
WRRRRR
CAREFUL, SUPERMAN. WE DON'T KNOW WHAT'S GOING ON YET.
FLORONIC MAN'S OUT. HIS PLANTS ARE HARMLESS NOW. BUT THAT STILL DOESN'T EXPLAIN OUR LITTLE DOPPELGANGERS.
THERE'S SOMETHING FAMILIAR ABOUT THEM. I CAN'T QUITE PLACE IT...
WHACKK
YUCK. I SMELL LIKE POISON IVY'S PERFUME.
BLUCH

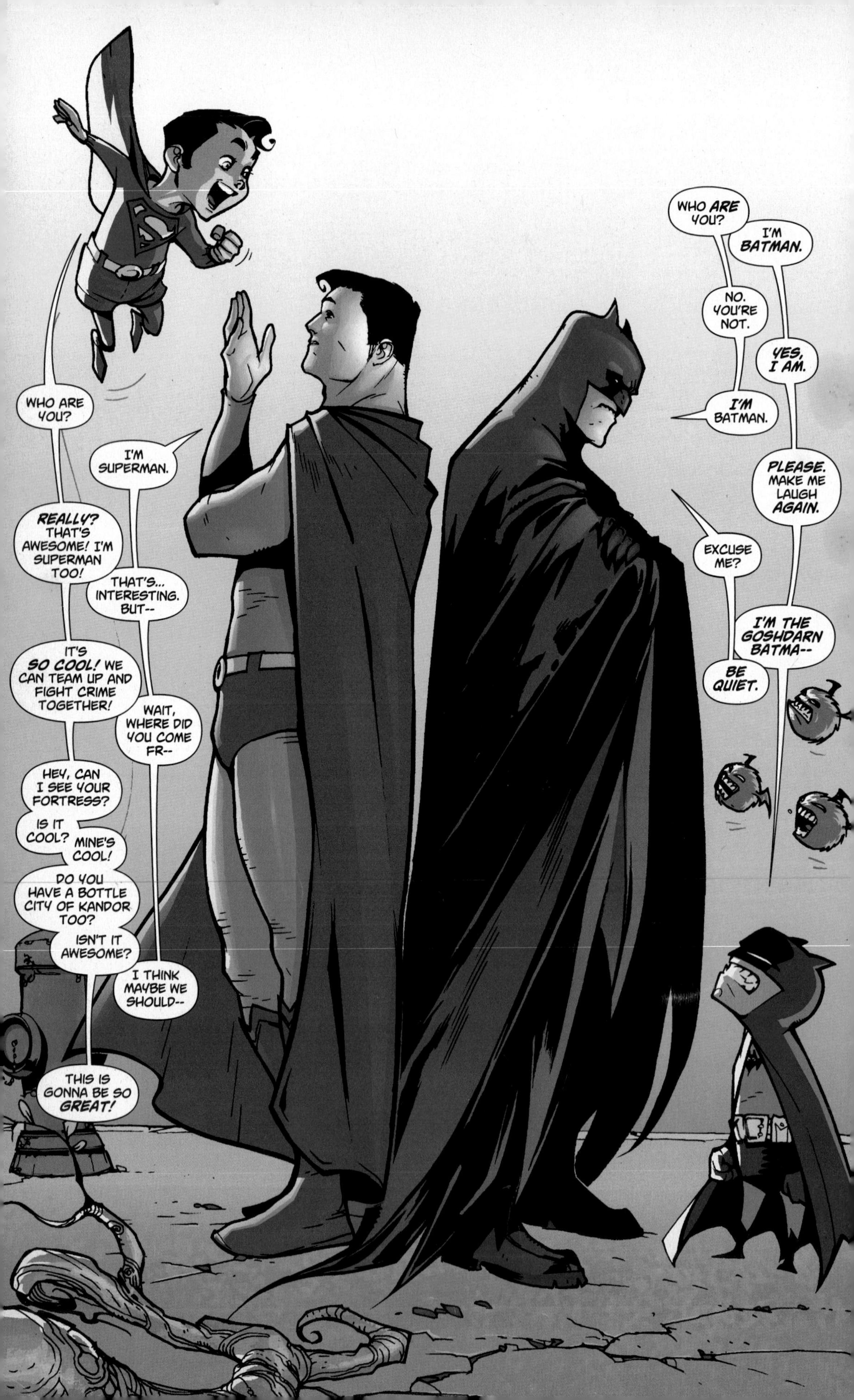
WHO ARE YOU?
I'M SUPERMAN.
REALLY? THAT'S AWESOME! I'M SUPERMAN TOO!
THAT'S... INTERESTING. BUT--
IT'S SO COOL! WE CAN TEAM UP AND FIGHT CRIME TOGETHER!
WAIT, WHERE DID YOU COME FR--
HEY, CAN I SEE YOUR FORTRESS?
IS IT COOL?
MINE'S COOL!
DO YOU HAVE A BOTTLE CITY OF KANDOR TOO?
ISN'T IT AWESOME?
I THINK MAYBE WE SHOULD--
THIS IS GONNA BE SO GREAT!
WHO ARE YOU?
I'M BATMAN.
NO. YOU'RE NOT.
YES, I AM.
I'M BATMAN.
PLEASE. MAKE ME LAUGH AGAIN.
EXCUSE ME?
I'M THE GOSHDARN BATMA--
BE QUIET.

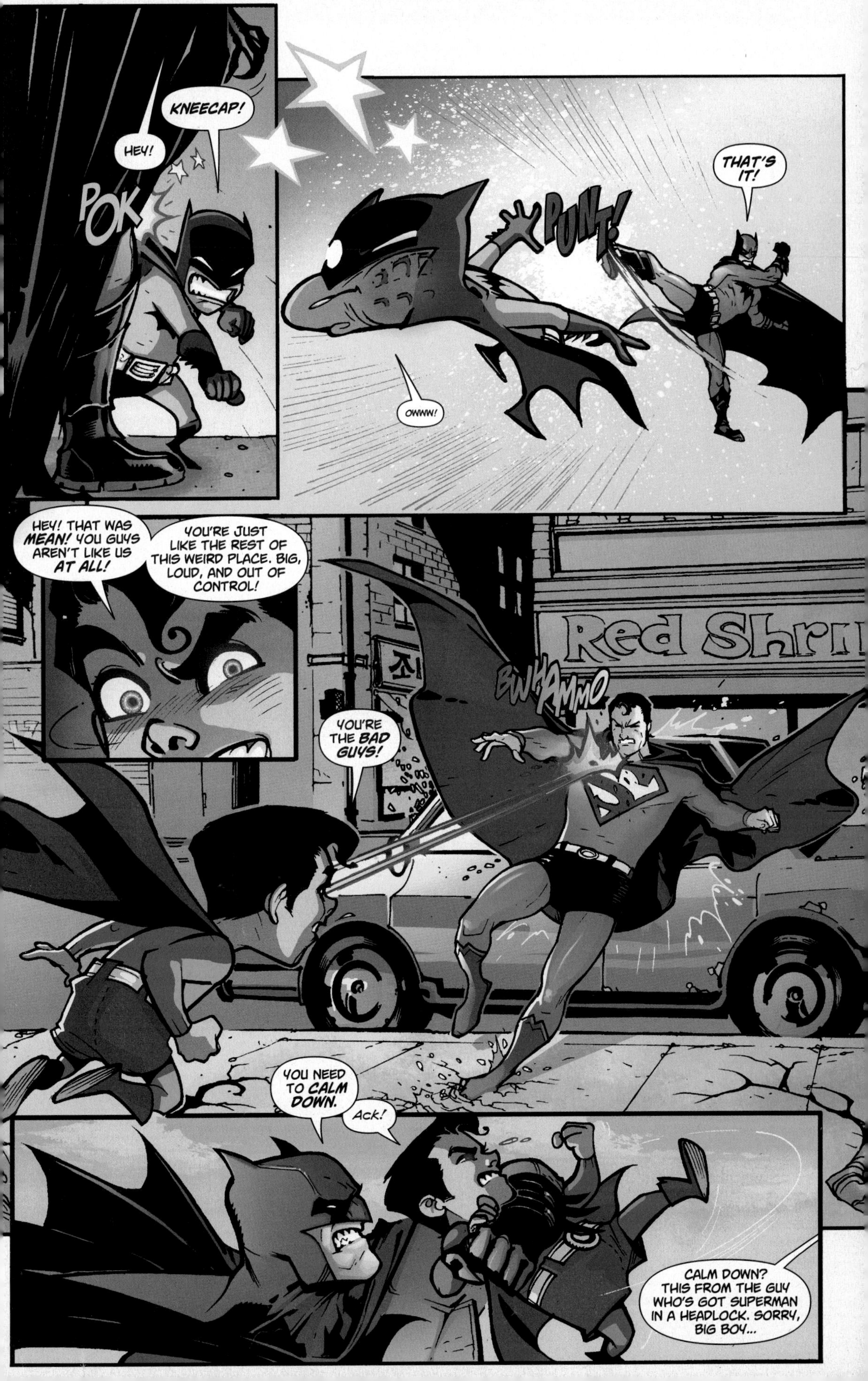
HEY!
KNEECAP!
POK
PUNT!
THAT'S IT!
OWWW!
HEY! THAT WAS MEAN! YOU GUYS AREN'T LIKE US AT ALL!
YOU'RE JUST LIKE THE REST OF THIS WEIRD PLACE. BIG, LOUD, AND OUT OF CONTROL!
Red Shr
BWHAMMO
YOU'RE THE BAD GUYS!
YOU NEED TO CALM DOWN.
Ack!
CALM DOWN? THIS FROM THE GUY WHO'S GOT SUPERMAN IN A HEADLOCK. SORRY, BIG BOY...

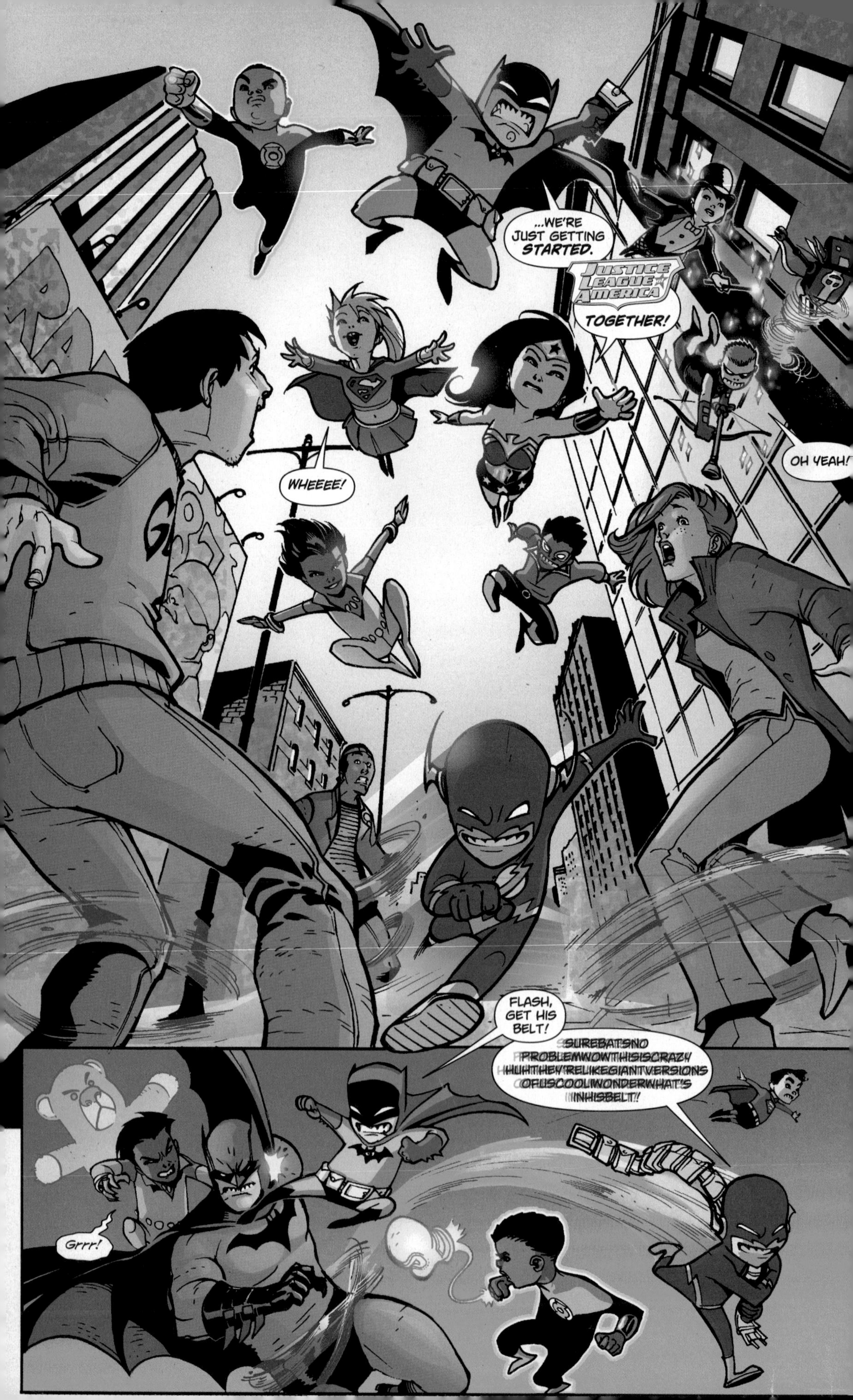
...WE'RE JUST GETTING STARTED.
TOGETHER!
WHEEEE!
OH YEAH!
FLASH, GET HIS BELT!
SUREBATSNO PROBLEMWOWTHISISCRAZY HUHTHEY'RELIKEGIANTVERSIONS OFUSCOOLIWONDERWHAT'S INHISBELT?!
Grrr!

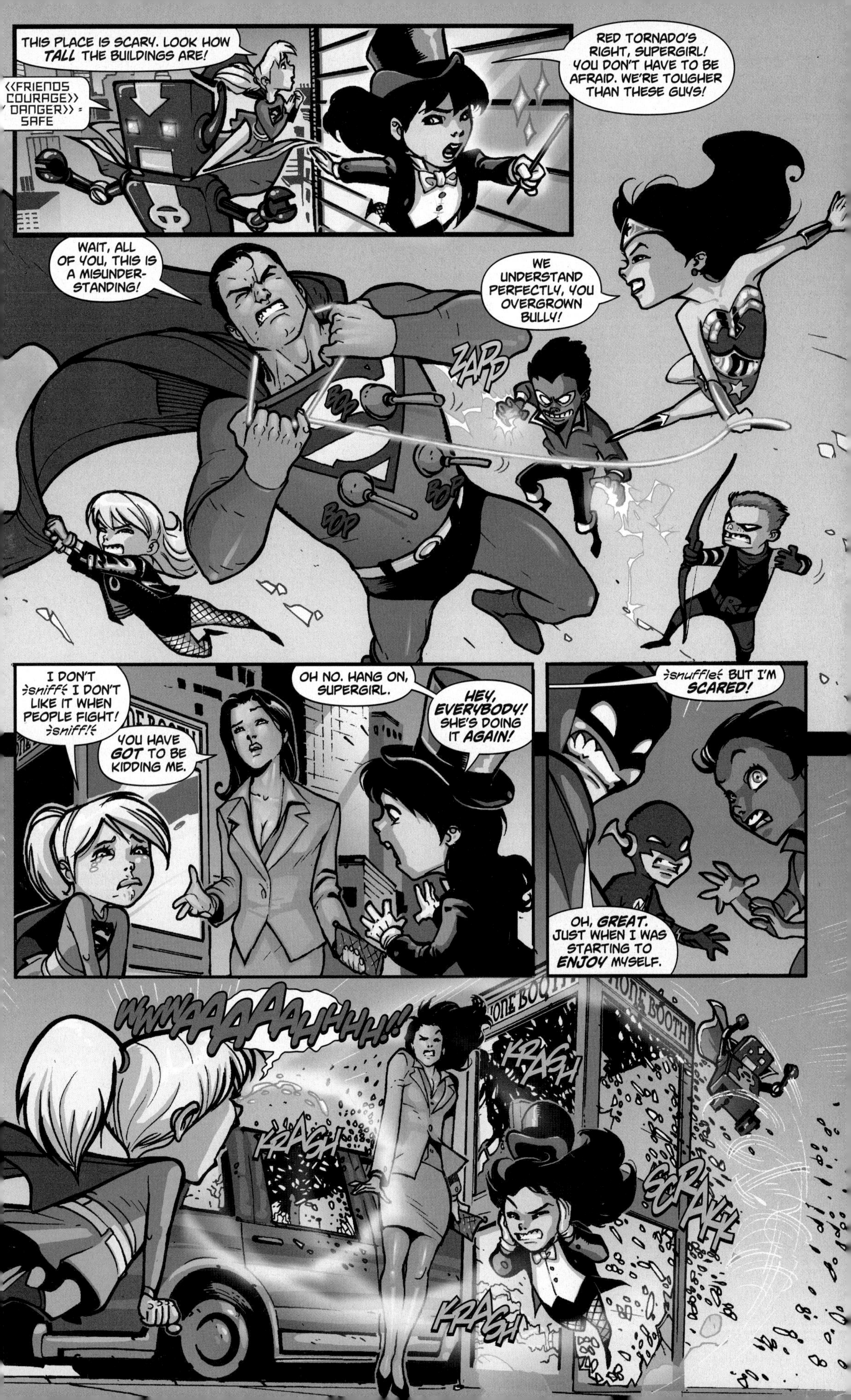
THIS PLACE IS SCARY. LOOK HOW TALL THE BUILDINGS ARE!
<<FRIENDS COURAGE>> <<DANGER>> = SAFE
RED TORNADO'S RIGHT, SUPERGIRL! YOU DON'T HAVE TO BE AFRAID. WE'RE TOUGHER THAN THESE GUYS!
WAIT, ALL OF YOU, THIS IS A MISUNDER-STANDING!
WE UNDERSTAND PERFECTLY, YOU OVERGROWN BULLY!
ZARP
BOP
BOP
BOP
I DON'T *sniff* I DON'T LIKE IT WHEN PEOPLE FIGHT! *sniff!*
YOU HAVE GOT TO BE KIDDING ME.
OH NO. HANG ON, SUPERGIRL.
HEY, EVERYBODY! SHE'S DOING IT AGAIN!
*snuffle* BUT I'M SCARED!
OH, GREAT. JUST WHEN I WAS STARTING TO ENJOY MYSELF.
WWAAAAAHHHH!!
KRASH
KRASH
SCRAKK
KRASH

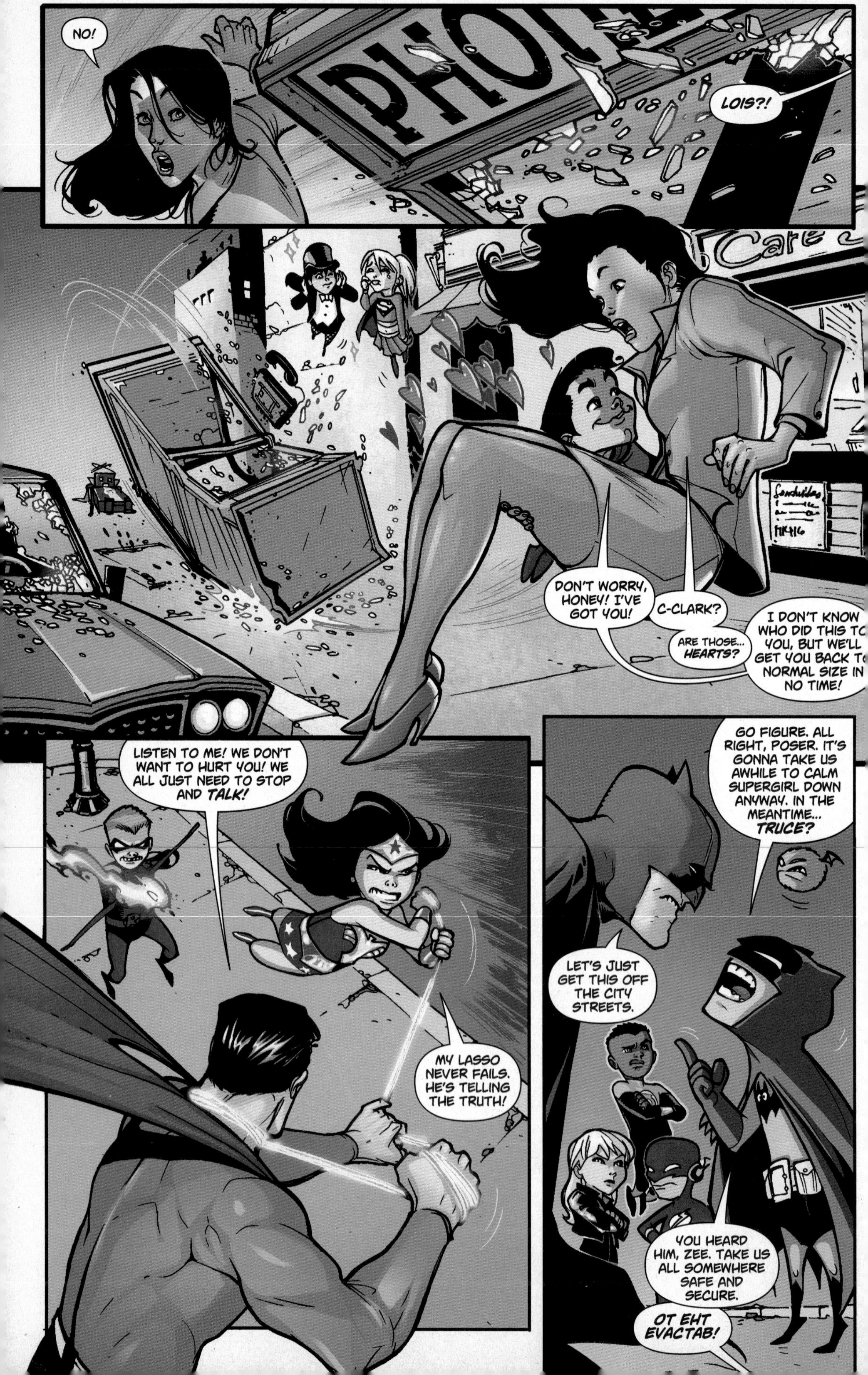

NO!
LOIS?!
DON'T WORRY, HONEY! I'VE GOT YOU!
C-CLARK?
ARE THOSE... HEARTS?
I DON'T KNOW WHO DID THIS TO YOU, BUT WE'LL GET YOU BACK TO NORMAL SIZE IN NO TIME!
LISTEN TO ME! WE DON'T WANT TO HURT YOU! WE ALL JUST NEED TO STOP AND TALK!
MY LASSO NEVER FAILS. HE'S TELLING THE TRUTH!
GO FIGURE. ALL RIGHT, POSER. IT'S GONNA TAKE US AWHILE TO CALM SUPERGIRL DOWN ANYWAY. IN THE MEANTIME... TRUCE?
LET'S JUST GET THIS OFF THE CITY STREETS.
YOU HEARD HIM, ZEE. TAKE US ALL SOMEWHERE SAFE AND SECURE.
OT EHT EVACTAB!

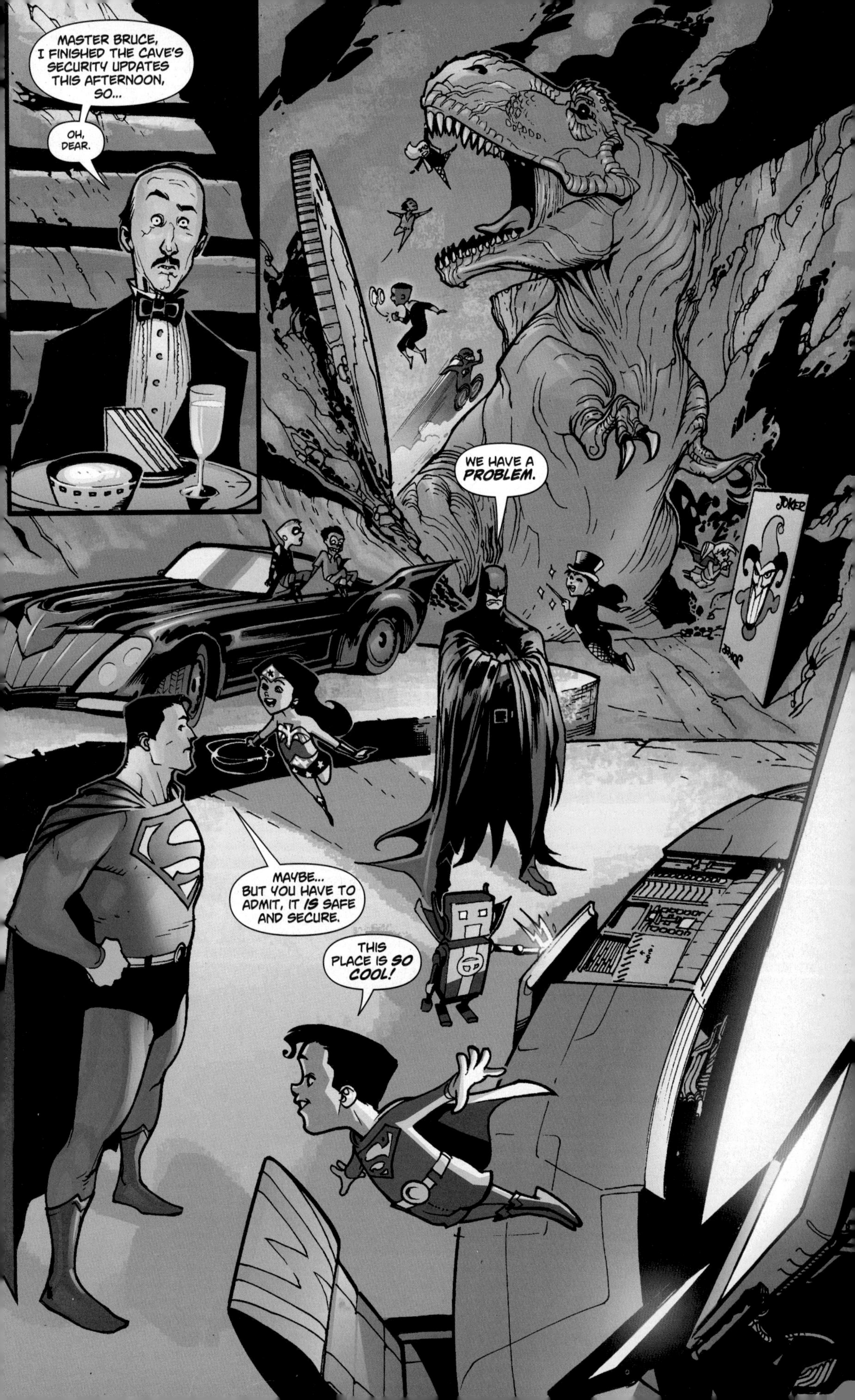
MASTER BRUCE, I FINISHED THE CAVE'S SECURITY UPDATES THIS AFTERNOON, SO...
OH, DEAR.
WE HAVE A *PROBLEM.*
JOKER
MAYBE... BUT YOU HAVE TO ADMIT, IT *IS* SAFE AND SECURE.
THIS PLACE IS *SO COOL!*

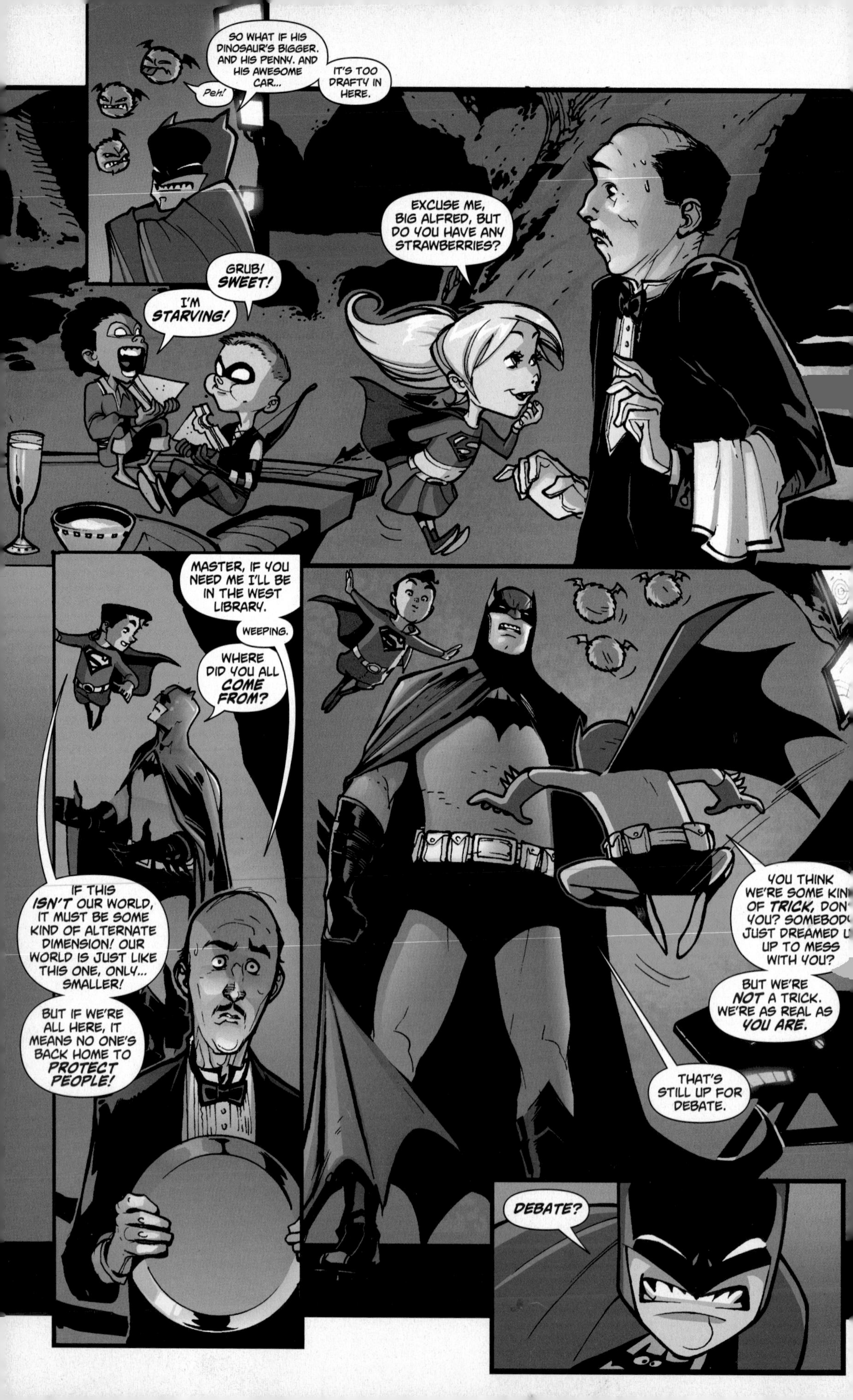
SO WHAT IF HIS DINOSAUR'S BIGGER. AND HIS PENNY. AND HIS AWESOME CAR...
Peh!
IT'S TOO DRAFTY IN HERE.
EXCUSE ME, BIG ALFRED, BUT DO YOU HAVE ANY STRAWBERRIES?
GRUB! SWEET!
I'M STARVING!
MASTER, IF YOU NEED ME I'LL BE IN THE WEST LIBRARY.
WEEPING.
WHERE DID YOU ALL COME FROM?
IF THIS ISN'T OUR WORLD, IT MUST BE SOME KIND OF ALTERNATE DIMENSION! OUR WORLD IS JUST LIKE THIS ONE, ONLY... SMALLER!
BUT IF WE'RE ALL HERE, IT MEANS NO ONE'S BACK HOME TO PROTECT PEOPLE!
YOU THINK WE'RE SOME KIN OF TRICK, DON' YOU? SOMEBOD JUST DREAMED U UP TO MESS WITH YOU?
BUT WE'RE NOT A TRICK. WE'RE AS REAL AS YOU ARE.
THAT'S STILL UP FOR DEBATE.
DEBATE?

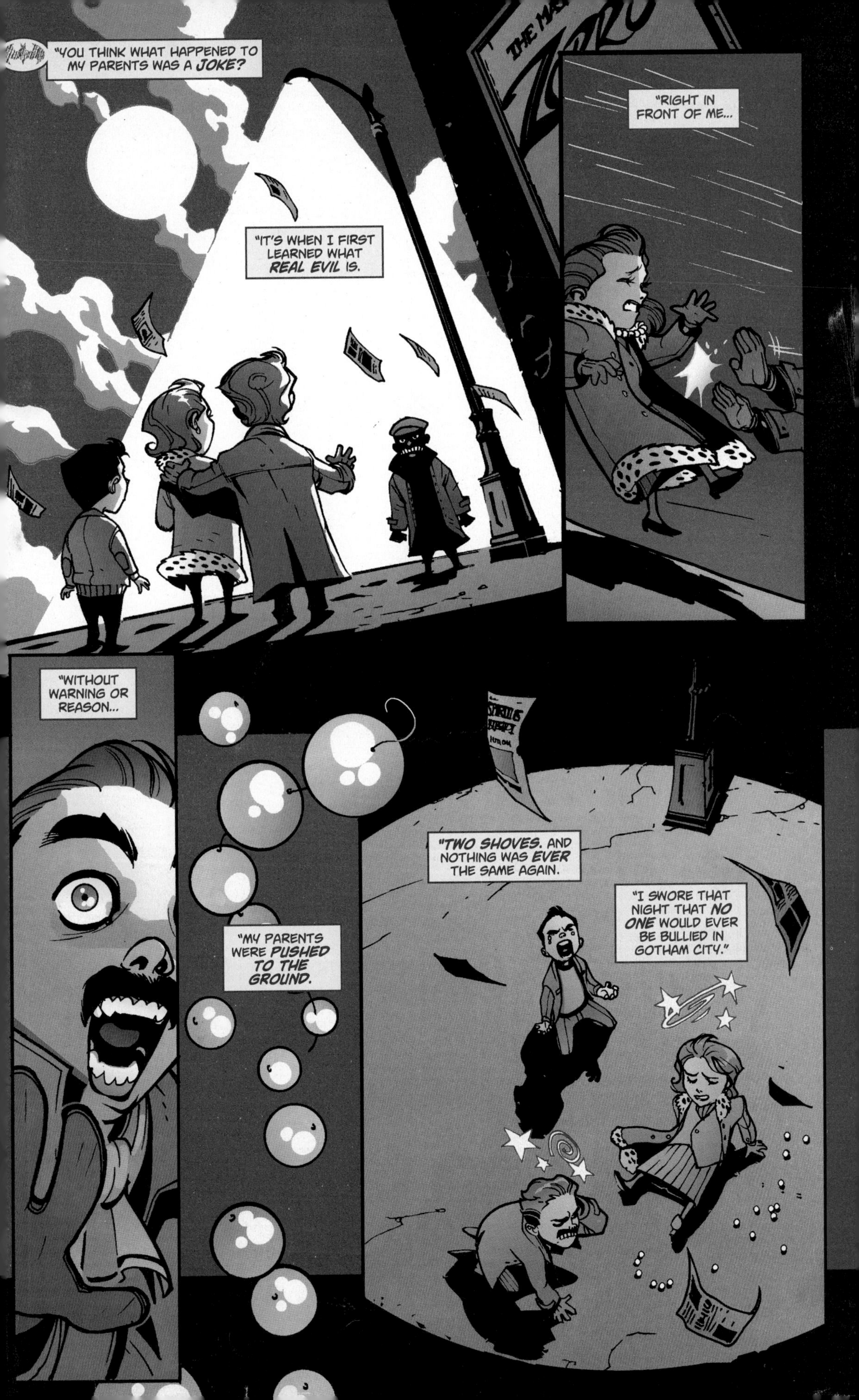
"YOU THINK WHAT HAPPENED TO MY PARENTS WAS A JOKE?
"IT'S WHEN I FIRST LEARNED WHAT REAL EVIL IS.
"RIGHT IN FRONT OF ME...
"WITHOUT WARNING OR REASON...
"MY PARENTS WERE PUSHED TO THE GROUND.
"TWO SHOVES. AND NOTHING WAS EVER THE SAME AGAIN.
"I SWORE THAT NIGHT THAT NO ONE WOULD EVER BE BULLIED IN GOTHAM CITY."

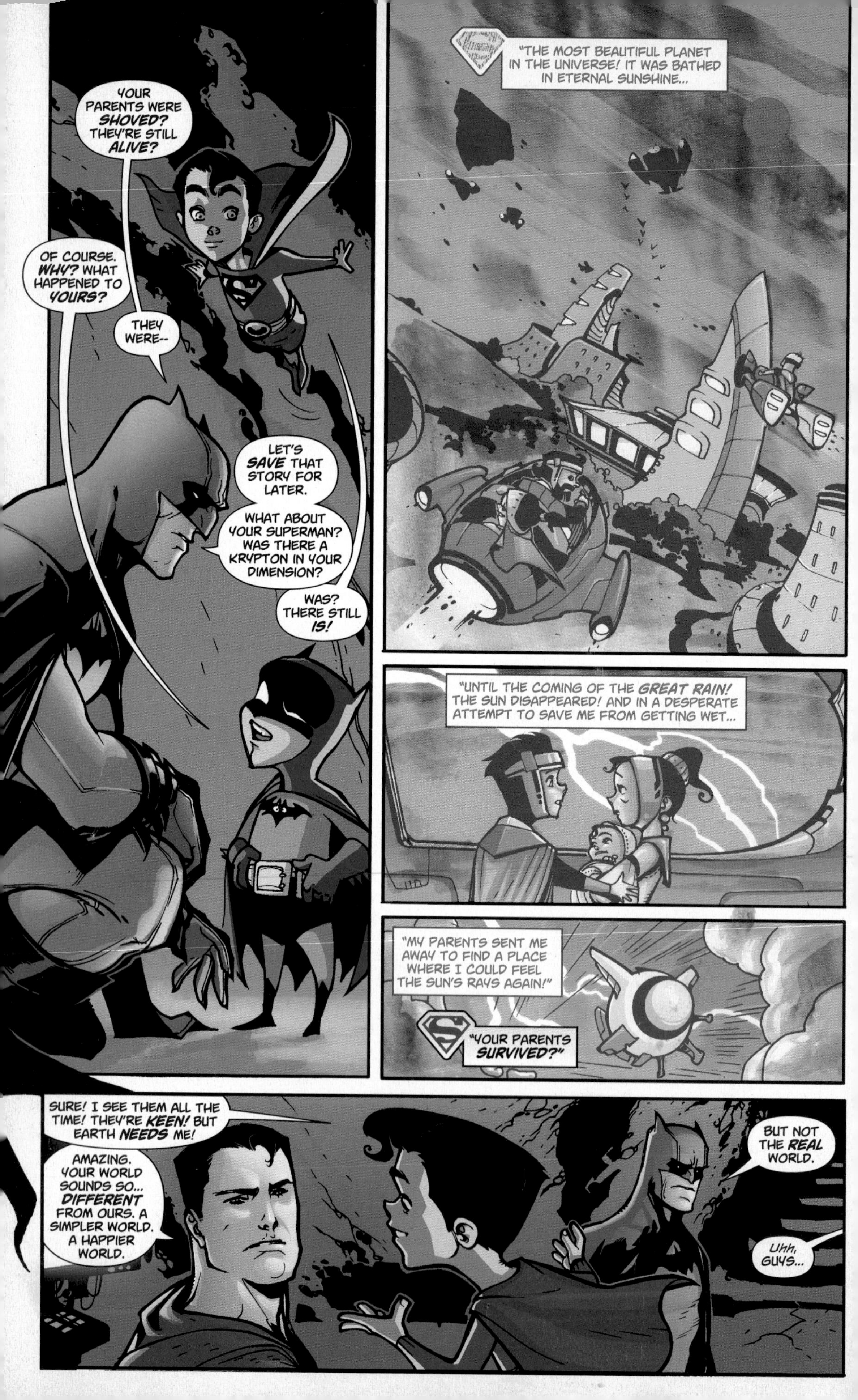
YOUR PARENTS WERE SHOVED? THEY'RE STILL ALIVE?
OF COURSE. WHY? WHAT HAPPENED TO YOURS?
THEY WERE--
LET'S SAVE THAT STORY FOR LATER.
WHAT ABOUT YOUR SUPERMAN? WAS THERE A KRYPTON IN YOUR DIMENSION?
WAS? THERE STILL IS!
"THE MOST BEAUTIFUL PLANET IN THE UNIVERSE! IT WAS BATHED IN ETERNAL SUNSHINE...
"UNTIL THE COMING OF THE GREAT RAIN! THE SUN DISAPPEARED! AND IN A DESPERATE ATTEMPT TO SAVE ME FROM GETTING WET...
"MY PARENTS SENT ME AWAY TO FIND A PLACE WHERE I COULD FEEL THE SUN'S RAYS AGAIN!"
"YOUR PARENTS SURVIVED?"
SURE! I SEE THEM ALL THE TIME! THEY'RE KEEN! BUT EARTH NEEDS ME!
AMAZING. YOUR WORLD SOUNDS SO... DIFFERENT FROM OURS. A SIMPLER WORLD. A HAPPIER WORLD.
BUT NOT THE REAL WORLD.
Uhh, GUYS...

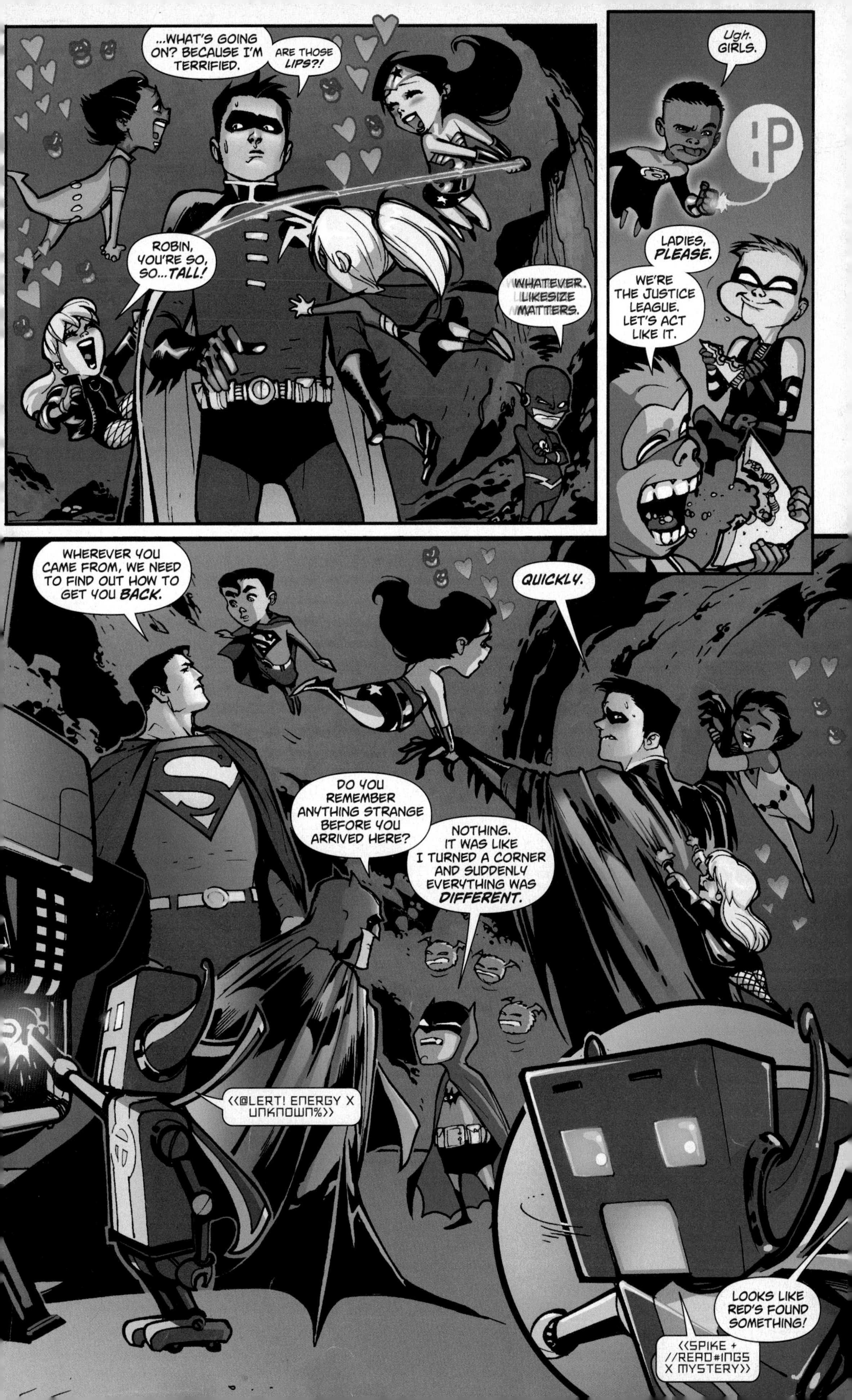

...WHAT'S GOING ON? BECAUSE I'M TERRIFIED.
ARE THOSE LIPS?!
ROBIN, YOU'RE SO, SO...TALL!
WHATEVER. LIKESIZE MATTERS.
Ugh. GIRLS.
:P
LADIES, PLEASE.
WE'RE THE JUSTICE LEAGUE. LET'S ACT LIKE IT.
WHEREVER YOU CAME FROM, WE NEED TO FIND OUT HOW TO GET YOU BACK.
QUICKLY.
DO YOU REMEMBER ANYTHING STRANGE BEFORE YOU ARRIVED HERE?
NOTHING. IT WAS LIKE I TURNED A CORNER AND SUDDENLY EVERYTHING WAS DIFFERENT.
<<@LERT! ENERGY X UNKNOWN%>>
LOOKS LIKE RED'S FOUND SOMETHING!
<<SPIKE + //READ#INGS X MYSTERY>>

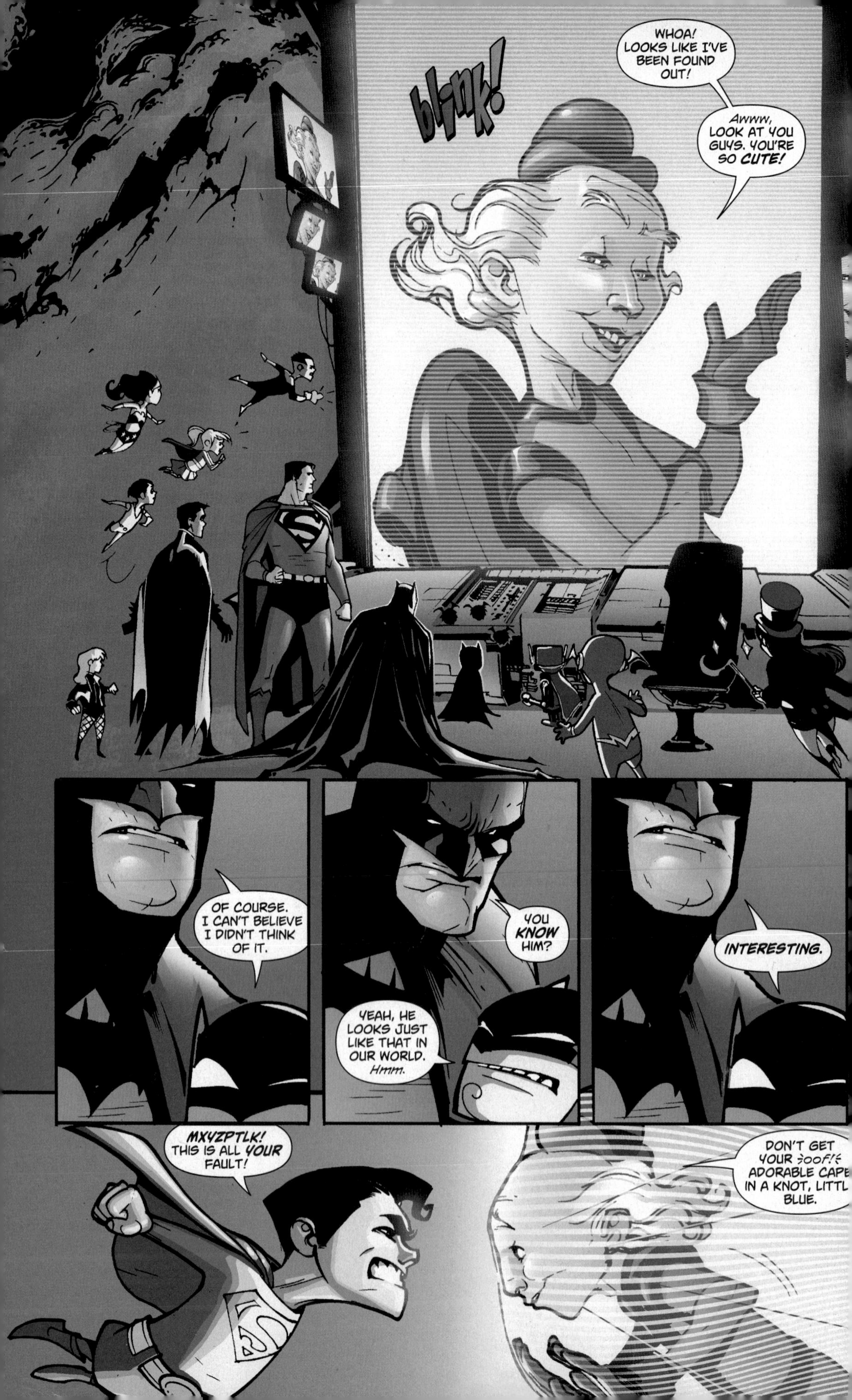
blink!
WHOA! LOOKS LIKE I'VE BEEN FOUND OUT!
*Awww,* LOOK AT YOU GUYS. YOU'RE SO ***CUTE!***
OF COURSE. I CAN'T BELIEVE I DIDN'T THINK OF IT.
YOU ***KNOW*** HIM?
YEAH, HE LOOKS JUST LIKE THAT IN OUR WORLD. *Hmm.*
***INTERESTING.***
***MXYZPTLK!*** THIS IS ALL ***YOUR*** FAULT!
DON'T GET YOUR OOF! ADORABLE CAPE IN A KNOT, LITTLE BLUE.

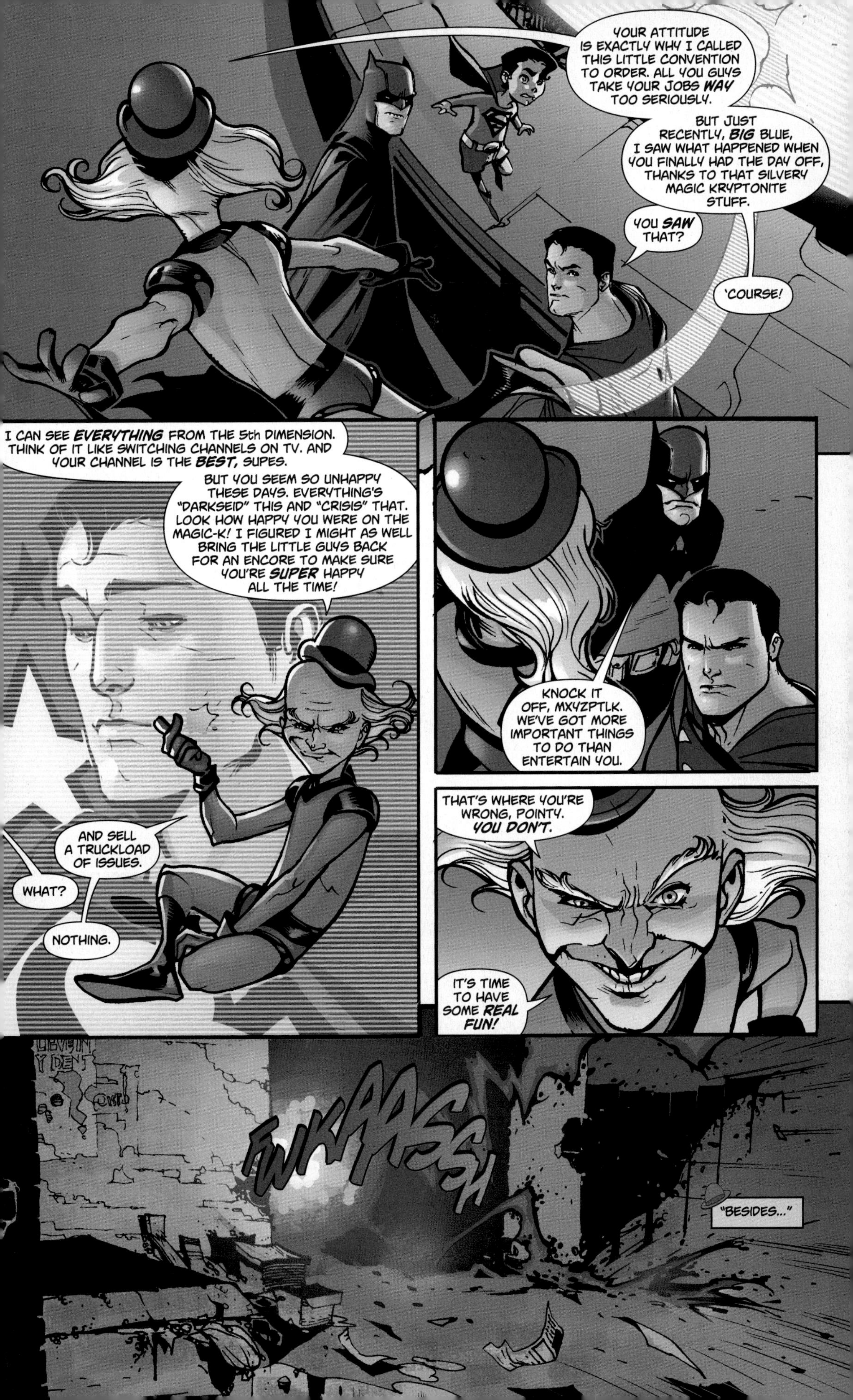

YOUR ATTITUDE IS EXACTLY WHY I CALLED THIS LITTLE CONVENTION TO ORDER. ALL YOU GUYS TAKE YOUR JOBS **WAY** TOO SERIOUSLY.
BUT JUST RECENTLY, **BIG** BLUE, I SAW WHAT HAPPENED WHEN YOU FINALLY HAD THE DAY OFF, THANKS TO THAT SILVERY MAGIC KRYPTONITE STUFF.
YOU **SAW** THAT?
'COURSE!
I CAN SEE **EVERYTHING** FROM THE 5th DIMENSION. THINK OF IT LIKE SWITCHING CHANNELS ON TV. AND YOUR CHANNEL IS THE **BEST**, SUPES.
BUT YOU SEEM SO UNHAPPY THESE DAYS. EVERYTHING'S "DARKSEID" THIS AND "CRISIS" THAT. LOOK HOW HAPPY YOU WERE ON THE MAGIC-K! I FIGURED I MIGHT AS WELL BRING THE LITTLE GUYS BACK FOR AN ENCORE TO MAKE SURE YOU'RE **SUPER** HAPPY ALL THE TIME!
AND SELL A TRUCKLOAD OF ISSUES.
WHAT?
NOTHING.
KNOCK IT OFF, MXYZPTLK. WE'VE GOT MORE IMPORTANT THINGS TO DO THAN ENTERTAIN YOU.
THAT'S WHERE YOU'RE WRONG, POINTY. ***YOU DON'T.***
IT'S TIME TO HAVE SOME ***REAL FUN!***
FWKAASSH
"BESIDES..."

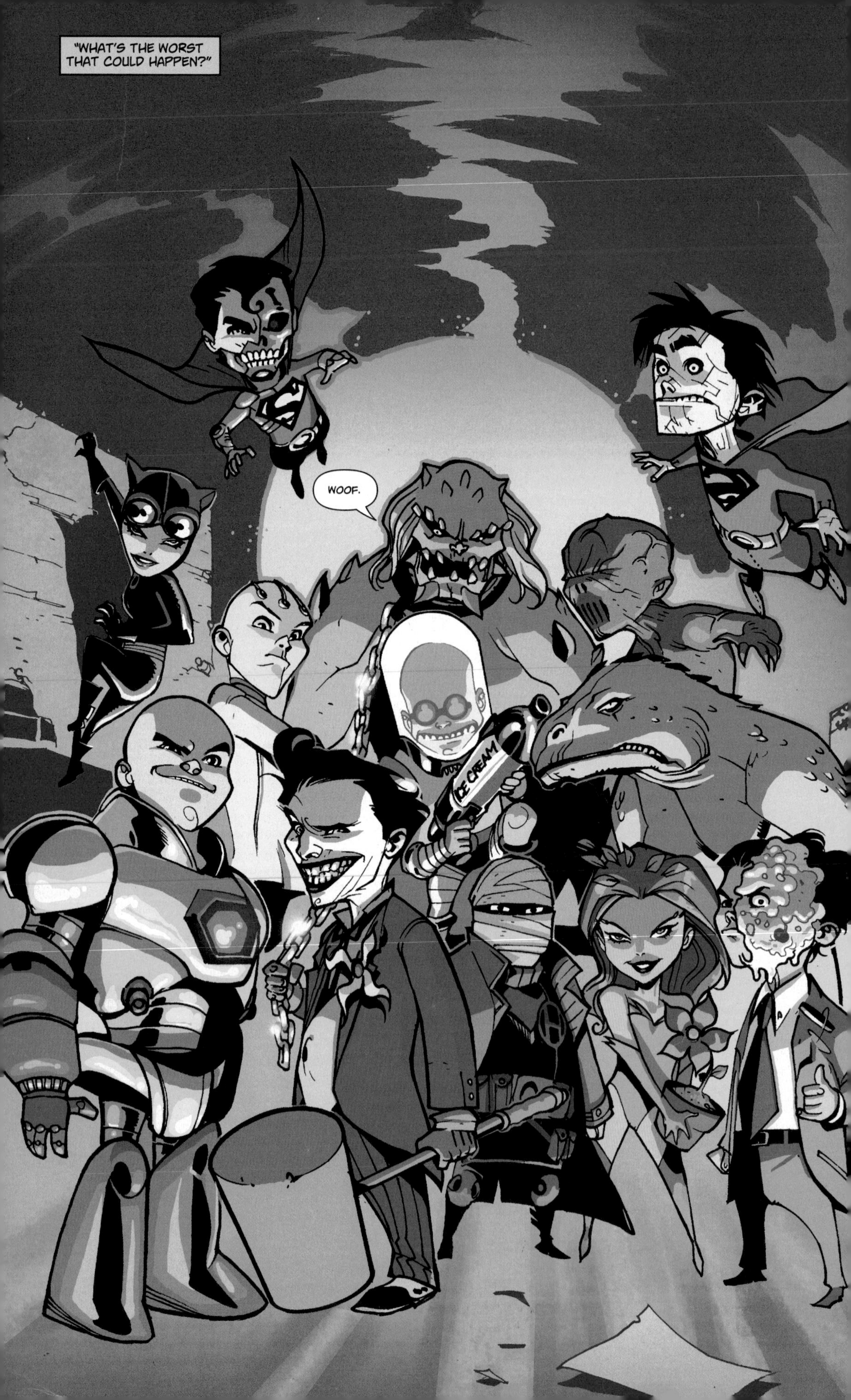
"WHAT'S THE WORST THAT COULD HAPPEN?"
WOOF.
ICE CREAM

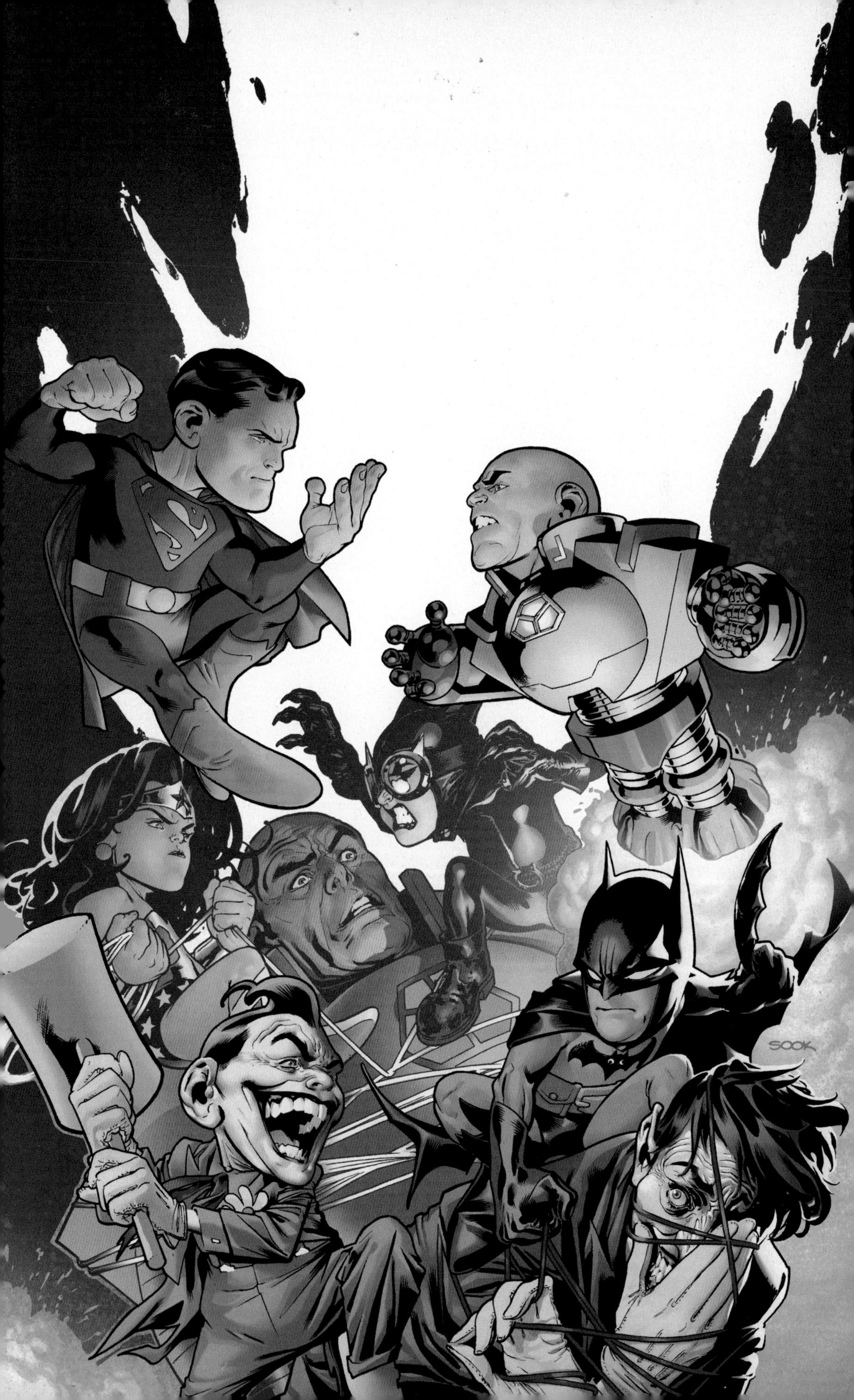
SOOK

SUPERMAN/BATMAN 52

LIL' LEAGUERS
part two

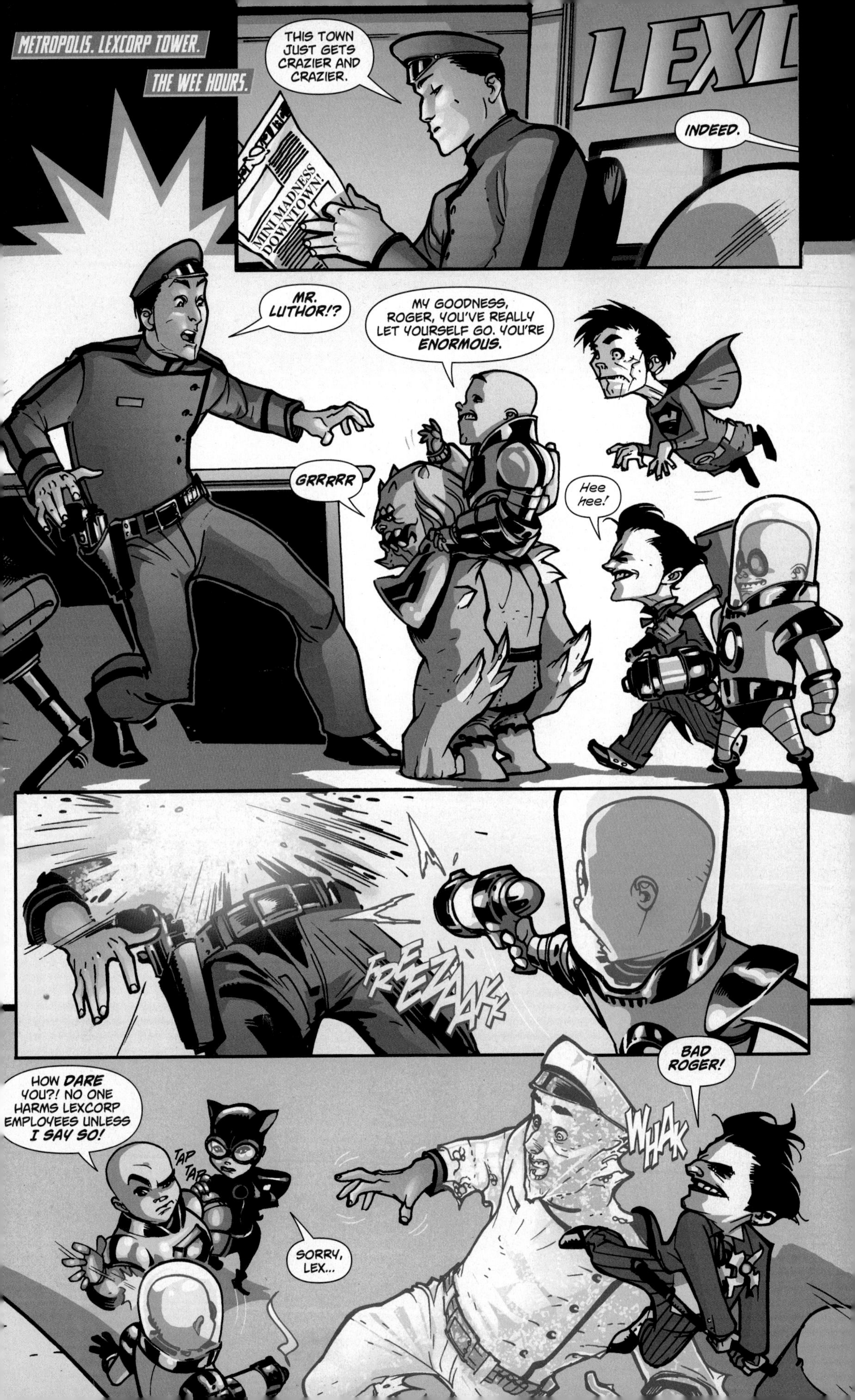
METROPOLIS. LEXCORP TOWER.
THE WEE HOURS.
THIS TOWN JUST GETS CRAZIER AND CRAZIER.
MINI MADNESS DOWNTOWN!
LEX
INDEED.
MR. LUTHOR!?
MY GOODNESS, ROGER, YOU'VE REALLY LET YOURSELF GO. YOU'RE ENORMOUS.
GRRRRR
Hee hee!
FREEZAAAK
HOW DARE YOU?! NO ONE HARMS LEXCORP EMPLOYEES UNLESS I SAY SO!
TAP TAP
SORRY, LEX...
BAD ROGER!
WHAK

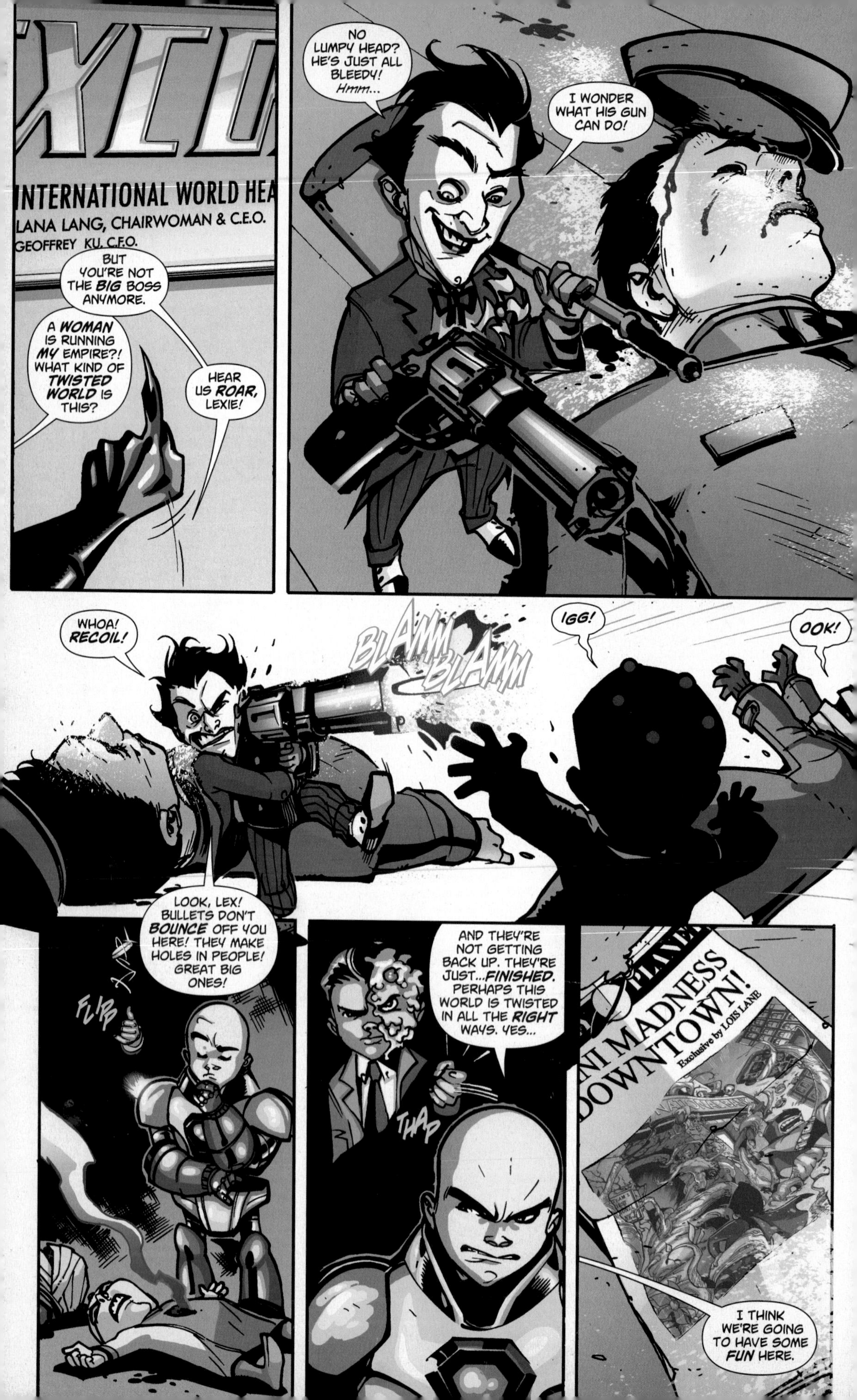

INTERNATIONAL WORLD HEA
LANA LANG, CHAIRWOMAN & C.E.O.
GEOFFREY KU, C.F.O.
BUT YOU'RE NOT THE BIG BOSS ANYMORE.
A WOMAN IS RUNNING MY EMPIRE?! WHAT KIND OF TWISTED WORLD IS THIS?
HEAR US ROAR, LEXIE!
NO LUMPY HEAD? HE'S JUST ALL BLEEDY! Hmm...
I WONDER WHAT HIS GUN CAN DO!
WHOA! RECOIL!
BLAMM BLAMM
IGG!
OOK!
LOOK, LEX! BULLETS DON'T BOUNCE OFF YOU HERE! THEY MAKE HOLES IN PEOPLE! GREAT BIG ONES!
FLIPP
AND THEY'RE NOT GETTING BACK UP. THEY'RE JUST...FINISHED. PERHAPS THIS WORLD IS TWISTED IN ALL THE RIGHT WAYS. YES...
THAP
PLANET
NI MADNESS DOWNTOWN!
Exclusive by LOIS LANE
I THINK WE'RE GOING TO HAVE SOME FUN HERE.

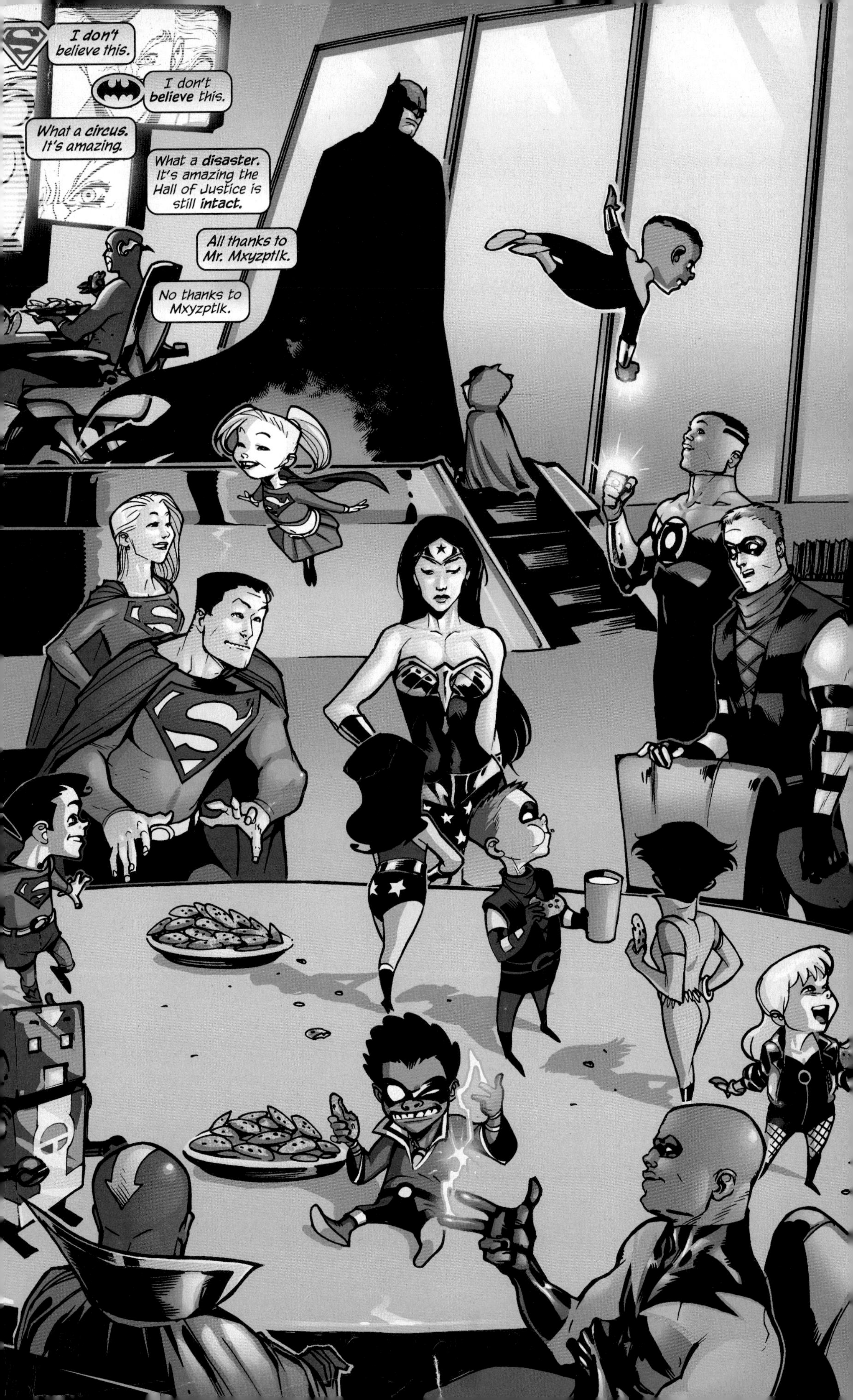
I don't believe this.
I don't believe this.
What a circus. It's amazing.
What a disaster. It's amazing the Hall of Justice is still intact.
All thanks to Mr. Mxyzptlk.
No thanks to Mxyzptlk.

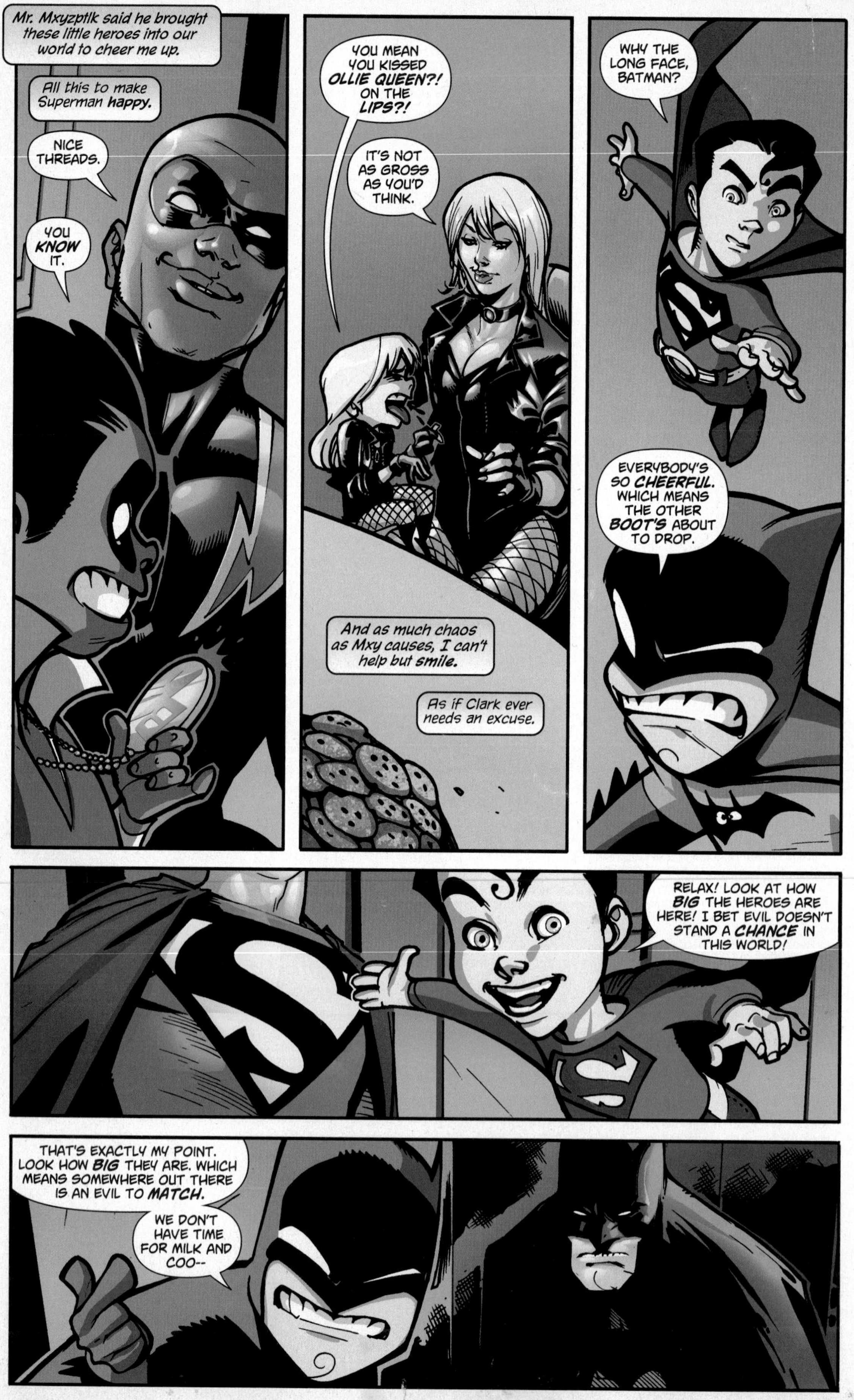

Mr. Mxyzptlk said he brought these little heroes into our world to cheer me up.
All this to make Superman happy.
NICE THREADS.
YOU KNOW IT.
YOU MEAN YOU KISSED OLLIE QUEEN?! ON THE LIPS?!
IT'S NOT AS GROSS AS YOU'D THINK.
And as much chaos as Mxy causes, I can't help but smile.
As if Clark ever needs an excuse.
WHY THE LONG FACE, BATMAN?
EVERYBODY'S SO CHEERFUL. WHICH MEANS THE OTHER BOOT'S ABOUT TO DROP.
RELAX! LOOK AT HOW BIG THE HEROES ARE HERE! I BET EVIL DOESN'T STAND A CHANCE IN THIS WORLD!
THAT'S EXACTLY MY POINT. LOOK HOW BIG THEY ARE. WHICH MEANS SOMEWHERE OUT THERE IS AN EVIL TO MATCH.
WE DON'T HAVE TIME FOR MILK AND COO--

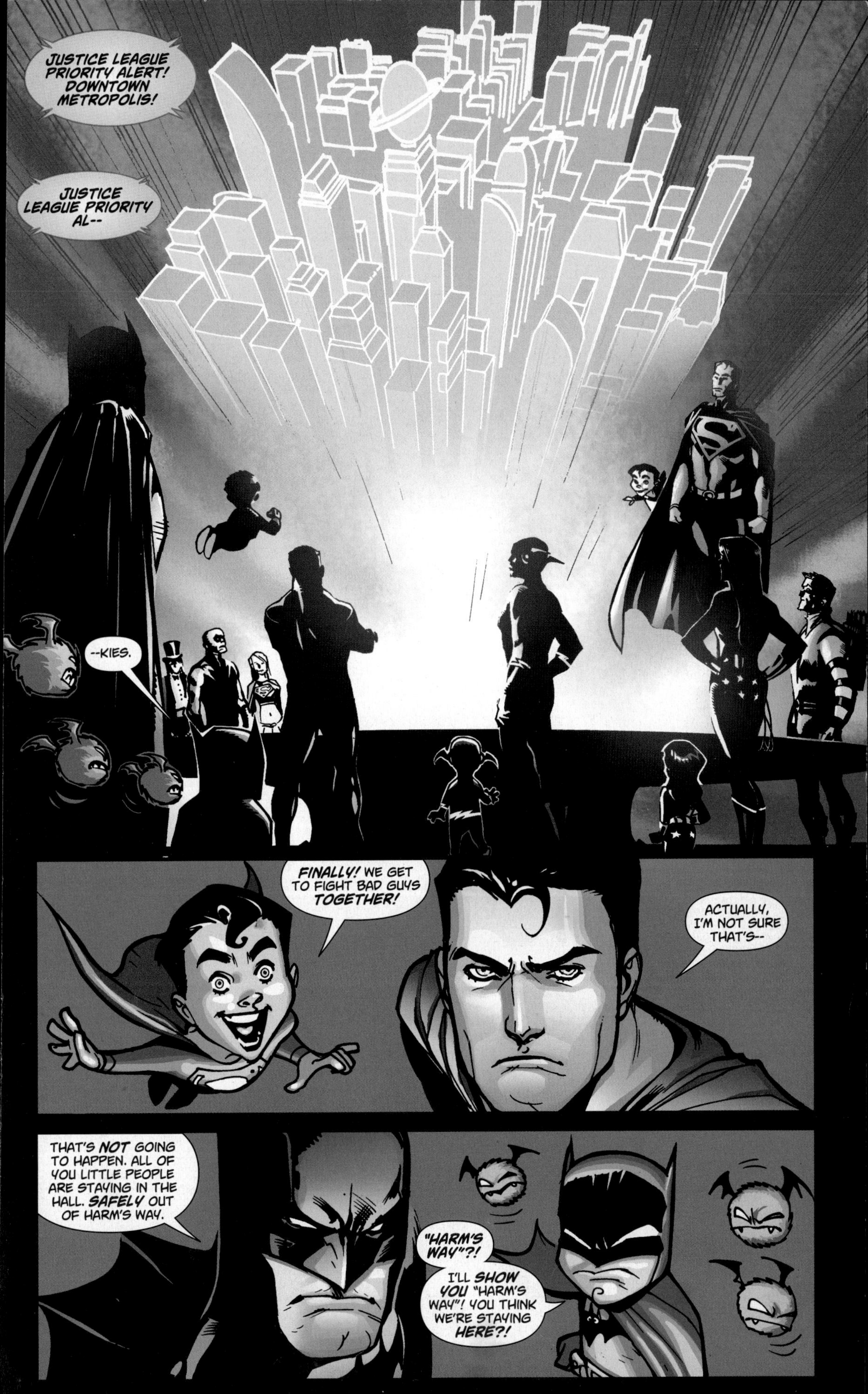
JUSTICE LEAGUE PRIORITY ALERT! DOWNTOWN METROPOLIS!
JUSTICE LEAGUE PRIORITY AL--
--KIES.
FINALLY! WE GET TO FIGHT BAD GUYS TOGETHER!
ACTUALLY, I'M NOT SURE THAT'S--
THAT'S NOT GOING TO HAPPEN. ALL OF YOU LITTLE PEOPLE ARE STAYING IN THE HALL. SAFELY OUT OF HARM'S WAY.
"HARM'S WAY"?!
I'LL SHOW YOU "HARM'S WAY"! YOU THINK WE'RE STAYING HERE?!

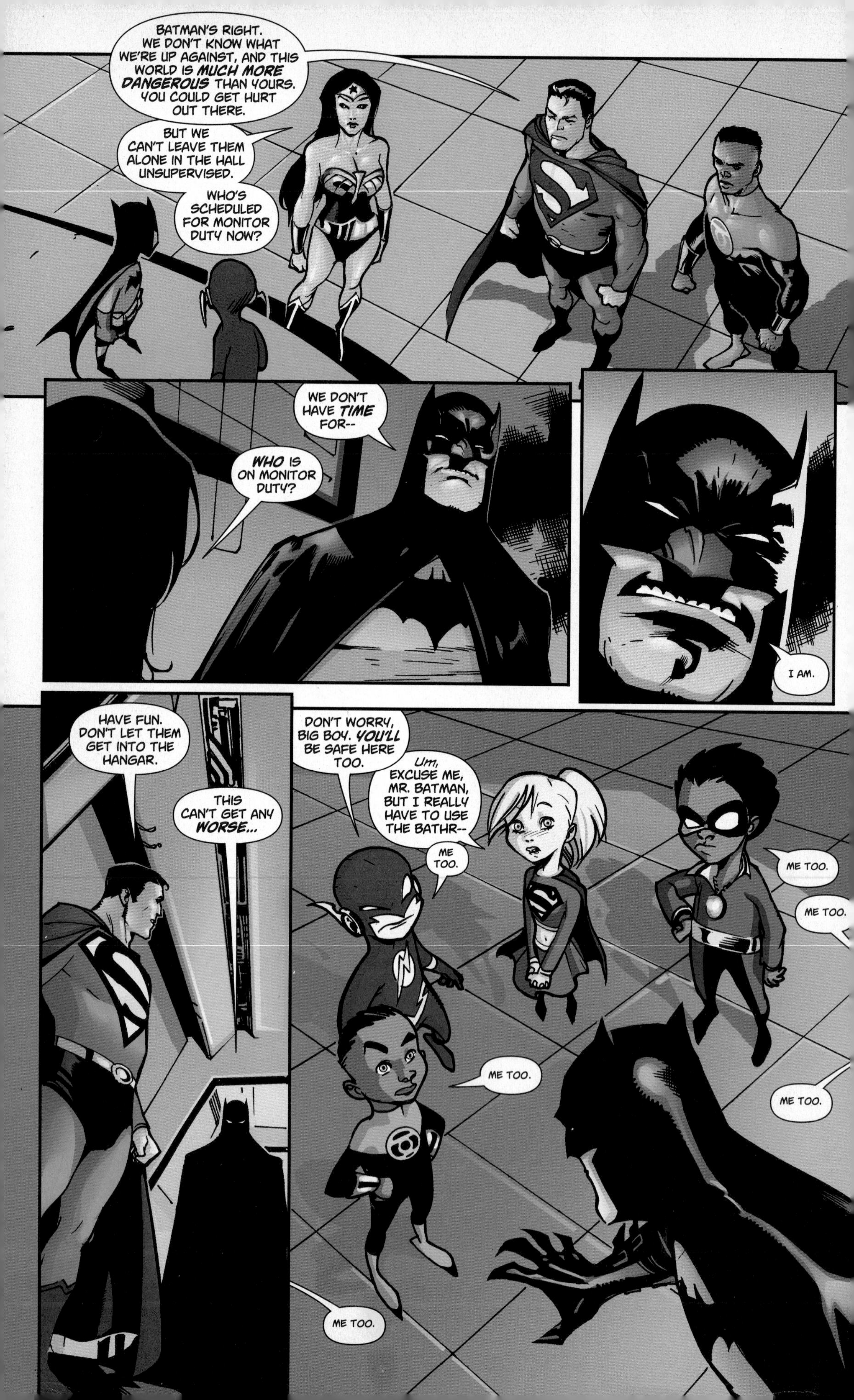
BATMAN'S RIGHT. WE DON'T KNOW WHAT WE'RE UP AGAINST, AND THIS WORLD IS MUCH MORE DANGEROUS THAN YOURS. YOU COULD GET HURT OUT THERE.
BUT WE CAN'T LEAVE THEM ALONE IN THE HALL UNSUPERVISED.
WHO'S SCHEDULED FOR MONITOR DUTY NOW?
WE DON'T HAVE TIME FOR--
WHO IS ON MONITOR DUTY?
I AM.
HAVE FUN. DON'T LET THEM GET INTO THE HANGAR.
THIS CAN'T GET ANY WORSE...
DON'T WORRY, BIG BOY. YOU'LL BE SAFE HERE TOO.
UM, EXCUSE ME, MR. BATMAN, BUT I REALLY HAVE TO USE THE BATHR--
ME TOO.
ME TOO.
ME TOO.
ME TOO.
ME TOO.
ME TOO.

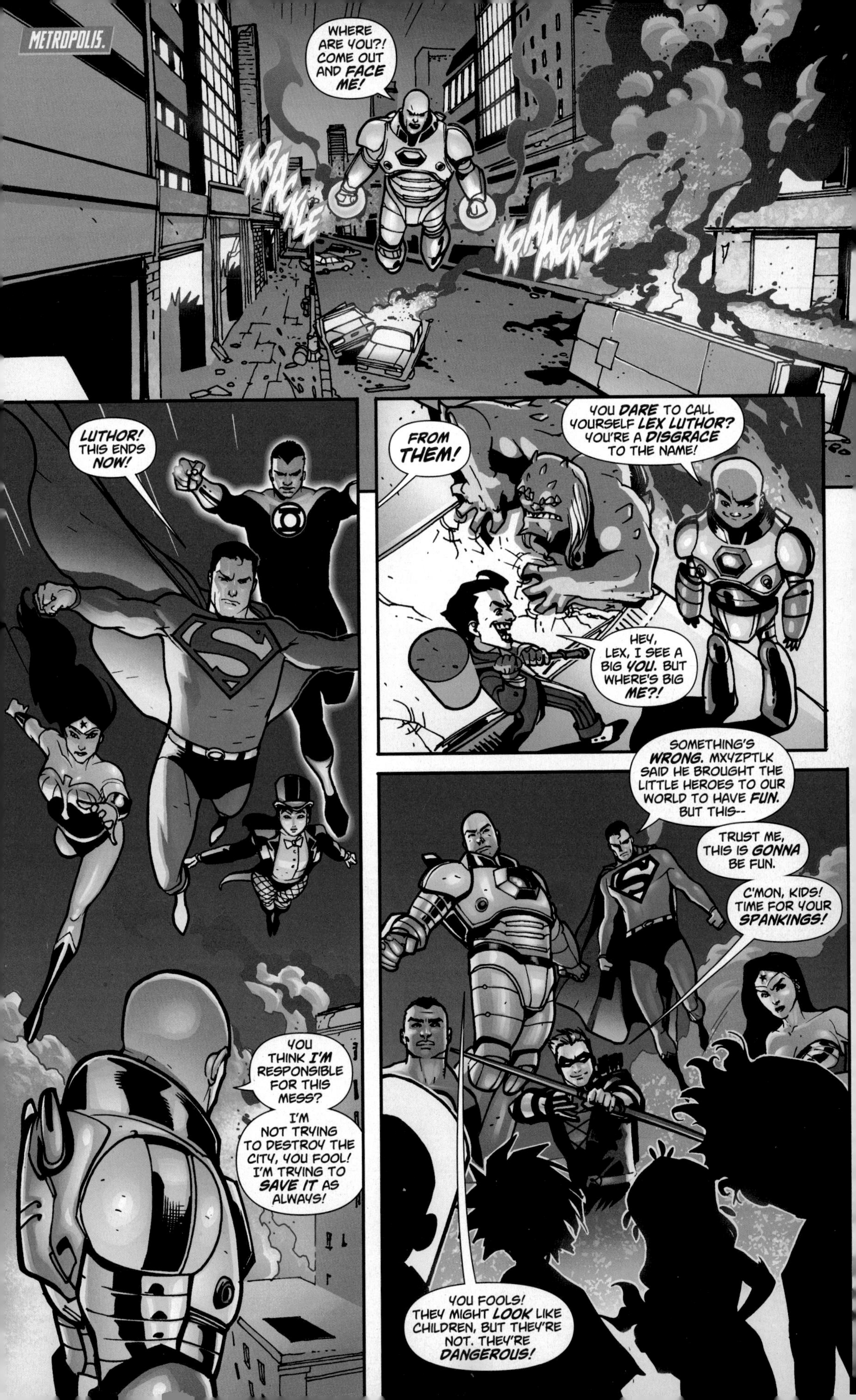
METROPOLIS.
WHERE ARE YOU?! COME OUT AND FACE ME!
KRRACKLE
KRRAACKLE
LUTHOR! THIS ENDS NOW!
YOU THINK I'M RESPONSIBLE FOR THIS MESS?
I'M NOT TRYING TO DESTROY THE CITY, YOU FOOL! I'M TRYING TO SAVE IT AS ALWAYS!
FROM THEM!
YOU DARE TO CALL YOURSELF LEX LUTHOR? YOU'RE A DISGRACE TO THE NAME!
HEY, LEX, I SEE A BIG YOU. BUT WHERE'S BIG ME?!
SOMETHING'S WRONG. MXYZPTLK SAID HE BROUGHT THE LITTLE HEROES TO OUR WORLD TO HAVE FUN. BUT THIS--
TRUST ME, THIS IS GONNA BE FUN.
C'MON, KIDS! TIME FOR YOUR SPANKINGS!
YOU FOOLS! THEY MIGHT LOOK LIKE CHILDREN, BUT THEY'RE NOT. THEY'RE DANGEROUS!

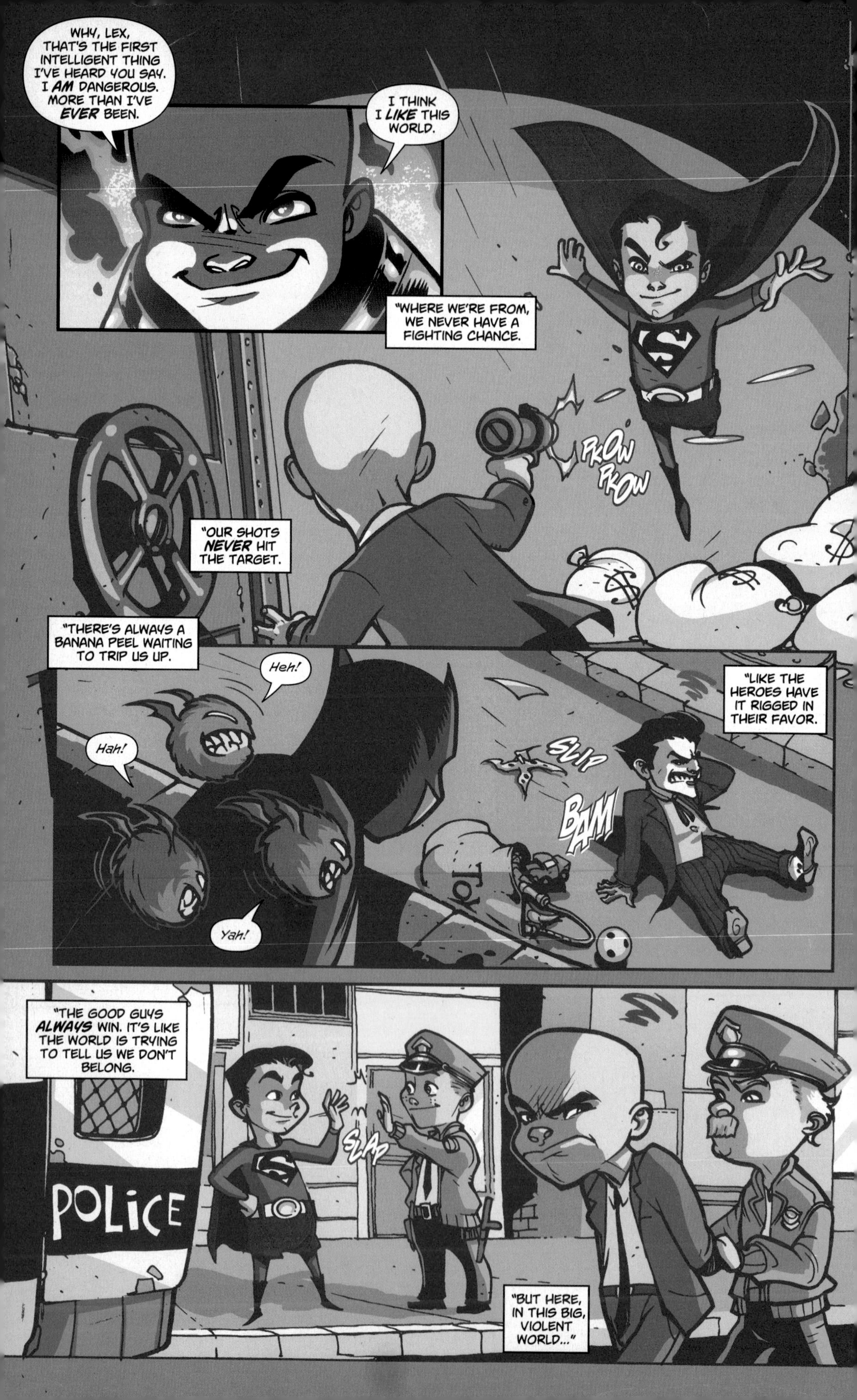
WHY, LEX, THAT'S THE FIRST INTELLIGENT THING I'VE HEARD YOU SAY. I AM DANGEROUS. MORE THAN I'VE EVER BEEN.
I THINK I LIKE THIS WORLD.
"WHERE WE'RE FROM, WE NEVER HAVE A FIGHTING CHANCE.
PKOW PKOW
"OUR SHOTS NEVER HIT THE TARGET.
"THERE'S ALWAYS A BANANA PEEL WAITING TO TRIP US UP.
Heh!
Hah!
Yah!
"LIKE THE HEROES HAVE IT RIGGED IN THEIR FAVOR.
SLIP
BAM
"THE GOOD GUYS ALWAYS WIN. IT'S LIKE THE WORLD IS TRYING TO TELL US WE DON'T BELONG.
SLAP
POLICE
"BUT HERE, IN THIS BIG, VIOLENT WORLD..."

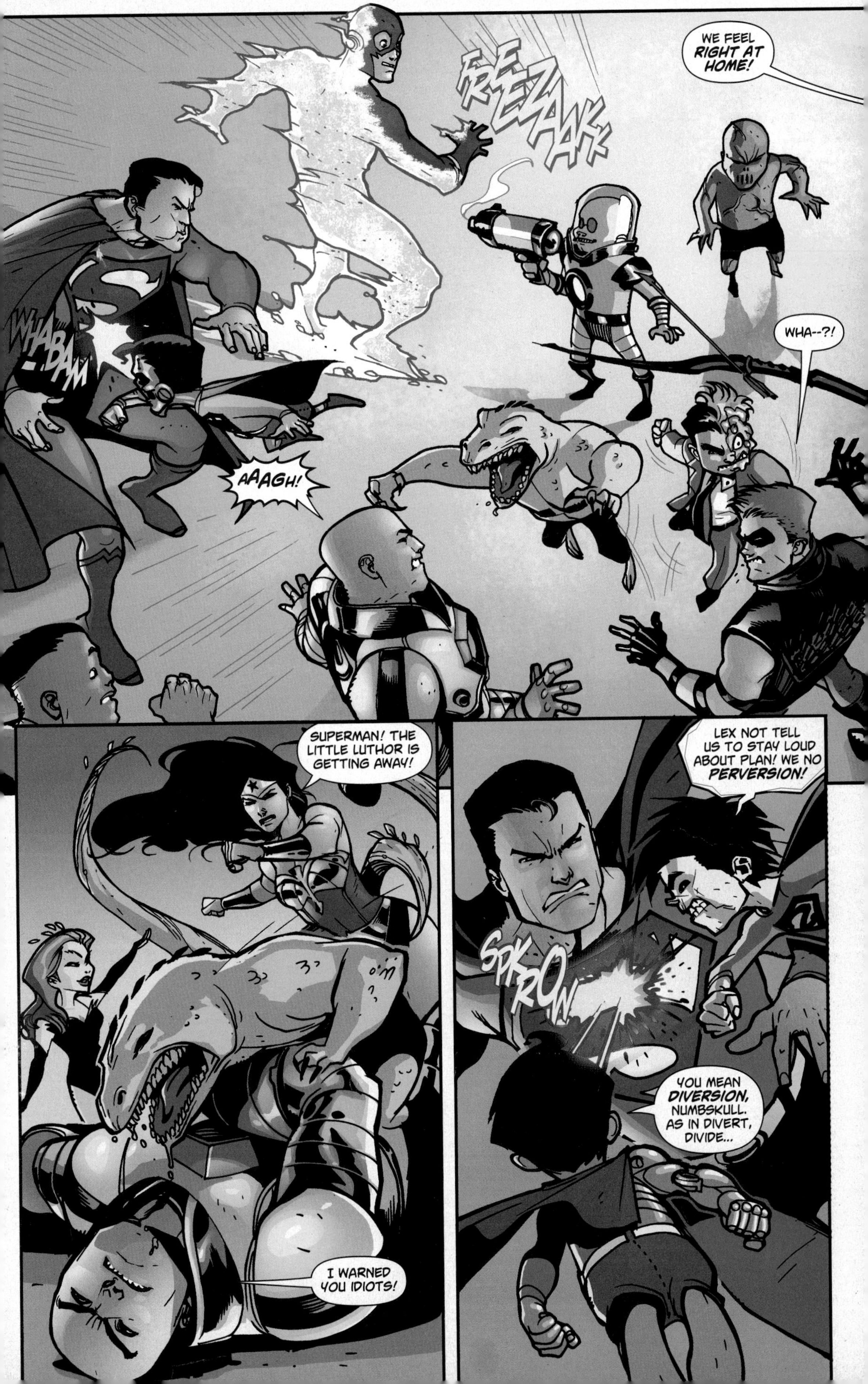

FREEZAAAK
WE FEEL RIGHT AT HOME!
WHABAM
WHA--?!
AAAGH!
SUPERMAN! THE LITTLE LUTHOR IS GETTING AWAY!
I WARNED YOU IDIOTS!
LEX NOT TELL US TO STAY LOUD ABOUT PLAN! WE NO PERVERSION!
SPKRON
YOU MEAN DIVERSION, NUMBSKULL. AS IN DIVERT, DIVIDE...

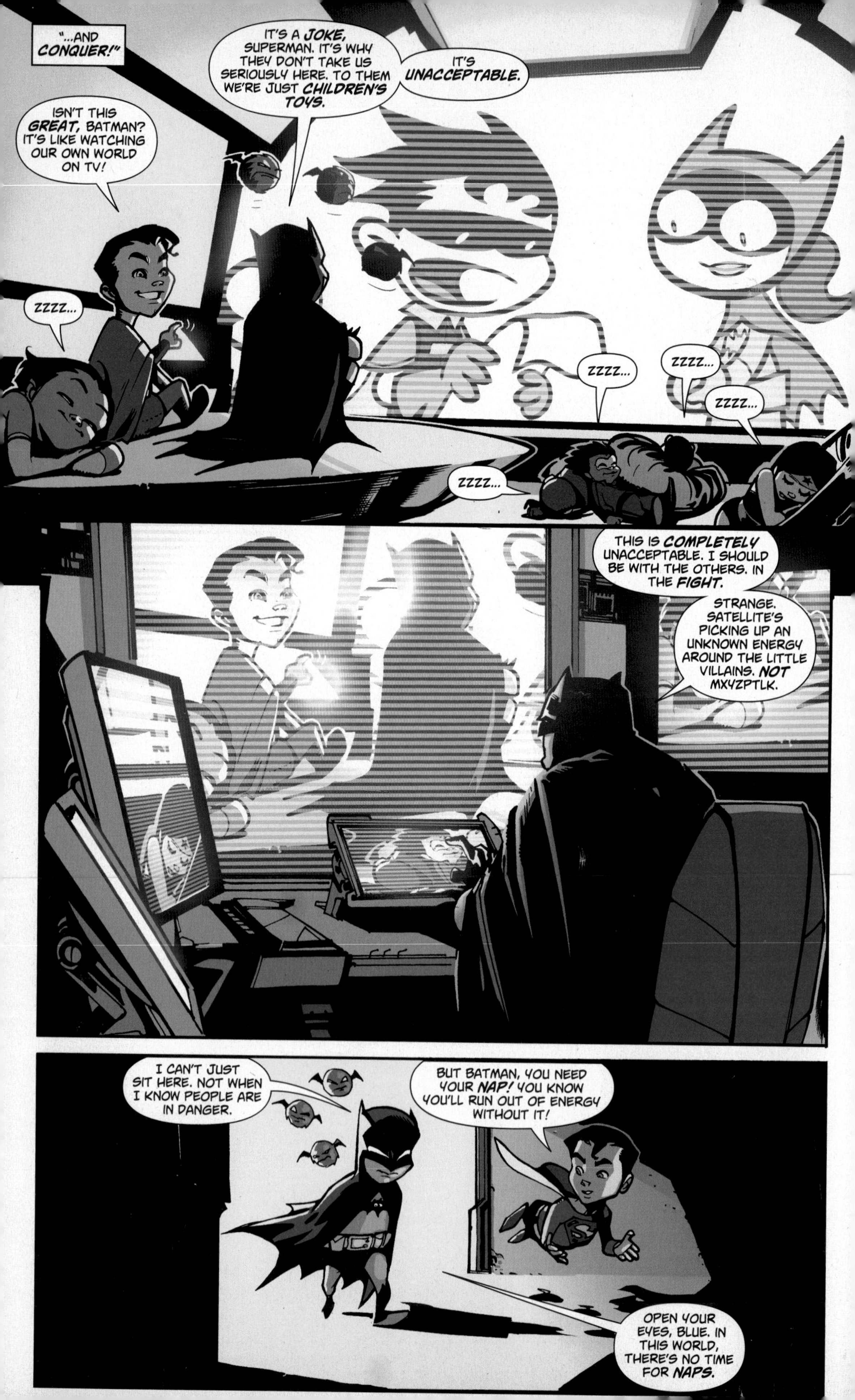

"...AND CONQUER!"
IT'S A JOKE, SUPERMAN. IT'S WHY THEY DON'T TAKE US SERIOUSLY HERE. TO THEM WE'RE JUST CHILDREN'S TOYS.
IT'S UNACCEPTABLE.
ISN'T THIS GREAT, BATMAN? IT'S LIKE WATCHING OUR OWN WORLD ON TV!
ZZZZ...
ZZZZ...
ZZZZ...
ZZZZ...
ZZZZ...
THIS IS COMPLETELY UNACCEPTABLE. I SHOULD BE WITH THE OTHERS. IN THE FIGHT.
STRANGE. SATELLITE'S PICKING UP AN UNKNOWN ENERGY AROUND THE LITTLE VILLAINS. NOT MXYZPTLK.
I CAN'T JUST SIT HERE. NOT WHEN I KNOW PEOPLE ARE IN DANGER.
BUT BATMAN, YOU NEED YOUR NAP! YOU KNOW YOU'LL RUN OUT OF ENERGY WITHOUT IT!
OPEN YOUR EYES, BLUE. IN THIS WORLD, THERE'S NO TIME FOR NAPS.

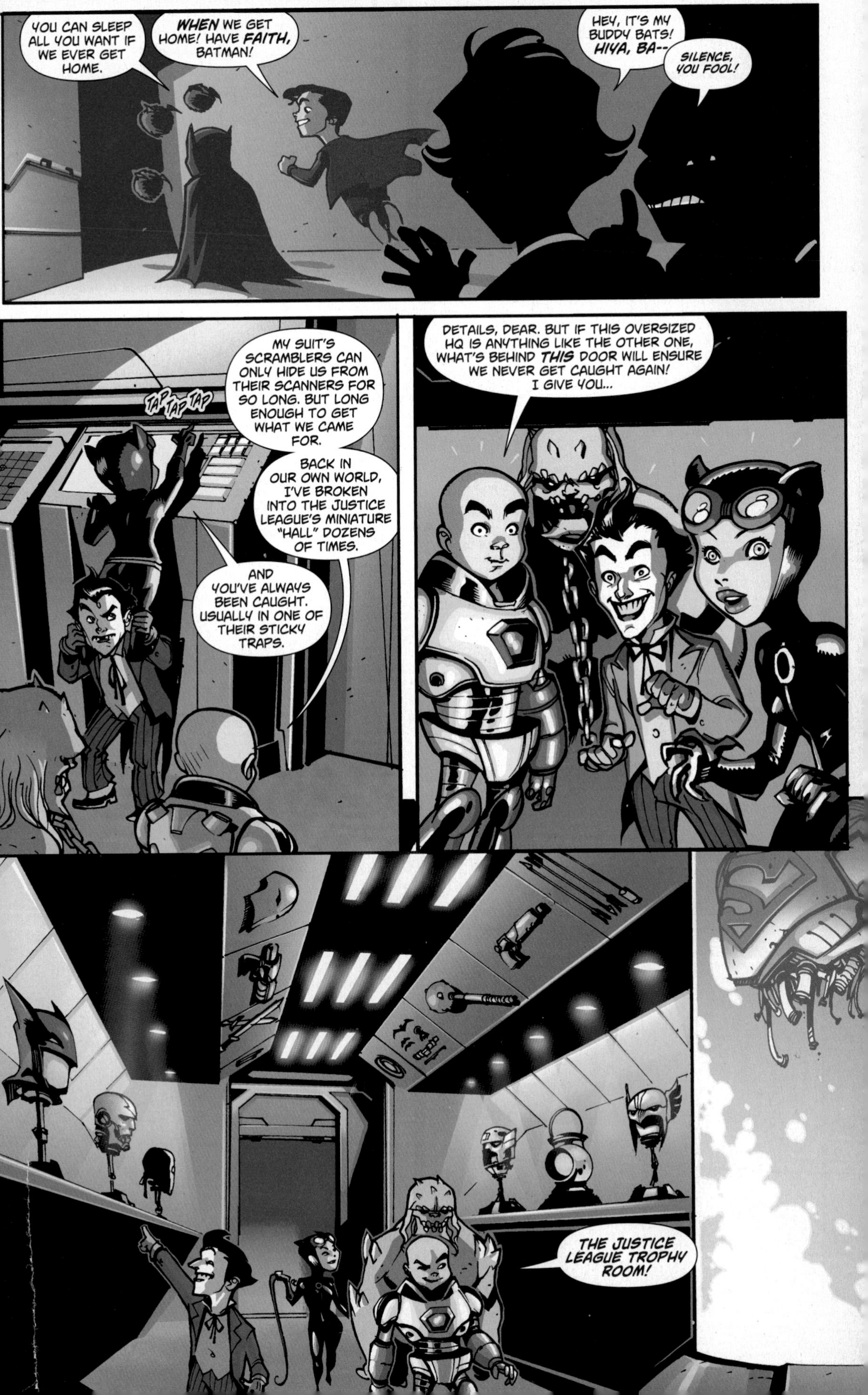
YOU CAN SLEEP ALL YOU WANT IF WE EVER GET HOME.
WHEN WE GET HOME! HAVE FAITH, BATMAN!
HEY, IT'S MY BUDDY BATS! HIYA, BA--
SILENCE, YOU FOOL!
TAP TAP TAP
MY SUIT'S SCRAMBLERS CAN ONLY HIDE US FROM THEIR SCANNERS FOR SO LONG. BUT LONG ENOUGH TO GET WHAT WE CAME FOR.
BACK IN OUR OWN WORLD, I'VE BROKEN INTO THE JUSTICE LEAGUE'S MINIATURE "HALL" DOZENS OF TIMES.
AND YOU'VE ALWAYS BEEN CAUGHT. USUALLY IN ONE OF THEIR STICKY TRAPS.
DETAILS, DEAR. BUT IF THIS OVERSIZED HQ IS ANYTHING LIKE THE OTHER ONE, WHAT'S BEHIND THIS DOOR WILL ENSURE WE NEVER GET CAUGHT AGAIN! I GIVE YOU...
THE JUSTICE LEAGUE TROPHY ROOM!

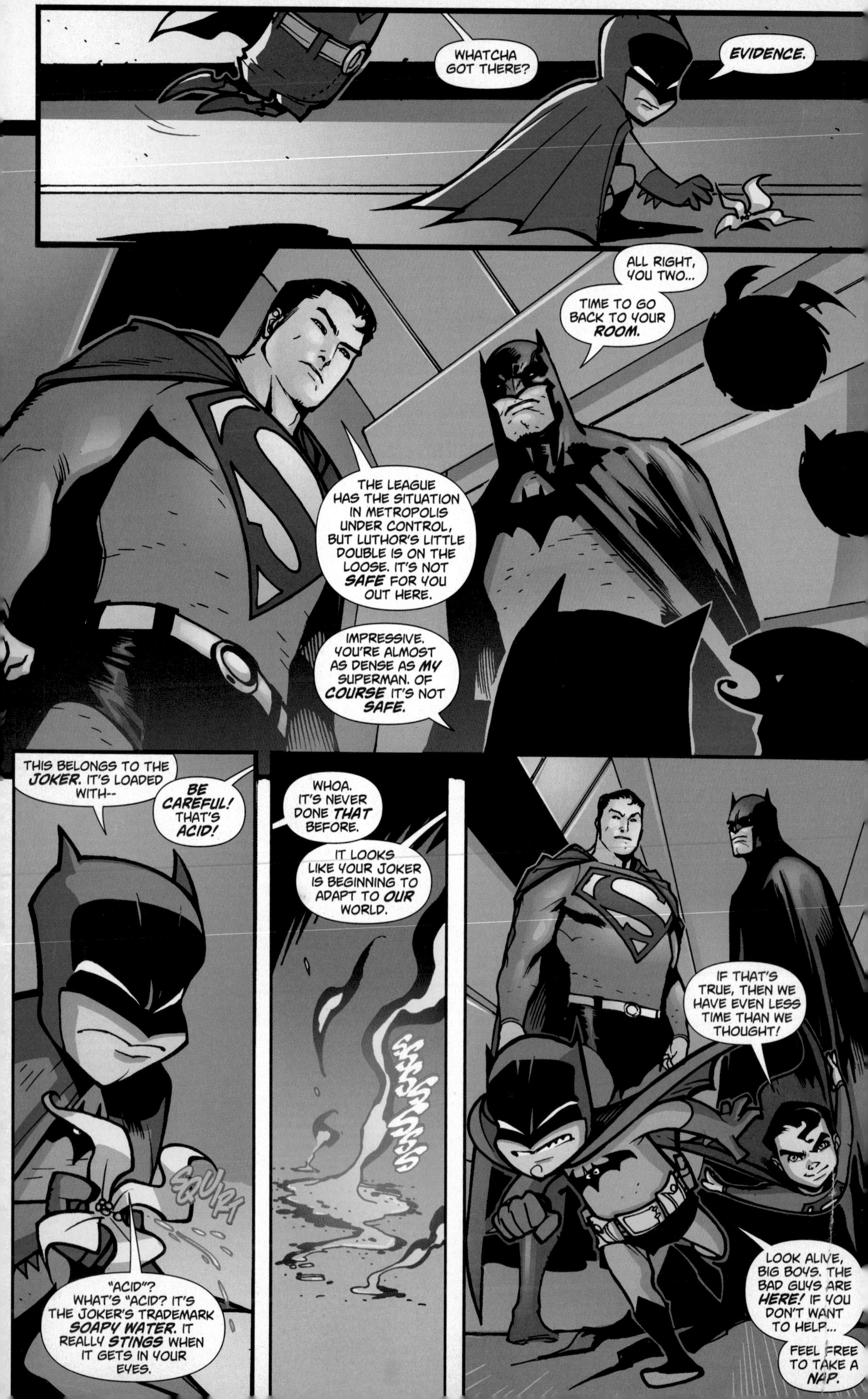
WHATCHA GOT THERE?
EVIDENCE.
ALL RIGHT, YOU TWO...
TIME TO GO BACK TO YOUR ROOM.
THE LEAGUE HAS THE SITUATION IN METROPOLIS UNDER CONTROL, BUT LUTHOR'S LITTLE DOUBLE IS ON THE LOOSE. IT'S NOT SAFE FOR YOU OUT HERE.
IMPRESSIVE. YOU'RE ALMOST AS DENSE AS MY SUPERMAN. OF COURSE IT'S NOT SAFE.
THIS BELONGS TO THE JOKER. IT'S LOADED WITH--
BE CAREFUL! THAT'S ACID!
SQUIRT
"ACID"? WHAT'S "ACID? IT'S THE JOKER'S TRADEMARK SOAPY WATER. IT REALLY STINGS WHEN IT GETS IN YOUR EYES.
WHOA. IT'S NEVER DONE THAT BEFORE.
IT LOOKS LIKE YOUR JOKER IS BEGINNING TO ADAPT TO OUR WORLD.
SSSSSSSSSS
IF THAT'S TRUE, THEN WE HAVE EVEN LESS TIME THAN WE THOUGHT!
LOOK ALIVE, BIG BOYS. THE BAD GUYS ARE HERE! IF YOU DON'T WANT TO HELP...
FEEL FREE TO TAKE A NAP.

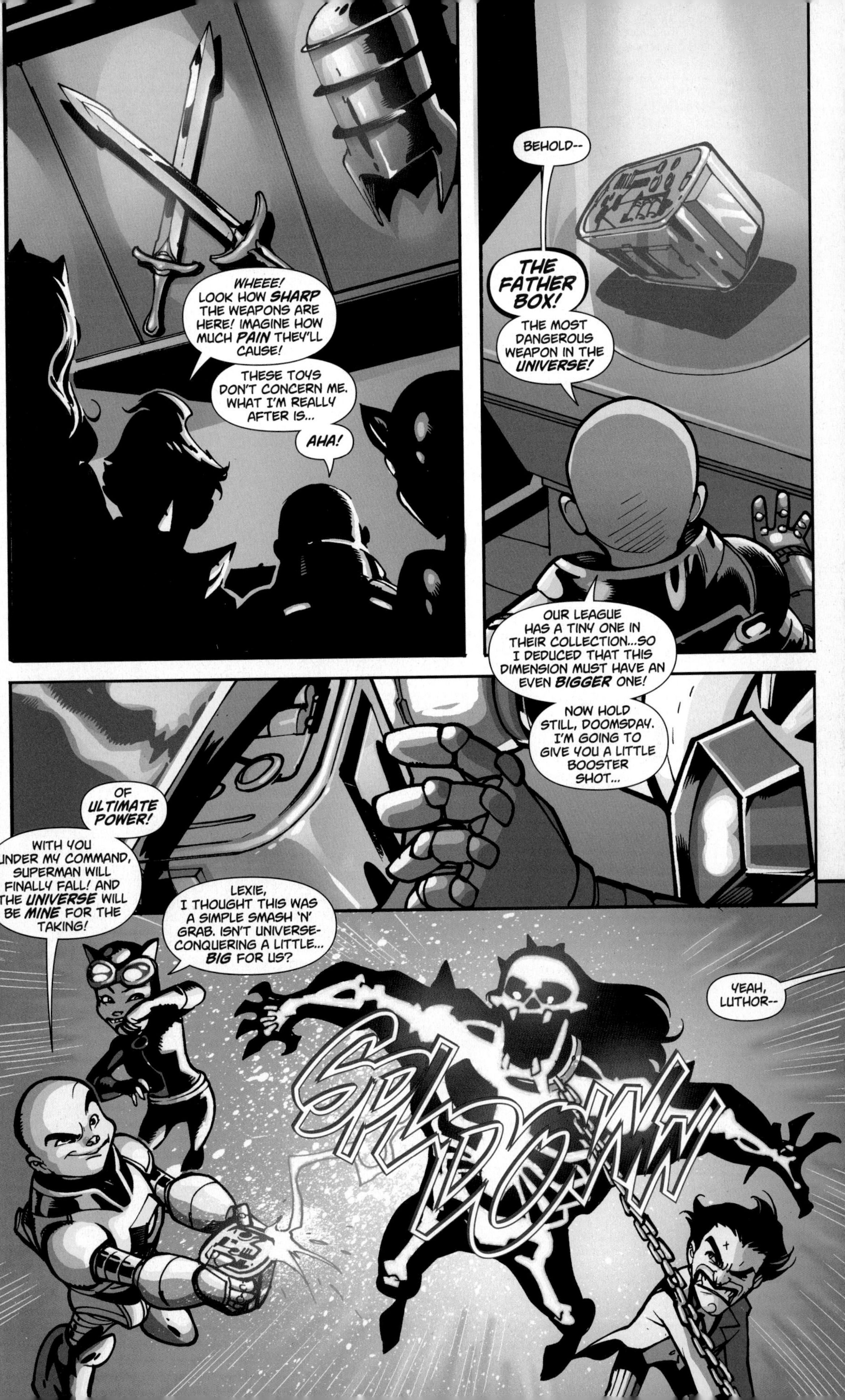
WHEEE! LOOK HOW SHARP THE WEAPONS ARE HERE! IMAGINE HOW MUCH PAIN THEY'LL CAUSE!
THESE TOYS DON'T CONCERN ME. WHAT I'M REALLY AFTER IS...
AHA!
BEHOLD--
THE FATHER BOX!
THE MOST DANGEROUS WEAPON IN THE UNIVERSE!
OUR LEAGUE HAS A TINY ONE IN THEIR COLLECTION...SO I DEDUCED THAT THIS DIMENSION MUST HAVE AN EVEN BIGGER ONE!
NOW HOLD STILL, DOOMSDAY. I'M GOING TO GIVE YOU A LITTLE BOOSTER SHOT...
OF ULTIMATE POWER!
WITH YOU UNDER MY COMMAND, SUPERMAN WILL FINALLY FALL! AND THE UNIVERSE WILL BE MINE FOR THE TAKING!
LEXIE, I THOUGHT THIS WAS A SIMPLE SMASH 'N' GRAB. ISN'T UNIVERSE-CONQUERING A LITTLE... BIG FOR US?
YEAH, LUTHOR--
SPLDOWN

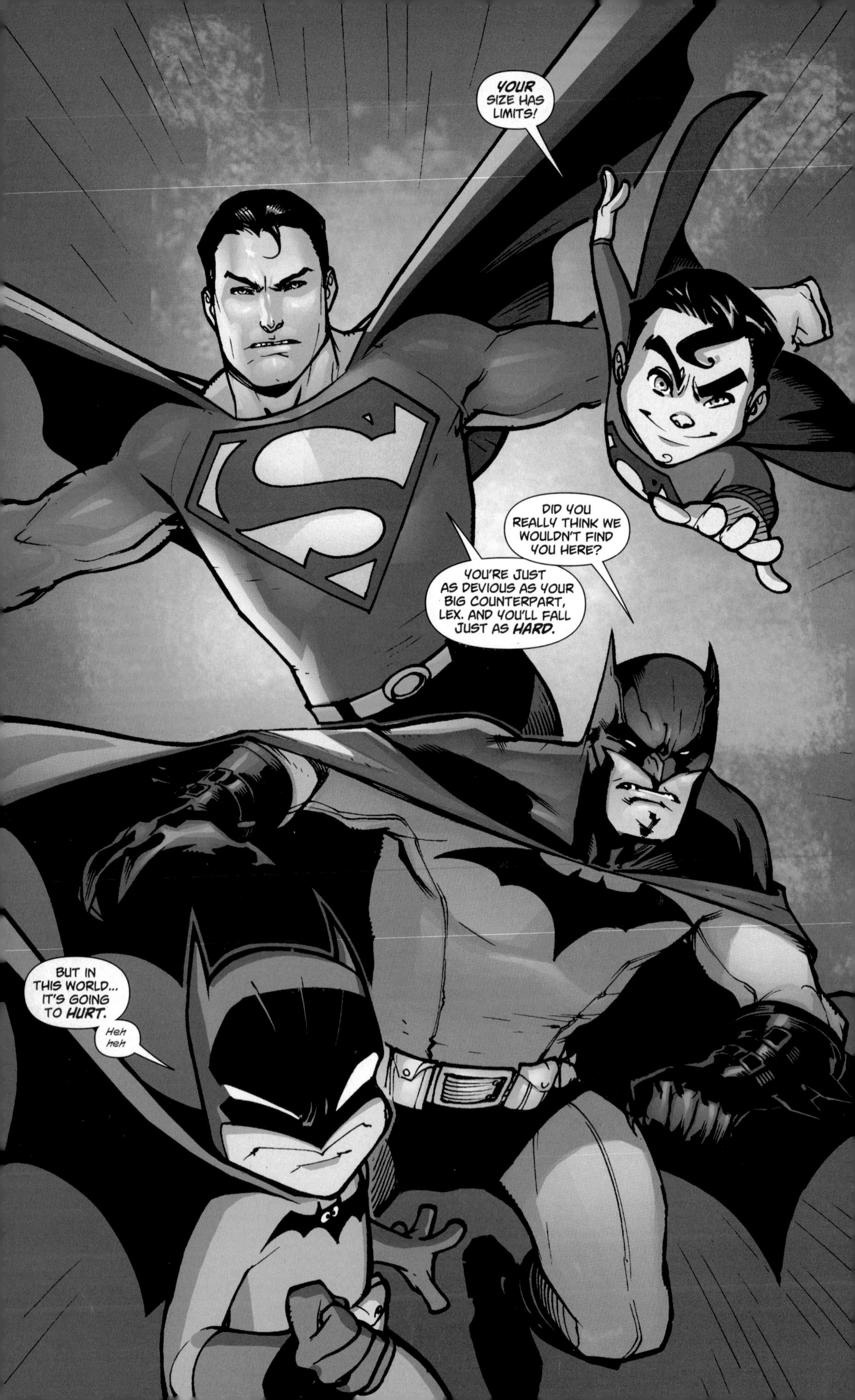

*YOUR* SIZE HAS LIMITS!
DID YOU REALLY THINK WE WOULDN'T FIND YOU HERE?
YOU'RE JUST AS DEVIOUS AS YOUR BIG COUNTERPART, LEX. AND YOU'LL FALL JUST AS *HARD*.
BUT IN THIS WORLD... IT'S GOING TO *HURT*.
Heh heh

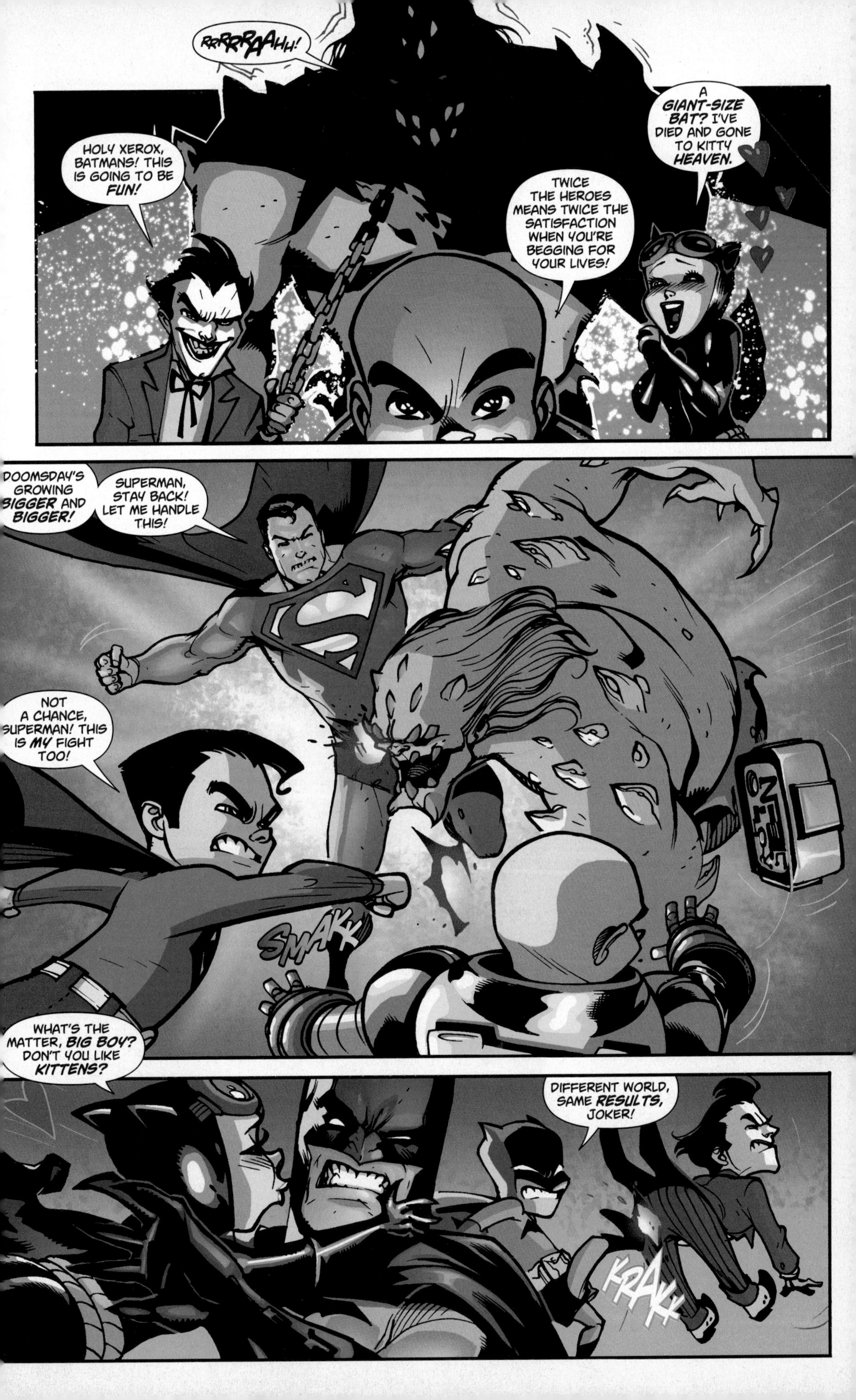
RRRRRAAHH!
HOLY XEROX, BATMANS! THIS IS GOING TO BE FUN!
TWICE THE HEROES MEANS TWICE THE SATISFACTION WHEN YOU'RE BEGGING FOR YOUR LIVES!
A GIANT-SIZE BAT? I'VE DIED AND GONE TO KITTY HEAVEN.
DOOMSDAY'S GROWING BIGGER AND BIGGER!
SUPERMAN, STAY BACK! LET ME HANDLE THIS!
NOT A CHANCE, SUPERMAN! THIS IS MY FIGHT TOO!
SMAKK
WHAT'S THE MATTER, BIG BOY? DON'T YOU LIKE KITTENS?
DIFFERENT WORLD, SAME RESULTS, JOKER!
KRAKK

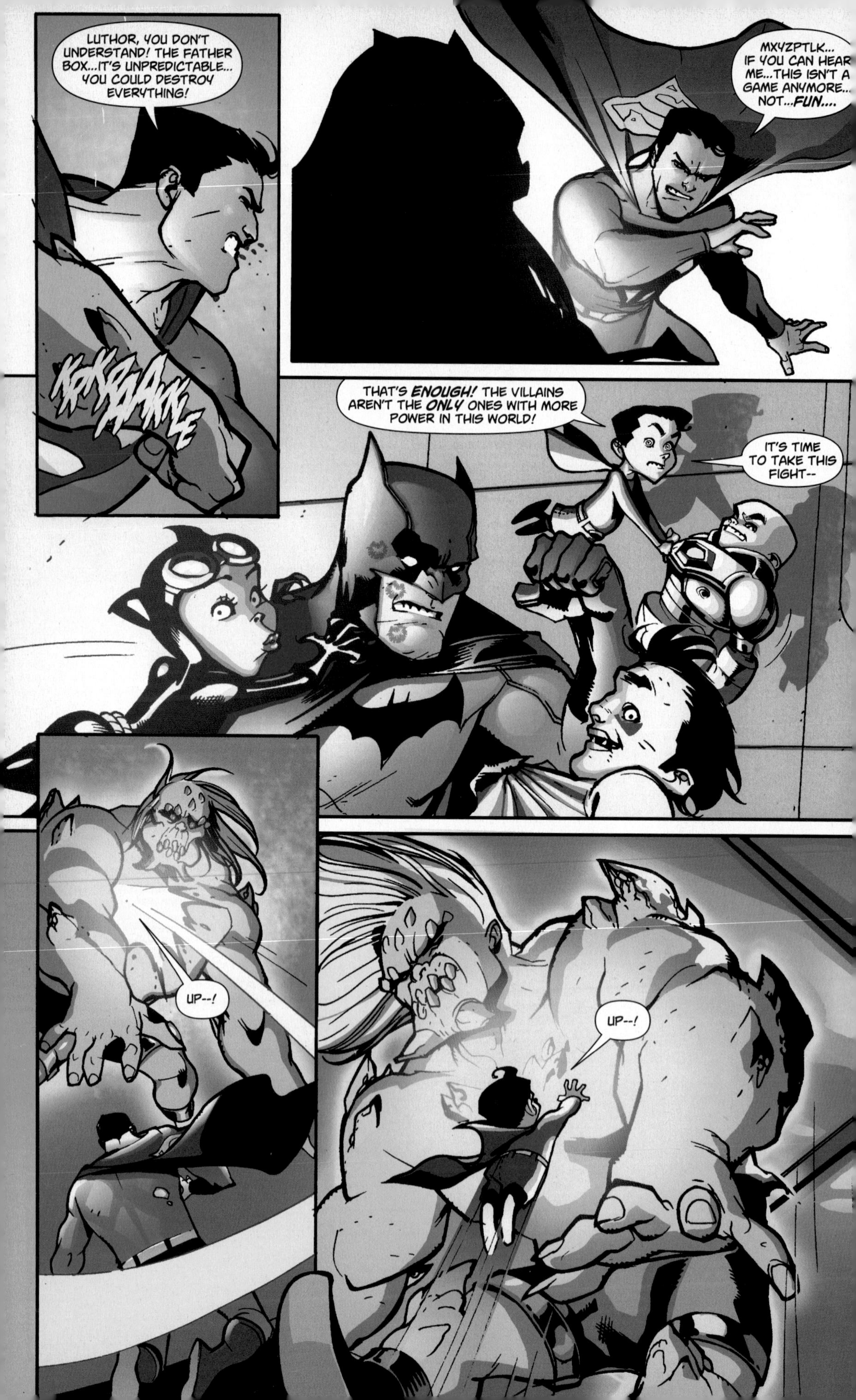

LUTHOR, YOU DON'T UNDERSTAND! THE FATHER BOX...IT'S UNPREDICTABLE... YOU COULD DESTROY EVERYTHING!
KRAKRAAKKLE
MXYZPTLK... IF YOU CAN HEAR ME...THIS ISN'T A GAME ANYMORE... NOT...FUN....
THAT'S ENOUGH! THE VILLAINS AREN'T THE ONLY ONES WITH MORE POWER IN THIS WORLD!
IT'S TIME TO TAKE THIS FIGHT--
UP--!
UP--!

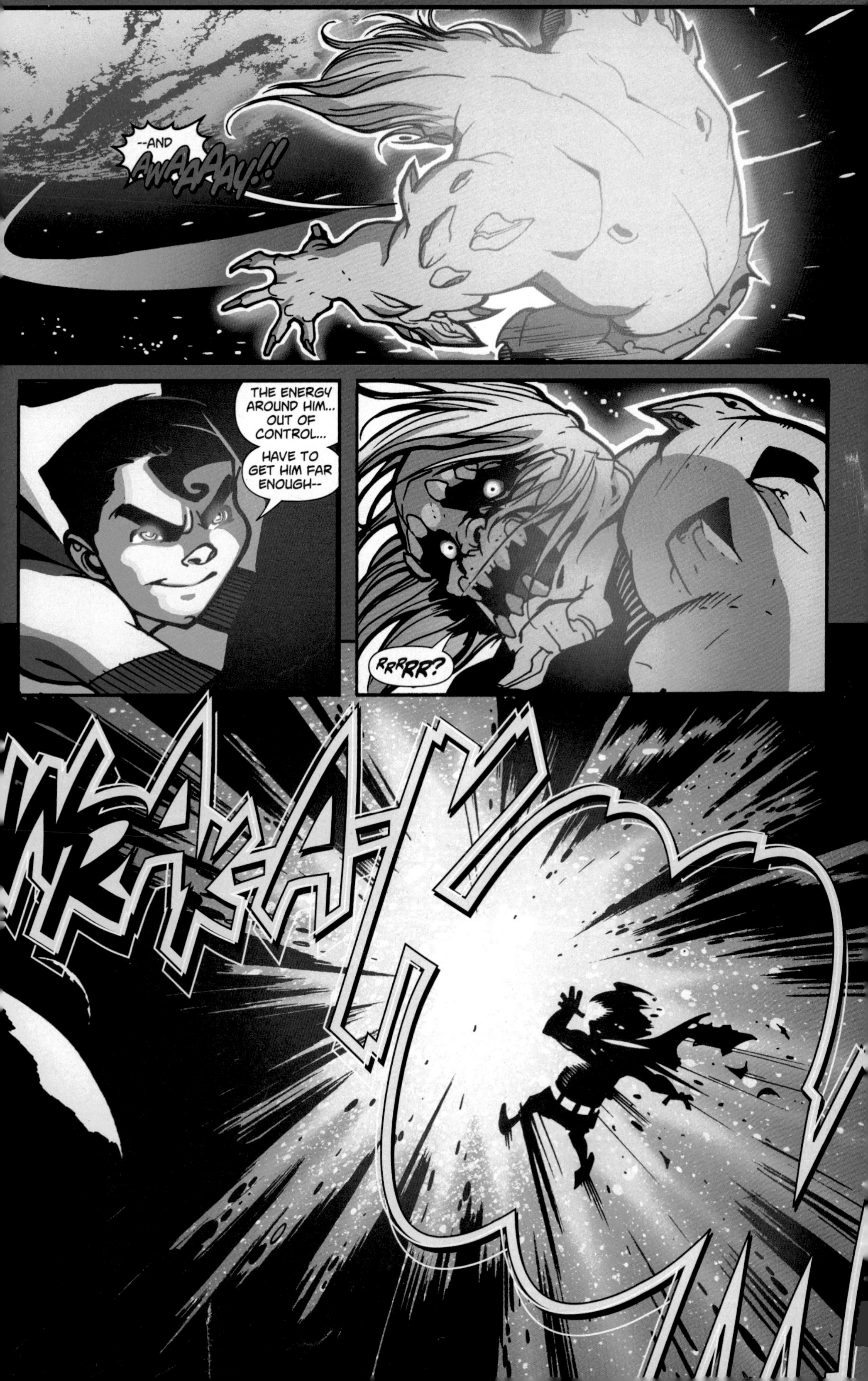
--AND AWAAAAY!!
THE ENERGY AROUND HIM... OUT OF CONTROL...
HAVE TO GET HIM FAR ENOUGH--
RRRRR?
WHAAAM

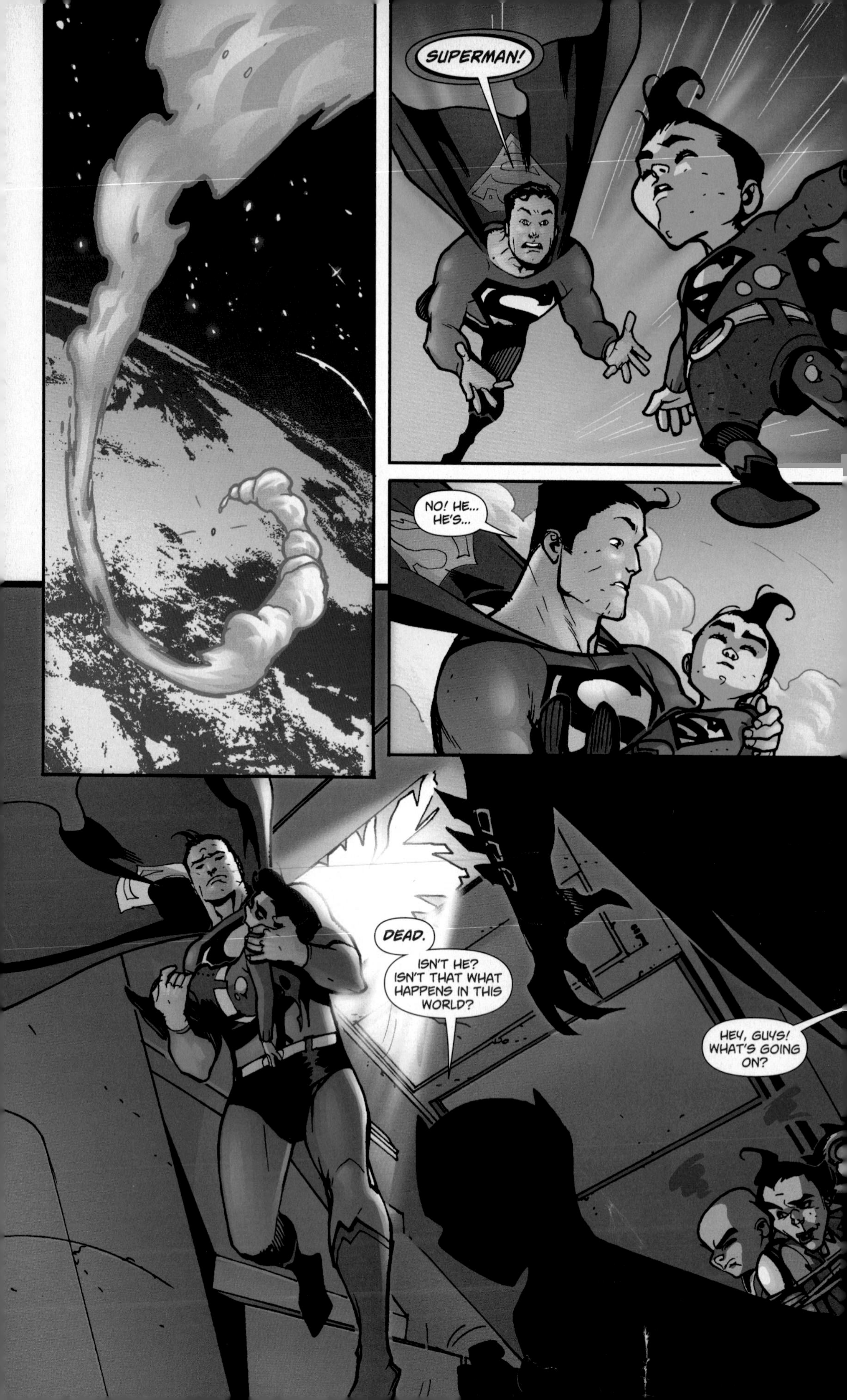
SUPERMAN!
NO! HE... HE'S...
DEAD.
ISN'T HE? ISN'T THAT WHAT HAPPENS IN THIS WORLD?
HEY, GUYS! WHAT'S GOING ON?

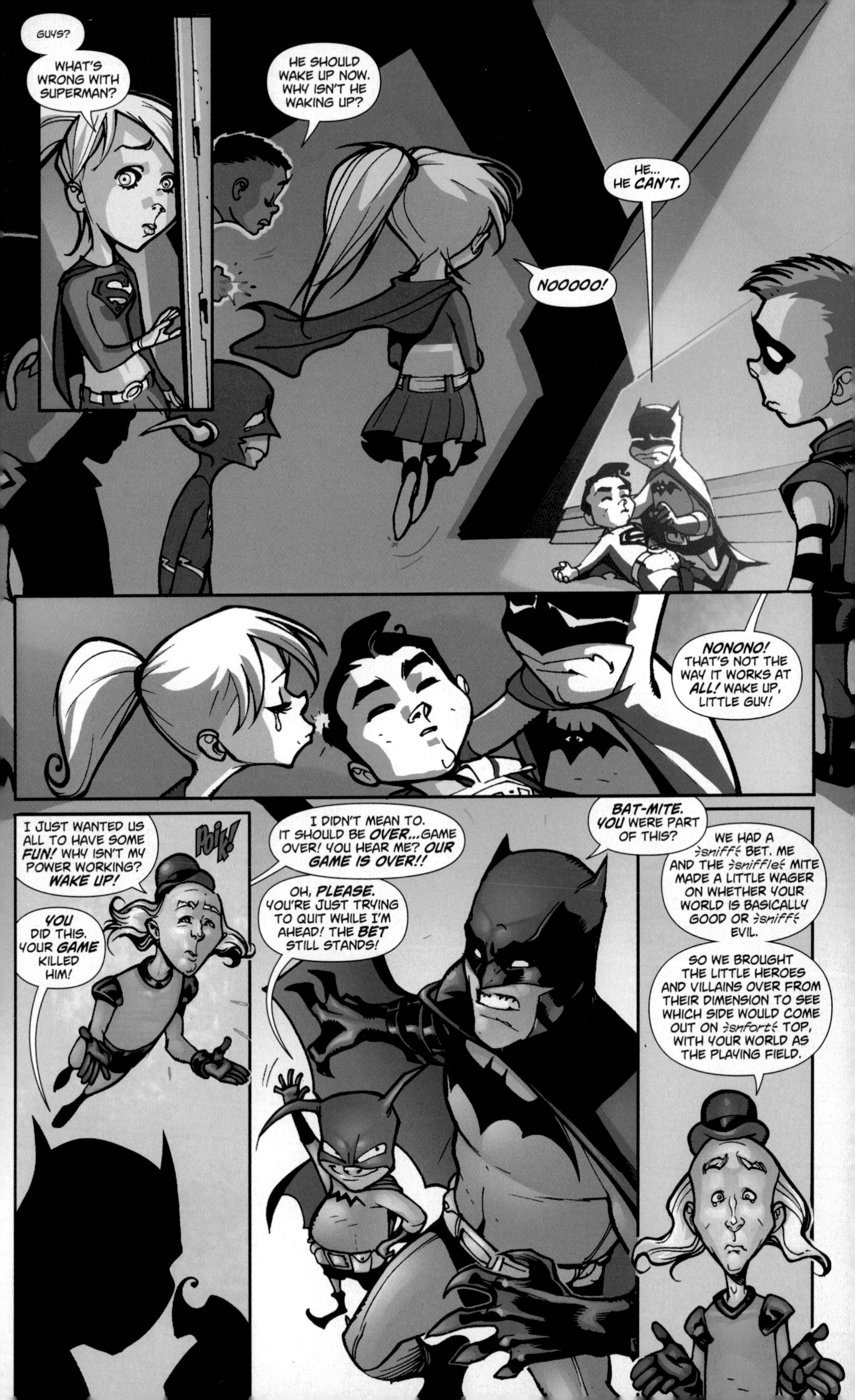
GUYS?
WHAT'S WRONG WITH SUPERMAN?
HE SHOULD WAKE UP NOW. WHY ISN'T HE WAKING UP?
HE... HE CAN'T.
NOOOOO!
NONONO! THAT'S NOT THE WAY IT WORKS AT ALL! WAKE UP, LITTLE GUY!
I JUST WANTED US ALL TO HAVE SOME FUN! WHY ISN'T MY POWER WORKING? WAKE UP!
POIK!
YOU DID THIS. YOUR GAME KILLED HIM!
I DIDN'T MEAN TO. IT SHOULD BE OVER...GAME OVER! YOU HEAR ME? OUR GAME IS OVER!!
OH, PLEASE. YOU'RE JUST TRYING TO QUIT WHILE I'M AHEAD! THE BET STILL STANDS!
BAT-MITE. YOU WERE PART OF THIS?
WE HAD A *sniff* BET. ME AND THE *sniffle* MITE MADE A LITTLE WAGER ON WHETHER YOUR WORLD IS BASICALLY GOOD OR *sniff* EVIL.
SO WE BROUGHT THE LITTLE HEROES AND VILLAINS OVER FROM THEIR DIMENSION TO SEE WHICH SIDE WOULD COME OUT ON *snfort* TOP, WITH YOUR WORLD AS THE PLAYING FIELD.

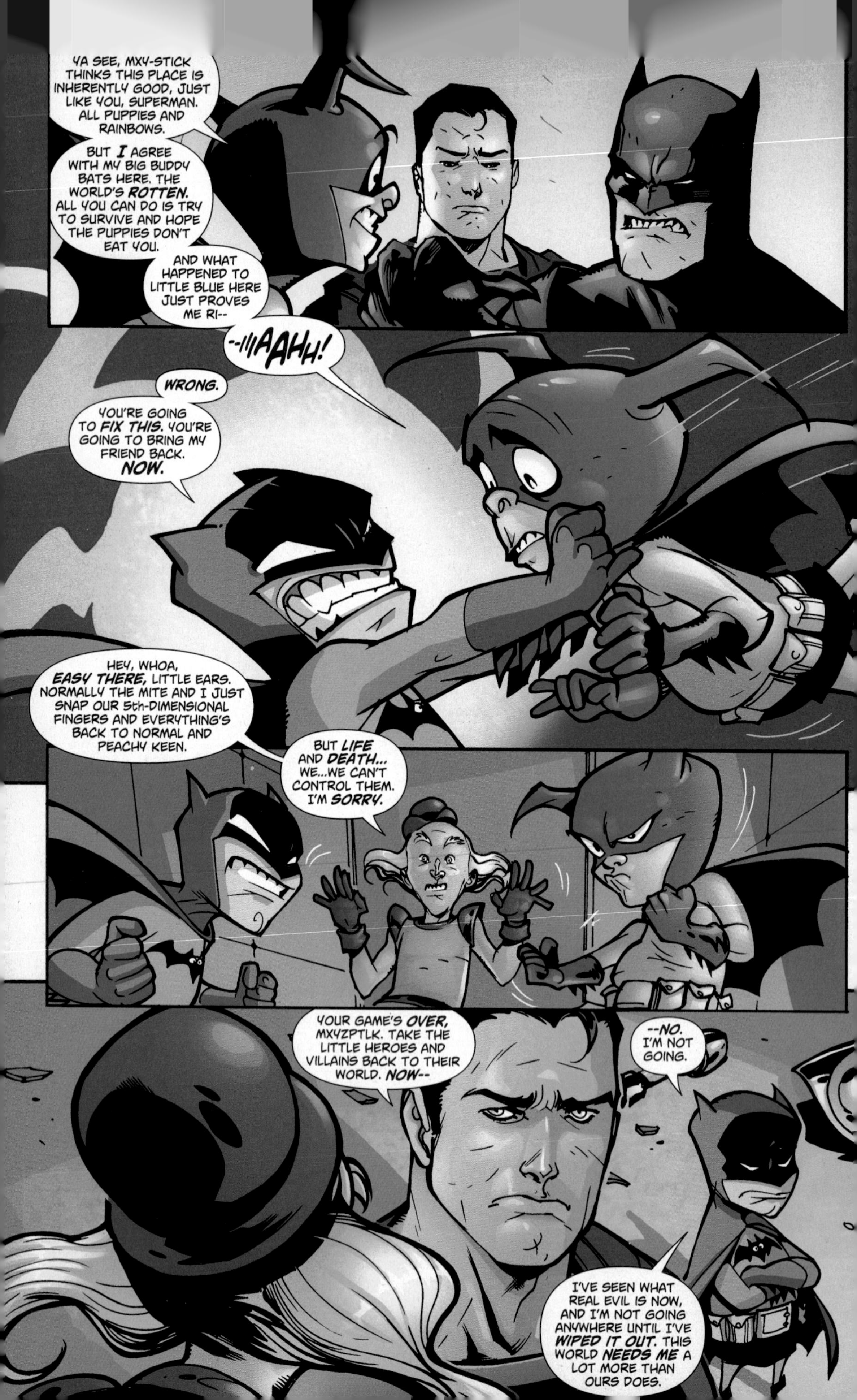

YA SEE, MXY-STICK THINKS THIS PLACE IS INHERENTLY GOOD, JUST LIKE YOU, SUPERMAN. ALL PUPPIES AND RAINBOWS.
BUT I AGREE WITH MY BIG BUDDY BATS HERE. THE WORLD'S ROTTEN. ALL YOU CAN DO IS TRY TO SURVIVE AND HOPE THE PUPPIES DON'T EAT YOU.
AND WHAT HAPPENED TO LITTLE BLUE HERE JUST PROVES ME RI--
--IIIAAHH!
WRONG.
YOU'RE GOING TO FIX THIS. YOU'RE GOING TO BRING MY FRIEND BACK. NOW.
HEY, WHOA, EASY THERE, LITTLE EARS. NORMALLY THE MITE AND I JUST SNAP OUR 5th-DIMENSIONAL FINGERS AND EVERYTHING'S BACK TO NORMAL AND PEACHY KEEN.
BUT LIFE AND DEATH... WE...WE CAN'T CONTROL THEM. I'M SORRY.
YOUR GAME'S OVER, MXYZPTLK. TAKE THE LITTLE HEROES AND VILLAINS BACK TO THEIR WORLD. NOW--
--NO. I'M NOT GOING.
I'VE SEEN WHAT REAL EVIL IS NOW, AND I'M NOT GOING ANYWHERE UNTIL I'VE WIPED IT OUT. THIS WORLD NEEDS ME A LOT MORE THAN OURS DOES.

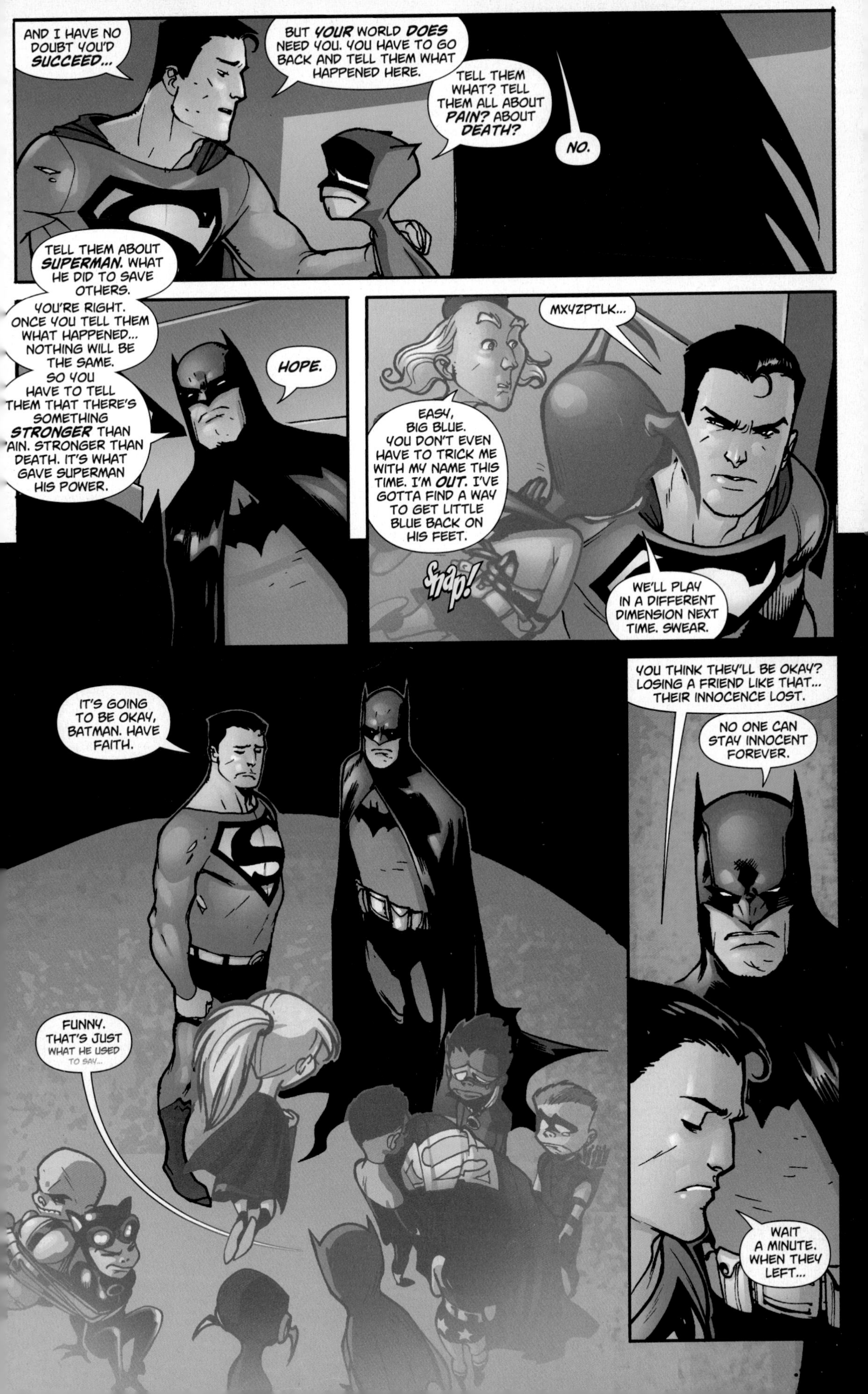
AND I HAVE NO DOUBT YOU'D SUCCEED...
BUT YOUR WORLD DOES NEED YOU. YOU HAVE TO GO BACK AND TELL THEM WHAT HAPPENED HERE.
TELL THEM WHAT? TELL THEM ALL ABOUT PAIN? ABOUT DEATH?
NO.
TELL THEM ABOUT SUPERMAN. WHAT HE DID TO SAVE OTHERS.
YOU'RE RIGHT. ONCE YOU TELL THEM WHAT HAPPENED... NOTHING WILL BE THE SAME.
SO YOU HAVE TO TELL THEM THAT THERE'S SOMETHING STRONGER THAN PAIN. STRONGER THAN DEATH. IT'S WHAT GAVE SUPERMAN HIS POWER.
HOPE.
MXYZPTLK...
EASY, BIG BLUE. YOU DON'T EVEN HAVE TO TRICK ME WITH MY NAME THIS TIME. I'M OUT. I'VE GOTTA FIND A WAY TO GET LITTLE BLUE BACK ON HIS FEET.
SNAP!
WE'LL PLAY IN A DIFFERENT DIMENSION NEXT TIME. SWEAR.
IT'S GOING TO BE OKAY, BATMAN. HAVE FAITH.
FUNNY. THAT'S JUST WHAT HE USED TO SAY...
YOU THINK THEY'LL BE OKAY? LOSING A FRIEND LIKE THAT... THEIR INNOCENCE LOST.
NO ONE CAN STAY INNOCENT FOREVER.
WAIT A MINUTE. WHEN THEY LEFT...

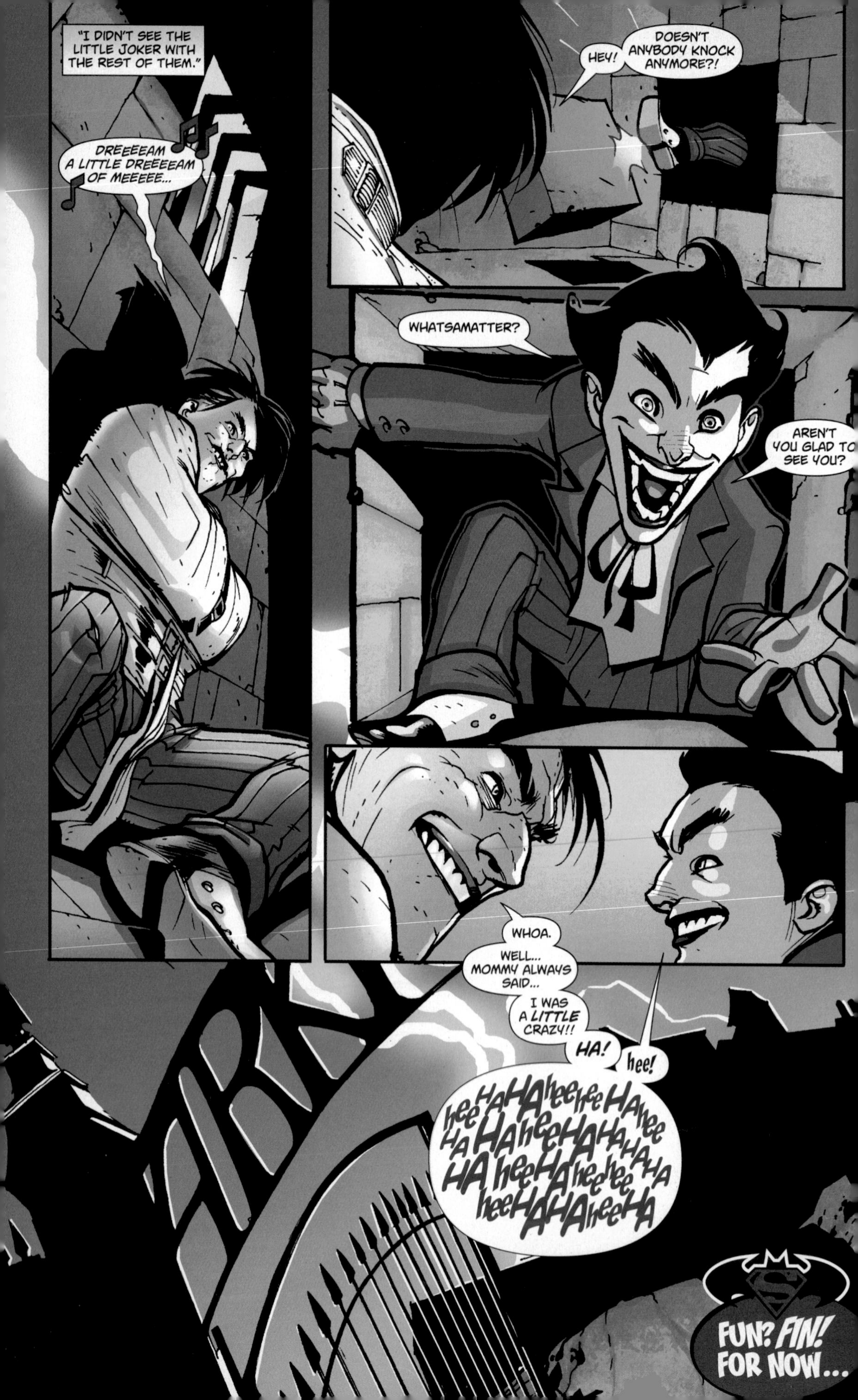
"I DIDN'T SEE THE LITTLE JOKER WITH THE REST OF THEM."
DREEEEAM A LITTLE DREEEEAM OF MEEEEE...
HEY!
DOESN'T ANYBODY KNOCK ANYMORE?!
WHATSAMATTER?
AREN'T YOU GLAD TO SEE YOU?
WHOA.
WELL... MOMMY ALWAYS SAID...
I WAS A LITTLE CRAZY!!
HA!
hee!
heeHAHAheeheeHAhee HAHAheeHAHAHAHA HA heeHAheeheeHA heeHAHAheeHA
FUN? FIN! FOR NOW...

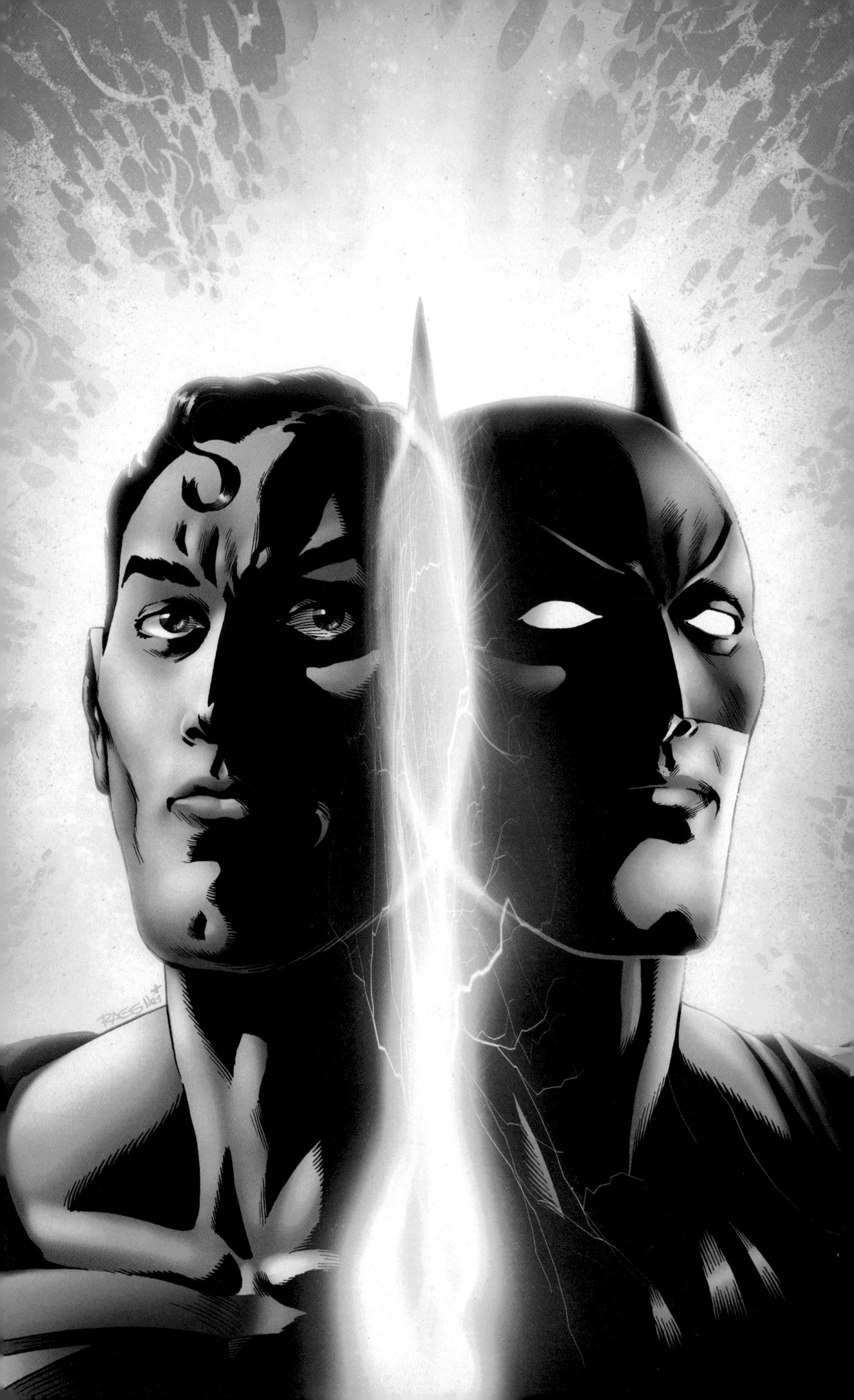

# SUPERMAN/BATMAN 53

## SUPERBAT
part one

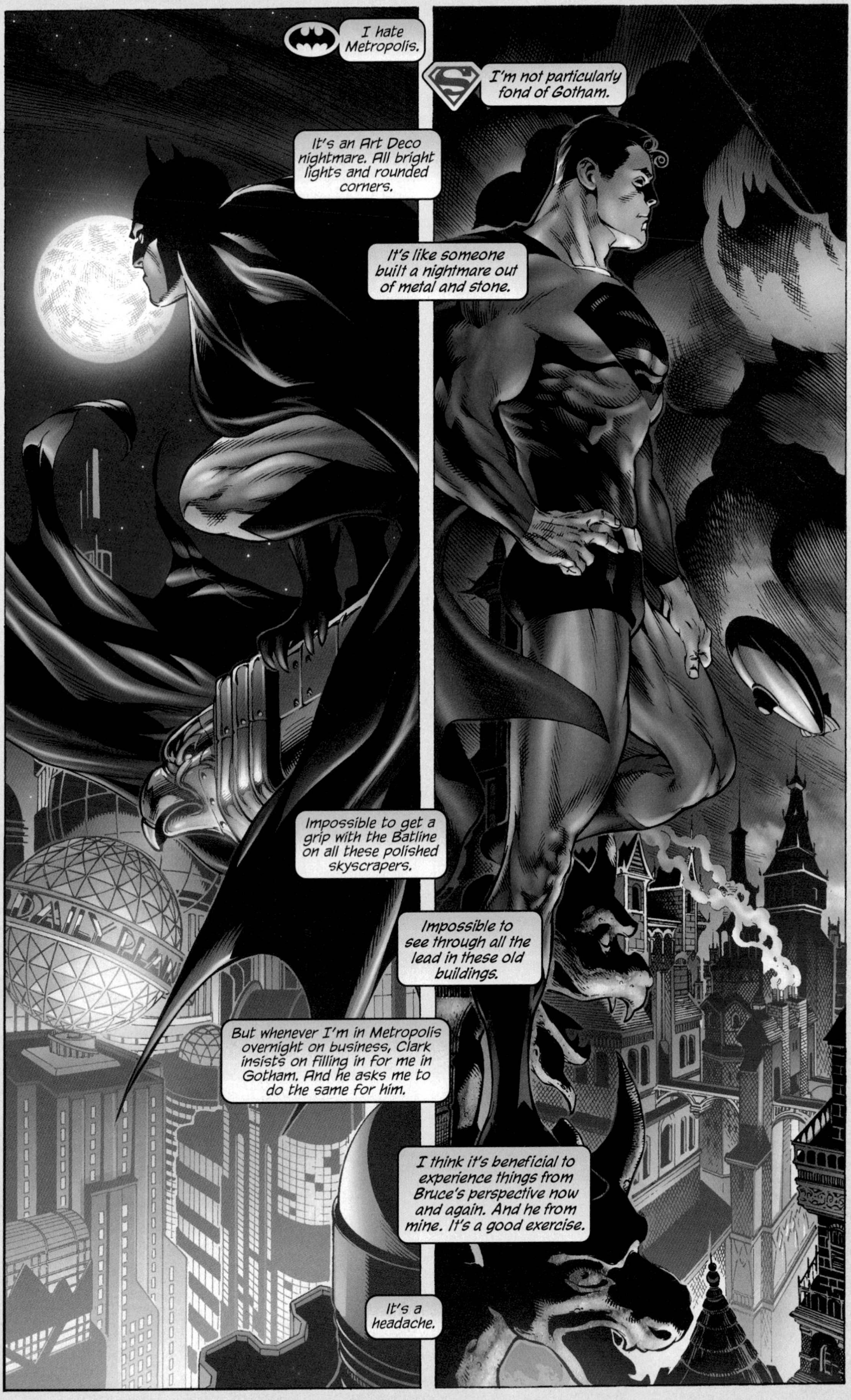
I hate Metropolis.
I'm not particularly fond of Gotham.
It's an Art Deco nightmare. All bright lights and rounded corners.
It's like someone built a nightmare out of metal and stone.
Impossible to get a grip with the Batline on all these polished skyscrapers.
Impossible to see through all the lead in these old buildings.
But whenever I'm in Metropolis overnight on business, Clark insists on filling in for me in Gotham. And he asks me to do the same for him.
I think it's beneficial to experience things from Bruce's perspective now and again. And he from mine. It's a good exercise.
It's a headache.
DAILY PLANET

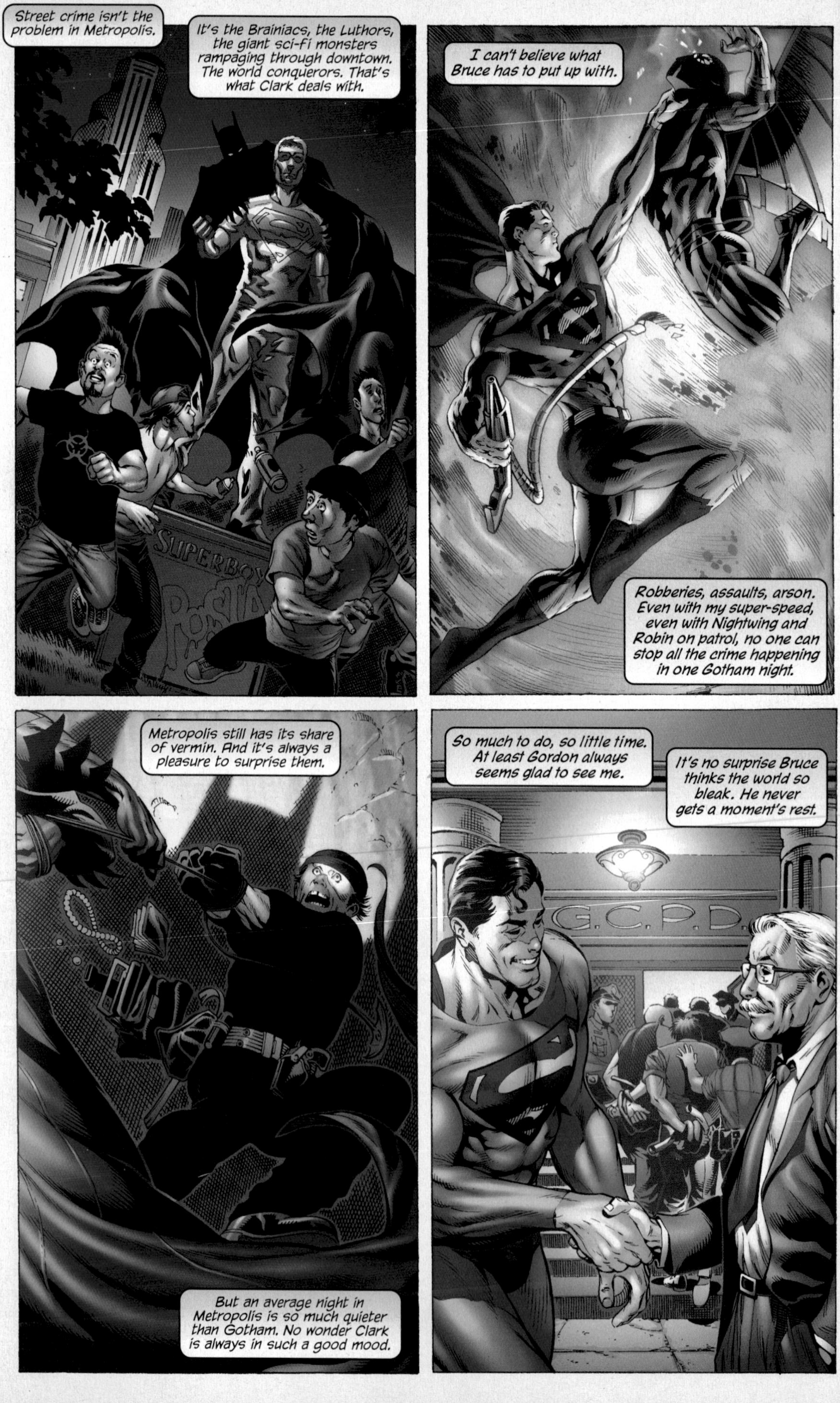
Street crime isn't the problem in Metropolis.
It's the Brainiacs, the Luthors, the giant sci-fi monsters rampaging through downtown. The world conquerors. That's what Clark deals with.
I can't believe what Bruce has to put up with.
Robberies, assaults, arson. Even with my super-speed, even with Nightwing and Robin on patrol, no one can stop all the crime happening in one Gotham night.
Metropolis still has its share of vermin. And it's always a pleasure to surprise them.
But an average night in Metropolis is so much quieter than Gotham. No wonder Clark is always in such a good mood.
So much to do, so little time. At least Gordon always seems glad to see me.
It's no surprise Bruce thinks the world so bleak. He never gets a moment's rest.
G.C.P.D.

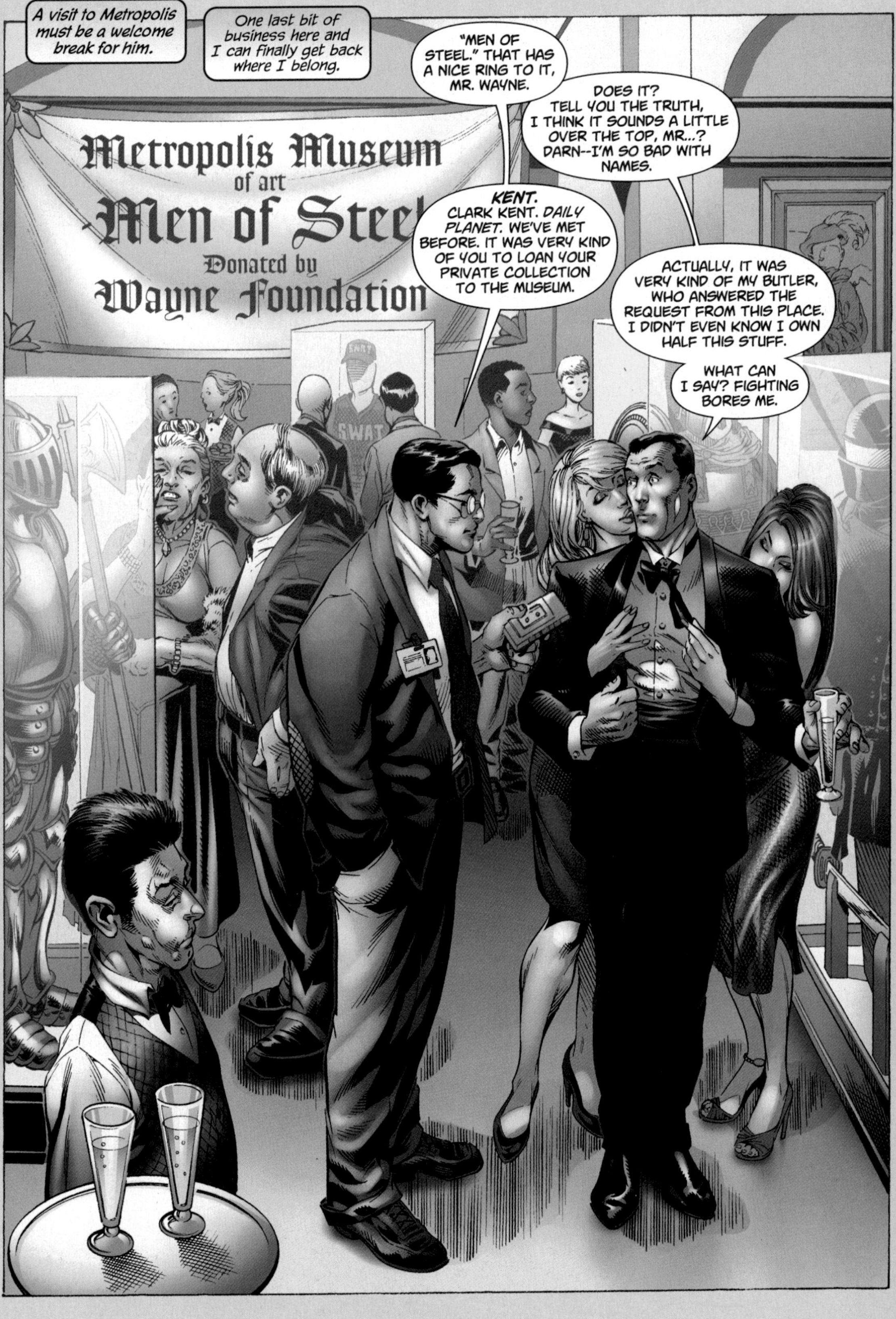

A visit to Metropolis must be a welcome break for him.
One last bit of business here and I can finally get back where I belong.
"MEN OF STEEL." THAT HAS A NICE RING TO IT, MR. WAYNE.
DOES IT? TELL YOU THE TRUTH, I THINK IT SOUNDS A LITTLE OVER THE TOP, MR...? DARN--I'M SO BAD WITH NAMES.
KENT. CLARK KENT. DAILY PLANET. WE'VE MET BEFORE. IT WAS VERY KIND OF YOU TO LOAN YOUR PRIVATE COLLECTION TO THE MUSEUM.
ACTUALLY, IT WAS VERY KIND OF MY BUTLER, WHO ANSWERED THE REQUEST FROM THIS PLACE. I DIDN'T EVEN KNOW I OWN HALF THIS STUFF.
WHAT CAN I SAY? FIGHTING BORES ME.
Metropolis Museum of art
Men of Steel
Donated by Wayne Foundation
SWAT

REALLY? I WOULD THINK A MAN OF YOUR...

ADVENTUROUS REPUTATION...

WOULD LOVE ALL THESE OLD SWORDS AND SHIELDS.

DON'T JUMP TO CONCLUSIONS, MR. CLARK.

HISTORY'S JUST NOT MY THING. WHAT'S PAST IS PAST. I LIVE IN THE *MOMENT*. I FIND IT MORE...

*STIMULATING.*

Tee!

Hee!

I THINK THAT'S MY CUE TO WRAP UP THE INTERVIEW.

FINE BY ME.

*That woman. The white hair...*

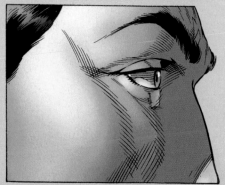

*That tattoo. I've seen it before.*

I'LL NEVER UNDERSTAND HOW GUYS COULD GO INTO BATTLE WEARING A DRESS.

NOW *YOUR* DRESS, ON THE OTHER HAND...

*She doesn't even blink. Not just ignoring a bad line. It's like she's hypnotized.*

CAWDOR.

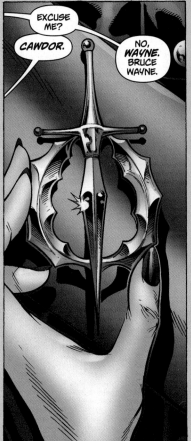

EXCUSE ME?

CAWDOR.

NO, *WAYNE.* BRUCE WAYNE.

BUT YOU GO AHEAD AND CALL ME ANYTHING YOU--*HEY!*

CAWDOR!

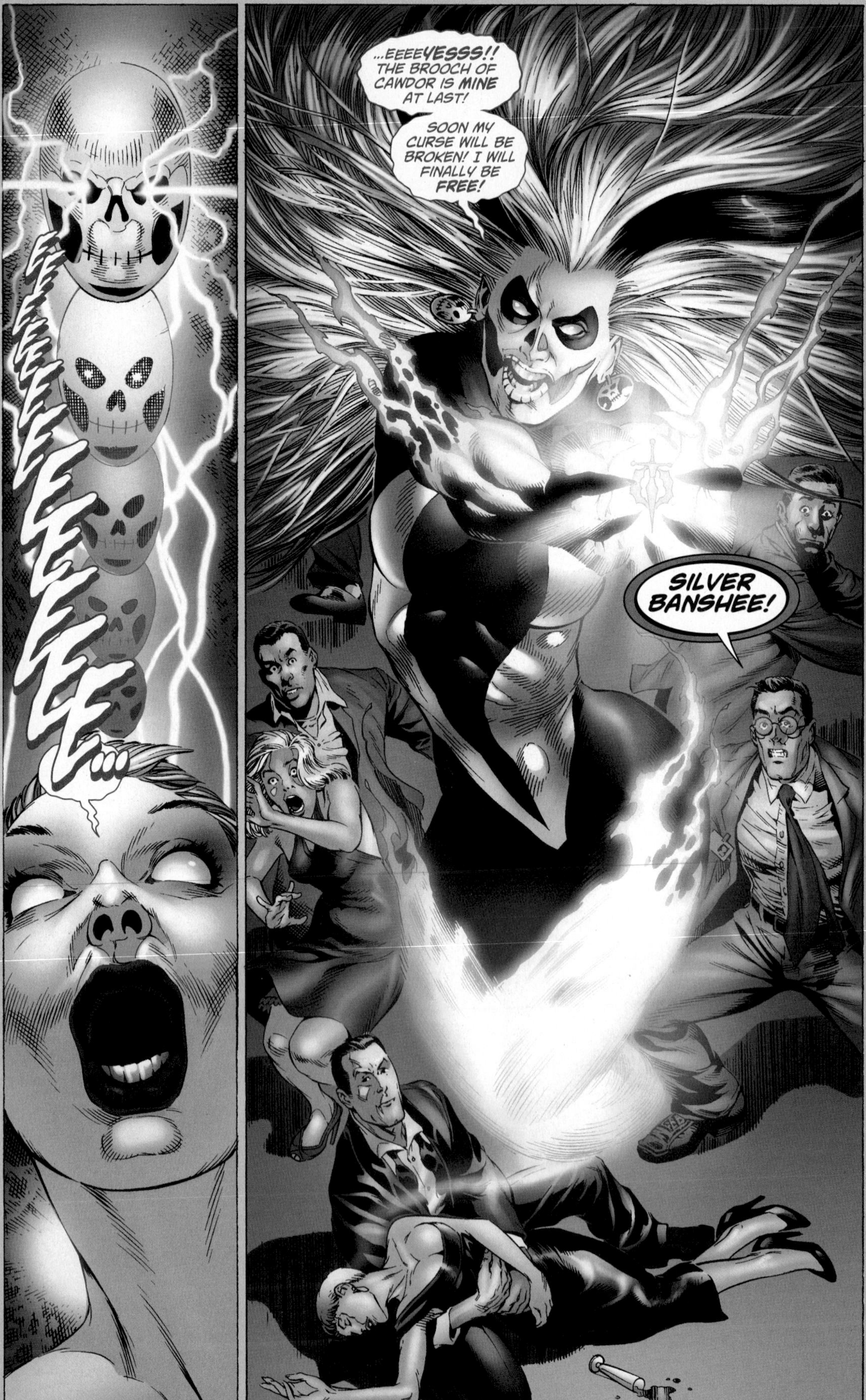

EEEEEEEEEEEEE...
...EEEEYESSS!! THE BROOCH OF CAWDOR IS MINE AT LAST!
SOON MY CURSE WILL BE BROKEN! I WILL FINALLY BE FREE!
SILVER BANSHEE!

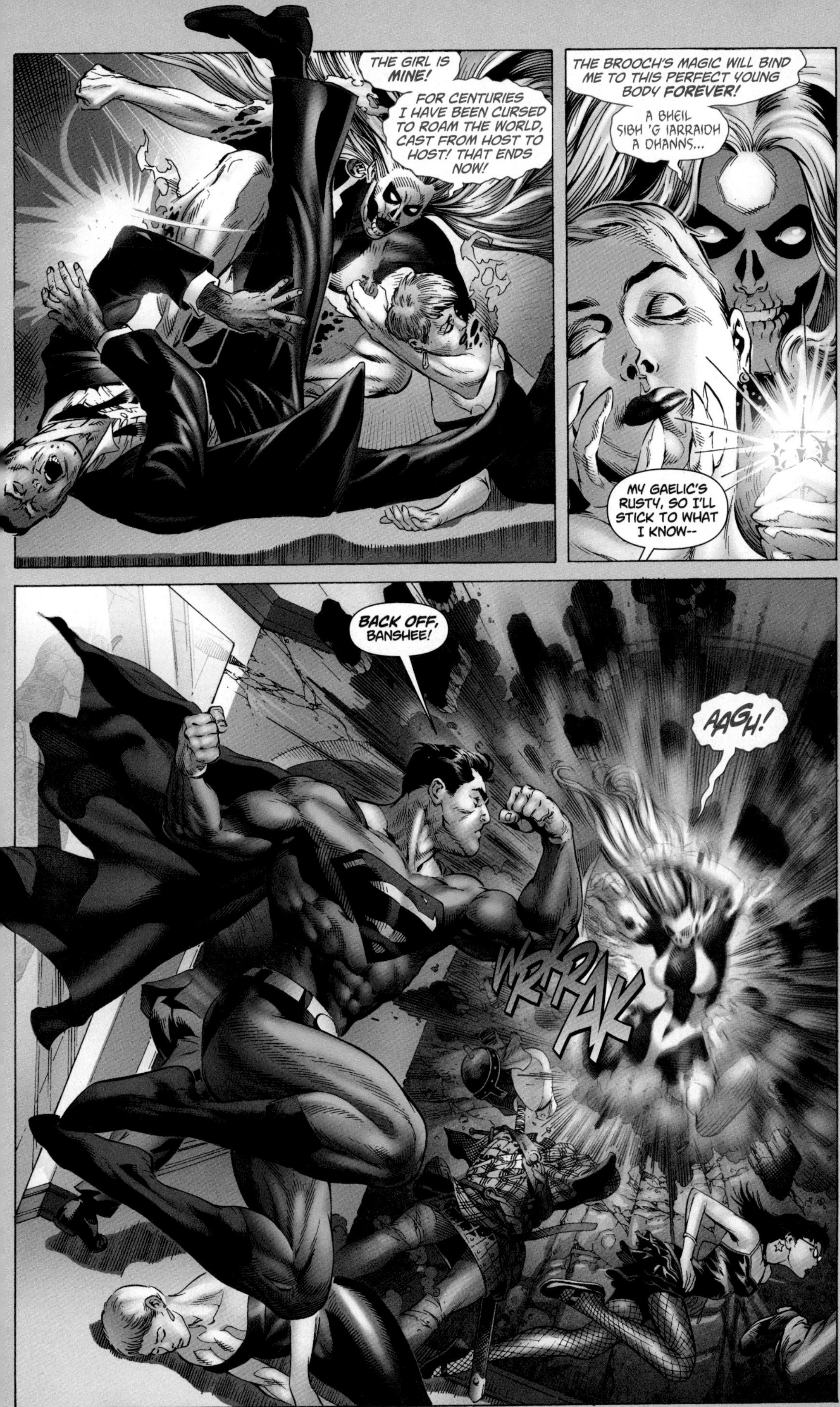
THE GIRL IS MINE!
FOR CENTURIES I HAVE BEEN CURSED TO ROAM THE WORLD, CAST FROM HOST TO HOST! THAT ENDS NOW!
THE BROOCH'S MAGIC WILL BIND ME TO THIS PERFECT YOUNG BODY FOREVER!
A BHEIL SIBH 'G IARRAIDH A DHANNS...
MY GAELIC'S RUSTY, SO I'LL STICK TO WHAT I KNOW--
BACK OFF, BANSHEE!
AAGH!
WRKRAK

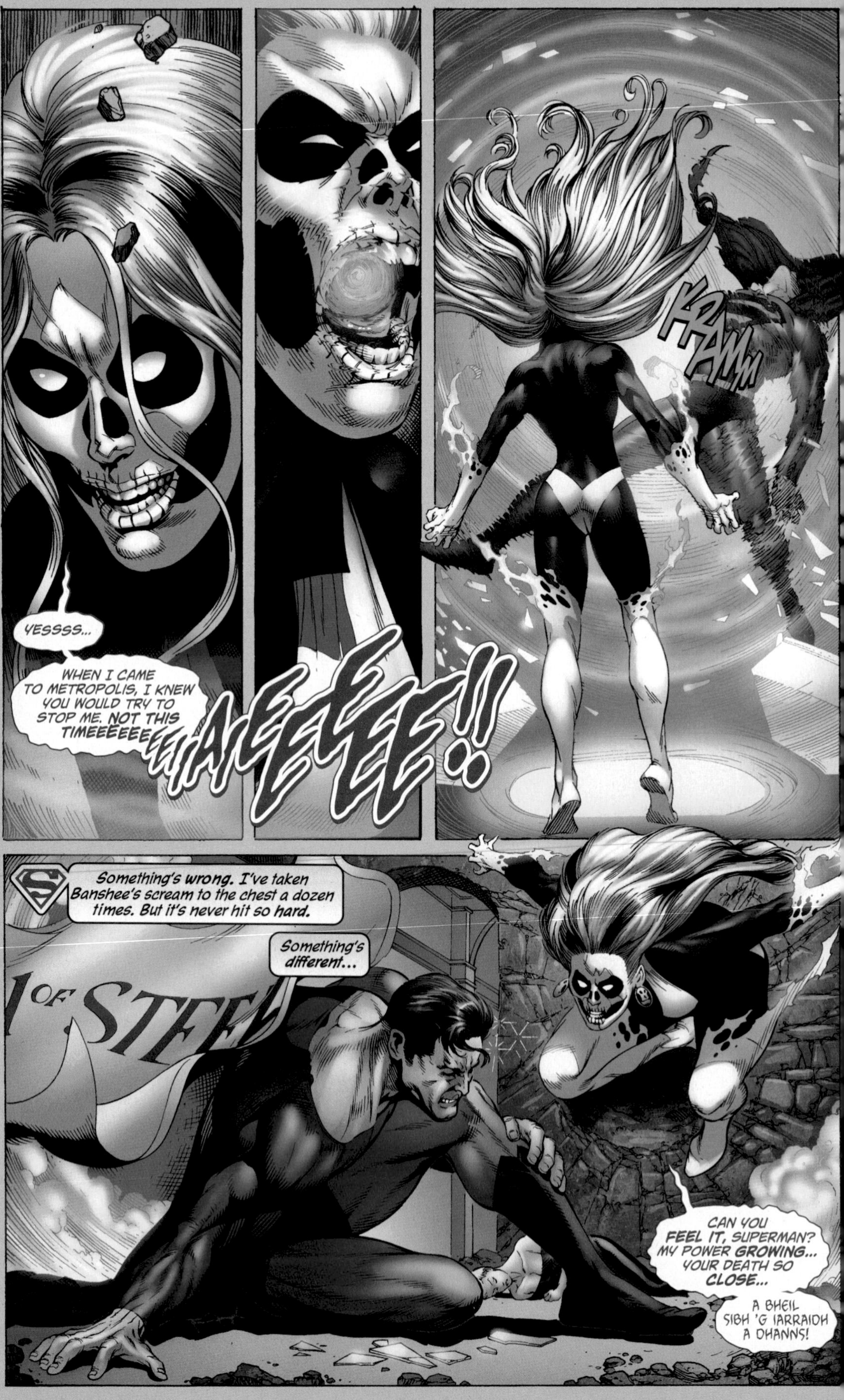
YESSSS...
WHEN I CAME TO METROPOLIS, I KNEW YOU WOULD TRY TO STOP ME. NOT THIS TIMEEEEEEE
EEEAAEEEEEEE!!
KRAMM
Something's wrong. I've taken Banshee's scream to the chest a dozen times. But it's never hit so hard.
Something's different...
CAN YOU FEEL IT, SUPERMAN? MY POWER GROWING... YOUR DEATH SO CLOSE...
A BHEIL SIBH 'G IARRAIDH A DHANNS!

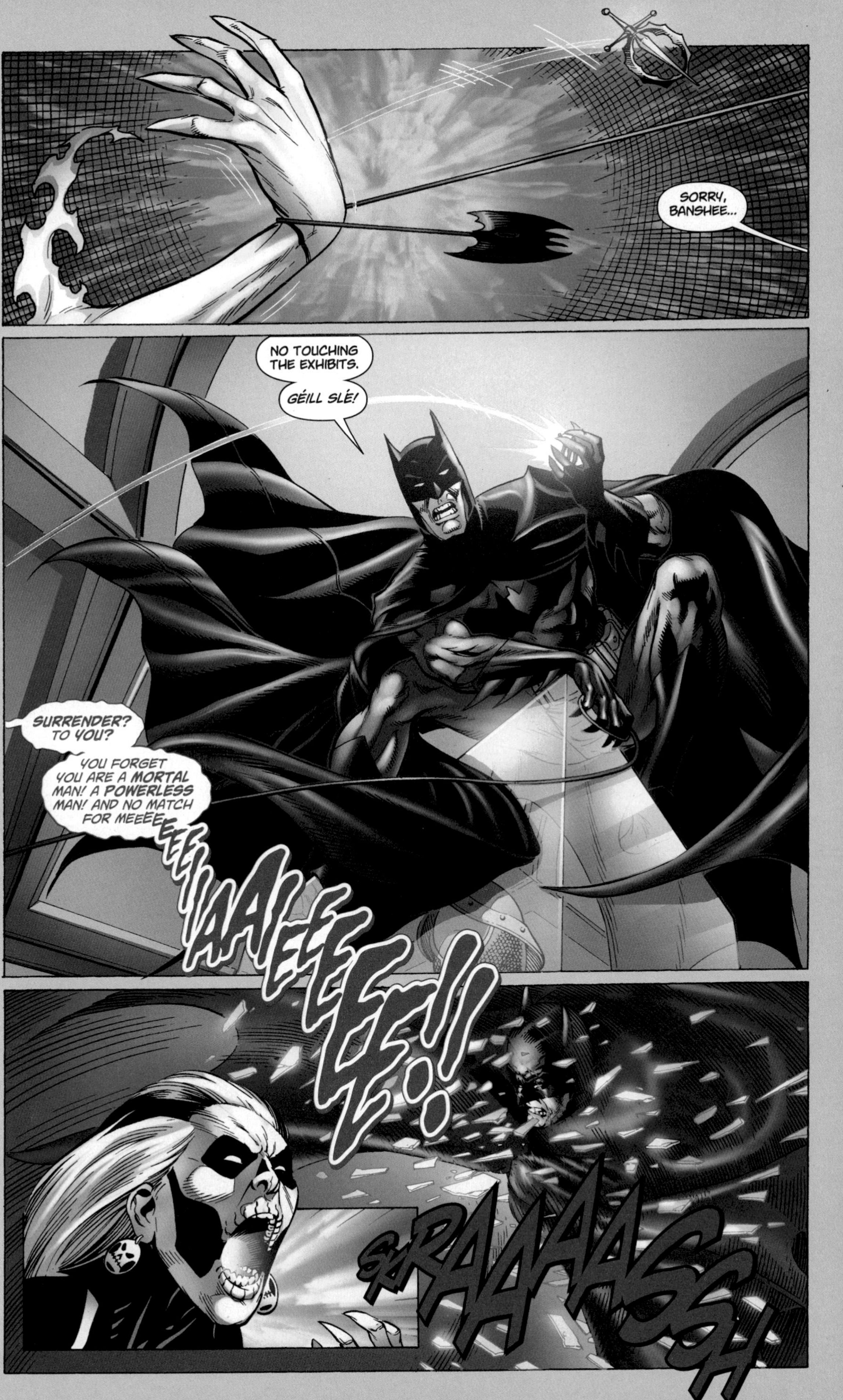
SORRY, BANSHEE...
NO TOUCHING THE EXHIBITS.
GÉILL SLÉ!
SURRENDER? TO YOU?
YOU FORGET YOU ARE A MORTAL MAN! A POWERLESS MAN! AND NO MATCH FOR MEEEE
EEIIAAEEEEEE!!
SKRAAAAASGH

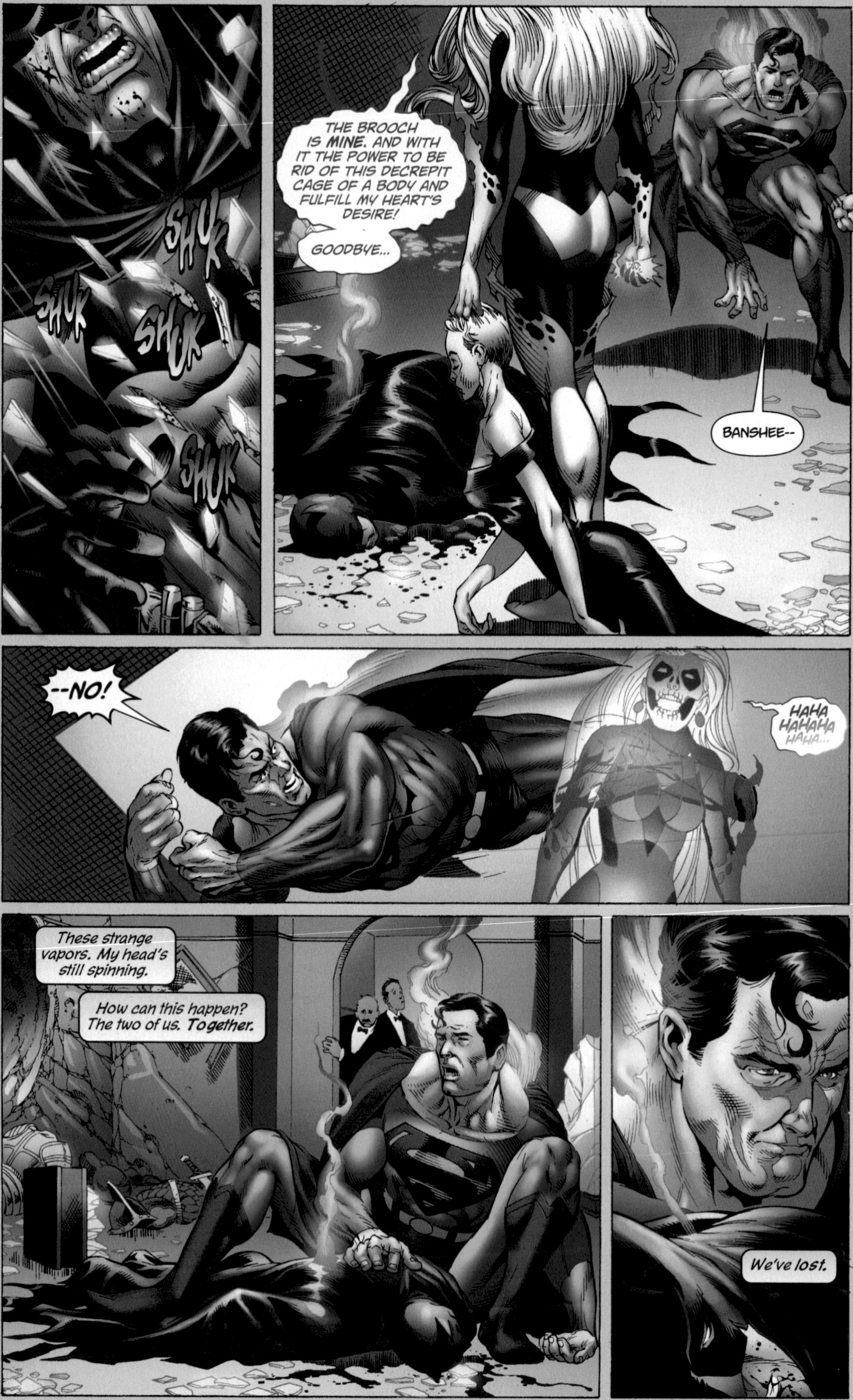
SHUK
SHUK
SHUK
SHUK
THE BROOCH IS MINE. AND WITH IT THE POWER TO BE RID OF THIS DECREPIT CAGE OF A BODY AND FULFILL MY HEART'S DESIRE!
GOODBYE...
BANSHEE--
--NO!
HAHA HAHAHA HAHA...
These strange vapors. My head's still spinning.
How can this happen? The two of us. Together.
We've lost.

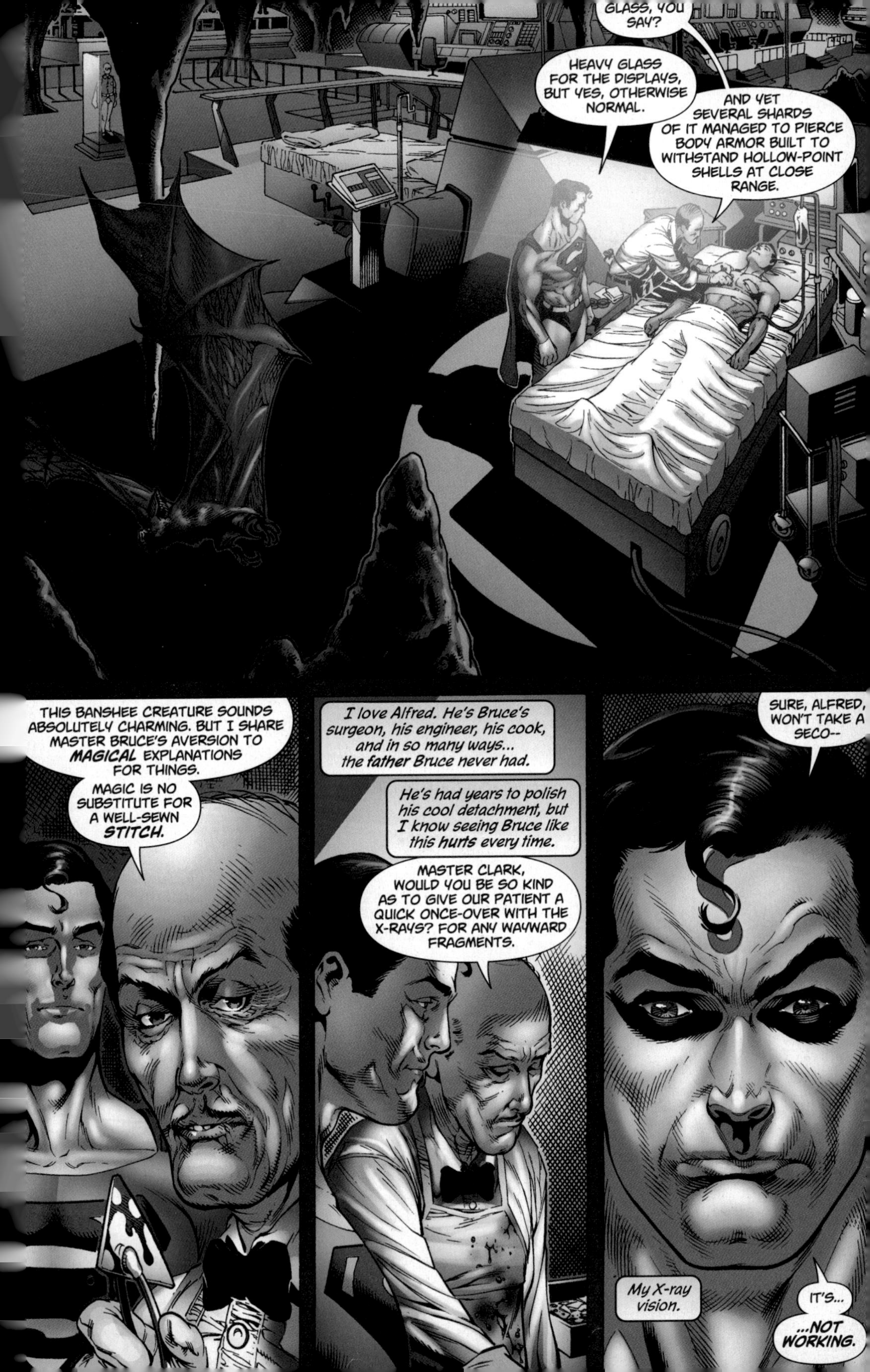
GLASS, YOU SAY?
HEAVY GLASS FOR THE DISPLAYS, BUT YES, OTHERWISE NORMAL.
AND YET SEVERAL SHARDS OF IT MANAGED TO PIERCE BODY ARMOR BUILT TO WITHSTAND HOLLOW-POINT SHELLS AT CLOSE RANGE.
THIS BANSHEE CREATURE SOUNDS ABSOLUTELY CHARMING. BUT I SHARE MASTER BRUCE'S AVERSION TO MAGICAL EXPLANATIONS FOR THINGS.
MAGIC IS NO SUBSTITUTE FOR A WELL-SEWN STITCH.
I love Alfred. He's Bruce's surgeon, his engineer, his cook, and in so many ways... the father Bruce never had.
He's had years to polish his cool detachment, but I know seeing Bruce like this hurts every time.
MASTER CLARK, WOULD YOU BE SO KIND AS TO GIVE OUR PATIENT A QUICK ONCE-OVER WITH THE X-RAYS? FOR ANY WAYWARD FRAGMENTS.
SURE, ALFRED, WON'T TAKE A SECO--
My X-ray vision.
IT'S...
...NOT WORKING.

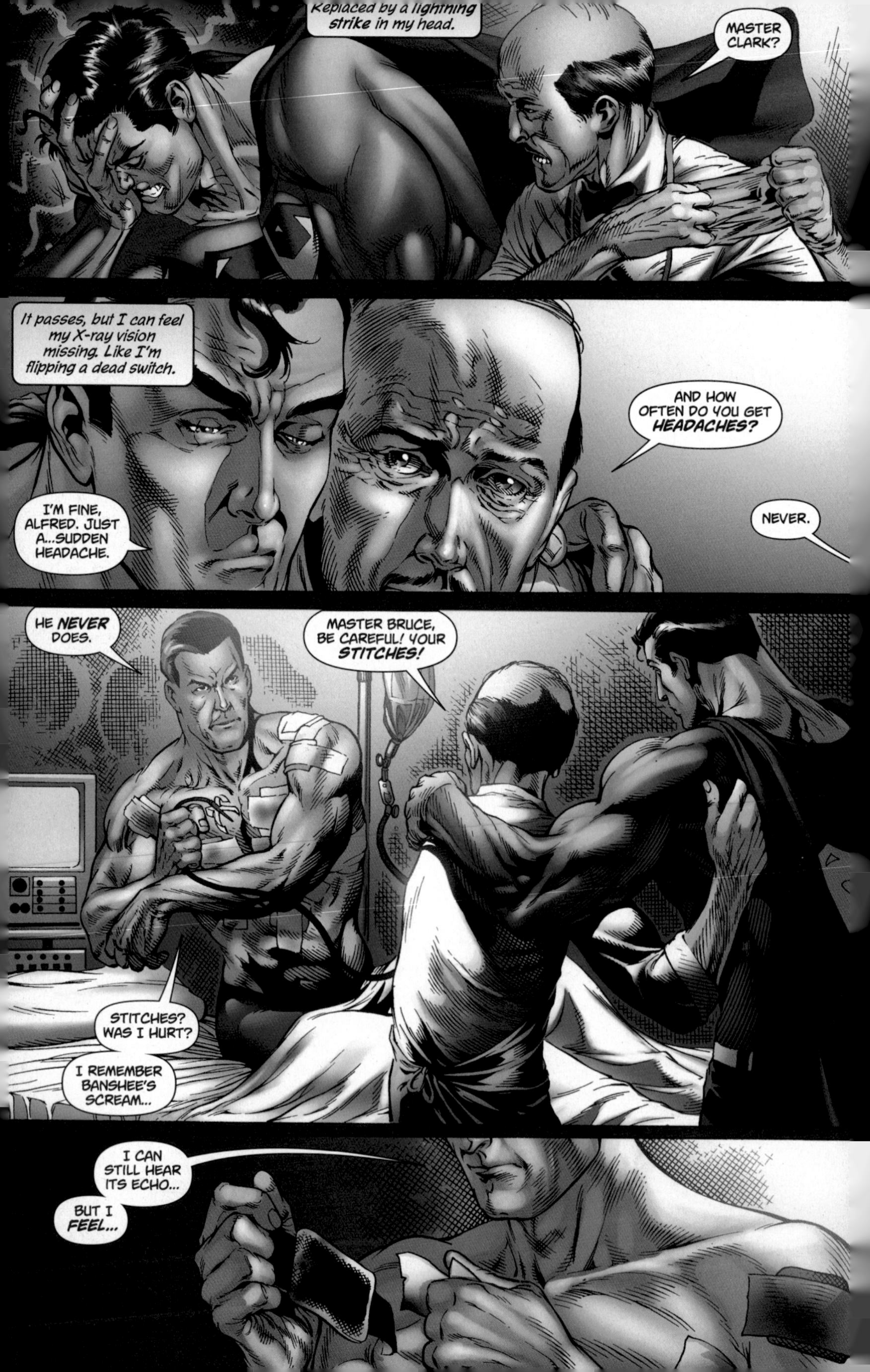
Replaced by a lightning strike in my head.
MASTER CLARK?
It passes, but I can feel my X-ray vision missing. Like I'm flipping a dead switch.
AND HOW OFTEN DO YOU GET HEADACHES?
I'M FINE, ALFRED. JUST A...SUDDEN HEADACHE.
NEVER.
HE NEVER DOES.
MASTER BRUCE, BE CAREFUL! YOUR STITCHES!
STITCHES? WAS I HURT?
I REMEMBER BANSHEE'S SCREAM...
I CAN STILL HEAR ITS ECHO...
BUT I FEEL...

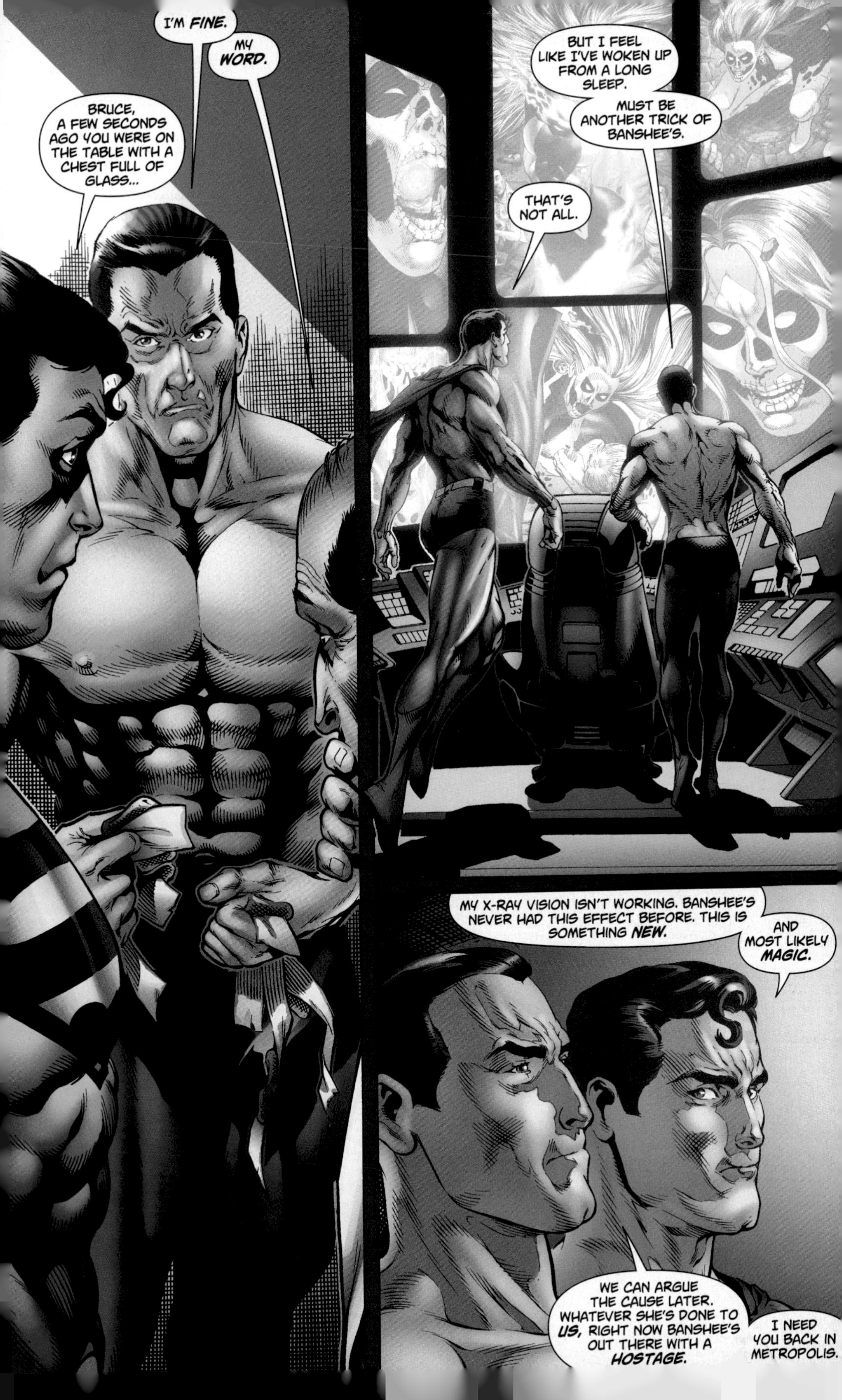
BRUCE, A FEW SECONDS AGO YOU WERE ON THE TABLE WITH A CHEST FULL OF GLASS...
I'M FINE.
MY WORD.
BUT I FEEL LIKE I'VE WOKEN UP FROM A LONG SLEEP.
MUST BE ANOTHER TRICK OF BANSHEE'S.
THAT'S NOT ALL.
MY X-RAY VISION ISN'T WORKING. BANSHEE'S NEVER HAD THIS EFFECT BEFORE. THIS IS SOMETHING NEW.
AND MOST LIKELY MAGIC.
WE CAN ARGUE THE CAUSE LATER. WHATEVER SHE'S DONE TO US, RIGHT NOW BANSHEE'S OUT THERE WITH A HOSTAGE.
I NEED YOU BACK IN METROPOLIS.

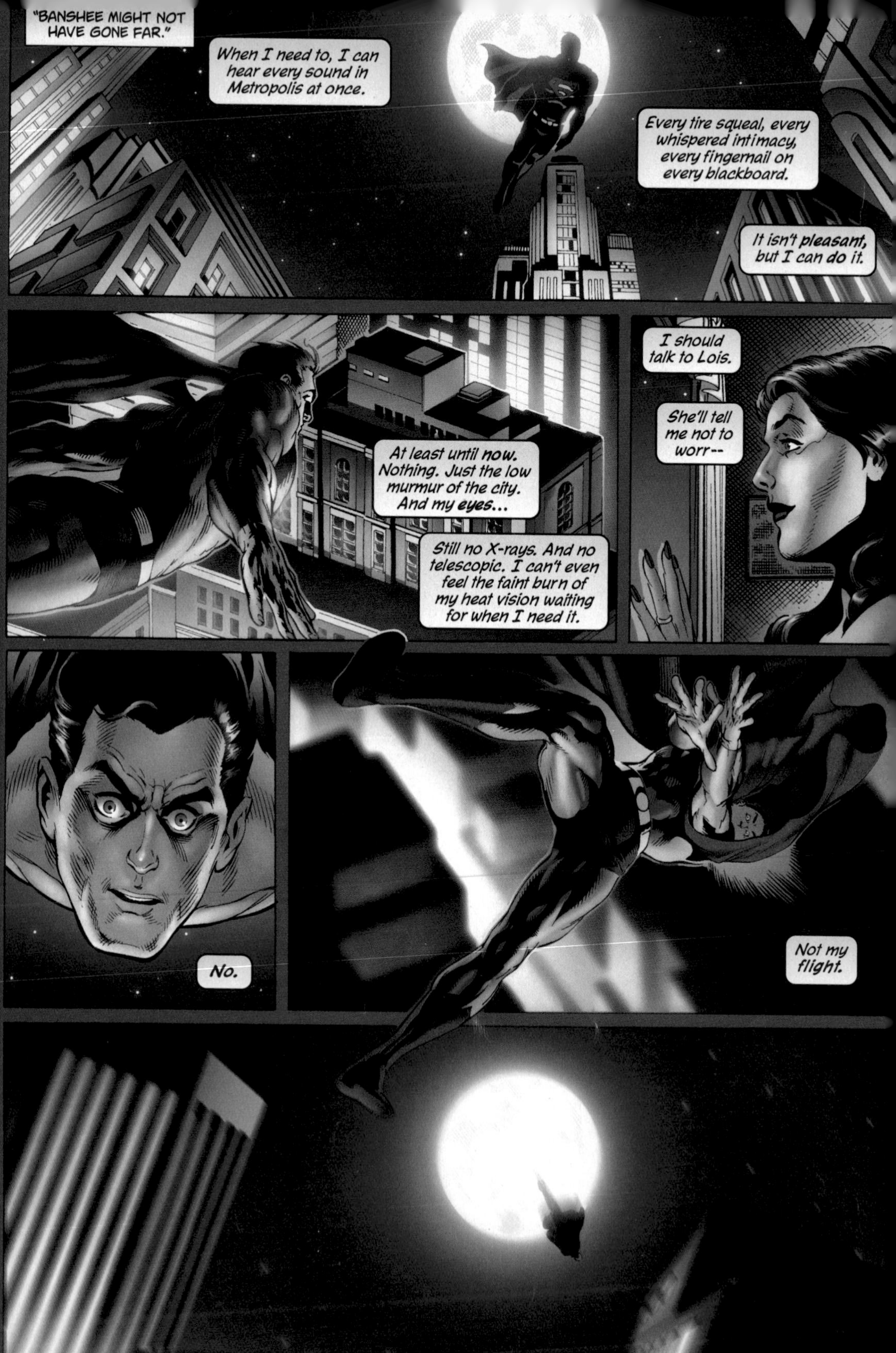
"BANSHEE MIGHT NOT HAVE GONE FAR."
When I need to, I can hear every sound in Metropolis at once.
Every tire squeal, every whispered intimacy, every fingernail on every blackboard.
It isn't pleasant, but I can do it.
At least until now. Nothing. Just the low murmur of the city. And my eyes...
Still no X-rays. And no telescopic. I can't even feel the faint burn of my heat vision waiting for when I need it.
I should talk to Lois.
She'll tell me not to worr--
No.
Not my flight.
Lois.

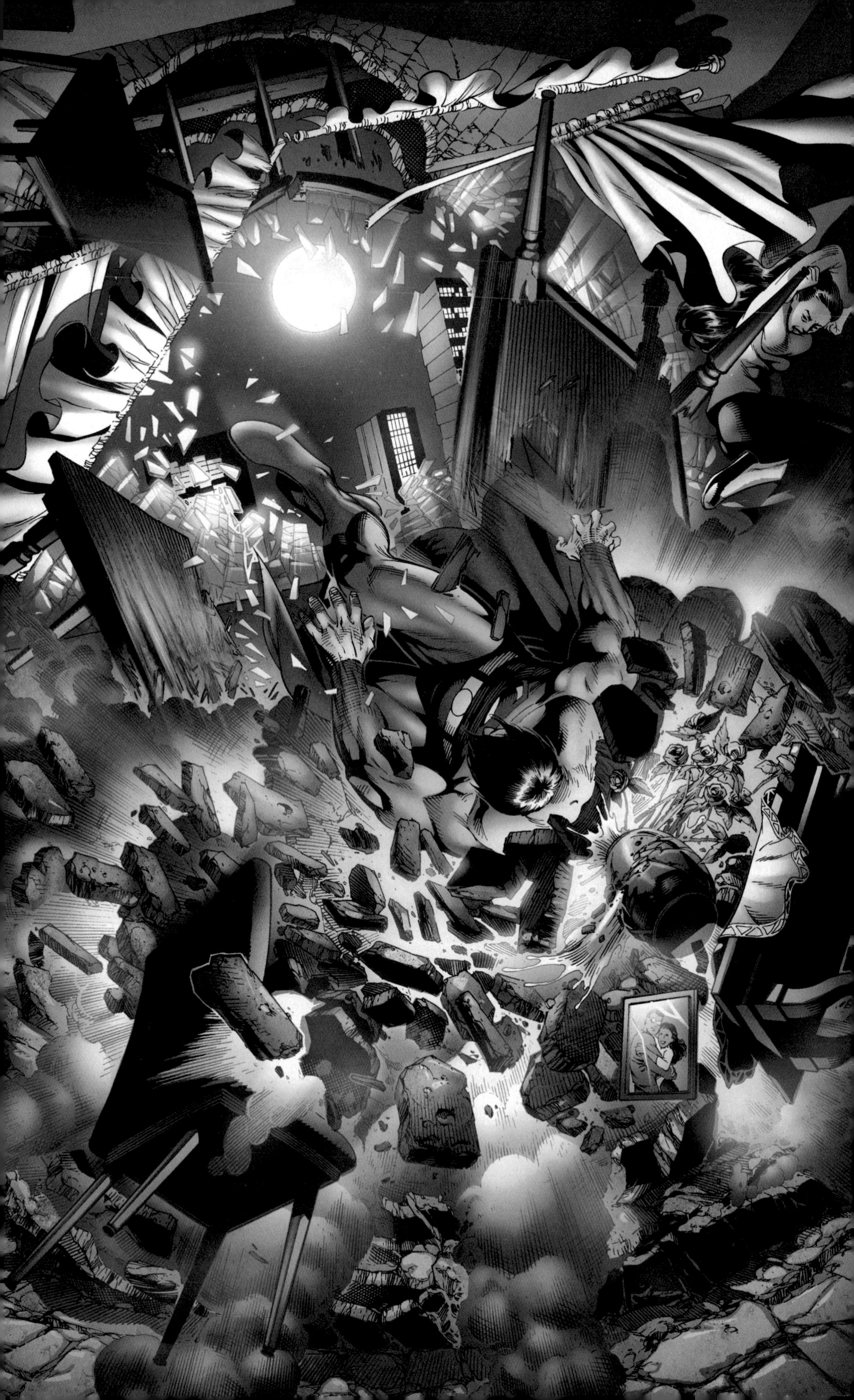

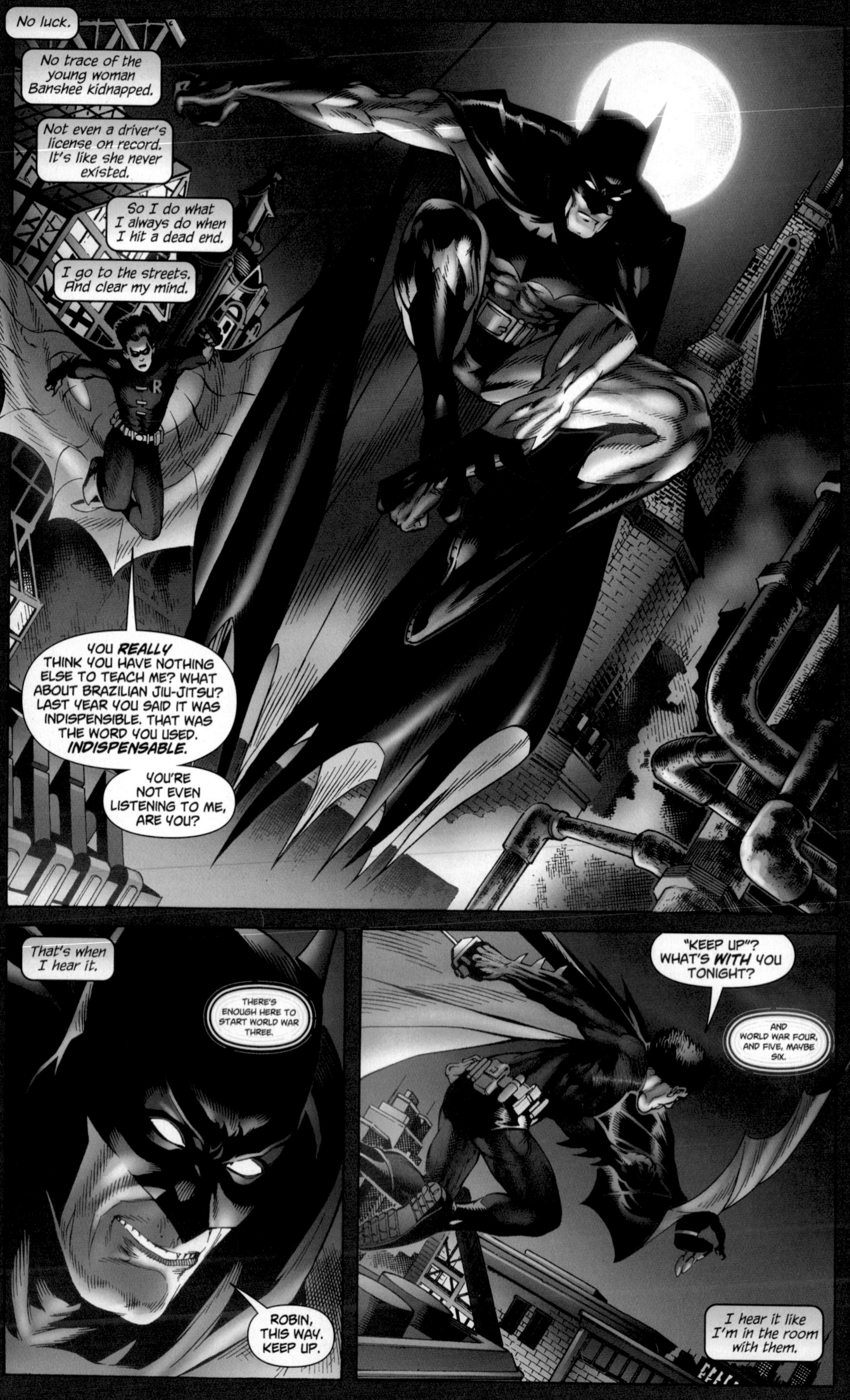
No luck.
No trace of the young woman Banshee kidnapped.
Not even a driver's license on record. It's like she never existed.
So I do what I always do when I hit a dead end.
I go to the streets. And clear my mind.
YOU REALLY THINK YOU HAVE NOTHING ELSE TO TEACH ME? WHAT ABOUT BRAZILIAN JIU-JITSU? LAST YEAR YOU SAID IT WAS INDISPENSIBLE. THAT WAS THE WORD YOU USED. INDISPENSABLE.
YOU'RE NOT EVEN LISTENING TO ME, ARE YOU?
That's when I hear it.
THERE'S ENOUGH HERE TO START WORLD WAR THREE.
ROBIN, THIS WAY. KEEP UP.
"KEEP UP"? WHAT'S WITH YOU TONIGHT?
AND WORLD WAR FOUR, AND FIVE, MAYBE SIX.
I hear it like I'm in the room with them.

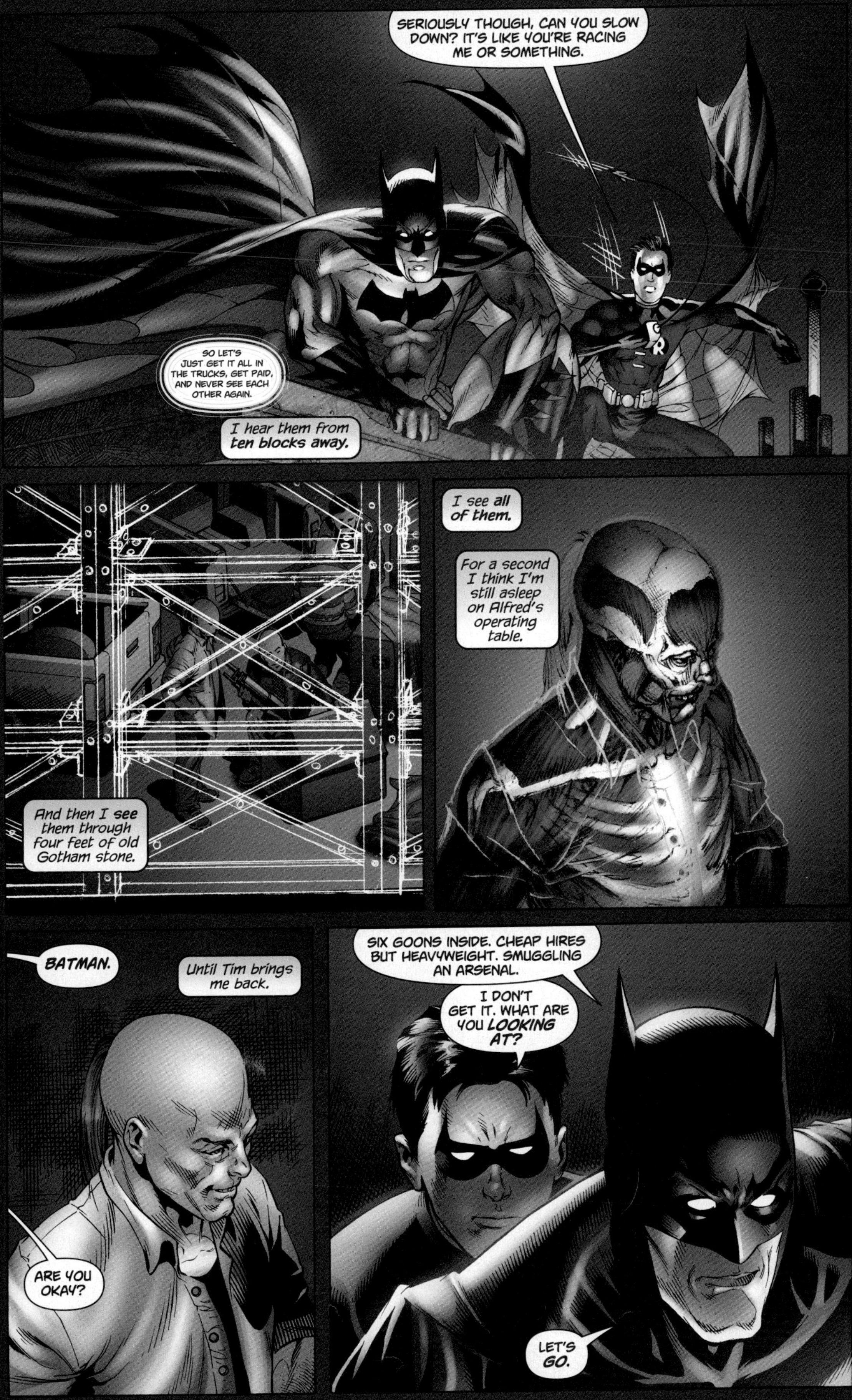
SERIOUSLY THOUGH, CAN YOU SLOW DOWN? IT'S LIKE YOU'RE RACING ME OR SOMETHING.
SO LET'S JUST GET IT ALL IN THE TRUCKS, GET PAID, AND NEVER SEE EACH OTHER AGAIN.
I hear them from ten blocks away.
And then I see them through four feet of old Gotham stone.
I see all of them.
For a second I think I'm still asleep on Alfred's operating table.
BATMAN.
Until Tim brings me back.
ARE YOU OKAY?
SIX GOONS INSIDE. CHEAP HIRES BUT HEAVYWEIGHT. SMUGGLING AN ARSENAL.
I DON'T GET IT. WHAT ARE YOU LOOKING AT?
LET'S GO.

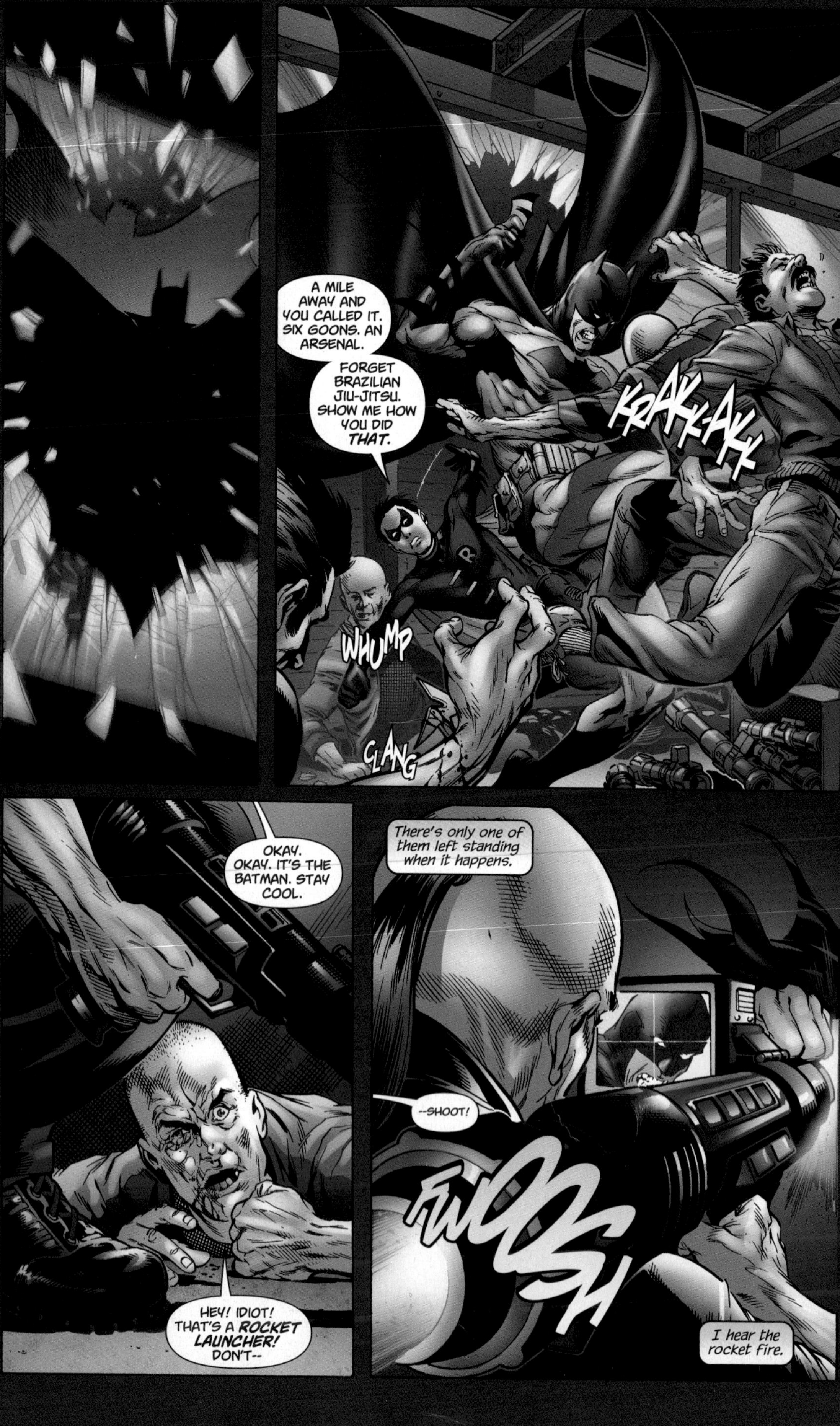
A MILE AWAY AND YOU CALLED IT. SIX GOONS. AN ARSENAL.
FORGET BRAZILIAN JIU-JITSU. SHOW ME HOW YOU DID *THAT.*
KRAKK-AKK
WHUMP
CLANG
OKAY. OKAY. IT'S THE BATMAN. STAY COOL.
HEY! IDIOT! THAT'S A *ROCKET LAUNCHER!* DON'T--
*There's only one of them left standing when it happens.*
--SHOOT!
FWOOSH
*I hear the rocket fire.*

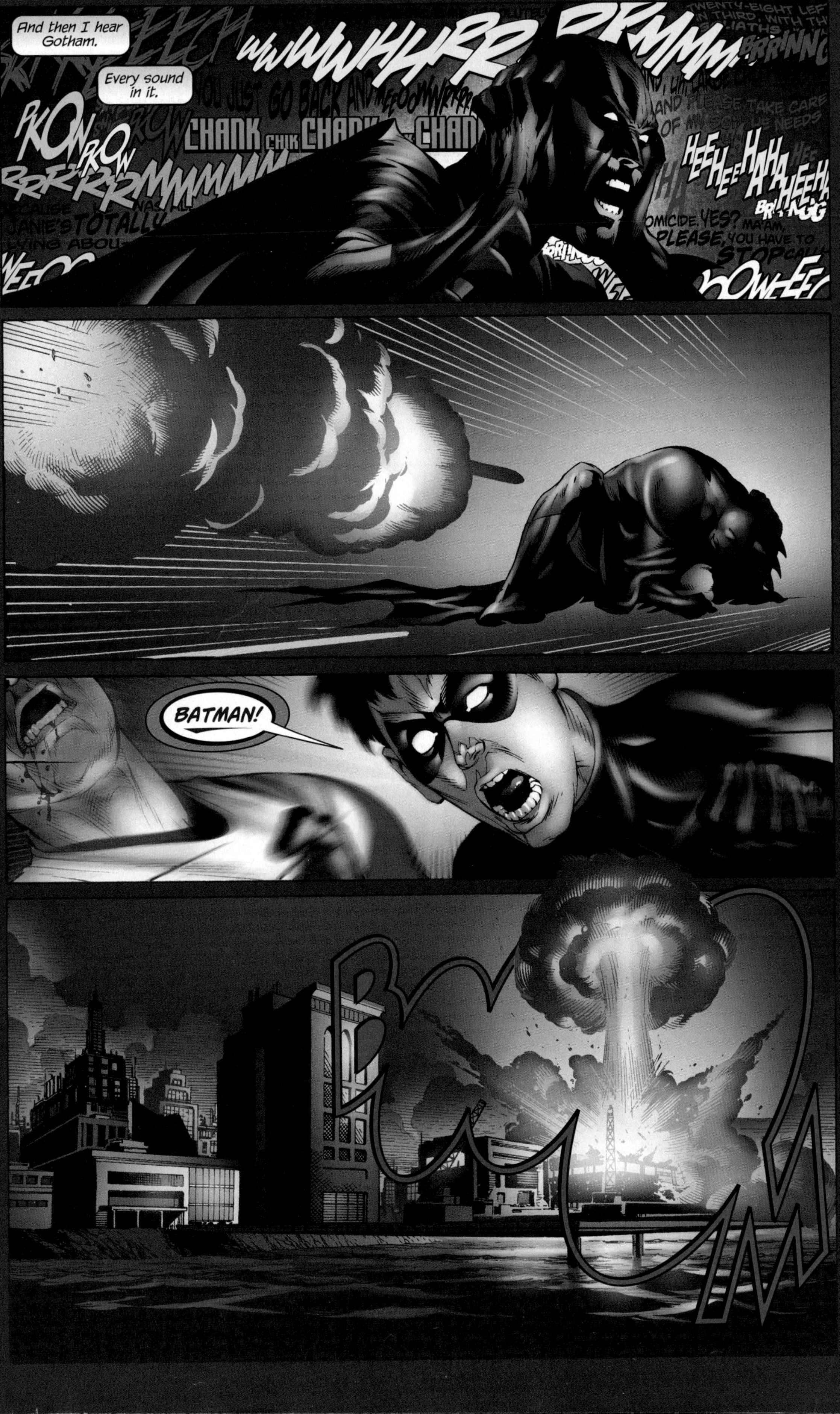
And then I hear Gotham.
Every sound in it.
WWWWWHHRR
PKOW
PROW
RRRRRRMMMMMN
YOU JUST GO BACK AND
MEEOOWRR
CHANK CHIK CHANK
TWENTY-EIGHT LEF IN THIRD, WITH TH
BRRINNG
AND PLEASE TAKE CARE
HEEHEEHAHAHEEHA
BRRINGG
JANIE'S TOTALLY
OMICIDE. YES? MA'AM, PLEASE, YOU HAVE TO STOP
BATMAN!
B
UM

huuuRgh
cough
chhough

BAT...
cough--

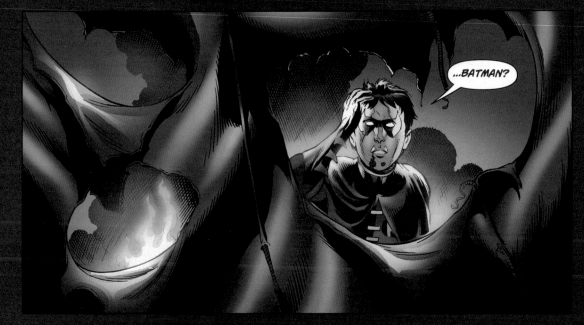

...BATMAN?

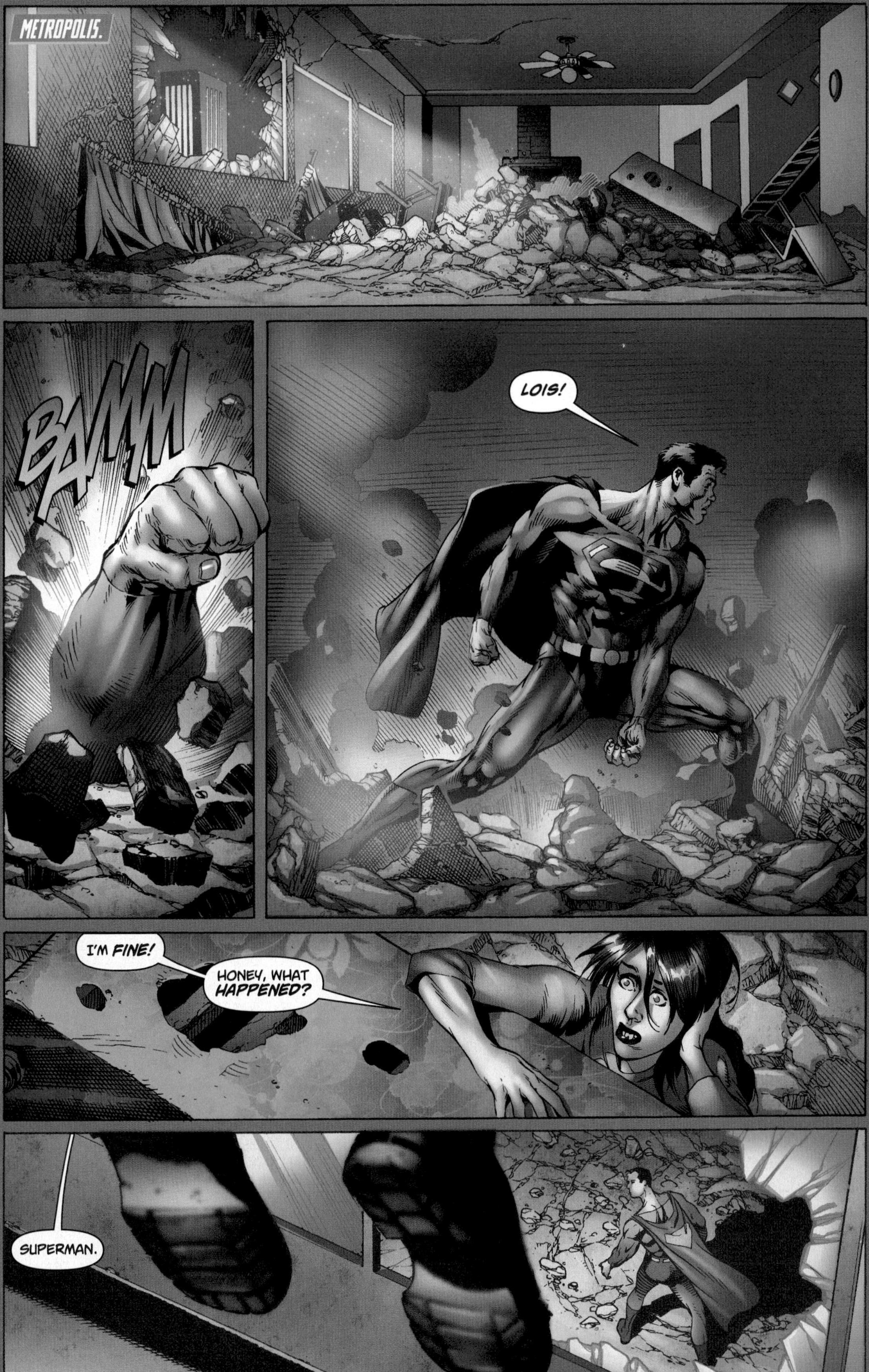
METROPOLIS.
BAMM
LOIS!
I'M FINE!
HONEY, WHAT HAPPENED?
SUPERMAN.

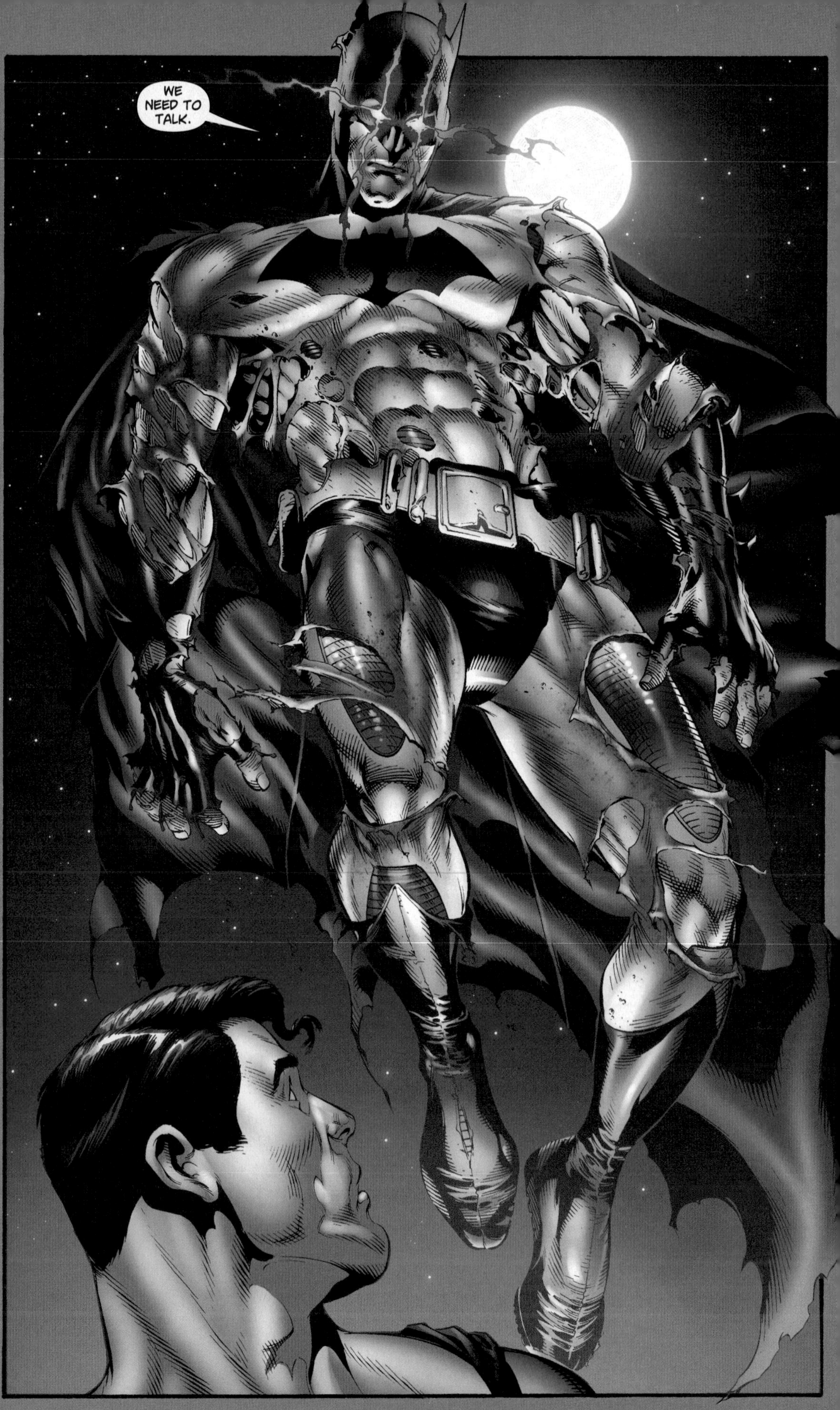
WE NEED TO TALK.

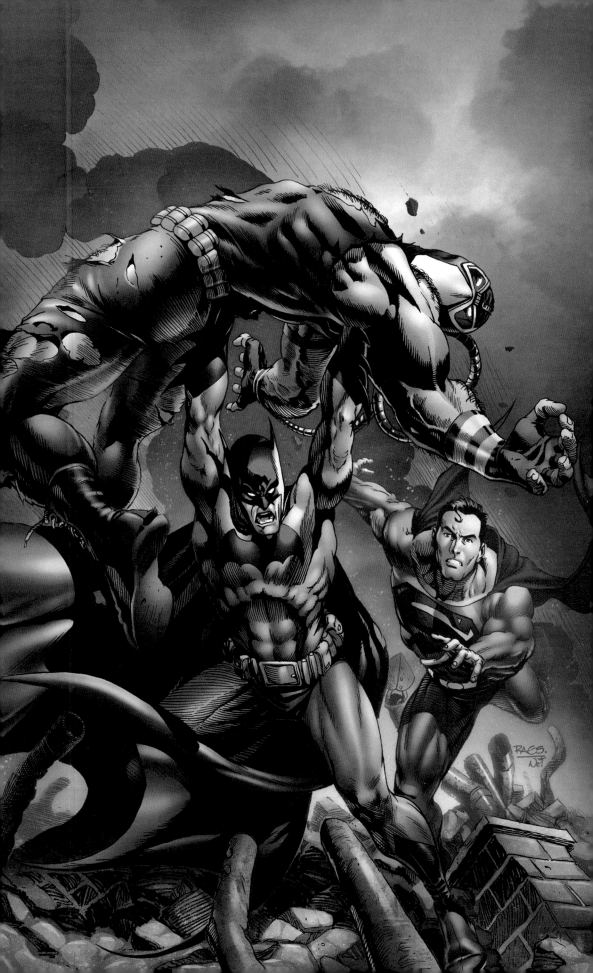

SUPERMAN/BATMAN 54

SUPERBAT
part two

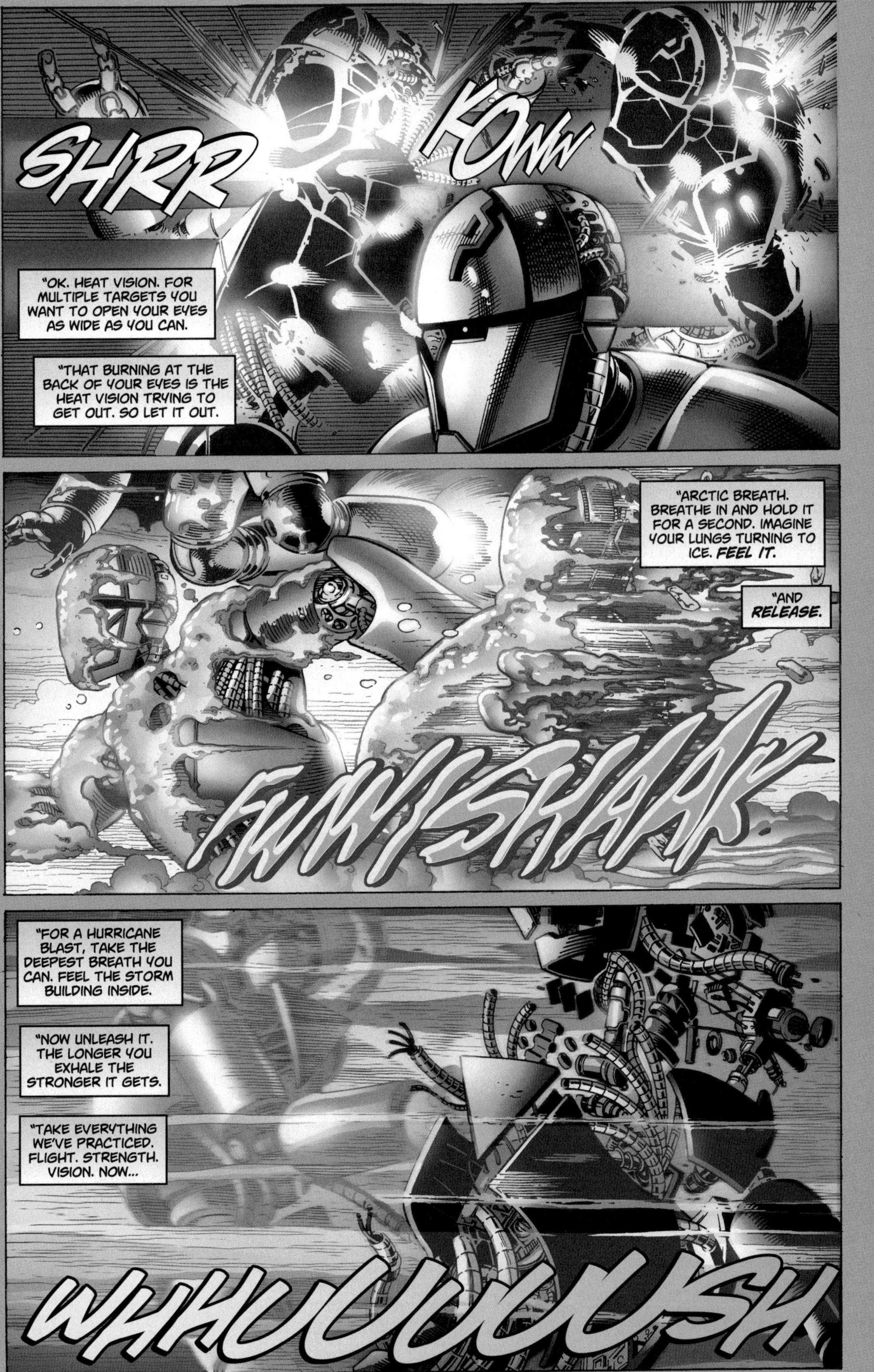
SHRR
KOWW
"OK. HEAT VISION. FOR MULTIPLE TARGETS YOU WANT TO OPEN YOUR EYES AS WIDE AS YOU CAN.
"THAT BURNING AT THE BACK OF YOUR EYES IS THE HEAT VISION TRYING TO GET OUT. SO LET IT OUT.
"ARCTIC BREATH. BREATHE IN AND HOLD IT FOR A SECOND. IMAGINE YOUR LUNGS TURNING TO ICE. FEEL IT.
"AND RELEASE.
FWWSHAAK
"FOR A HURRICANE BLAST, TAKE THE DEEPEST BREATH YOU CAN. FEEL THE STORM BUILDING INSIDE.
"NOW UNLEASH IT. THE LONGER YOU EXHALE THE STRONGER IT GETS.
"TAKE EVERYTHING WE'VE PRACTICED. FLIGHT. STRENGTH. VISION. NOW...
WHHUUUUUSH

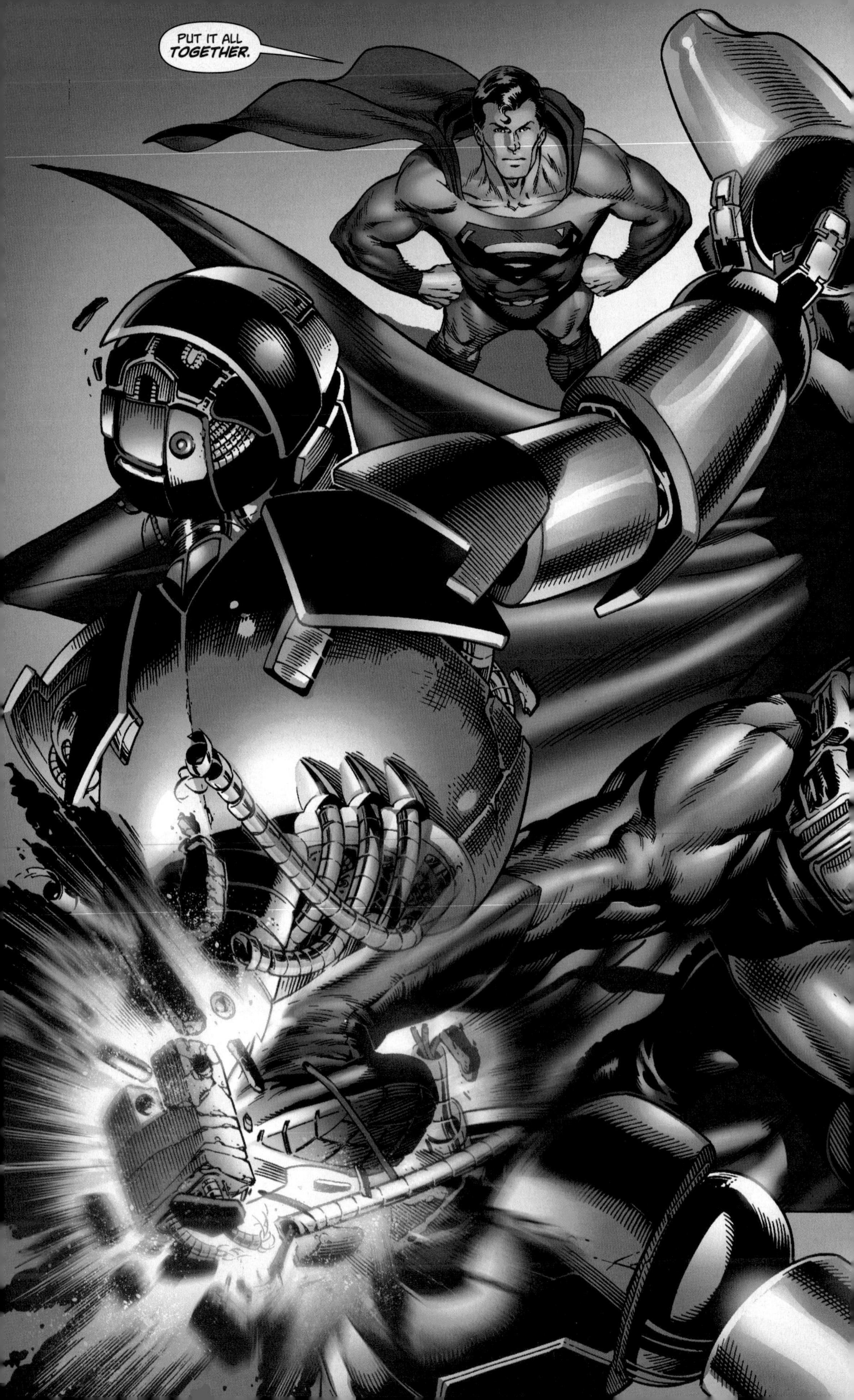
PUT IT ALL TOGETHER.

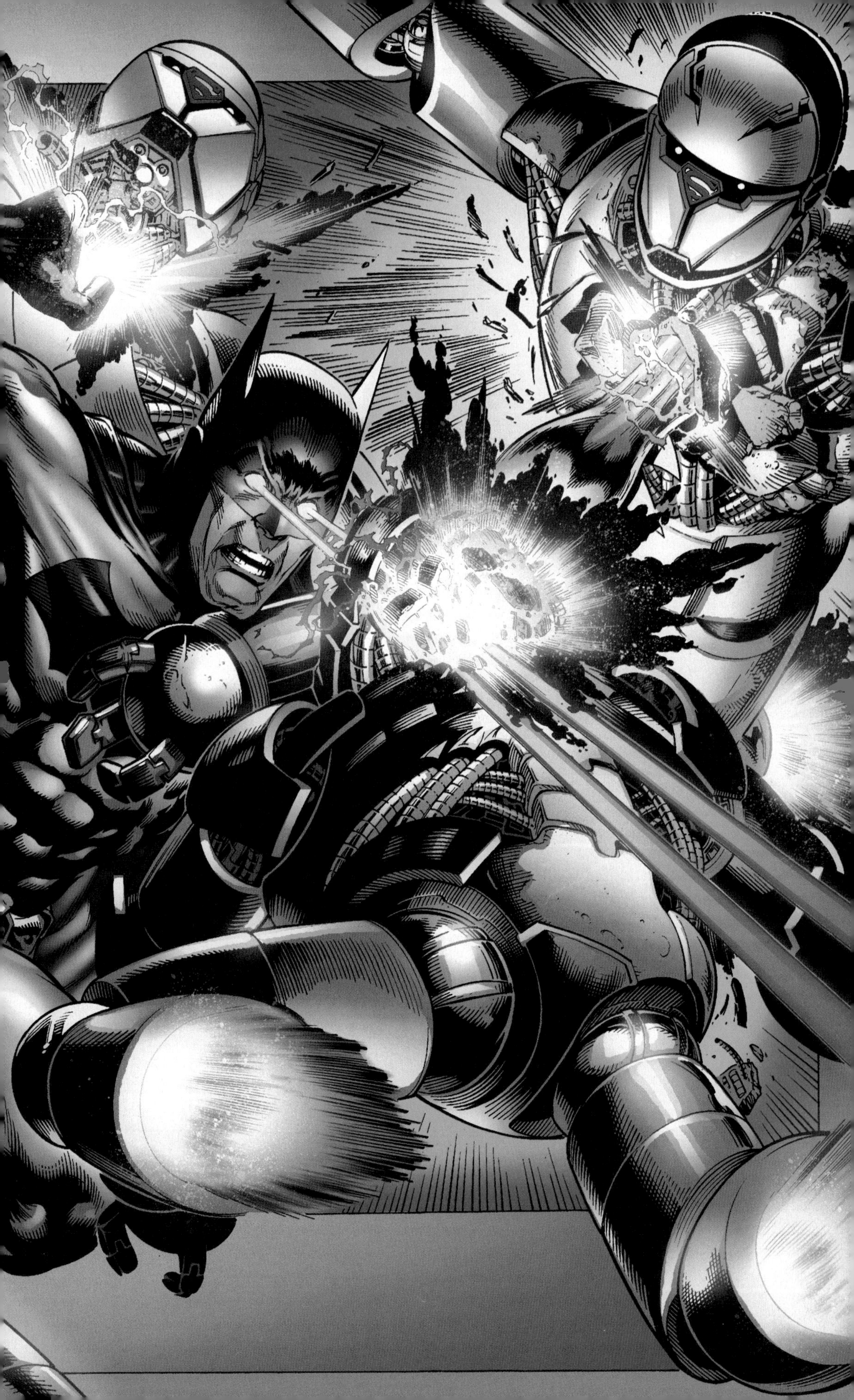

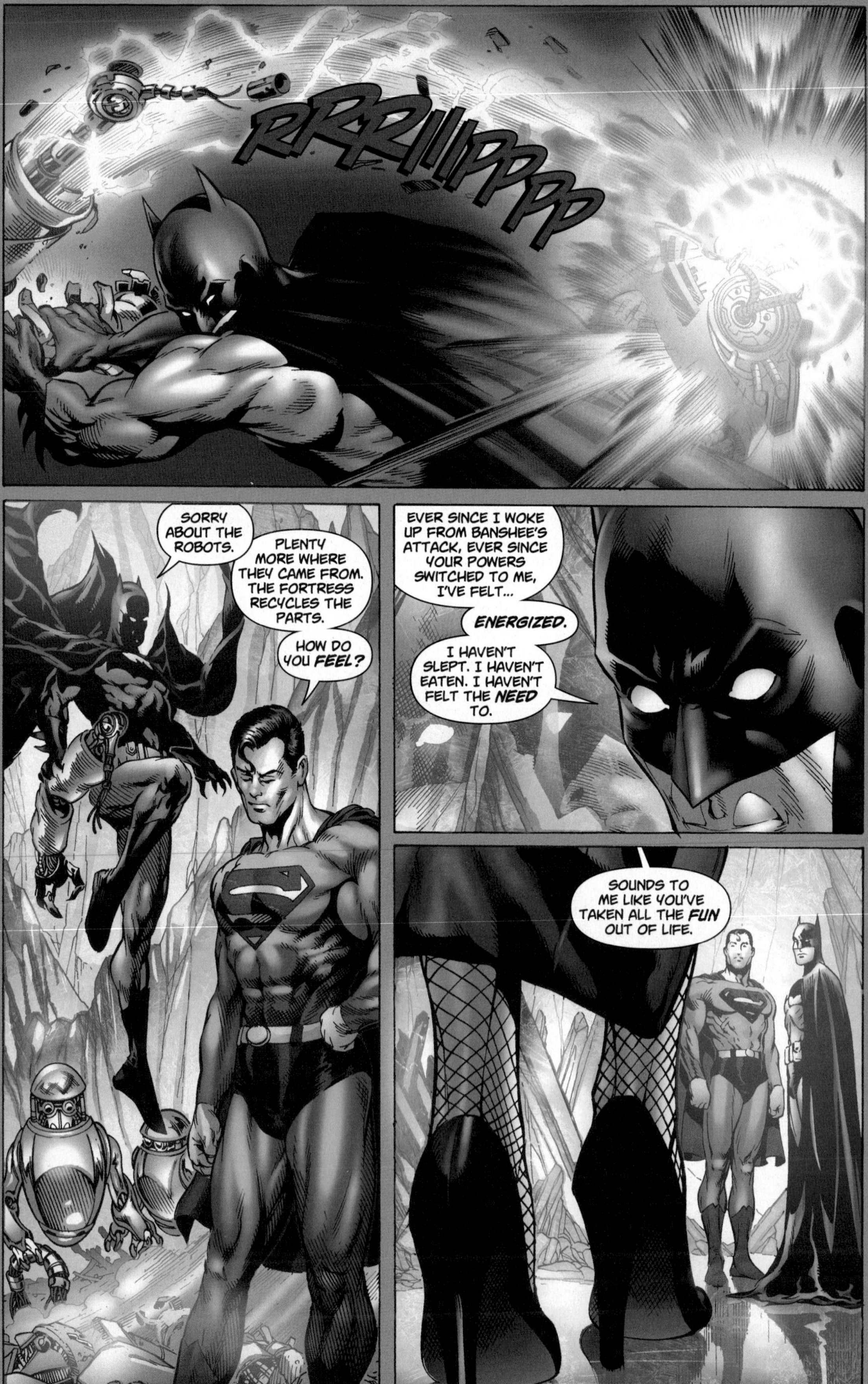
RRRIIIIPPPPP
SORRY ABOUT THE ROBOTS.
PLENTY MORE WHERE THEY CAME FROM. THE FORTRESS RECYCLES THE PARTS.
HOW DO YOU FEEL?
EVER SINCE I WOKE UP FROM BANSHEE'S ATTACK, EVER SINCE YOUR POWERS SWITCHED TO ME, I'VE FELT...
ENERGIZED.
I HAVEN'T SLEPT. I HAVEN'T EATEN. I HAVEN'T FELT THE NEED TO.
SOUNDS TO ME LIKE YOU'VE TAKEN ALL THE FUN OUT OF LIFE.

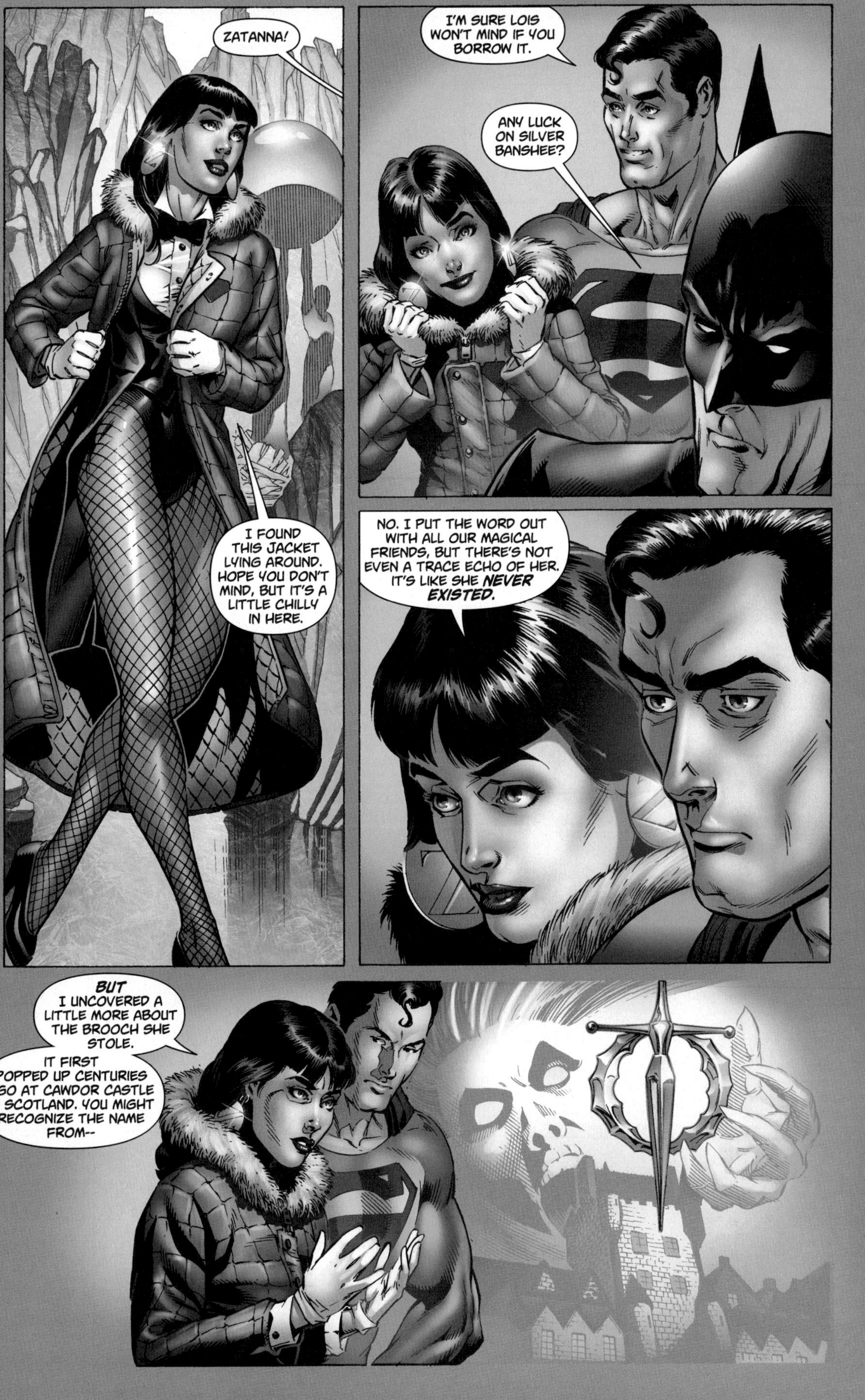
ZATANNA!
I FOUND THIS JACKET LYING AROUND. HOPE YOU DON'T MIND, BUT IT'S A LITTLE CHILLY IN HERE.
I'M SURE LOIS WON'T MIND IF YOU BORROW IT.
ANY LUCK ON SILVER BANSHEE?
NO. I PUT THE WORD OUT WITH ALL OUR MAGICAL FRIENDS, BUT THERE'S NOT EVEN A TRACE ECHO OF HER. IT'S LIKE SHE NEVER EXISTED.
BUT I UNCOVERED A LITTLE MORE ABOUT THE BROOCH SHE STOLE.
IT FIRST POPPED UP CENTURIES AGO AT CAWDOR CASTLE IN SCOTLAND. YOU MIGHT RECOGNIZE THE NAME FROM--

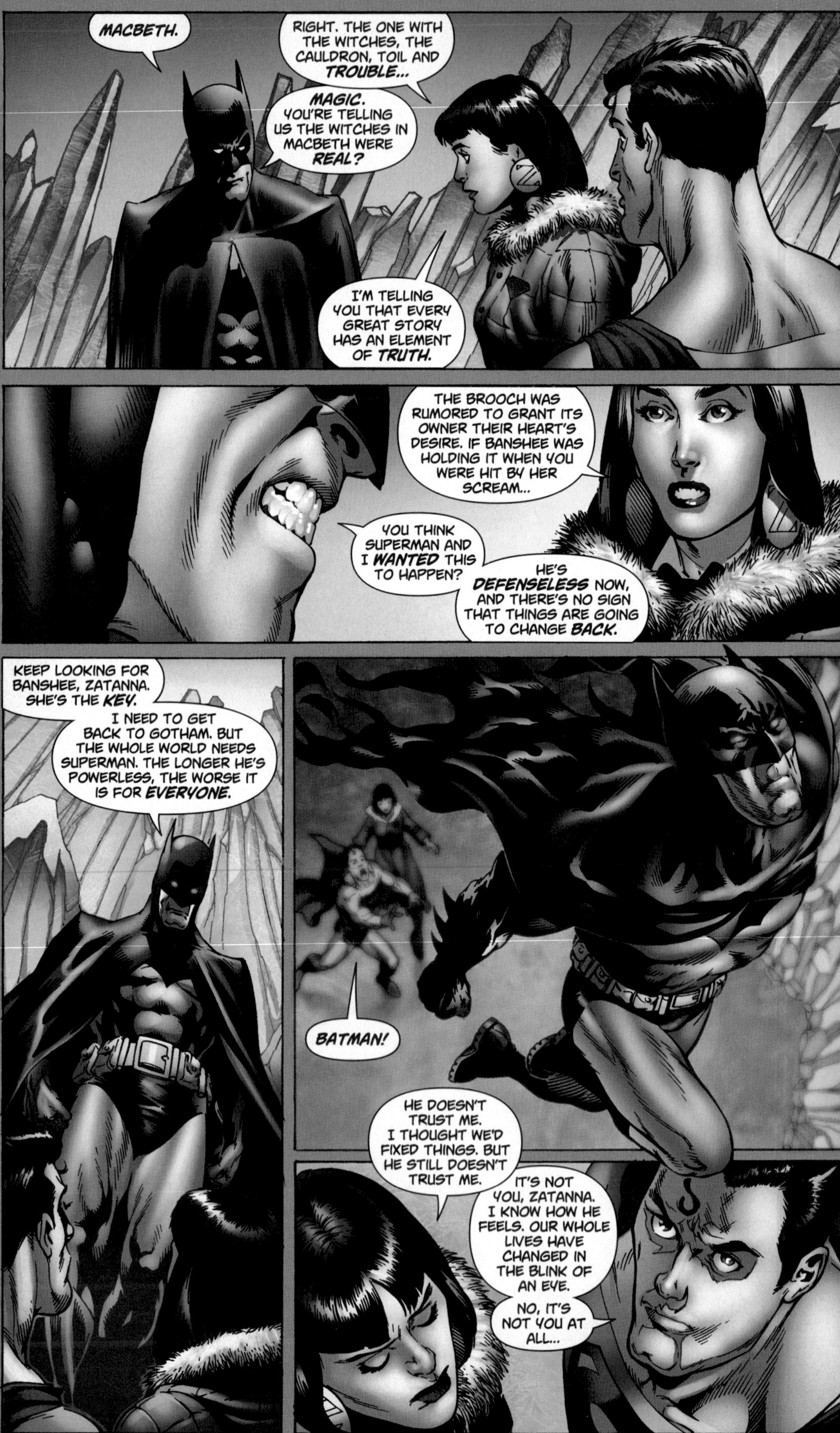
MACBETH.
RIGHT. THE ONE WITH THE WITCHES, THE CAULDRON, TOIL AND TROUBLE...
MAGIC. YOU'RE TELLING US THE WITCHES IN MACBETH WERE REAL?
I'M TELLING YOU THAT EVERY GREAT STORY HAS AN ELEMENT OF TRUTH.
THE BROOCH WAS RUMORED TO GRANT ITS OWNER THEIR HEART'S DESIRE. IF BANSHEE WAS HOLDING IT WHEN YOU WERE HIT BY HER SCREAM...
YOU THINK SUPERMAN AND I WANTED THIS TO HAPPEN?
HE'S DEFENSELESS NOW, AND THERE'S NO SIGN THAT THINGS ARE GOING TO CHANGE BACK.
KEEP LOOKING FOR BANSHEE, ZATANNA. SHE'S THE KEY.
I NEED TO GET BACK TO GOTHAM. BUT THE WHOLE WORLD NEEDS SUPERMAN. THE LONGER HE'S POWERLESS, THE WORSE IT IS FOR EVERYONE.
BATMAN!
HE DOESN'T TRUST ME. I THOUGHT WE'D FIXED THINGS. BUT HE STILL DOESN'T TRUST ME.
IT'S NOT YOU, ZATANNA. I KNOW HOW HE FEELS. OUR WHOLE LIVES HAVE CHANGED IN THE BLINK OF AN EYE.
NO, IT'S NOT YOU AT ALL...

HOW'S MY BIKE, ALFRED?

THE MOTORCYCLE IS BACK TO TOP FORM. BUT ITS *OWNER* REMAINS A GRAVE CONCERN. YOU SHOULD STILL BE RESTING FROM YOUR INJURIES.

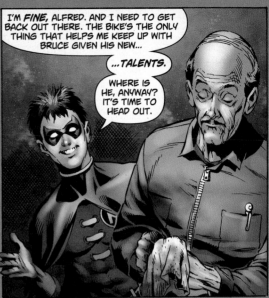

I'M *FINE*, ALFRED. AND I NEED TO GET BACK OUT THERE. THE BIKE'S THE ONLY THING THAT HELPS ME KEEP UP WITH BRUCE GIVEN HIS NEW...

...*TALENTS*.

WHERE IS HE, ANYWAY? IT'S TIME TO HEAD OUT.

I WISH I KNEW. MASTER BRUCE HAS BECOME RATHER...*DISTANT* OF LATE. EVEN MORE SO THAN USUAL. I BELIEVE HE IS HAVING SOME TROUBLE ADJUSTING TO THOSE VERY *TALENTS* YOU DESCRIBE.

NOW IF YOU'LL EXCUSE ME, THERE ARE SEVERAL KILOS OF *GUANO* I NEED TO DISPOSE OF BECAUSE A CERTAIN YOUNG LAYABOUT NEGLECTED HIS CHORES.

MY BAD, AL. I'LL DO DOUBLE NEXT TIME.

I SAY...

WHAT IS *THAT?*

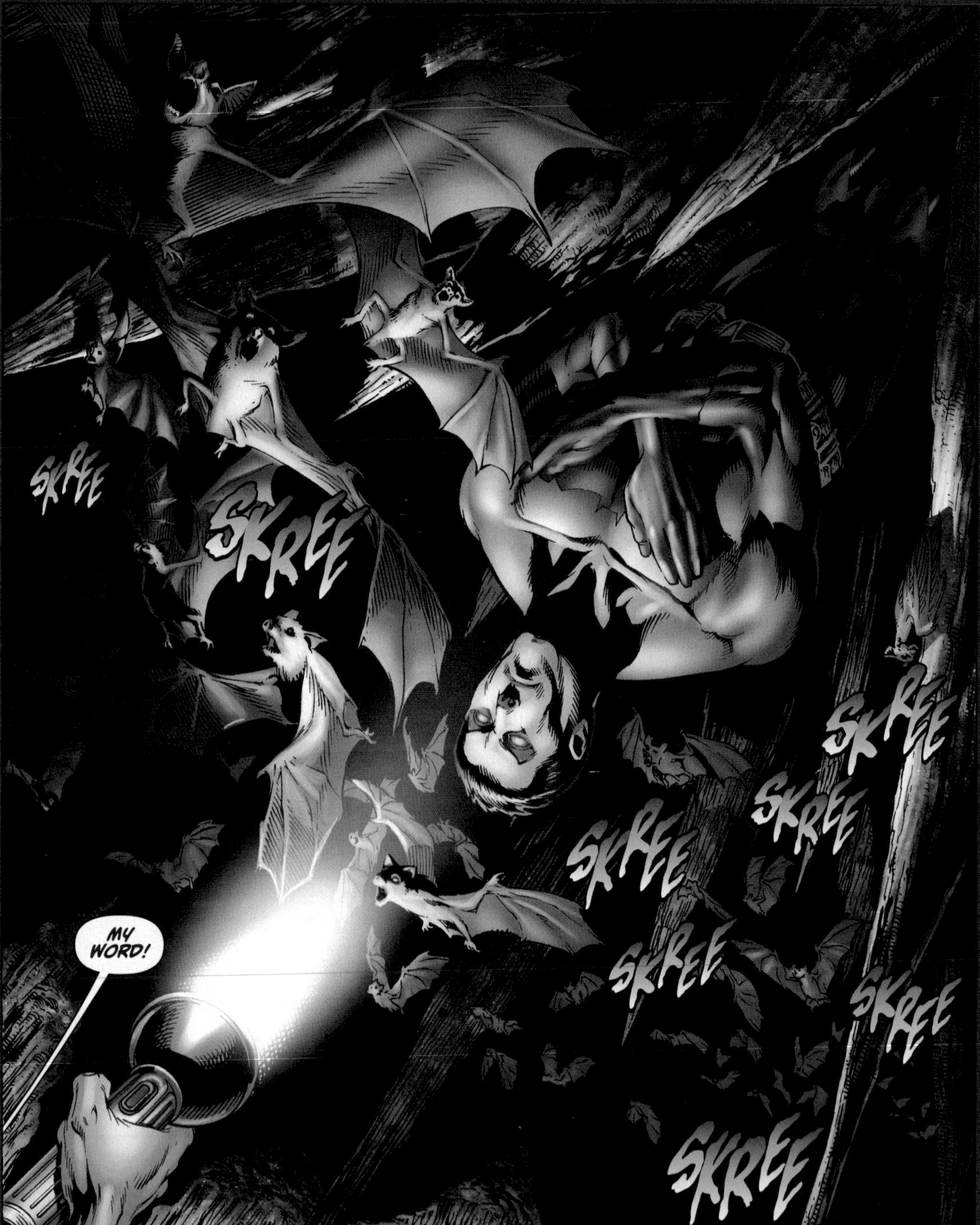
SKREE
SKREE
SKREE
SKREE
SKREE
SKREE
SKREE
SKREE
MY WORD!

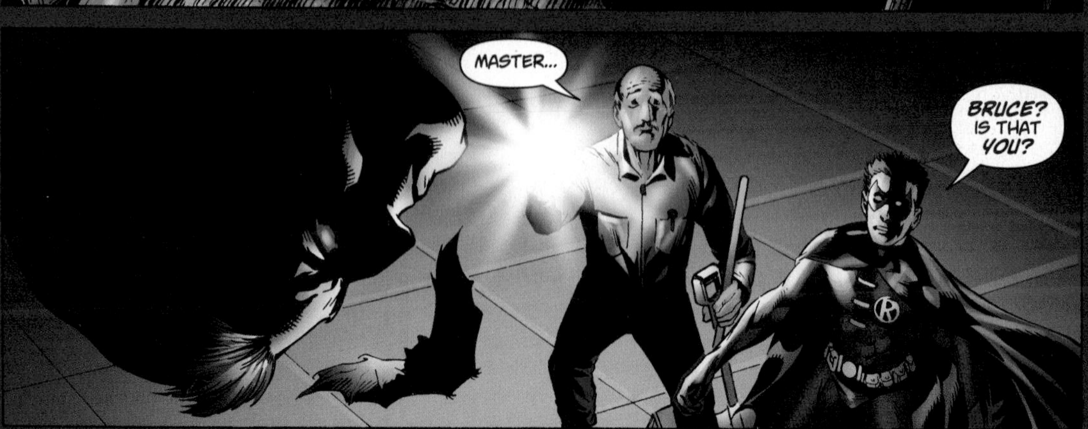
MASTER...
BRUCE? IS THAT YOU?

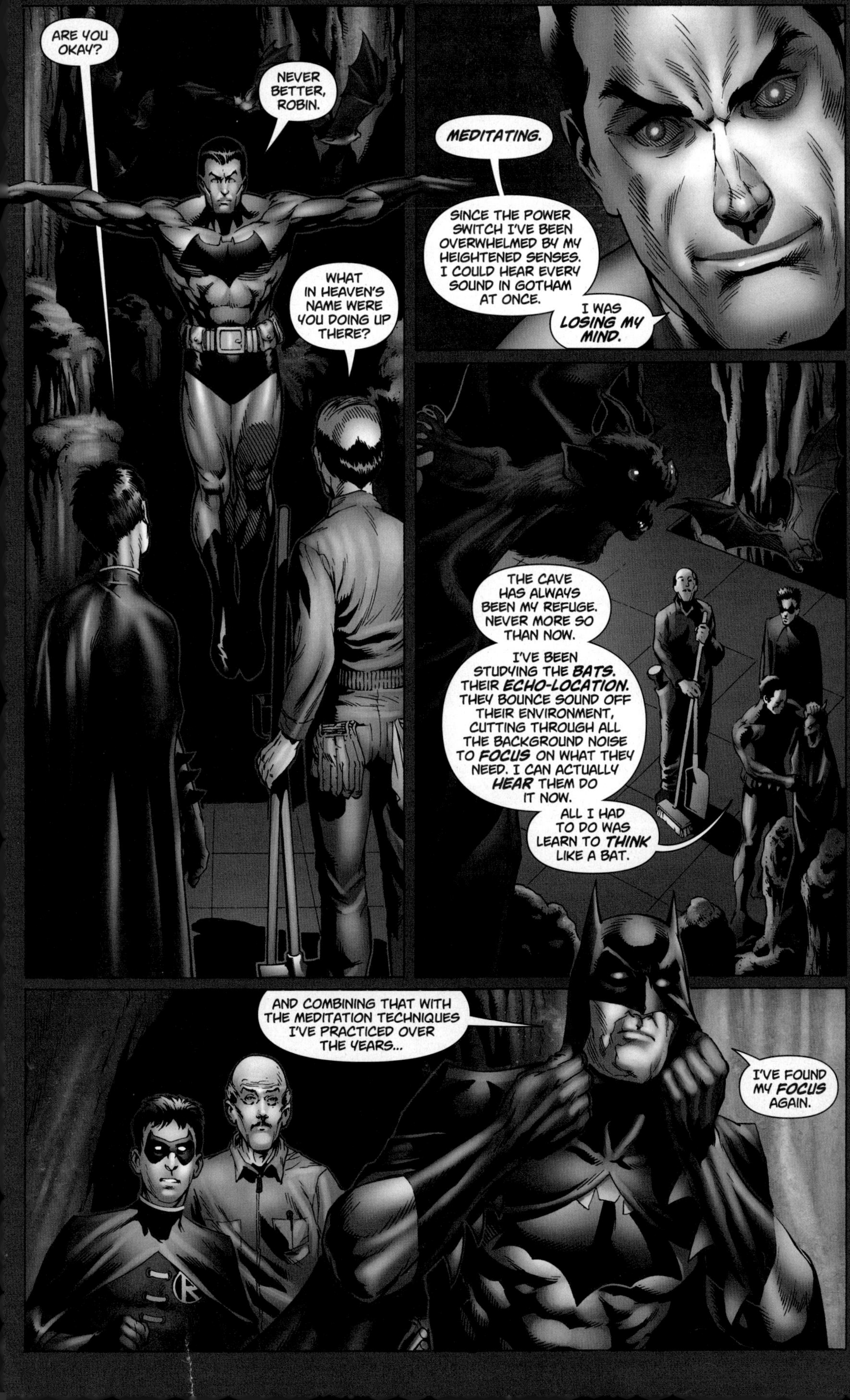
ARE YOU OKAY?
NEVER BETTER, ROBIN.
WHAT IN HEAVEN'S NAME WERE YOU DOING UP THERE?
MEDITATING.
SINCE THE POWER SWITCH I'VE BEEN OVERWHELMED BY MY HEIGHTENED SENSES. I COULD HEAR EVERY SOUND IN GOTHAM AT ONCE.
I WAS LOSING MY MIND.
THE CAVE HAS ALWAYS BEEN MY REFUGE. NEVER MORE SO THAN NOW.
I'VE BEEN STUDYING THE BATS. THEIR ECHO-LOCATION. THEY BOUNCE SOUND OFF THEIR ENVIRONMENT, CUTTING THROUGH ALL THE BACKGROUND NOISE TO FOCUS ON WHAT THEY NEED. I CAN ACTUALLY HEAR THEM DO IT NOW.
ALL I HAD TO DO WAS LEARN TO THINK LIKE A BAT.
AND COMBINING THAT WITH THE MEDITATION TECHNIQUES I'VE PRACTICED OVER THE YEARS...
I'VE FOUND MY FOCUS AGAIN.

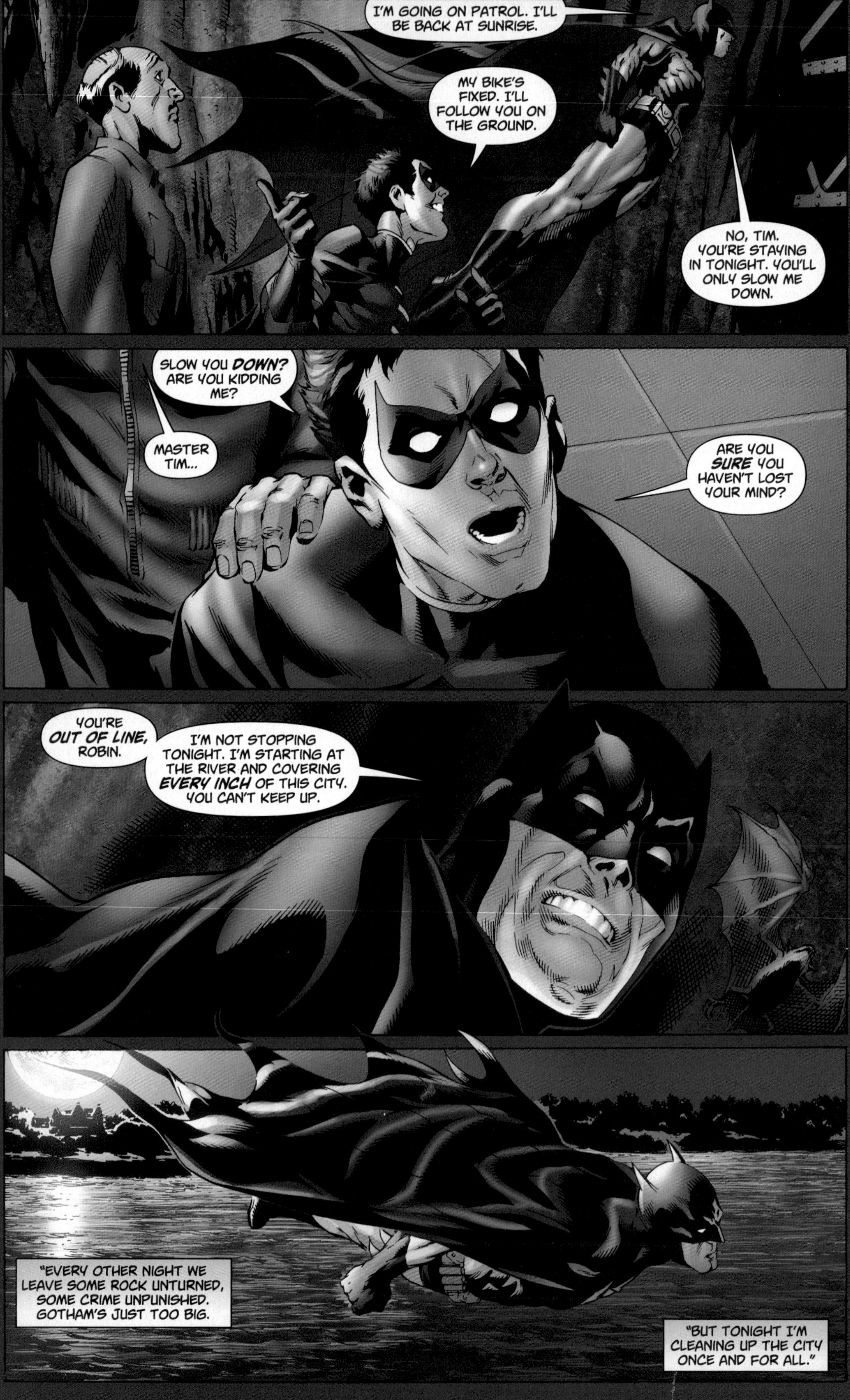
I'M GOING ON PATROL. I'LL BE BACK AT SUNRISE.
MY BIKE'S FIXED. I'LL FOLLOW YOU ON THE GROUND.
NO, TIM. YOU'RE STAYING IN TONIGHT. YOU'LL ONLY SLOW ME DOWN.
SLOW YOU DOWN? ARE YOU KIDDING ME?
MASTER TIM...
ARE YOU SURE YOU HAVEN'T LOST YOUR MIND?
YOU'RE OUT OF LINE, ROBIN.
I'M NOT STOPPING TONIGHT. I'M STARTING AT THE RIVER AND COVERING EVERY INCH OF THIS CITY. YOU CAN'T KEEP UP.
"EVERY OTHER NIGHT WE LEAVE SOME ROCK UNTURNED, SOME CRIME UNPUNISHED. GOTHAM'S JUST TOO BIG.
"BUT TONIGHT I'M CLEANING UP THE CITY ONCE AND FOR ALL."

"BECAUSE NOW I *CAN*."

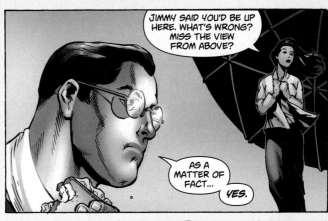

JIMMY SAID YOU'D BE UP HERE. WHAT'S WRONG? MISS THE VIEW FROM ABOVE?

AS A MATTER OF FACT... *YES*.

DO YOU *HAVE* TO SIT ON THE LEDGE? OR DO I NEED TO REMIND YOU WHAT WOULD HAPPEN IF YOU TRY TO LEAP A TALL BUILDING?

I KNOW. BUT I CAN *FEEL* MY FLIGHT MISSING. LIKE A PHANTOM LIMB. I JUST...

I WANTED TO REMEMBER WHAT IT FEELS LIKE FROM UP HIGH.

BUT ALL IT DOES IS REMIND ME THAT I'M POWERLESS NOW.

WAIT. IS THAT WHAT I THINK IT IS?

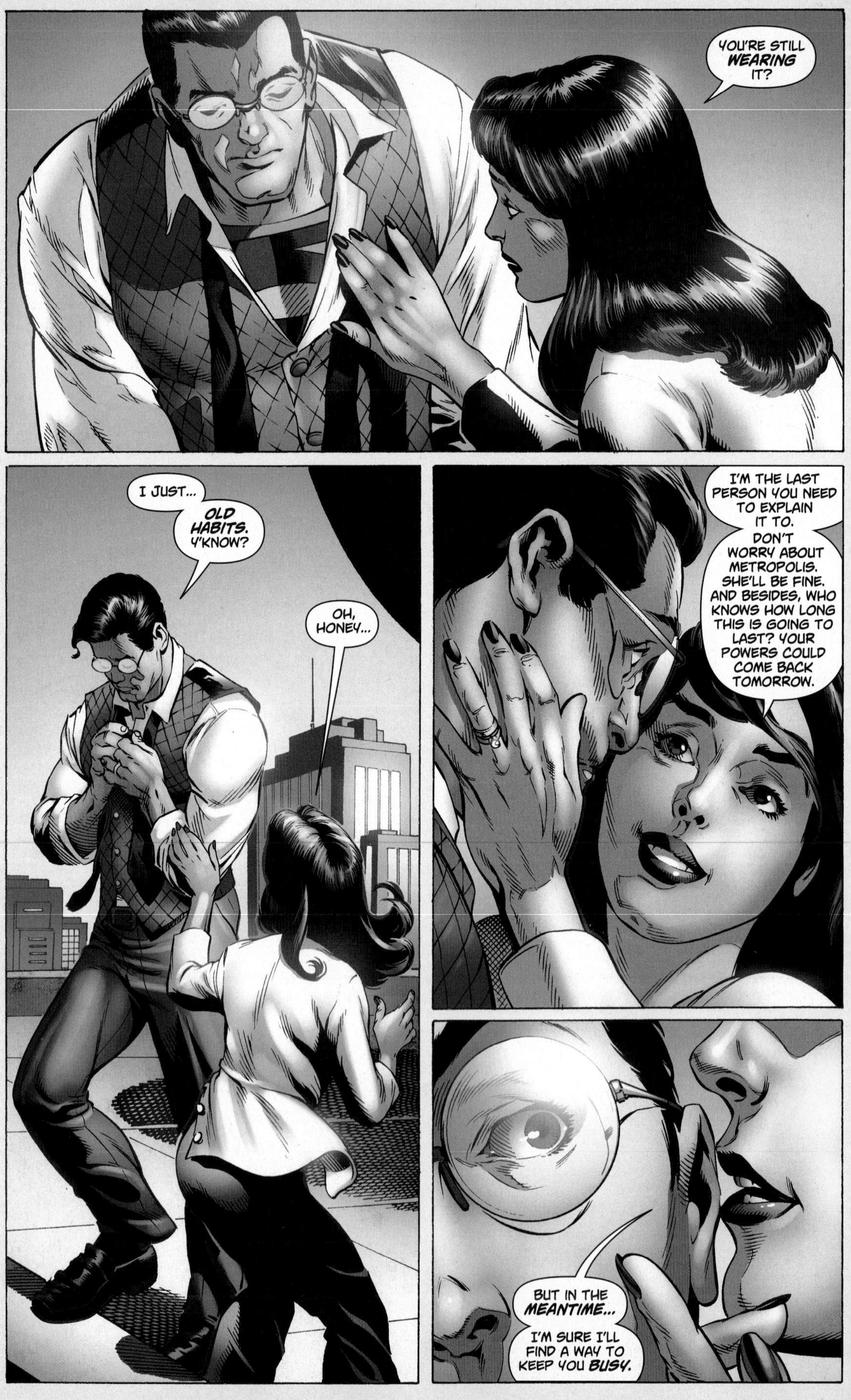
YOU'RE STILL WEARING IT?
I JUST... OLD HABITS. Y'KNOW?
OH, HONEY...
I'M THE LAST PERSON YOU NEED TO EXPLAIN IT TO.
DON'T WORRY ABOUT METROPOLIS. SHE'LL BE FINE. AND BESIDES, WHO KNOWS HOW LONG THIS IS GOING TO LAST? YOUR POWERS COULD COME BACK TOMORROW.
BUT IN THE MEANTIME...
I'M SURE I'LL FIND A WAY TO KEEP YOU BUSY.

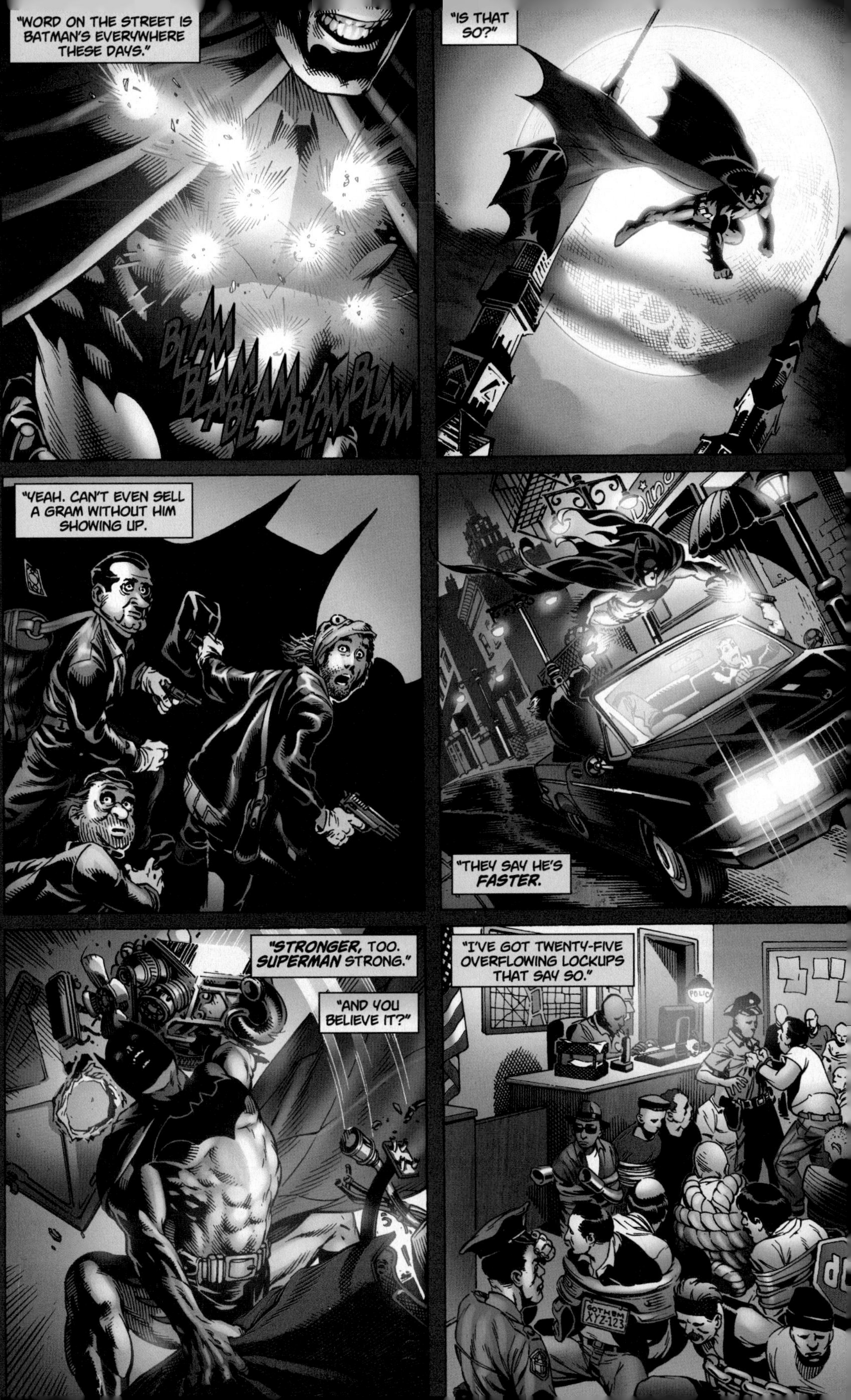
"WORD ON THE STREET IS BATMAN'S EVERYWHERE THESE DAYS."
BLAM BLAM BLAM BLAM BLAM BLAM BLAM BLAM
"IS THAT SO?"
"YEAH. CAN'T EVEN SELL A GRAM WITHOUT HIM SHOWING UP.
"THEY SAY HE'S FASTER.
"STRONGER, TOO. SUPERMAN STRONG."
"AND YOU BELIEVE IT?"
"I'VE GOT TWENTY-FIVE OVERFLOWING LOCKUPS THAT SAY SO."
POLICE
GOTHAM XYZ-123

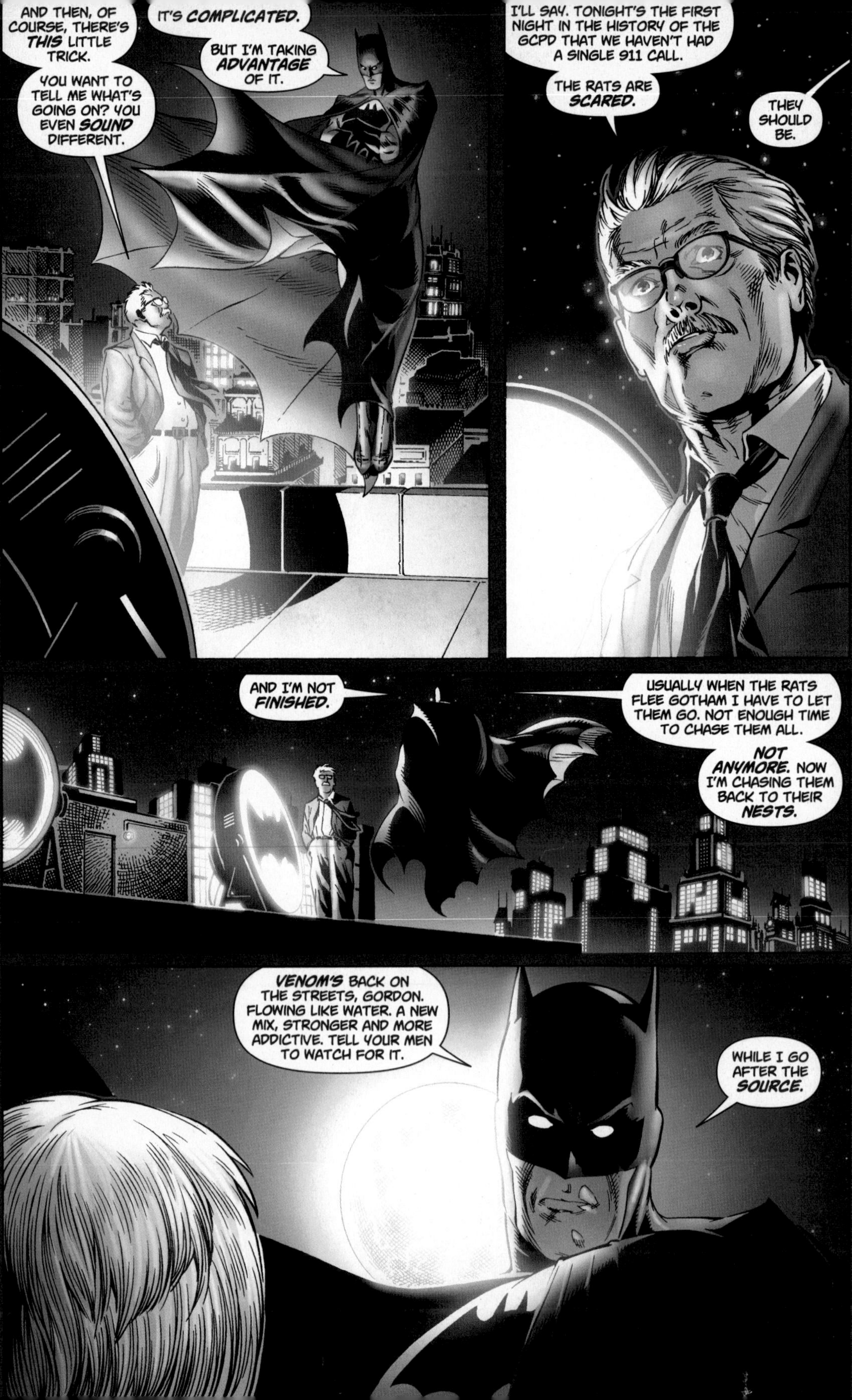
AND THEN, OF COURSE, THERE'S THIS LITTLE TRICK.
YOU WANT TO TELL ME WHAT'S GOING ON? YOU EVEN SOUND DIFFERENT.
IT'S COMPLICATED.
BUT I'M TAKING ADVANTAGE OF IT.
I'LL SAY. TONIGHT'S THE FIRST NIGHT IN THE HISTORY OF THE GCPD THAT WE HAVEN'T HAD A SINGLE 911 CALL.
THE RATS ARE SCARED.
THEY SHOULD BE.
AND I'M NOT FINISHED.
USUALLY WHEN THE RATS FLEE GOTHAM I HAVE TO LET THEM GO. NOT ENOUGH TIME TO CHASE THEM ALL.
NOT ANYMORE. NOW I'M CHASING THEM BACK TO THEIR NESTS.
VENOM'S BACK ON THE STREETS, GORDON. FLOWING LIKE WATER. A NEW MIX, STRONGER AND MORE ADDICTIVE. TELL YOUR MEN TO WATCH FOR IT.
WHILE I GO AFTER THE SOURCE.

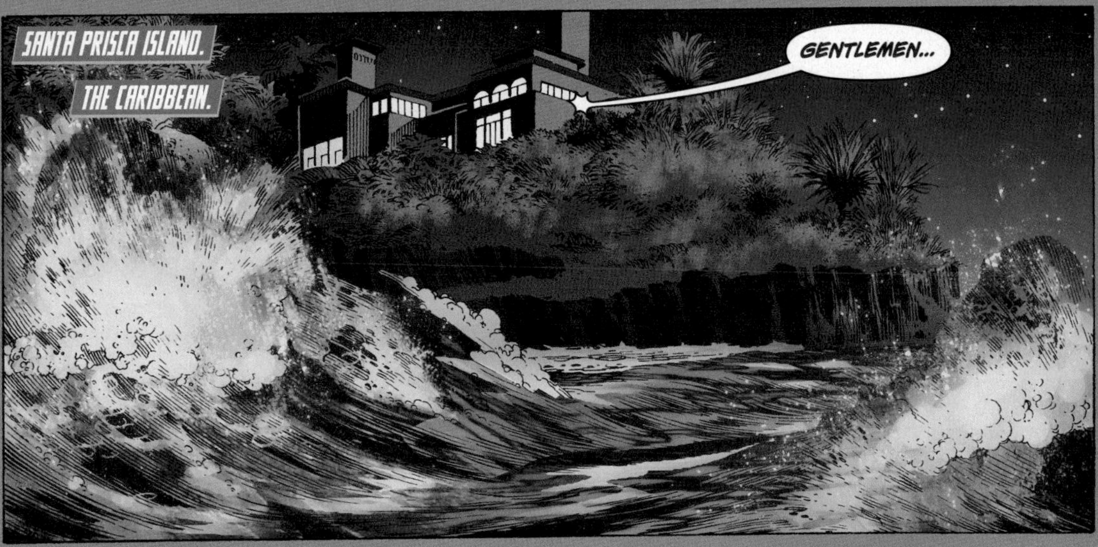
SANTA PRISCA ISLAND.
THE CARIBBEAN.
GENTLEMEN...

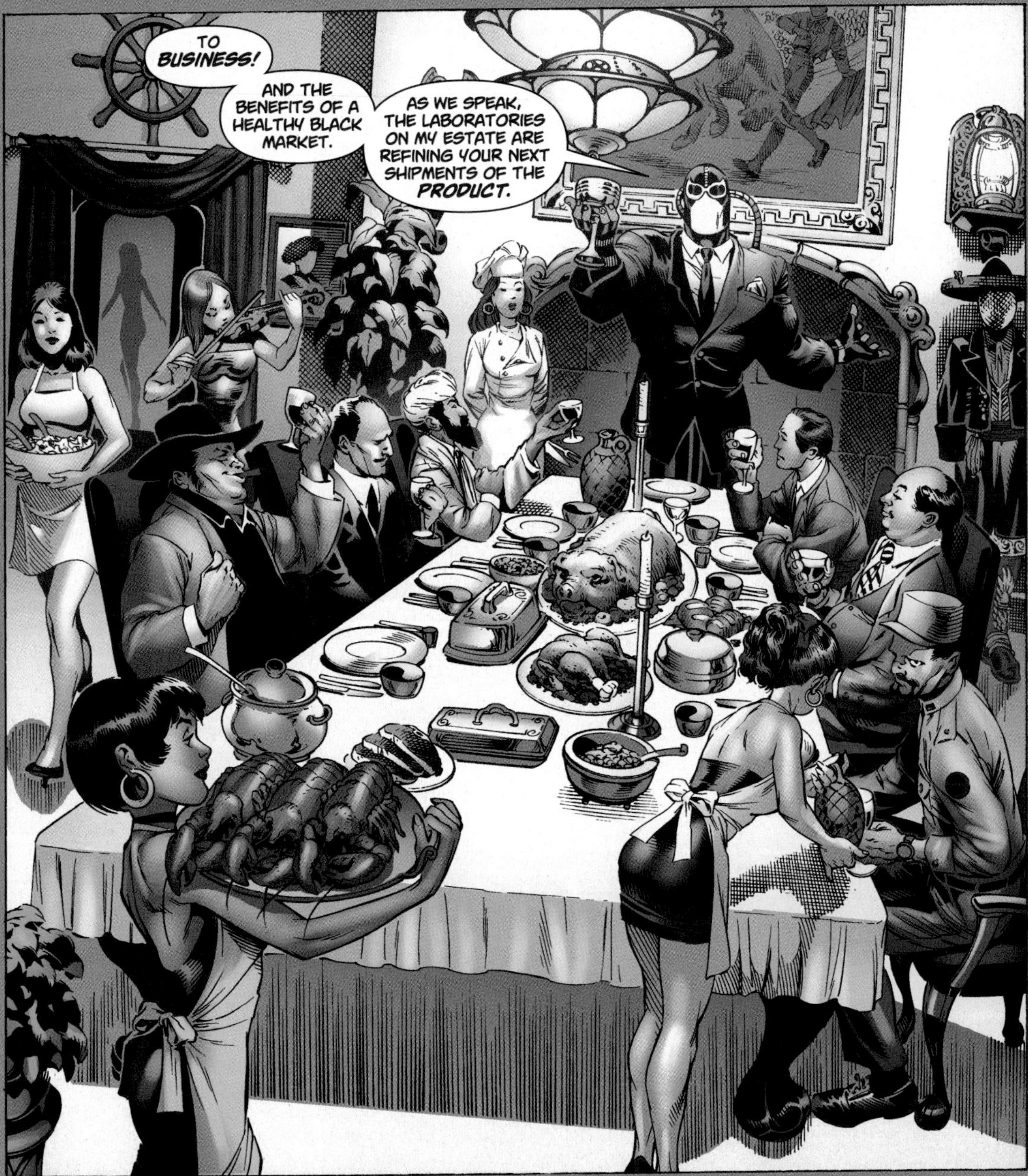
TO BUSINESS!
AND THE BENEFITS OF A HEALTHY BLACK MARKET.
AS WE SPEAK, THE LABORATORIES ON MY ESTATE ARE REFINING YOUR NEXT SHIPMENTS OF THE PRODUCT.

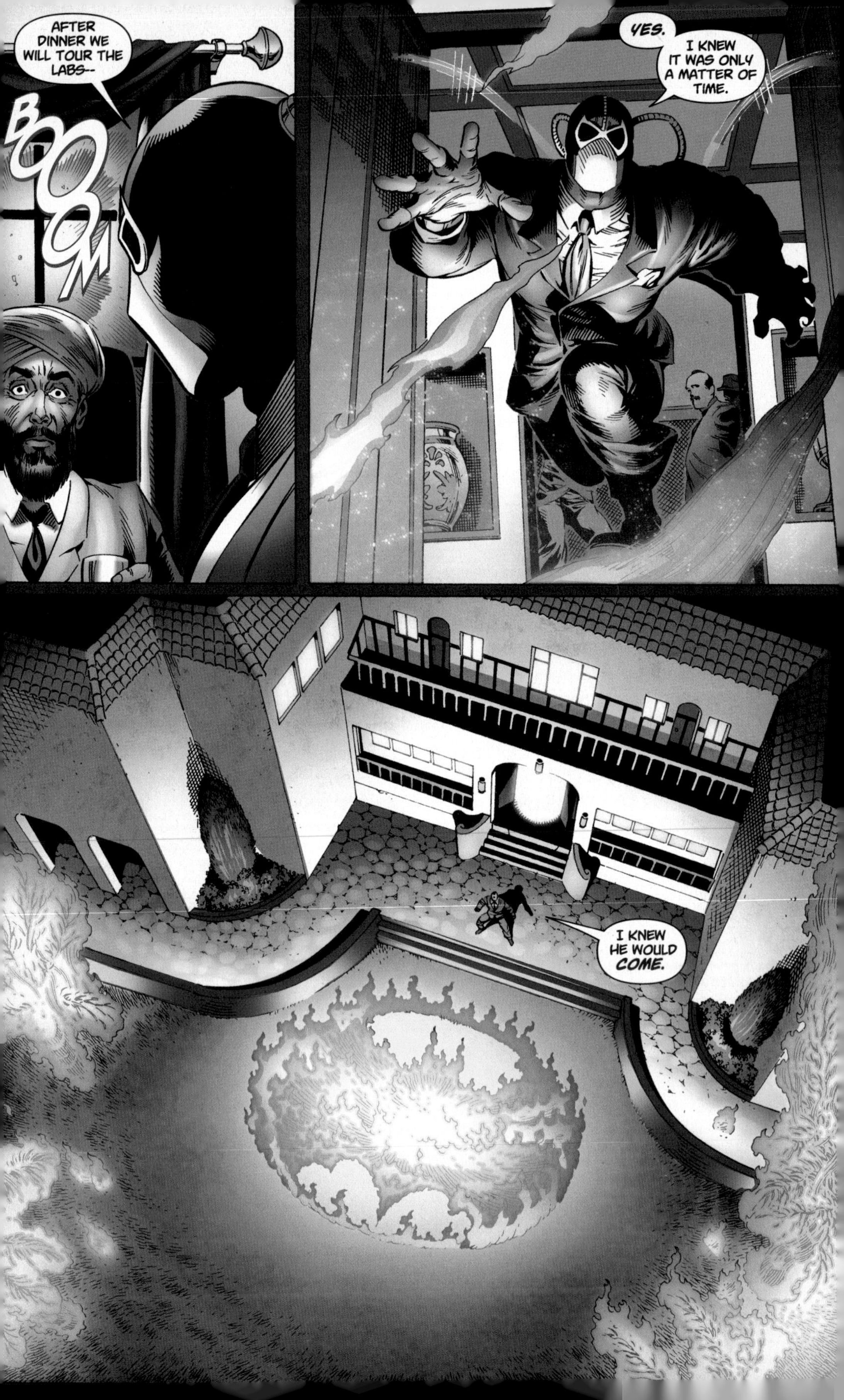
AFTER DINNER WE WILL TOUR THE LABS--
BOOOM
YES.
I KNEW IT WAS ONLY A MATTER OF TIME.
I KNEW HE WOULD COME.

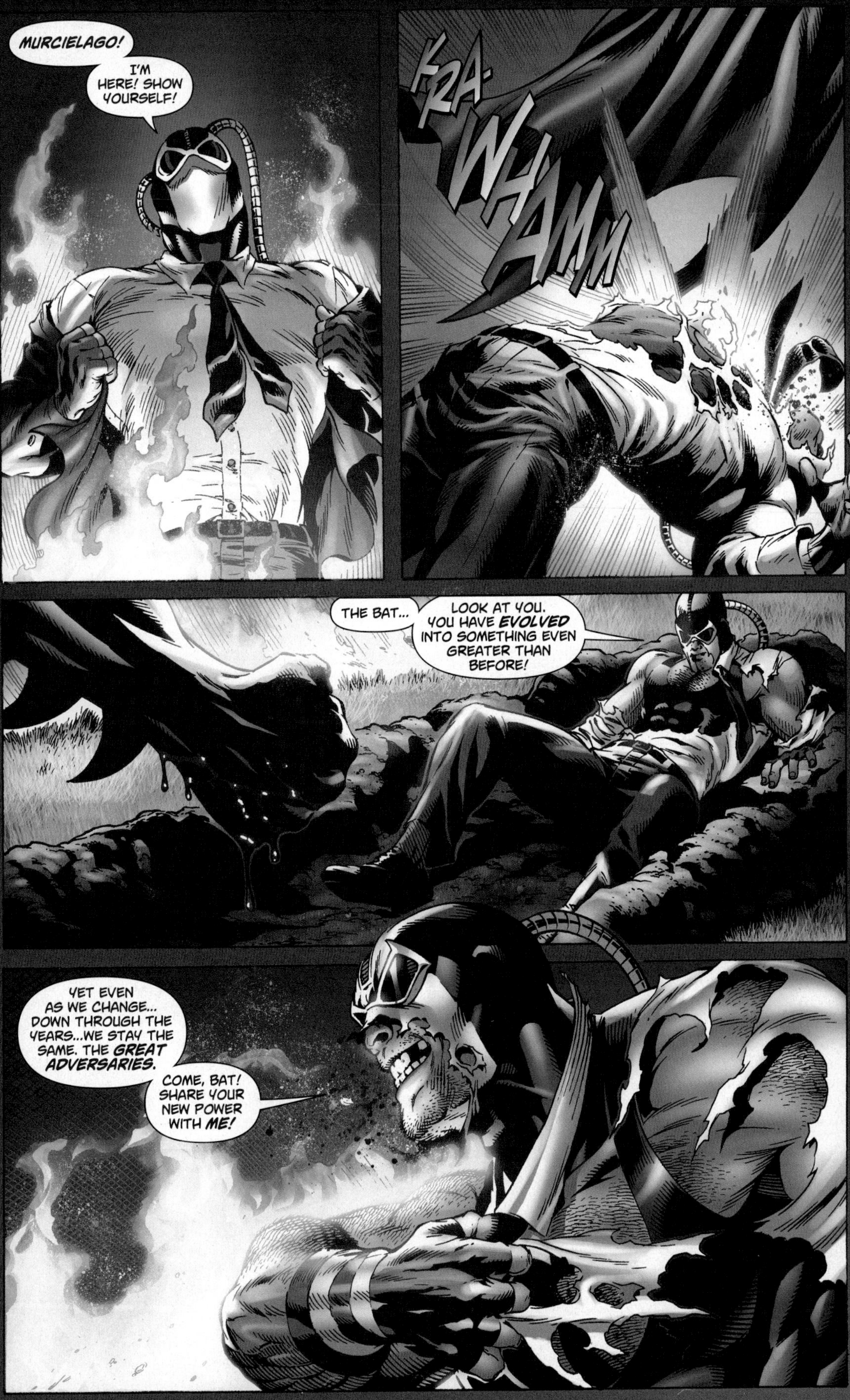
MURCIELAGO!
I'M HERE! SHOW YOURSELF!
KRA-WHAMM
THE BAT...
LOOK AT YOU. YOU HAVE EVOLVED INTO SOMETHING EVEN GREATER THAN BEFORE!
YET EVEN AS WE CHANGE... DOWN THROUGH THE YEARS...WE STAY THE SAME. THE GREAT ADVERSARIES.
COME, BAT! SHARE YOUR NEW POWER WITH ME!

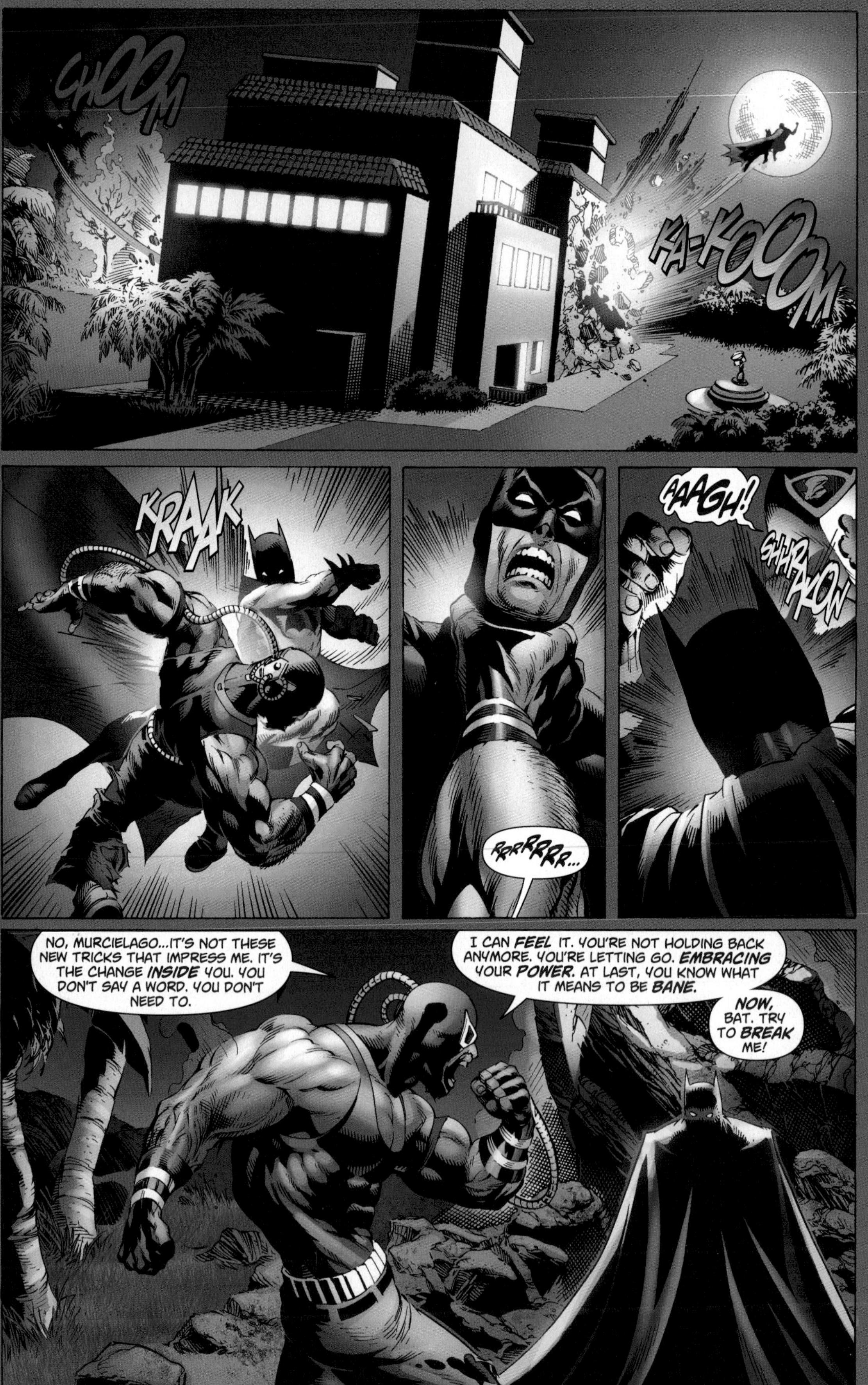
CHOOM
KA-KOOOM
KRAAK
AAAGH!
SHHRAKOW
RRRRRRR...
NO, MURCIELAGO...IT'S NOT THESE NEW TRICKS THAT IMPRESS ME. IT'S THE CHANGE INSIDE YOU. YOU DON'T SAY A WORD. YOU DON'T NEED TO.
I CAN FEEL IT. YOU'RE NOT HOLDING BACK ANYMORE. YOU'RE LETTING GO. EMBRACING YOUR POWER. AT LAST, YOU KNOW WHAT IT MEANS TO BE BANE.
NOW, BAT. TRY TO BREAK ME!

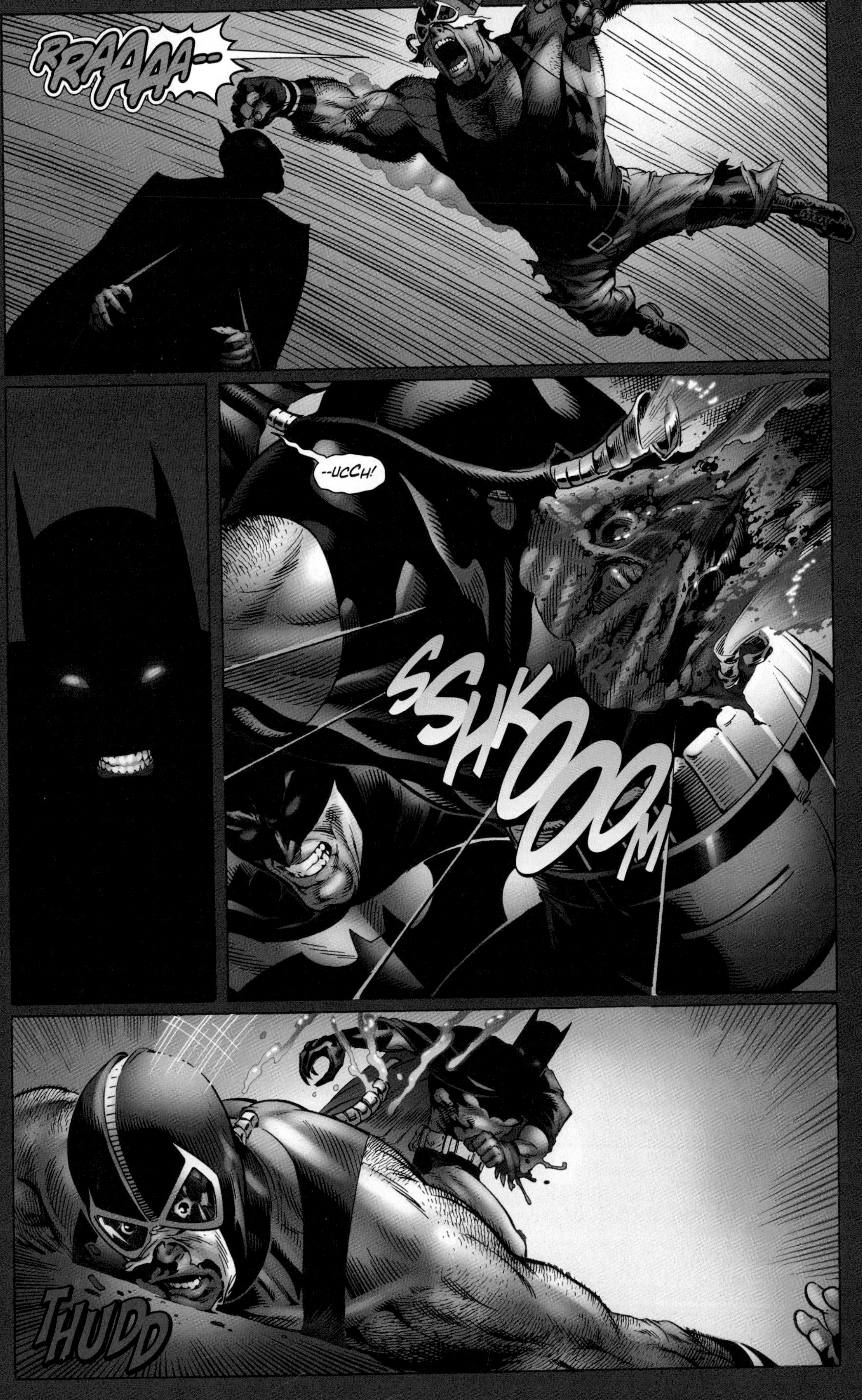
RRAAAA--
--UCCH!
SSHKOOOM
THUDD

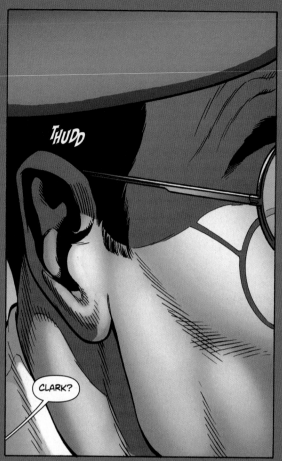

THUDD

CLARK?

HONEY, YOU OKAY?

YES, SORRY. I THOUGHT I... HEARD SOMETHING. JUST MY MIND PLAYING TRICKS ON ME.

YOUR *MIND* SHOULD BE FOCUSED ON JUST ONE THING, SWEETHEART. OUR FIRST REAL DATE NIGHT IN *MONTHS*.

AND THANKS FOR LEAVING THE COSTUME AT HOME.

NOO!

DID YOU HEAR THAT?

IT CAME FROM THE ALLEY.

IT SOUNDED LIKE SOMEONE'S *HURT*.

CLARK, WAIT...

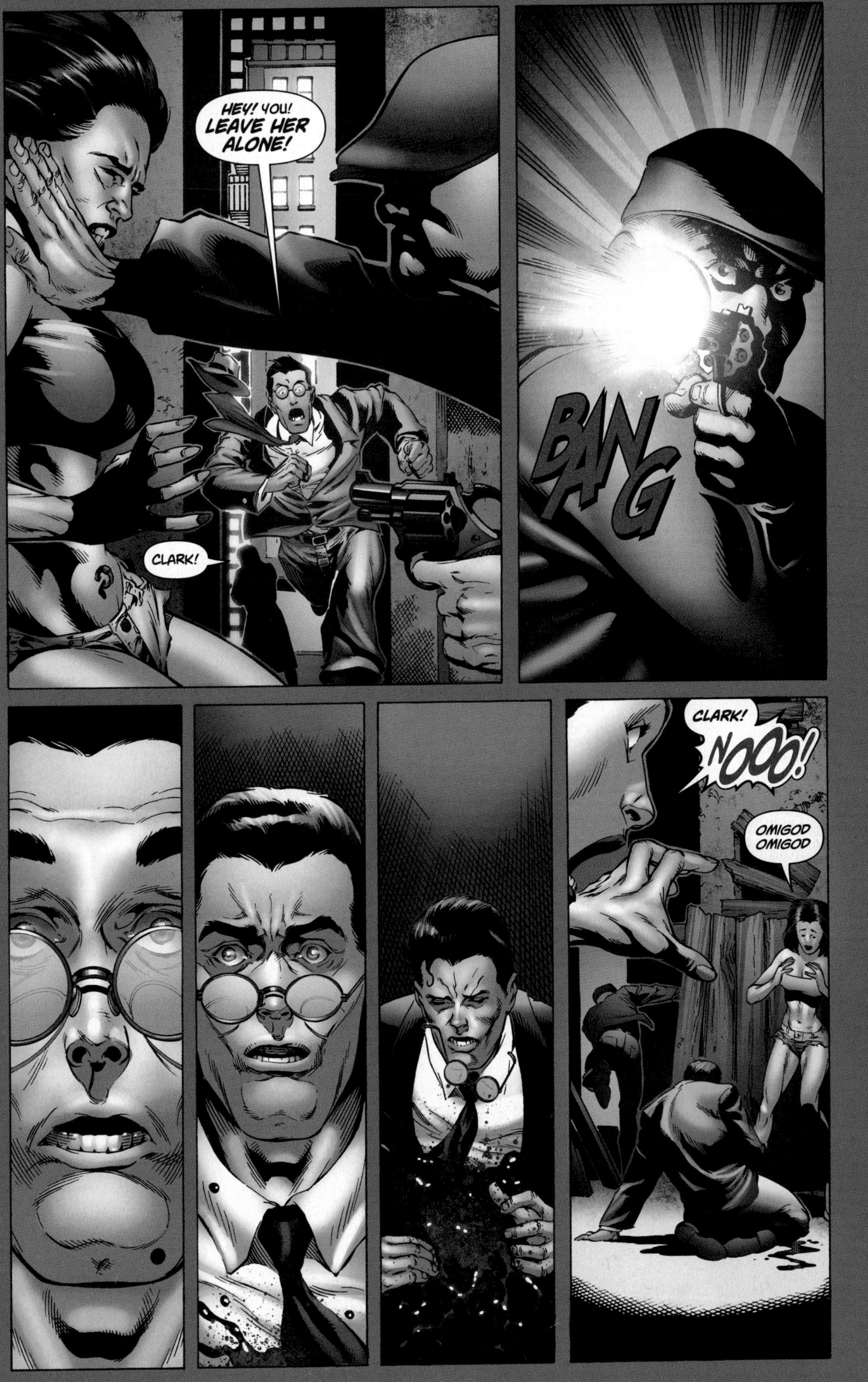
HEY! YOU! LEAVE HER ALONE!
CLARK!
BANG
CLARK!
NOOO!
OMIGOD OMIGOD

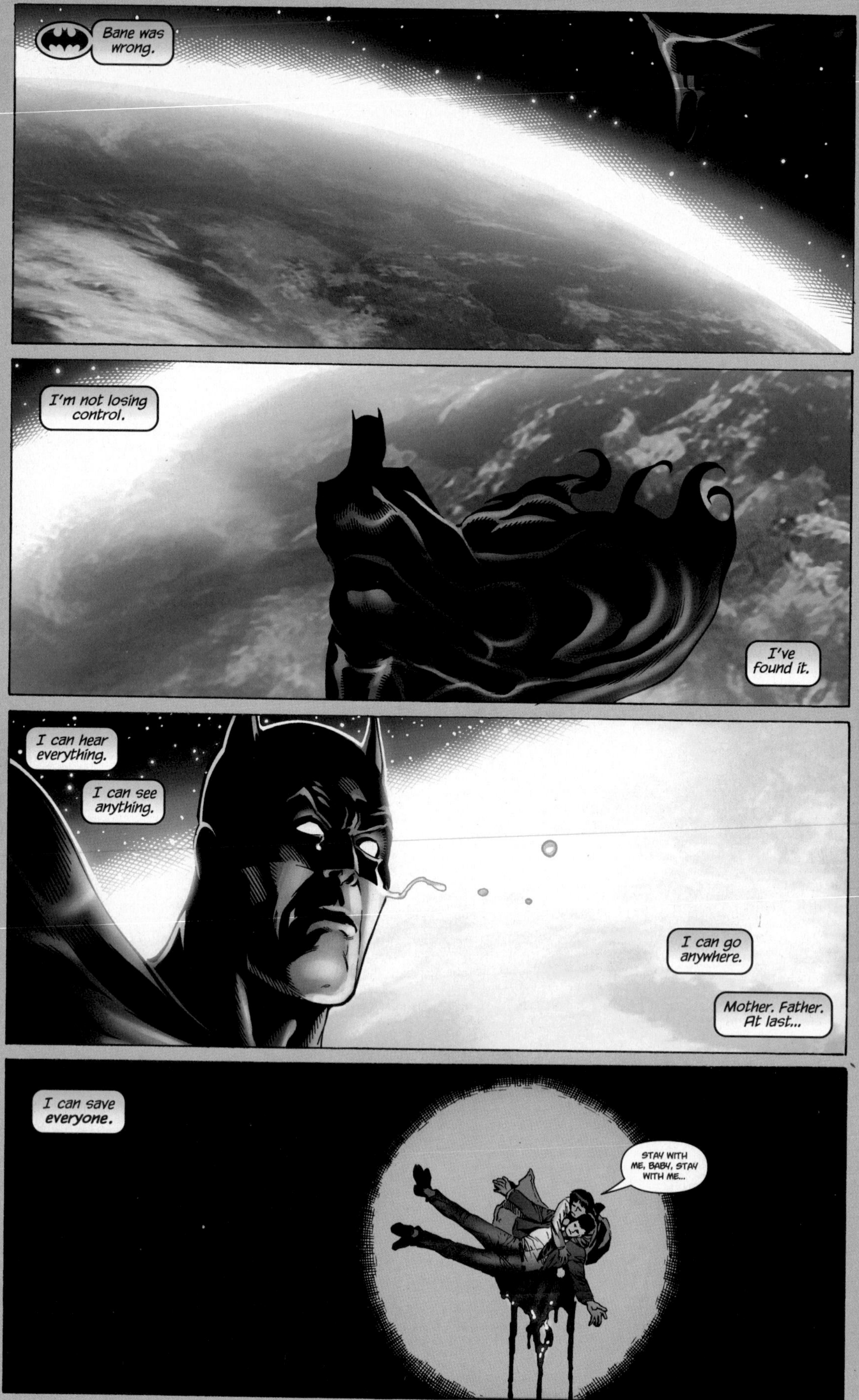
Bane was wrong.
I'm not losing control.
I've found it.
I can hear everything.
I can see anything.
I can go anywhere.
Mother. Father. At last...
I can save everyone.
STAY WITH ME, BABY, STAY WITH ME...

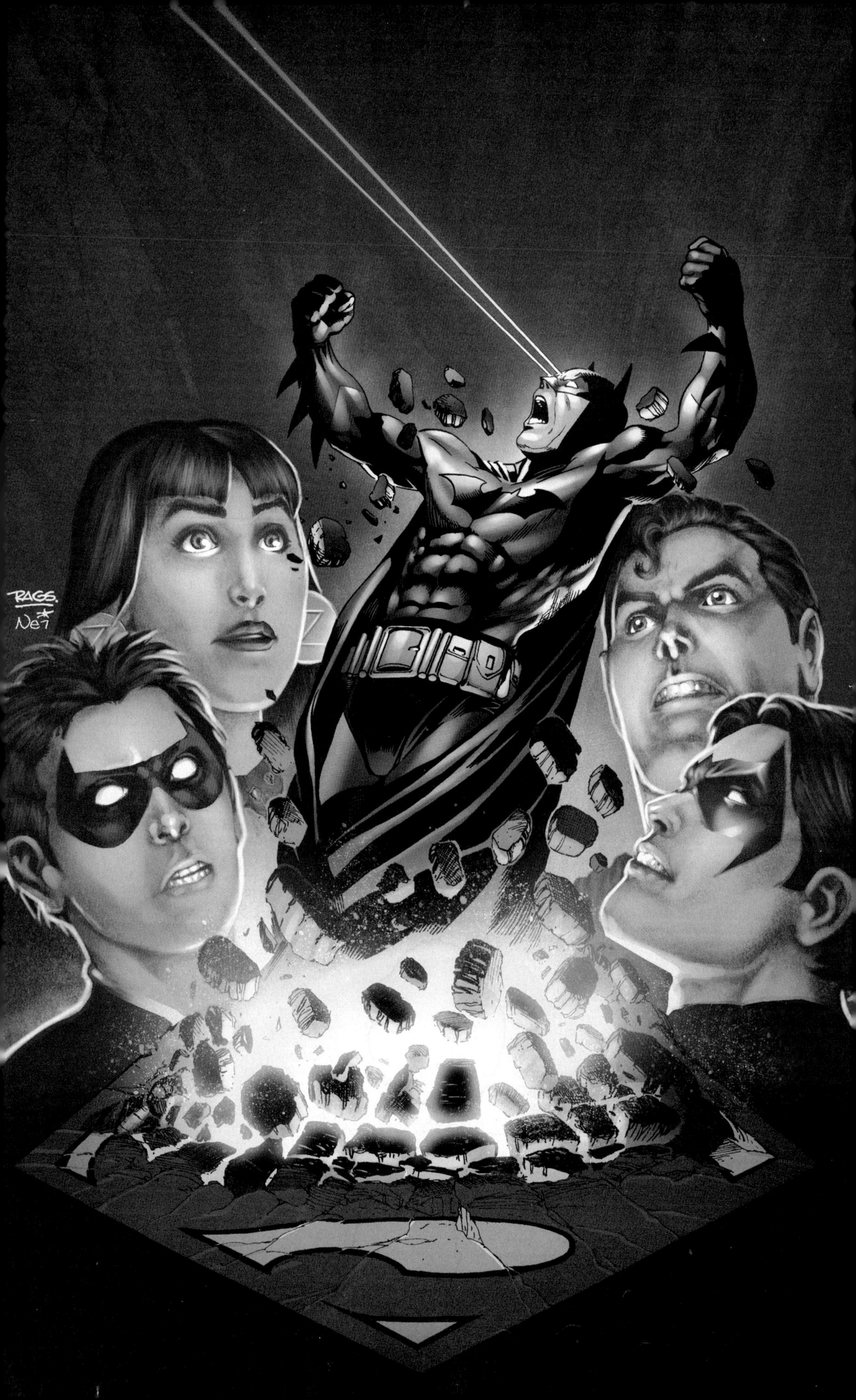

SUPERMAN/BATMAN 55

SUPERBAT
part three

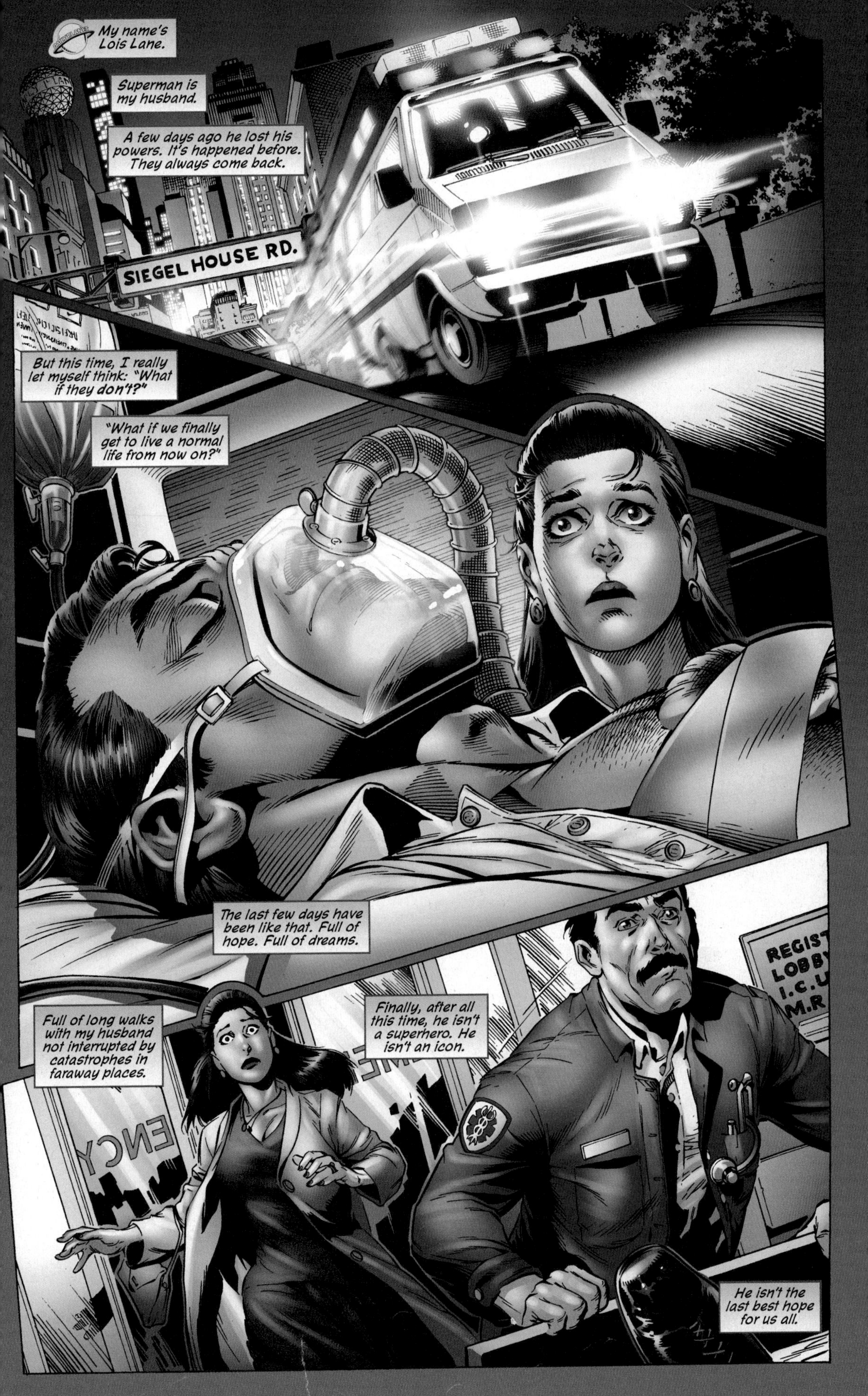
My name's Lois Lane.
Superman is my husband.
A few days ago he lost his powers. It's happened before. They always come back.
SIEGEL HOUSE RD.
But this time, I really let myself think: "What if they don't?"
"What if we finally get to live a normal life from now on?"
The last few days have been like that. Full of hope. Full of dreams.
Full of long walks with my husband not interrupted by catastrophes in faraway places.
Finally, after all this time, he isn't a superhero. He isn't an icon.
He isn't the last best hope for us all.

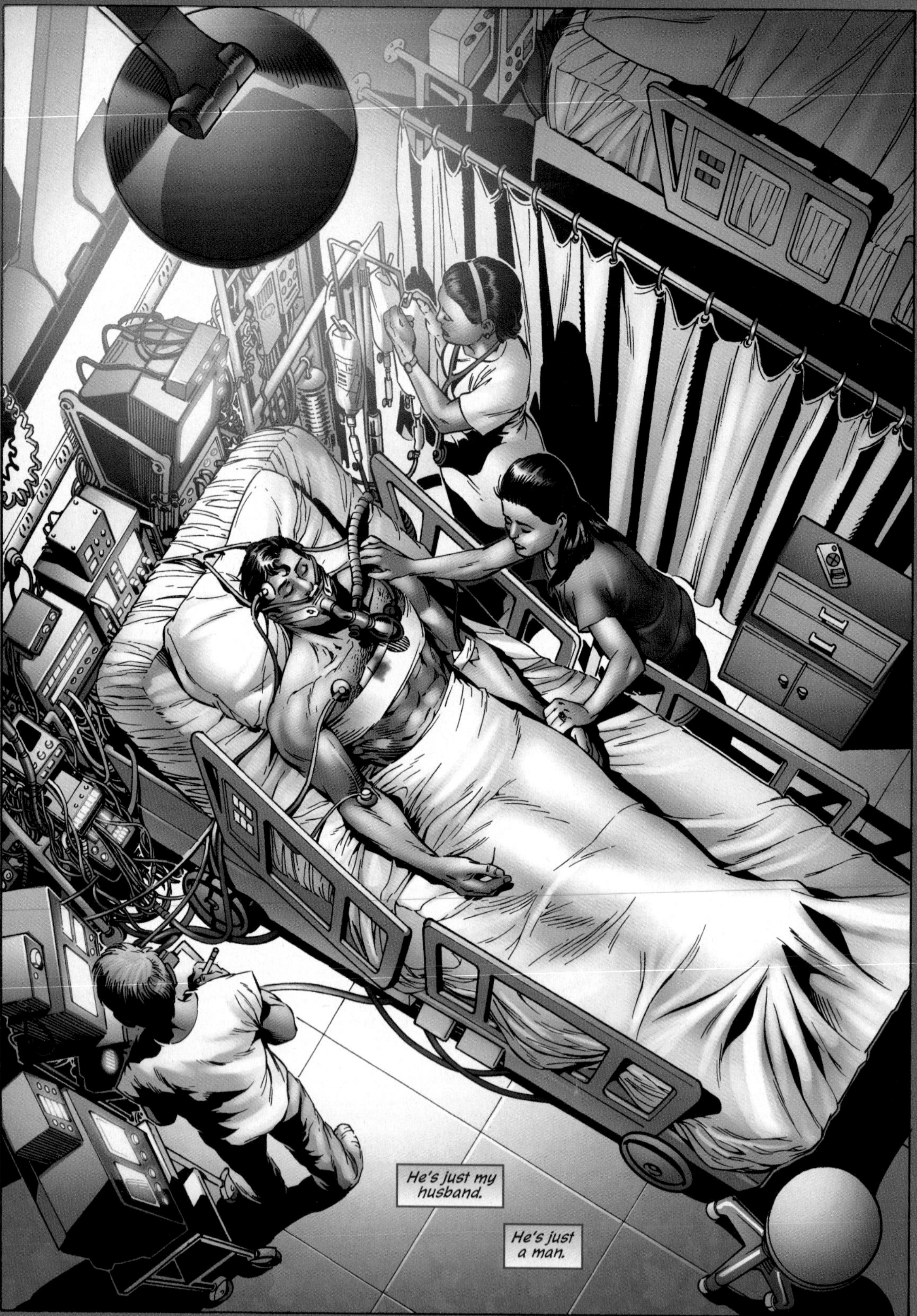
He's just my husband.
He's just a man.

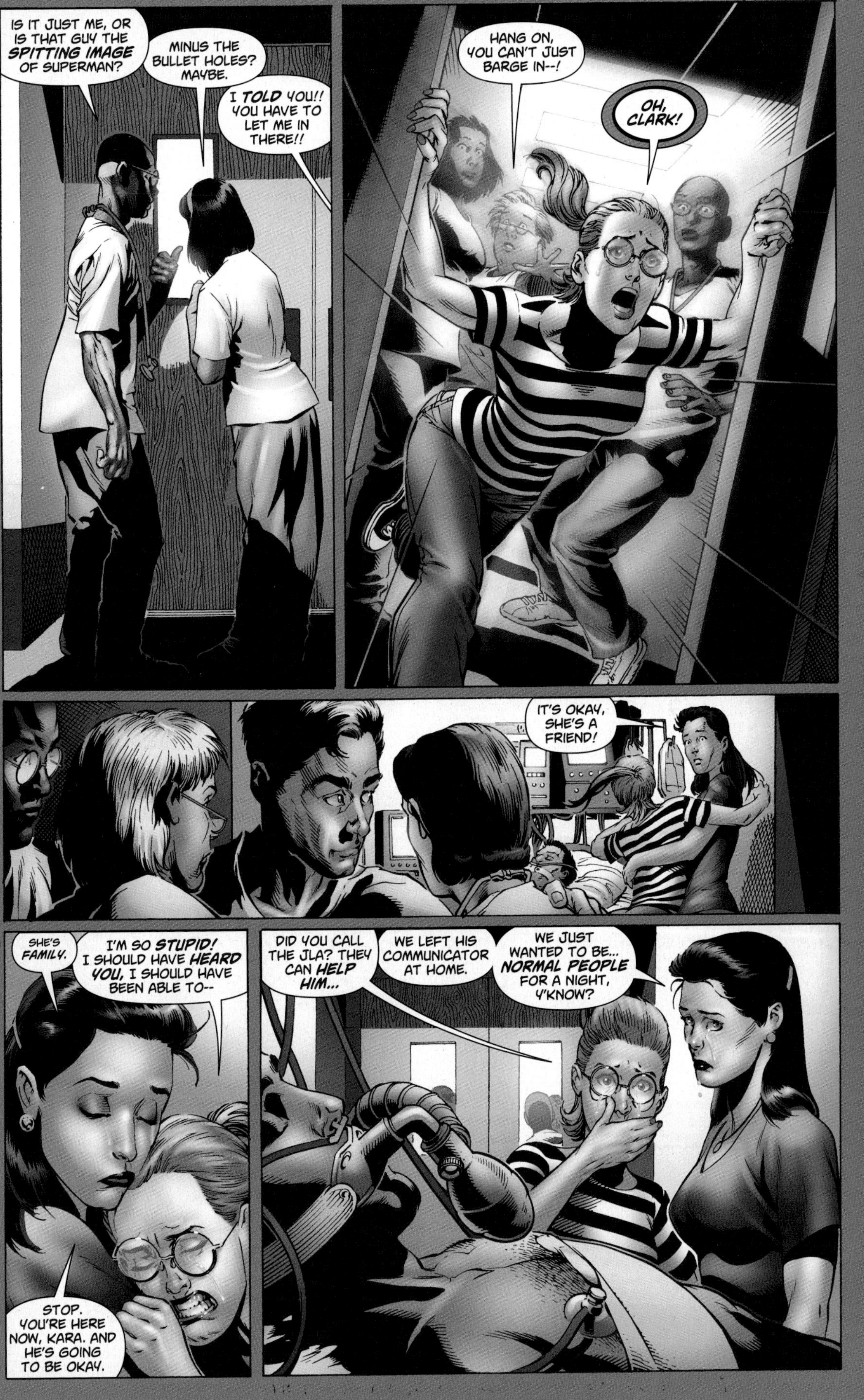

IS IT JUST ME, OR IS THAT GUY THE **SPITTING IMAGE** OF SUPERMAN?
MINUS THE BULLET HOLES? MAYBE.
I **TOLD** YOU!! YOU HAVE TO LET ME IN THERE!!
HANG ON, YOU CAN'T JUST BARGE IN--!
OH, CLARK!
IT'S OKAY, SHE'S A FRIEND!
SHE'S *FAMILY.*
I'M SO **STUPID!** I SHOULD HAVE **HEARD YOU,** I SHOULD HAVE BEEN ABLE TO--
STOP. YOU'RE HERE NOW, KARA. AND HE'S GOING TO BE OKAY.
DID YOU CALL THE JLA? THEY CAN **HELP HIM...**
WE LEFT HIS COMMUNICATOR AT HOME.
WE JUST WANTED TO BE... **NORMAL PEOPLE** FOR A NIGHT, Y'KNOW?

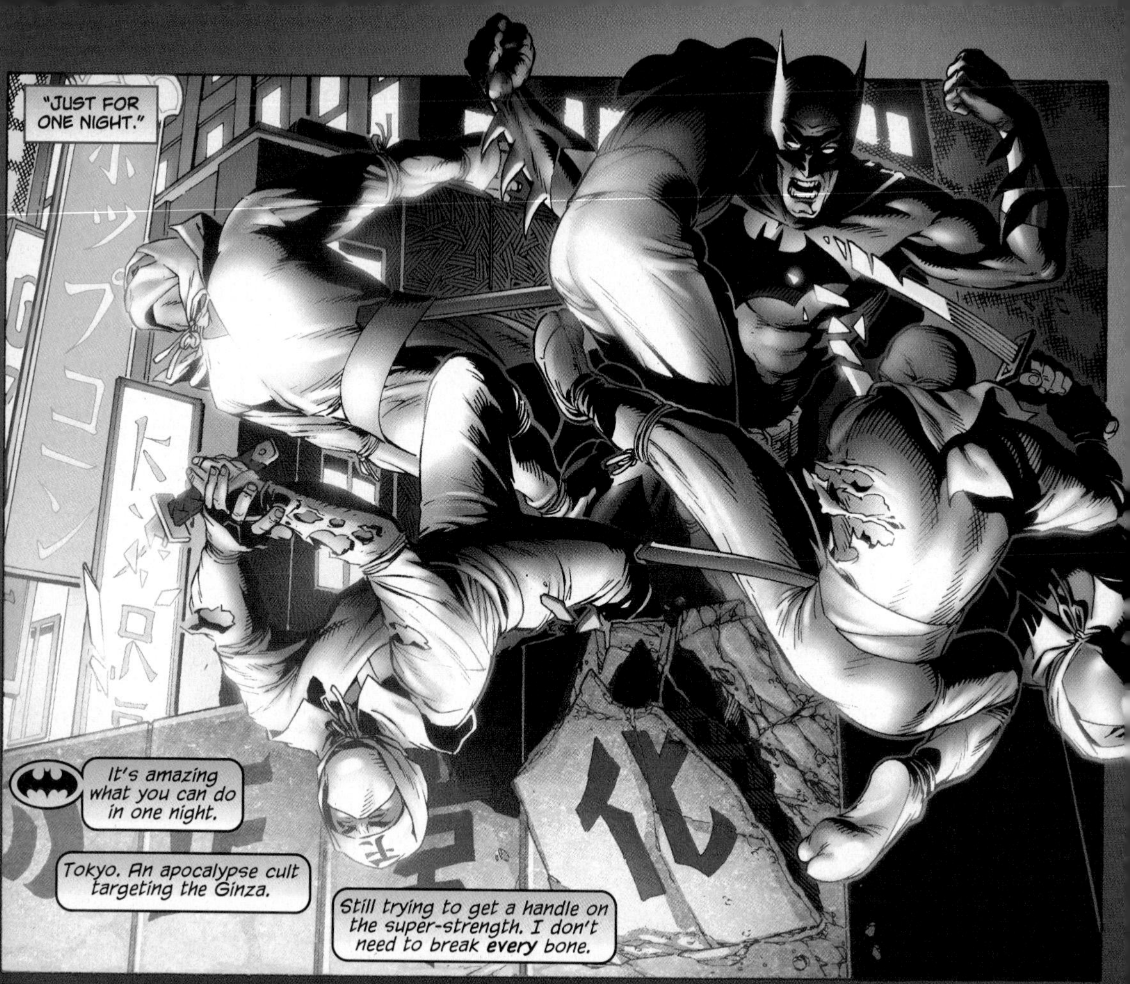
"JUST FOR ONE NIGHT."
It's amazing what you can do in one night.
Tokyo. An apocalypse cult targeting the Ginza.
Still trying to get a handle on the super-strength. I don't need to break **every** bone.


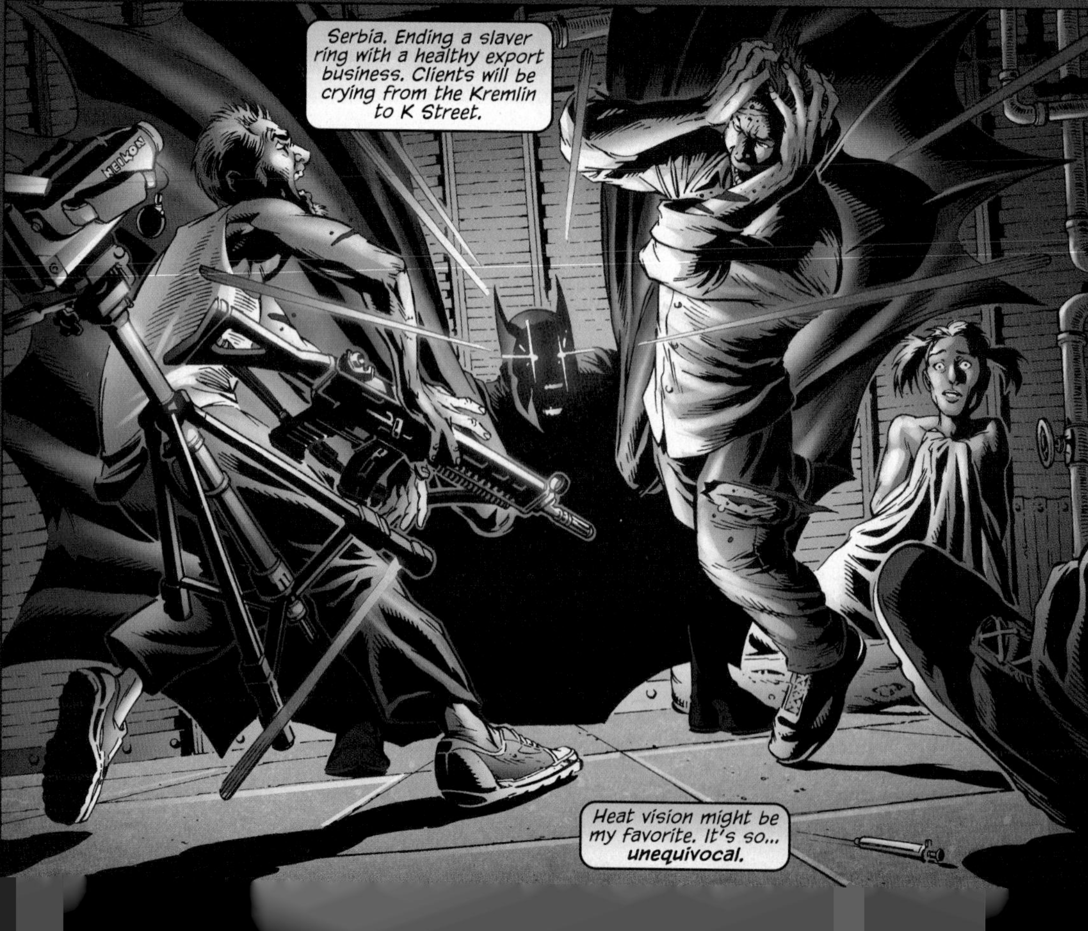
Serbia. Ending a slaver ring with a healthy export business. Clients will be crying from the Kremlin to K Street.
Heat vision might be my favorite. It's so... **unequivocal.**

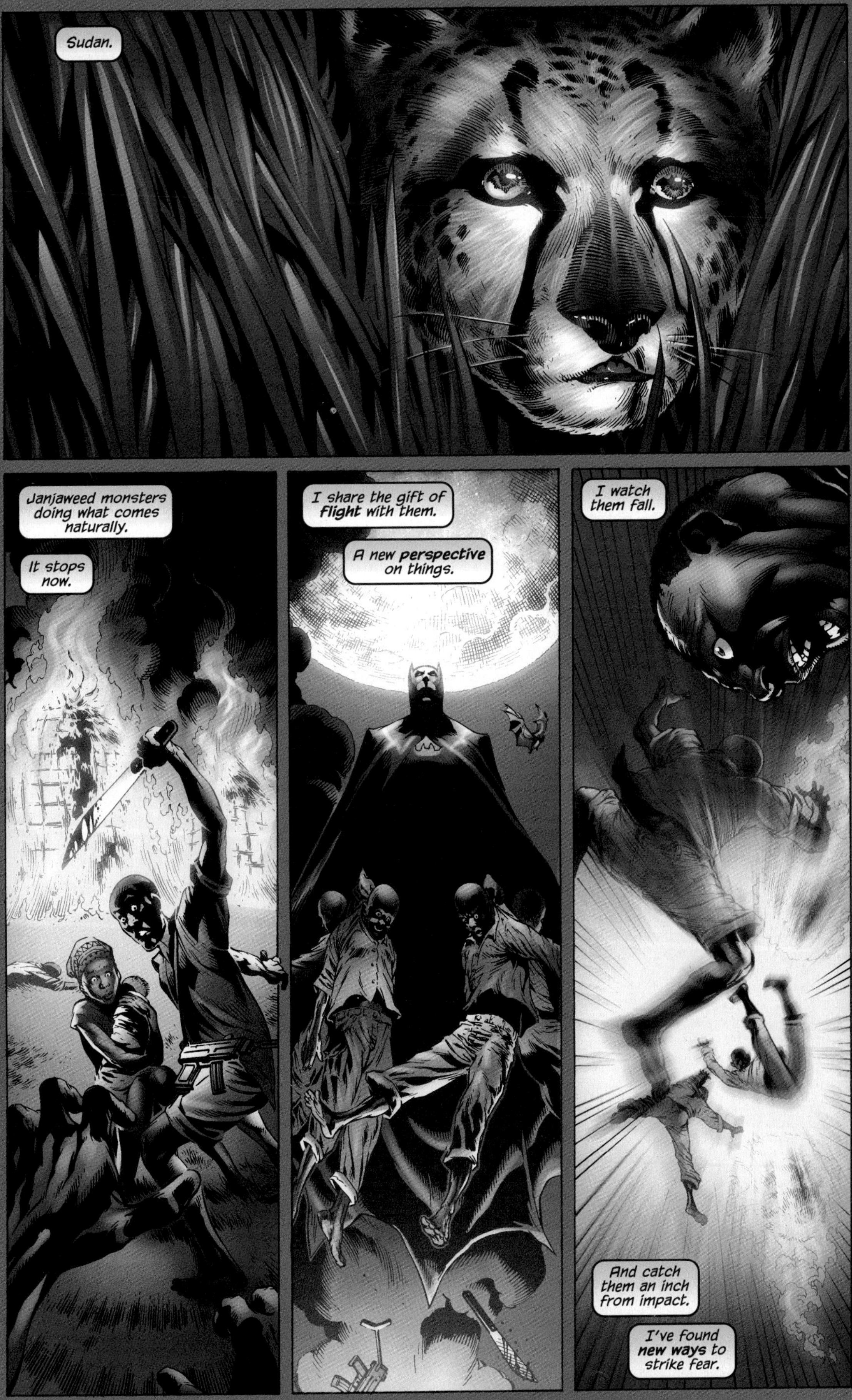

Sudan.
Janjaweed monsters doing what comes naturally.
It stops now.
I share the gift of **flight** with them.
A new **perspective** on things.
I watch them fall.
And catch them an inch from impact.
I've found **new ways** to strike fear.

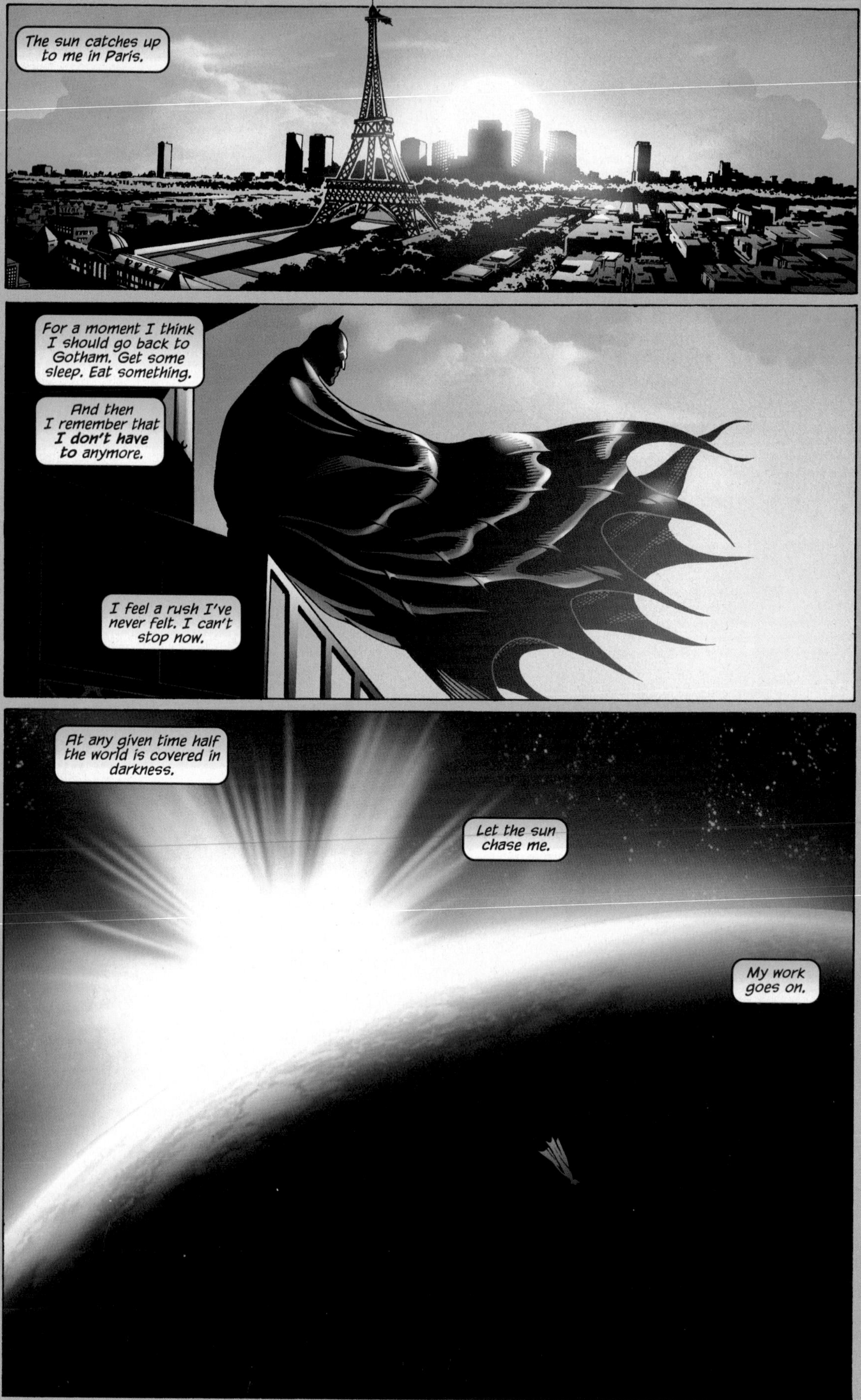
The sun catches up to me in Paris.
For a moment I think I should go back to Gotham. Get some sleep. Eat something.
And then I remember that I don't have to anymore.
I feel a rush I've never felt. I can't stop now.
At any given time half the world is covered in darkness.
Let the sun chase me.
My work goes on.

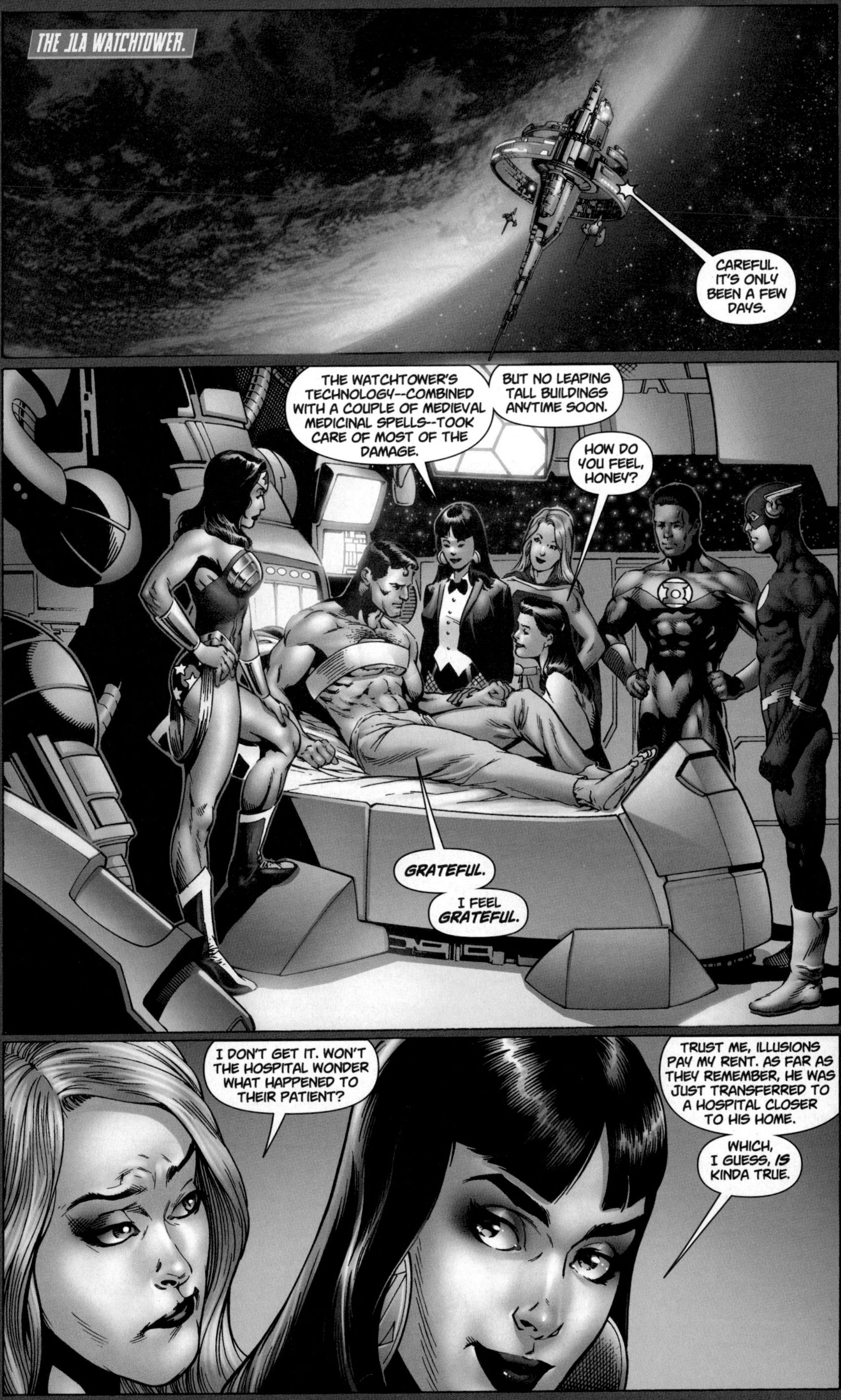
THE JLA WATCHTOWER.
CAREFUL. IT'S ONLY BEEN A FEW DAYS.
THE WATCHTOWER'S TECHNOLOGY--COMBINED WITH A COUPLE OF MEDIEVAL MEDICINAL SPELLS--TOOK CARE OF MOST OF THE DAMAGE.
BUT NO LEAPING TALL BUILDINGS ANYTIME SOON.
HOW DO YOU FEEL, HONEY?
GRATEFUL.
I FEEL GRATEFUL.
I DON'T GET IT. WON'T THE HOSPITAL WONDER WHAT HAPPENED TO THEIR PATIENT?
TRUST ME, ILLUSIONS PAY MY RENT. AS FAR AS THEY REMEMBER, HE WAS JUST TRANSFERRED TO A HOSPITAL CLOSER TO HIS HOME.
WHICH, I GUESS, IS KINDA TRUE.

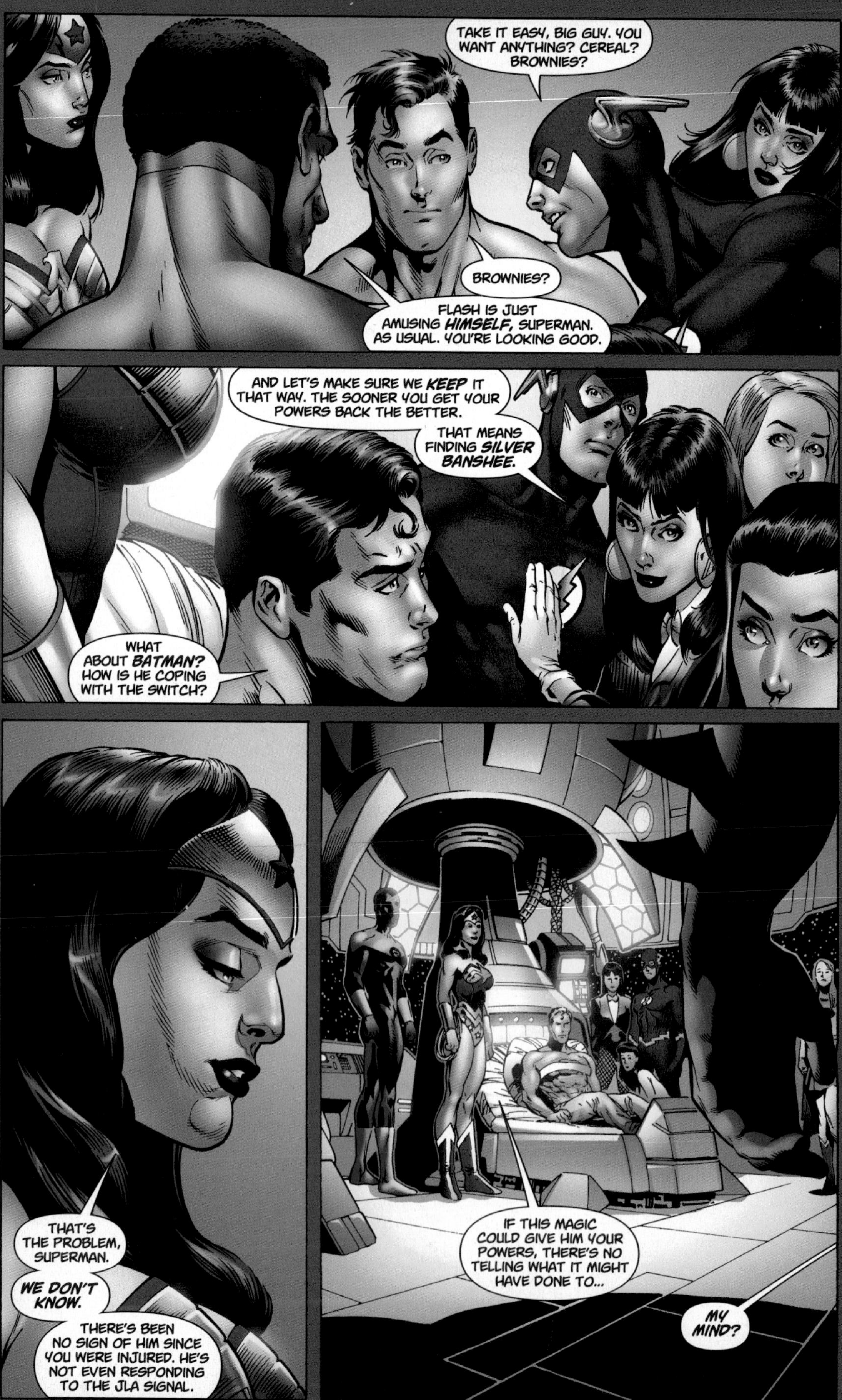
TAKE IT EASY, BIG GUY. YOU WANT ANYTHING? CEREAL? BROWNIES?
BROWNIES?
FLASH IS JUST AMUSING HIMSELF, SUPERMAN. AS USUAL. YOU'RE LOOKING GOOD.
AND LET'S MAKE SURE WE KEEP IT THAT WAY. THE SOONER YOU GET YOUR POWERS BACK THE BETTER.
THAT MEANS FINDING SILVER BANSHEE.
WHAT ABOUT BATMAN? HOW IS HE COPING WITH THE SWITCH?
THAT'S THE PROBLEM, SUPERMAN.
WE DON'T KNOW.
THERE'S BEEN NO SIGN OF HIM SINCE YOU WERE INJURED. HE'S NOT EVEN RESPONDING TO THE JLA SIGNAL.
IF THIS MAGIC COULD GIVE HIM YOUR POWERS, THERE'S NO TELLING WHAT IT MIGHT HAVE DONE TO...
MY MIND?

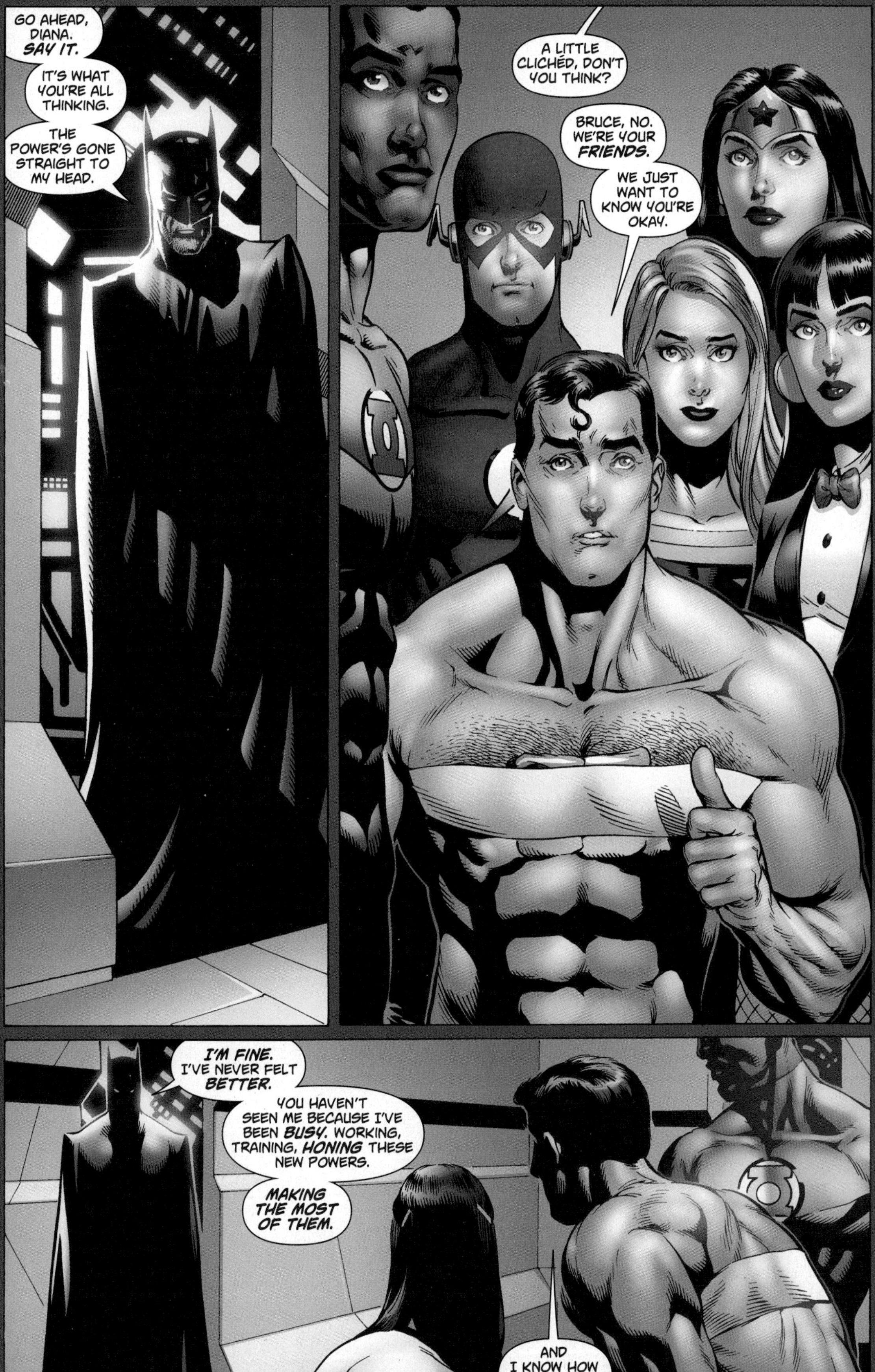
GO AHEAD, DIANA. SAY IT.
IT'S WHAT YOU'RE ALL THINKING.
THE POWER'S GONE STRAIGHT TO MY HEAD.
A LITTLE CLICHÉD, DON'T YOU THINK?
BRUCE, NO. WE'RE YOUR FRIENDS.
WE JUST WANT TO KNOW YOU'RE OKAY.
I'M FINE. I'VE NEVER FELT BETTER.
YOU HAVEN'T SEEN ME BECAUSE I'VE BEEN BUSY. WORKING, TRAINING, HONING THESE NEW POWERS.
MAKING THE MOST OF THEM.
AND I KNOW HOW HARD THAT MUST BE.

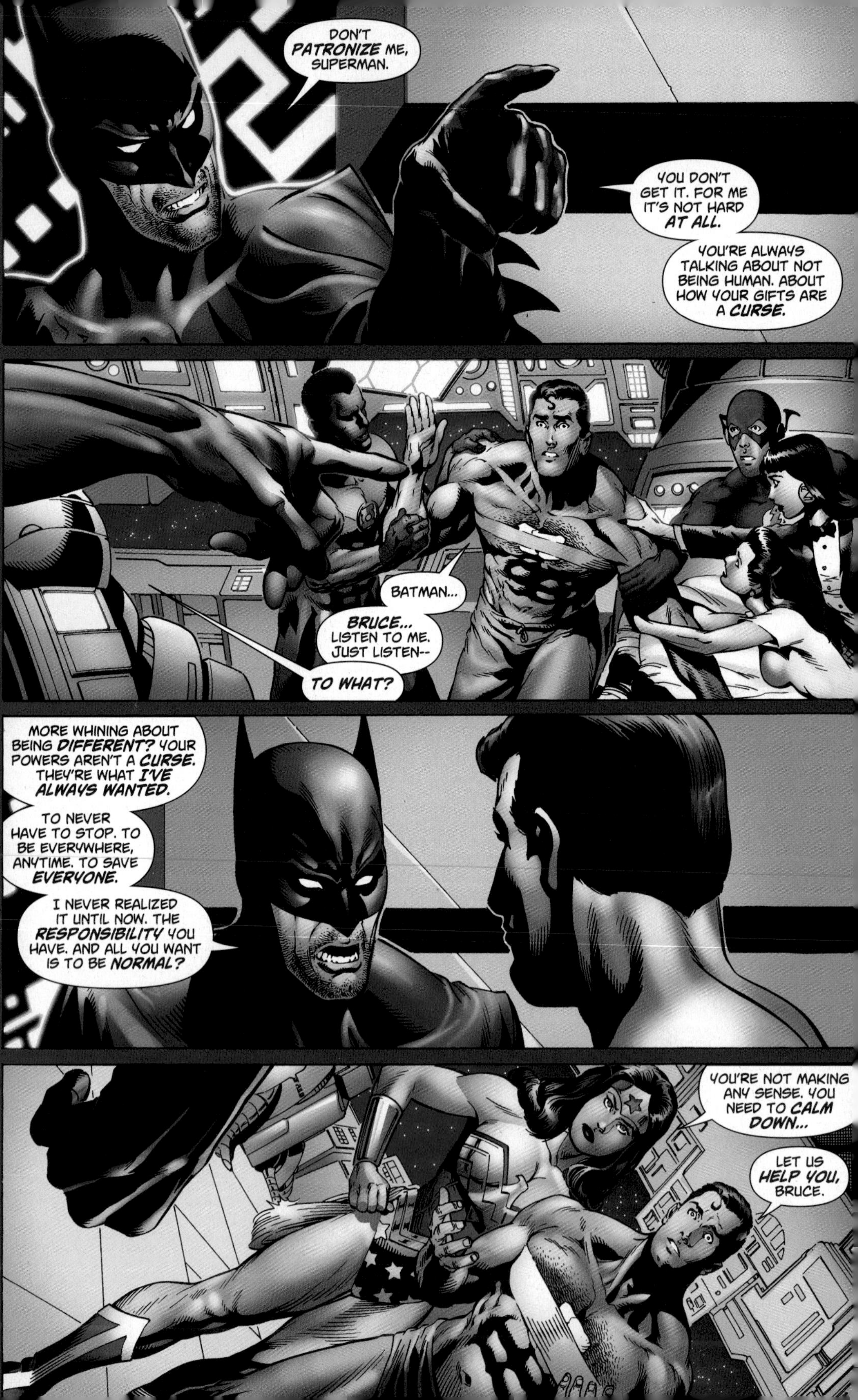
DON'T PATRONIZE ME, SUPERMAN.
YOU DON'T GET IT. FOR ME IT'S NOT HARD AT ALL.
YOU'RE ALWAYS TALKING ABOUT NOT BEING HUMAN. ABOUT HOW YOUR GIFTS ARE A CURSE.
BATMAN...
BRUCE... LISTEN TO ME. JUST LISTEN--
TO WHAT?
MORE WHINING ABOUT BEING DIFFERENT? YOUR POWERS AREN'T A CURSE. THEY'RE WHAT I'VE ALWAYS WANTED.
TO NEVER HAVE TO STOP. TO BE EVERYWHERE, ANYTIME. TO SAVE EVERYONE.
I NEVER REALIZED IT UNTIL NOW. THE RESPONSIBILITY YOU HAVE. AND ALL YOU WANT IS TO BE NORMAL?
YOU'RE NOT MAKING ANY SENSE. YOU NEED TO CALM DOWN...
LET US HELP YOU, BRUCE.

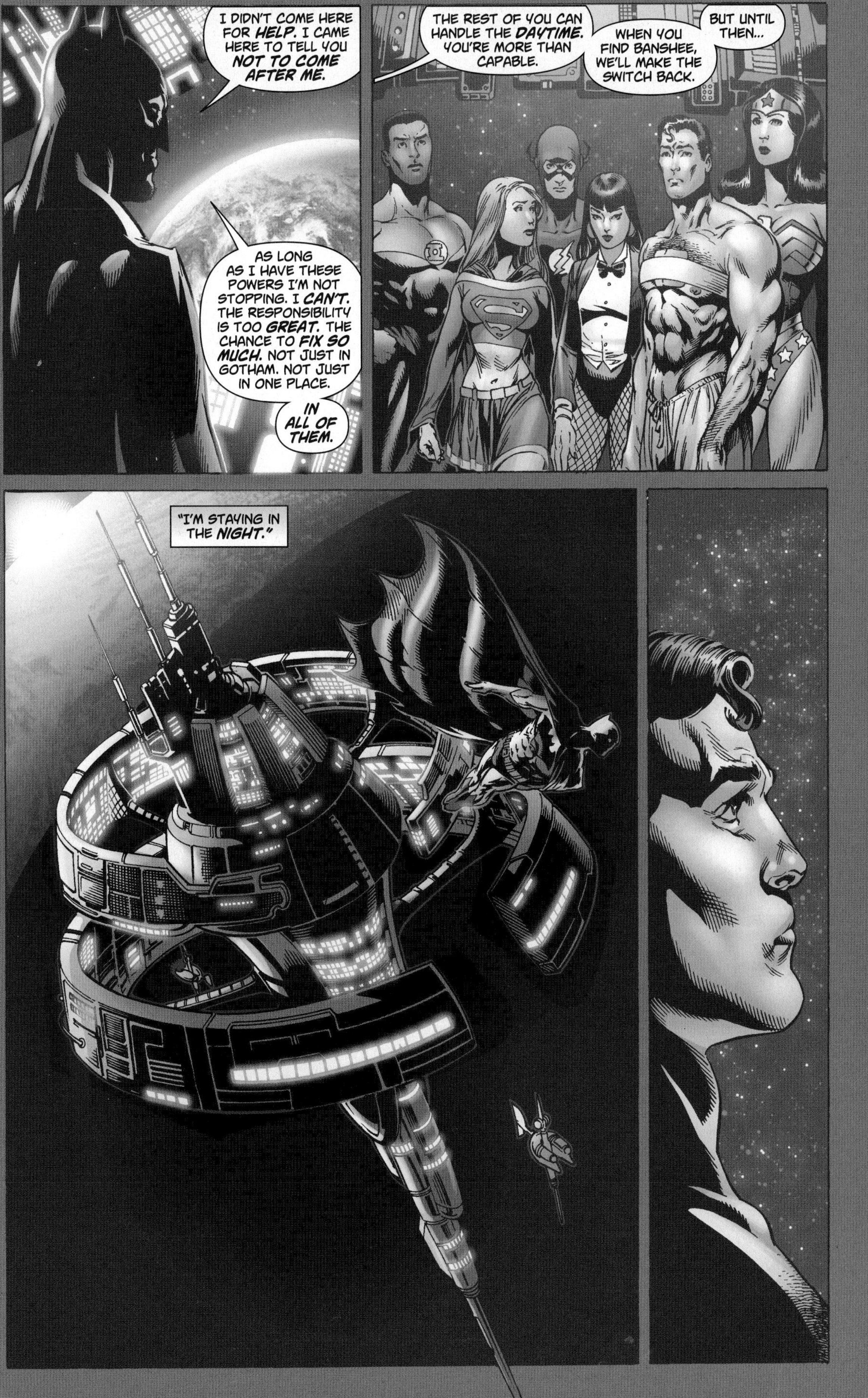

I DIDN'T COME HERE FOR HELP. I CAME HERE TO TELL YOU NOT TO COME AFTER ME.
AS LONG AS I HAVE THESE POWERS I'M NOT STOPPING. I CAN'T. THE RESPONSIBILITY IS TOO GREAT. THE CHANCE TO FIX SO MUCH. NOT JUST IN GOTHAM. NOT JUST IN ONE PLACE.
IN ALL OF THEM.
THE REST OF YOU CAN HANDLE THE DAYTIME. YOU'RE MORE THAN CAPABLE.
WHEN YOU FIND BANSHEE, WE'LL MAKE THE SWITCH BACK.
BUT UNTIL THEN...
"I'M STAYING IN THE NIGHT."

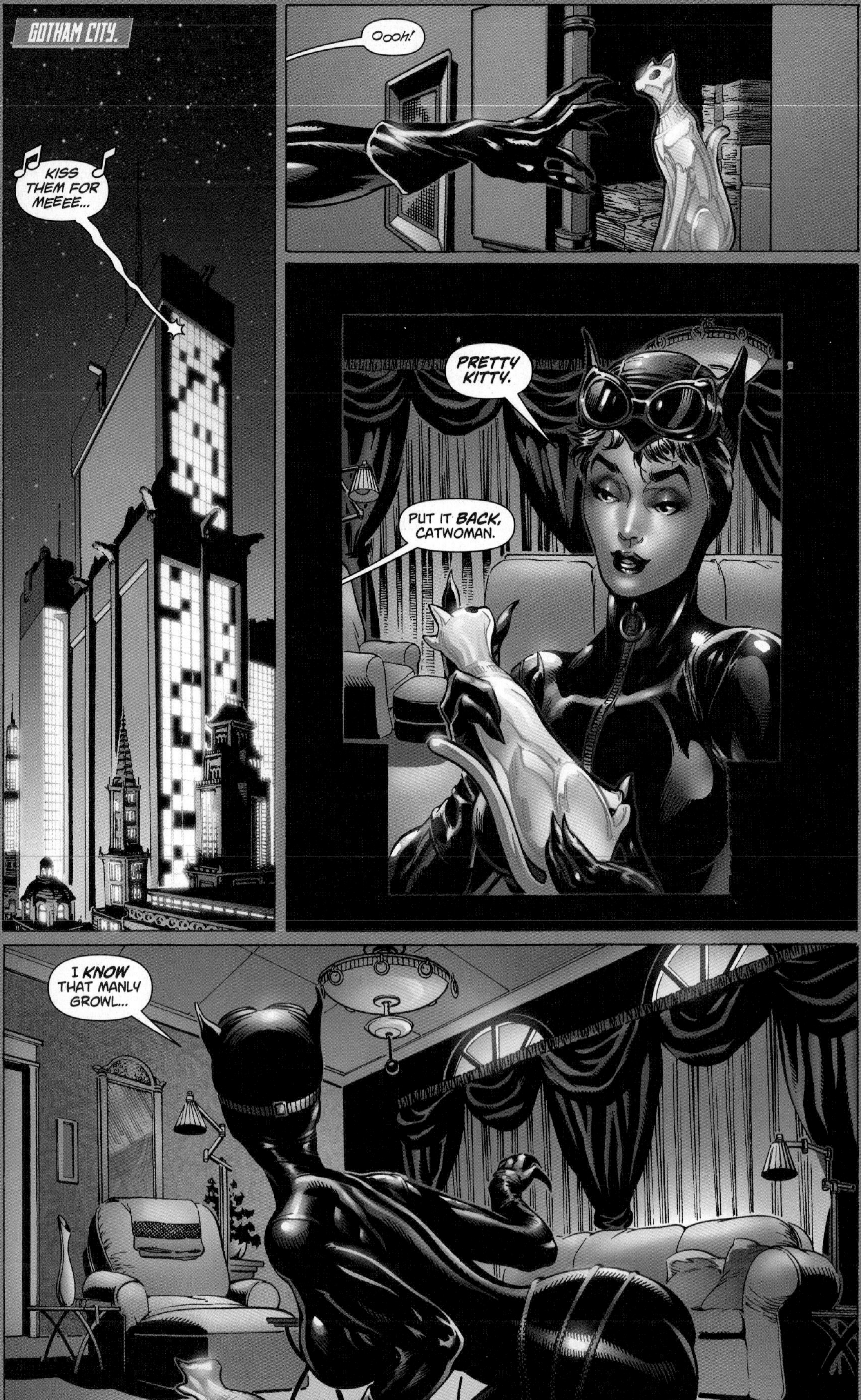
GOTHAM CITY.
KISS THEM FOR MEEEE...
Oooh!
PRETTY KITTY.
PUT IT BACK, CATWOMAN.
I KNOW THAT MANLY GROWL...

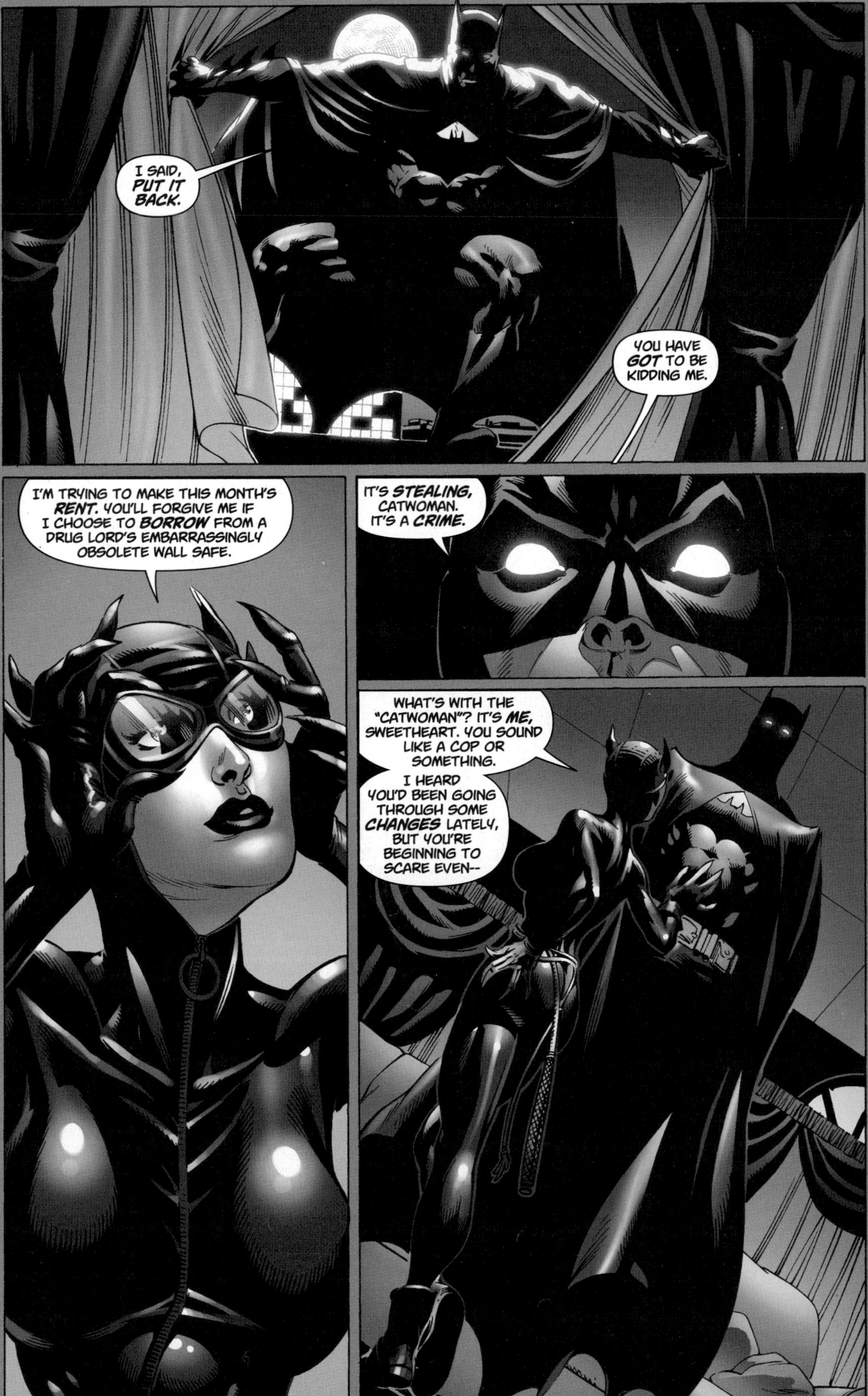
I SAID, PUT IT BACK.
YOU HAVE GOT TO BE KIDDING ME.
I'M TRYING TO MAKE THIS MONTH'S RENT. YOU'LL FORGIVE ME IF I CHOOSE TO BORROW FROM A DRUG LORD'S EMBARRASSINGLY OBSOLETE WALL SAFE.
IT'S STEALING, CATWOMAN. IT'S A CRIME.
WHAT'S WITH THE "CATWOMAN"? IT'S ME, SWEETHEART. YOU SOUND LIKE A COP OR SOMETHING.
I HEARD YOU'D BEEN GOING THROUGH SOME CHANGES LATELY, BUT YOU'RE BEGINNING TO SCARE EVEN--

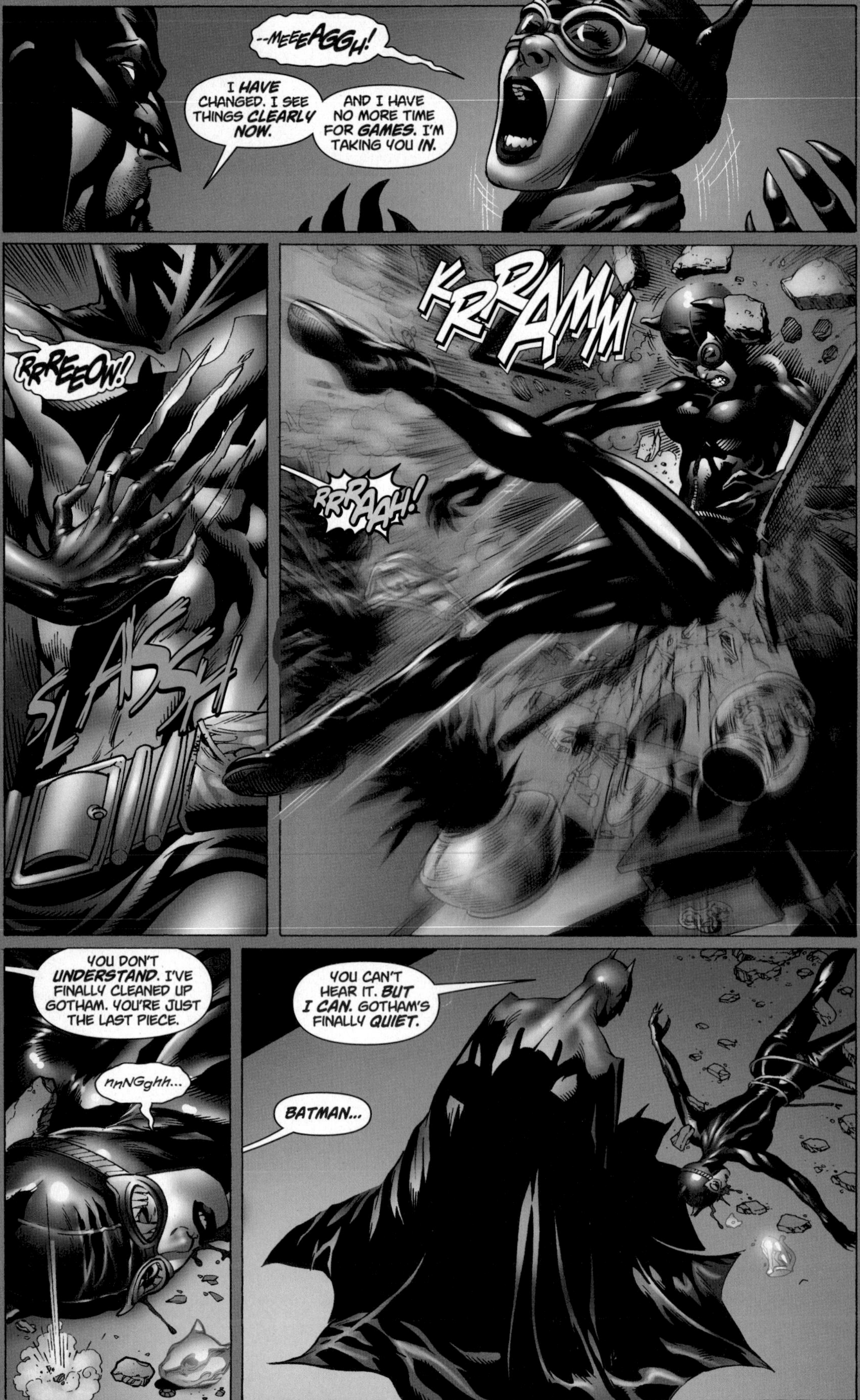
--MEEEAGGH!
I HAVE CHANGED. I SEE THINGS CLEARLY NOW.
AND I HAVE NO MORE TIME FOR GAMES. I'M TAKING YOU IN.
RRREEEOW!
SLASH
KRRAMM
RRRAAH!
YOU DON'T UNDERSTAND. I'VE FINALLY CLEANED UP GOTHAM. YOU'RE JUST THE LAST PIECE.
nnNGghh...
BATMAN...
YOU CAN'T HEAR IT. BUT I CAN. GOTHAM'S FINALLY QUIET.

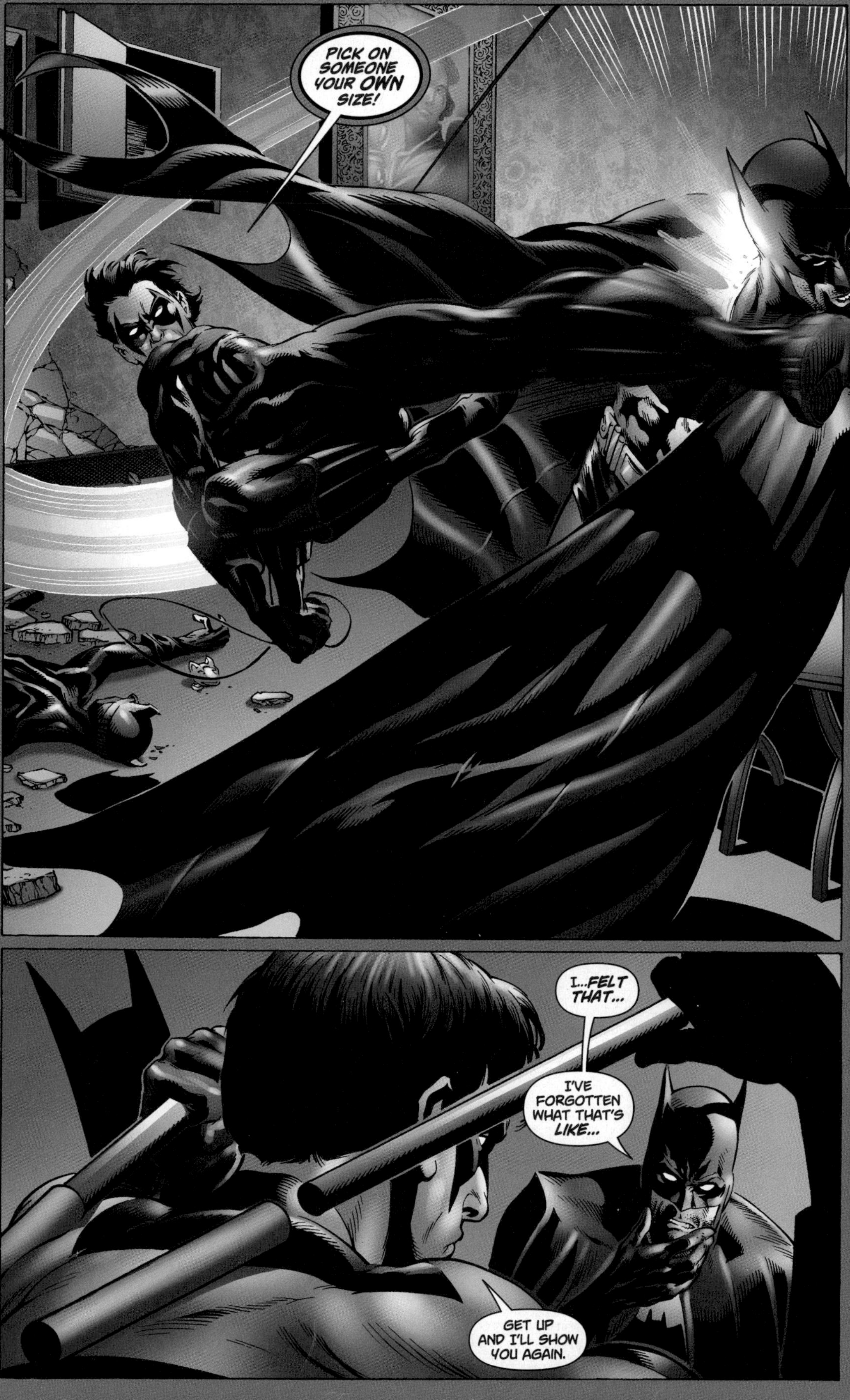
PICK ON SOMEONE YOUR OWN SIZE!
I...FELT THAT...
I'VE FORGOTTEN WHAT THAT'S LIKE...
GET UP AND I'LL SHOW YOU AGAIN.

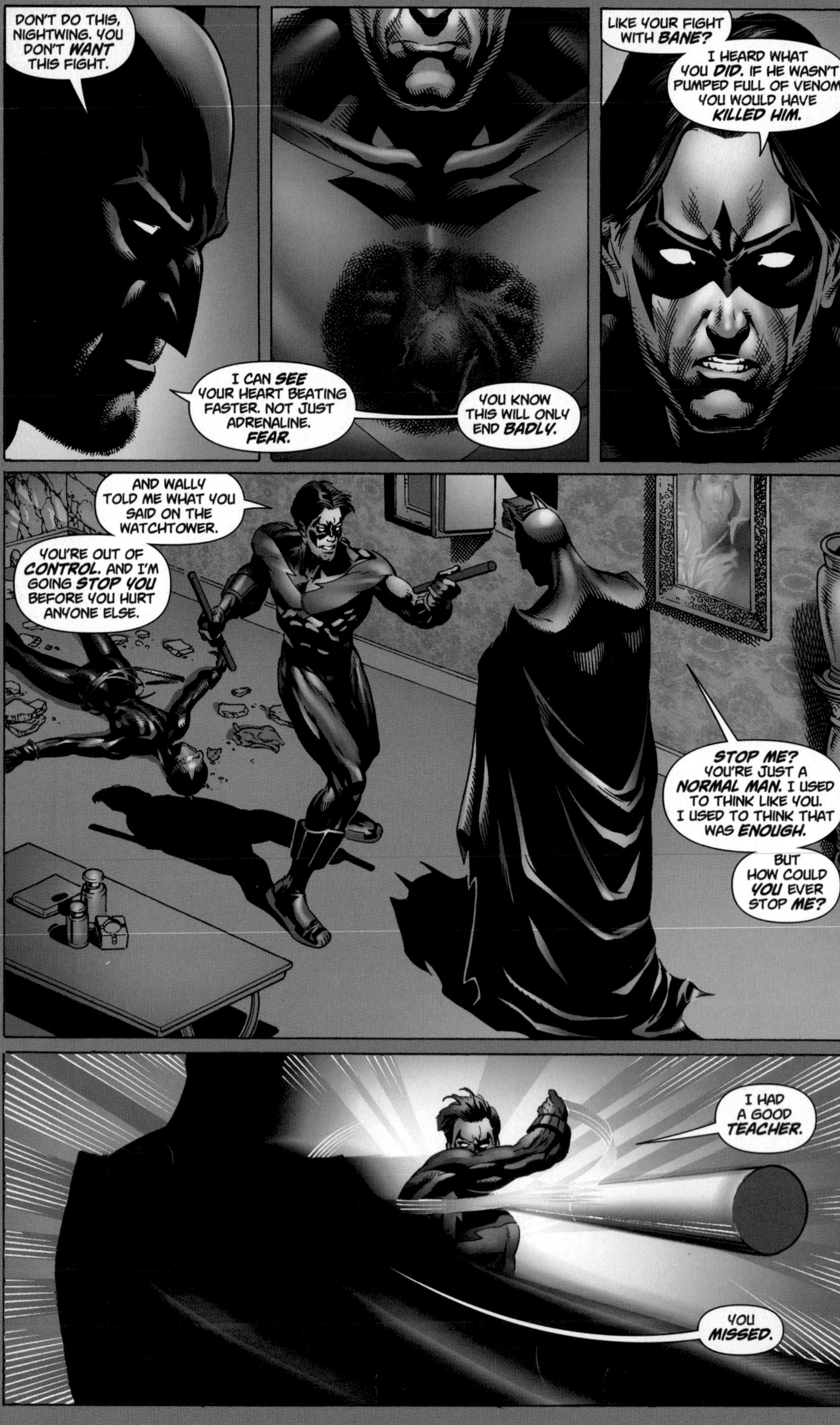
DON'T DO THIS, NIGHTWING. YOU DON'T WANT THIS FIGHT.
I CAN SEE YOUR HEART BEATING FASTER. NOT JUST ADRENALINE. FEAR.
YOU KNOW THIS WILL ONLY END BADLY.
LIKE YOUR FIGHT WITH BANE?
I HEARD WHAT YOU DID. IF HE WASN'T PUMPED FULL OF VENOM YOU WOULD HAVE KILLED HIM.
AND WALLY TOLD ME WHAT YOU SAID ON THE WATCHTOWER.
YOU'RE OUT OF CONTROL. AND I'M GOING STOP YOU BEFORE YOU HURT ANYONE ELSE.
STOP ME? YOU'RE JUST A NORMAL MAN. I USED TO THINK LIKE YOU. I USED TO THINK THAT WAS ENOUGH.
BUT HOW COULD YOU EVER STOP ME?
I HAD A GOOD TEACHER.
YOU MISSED.

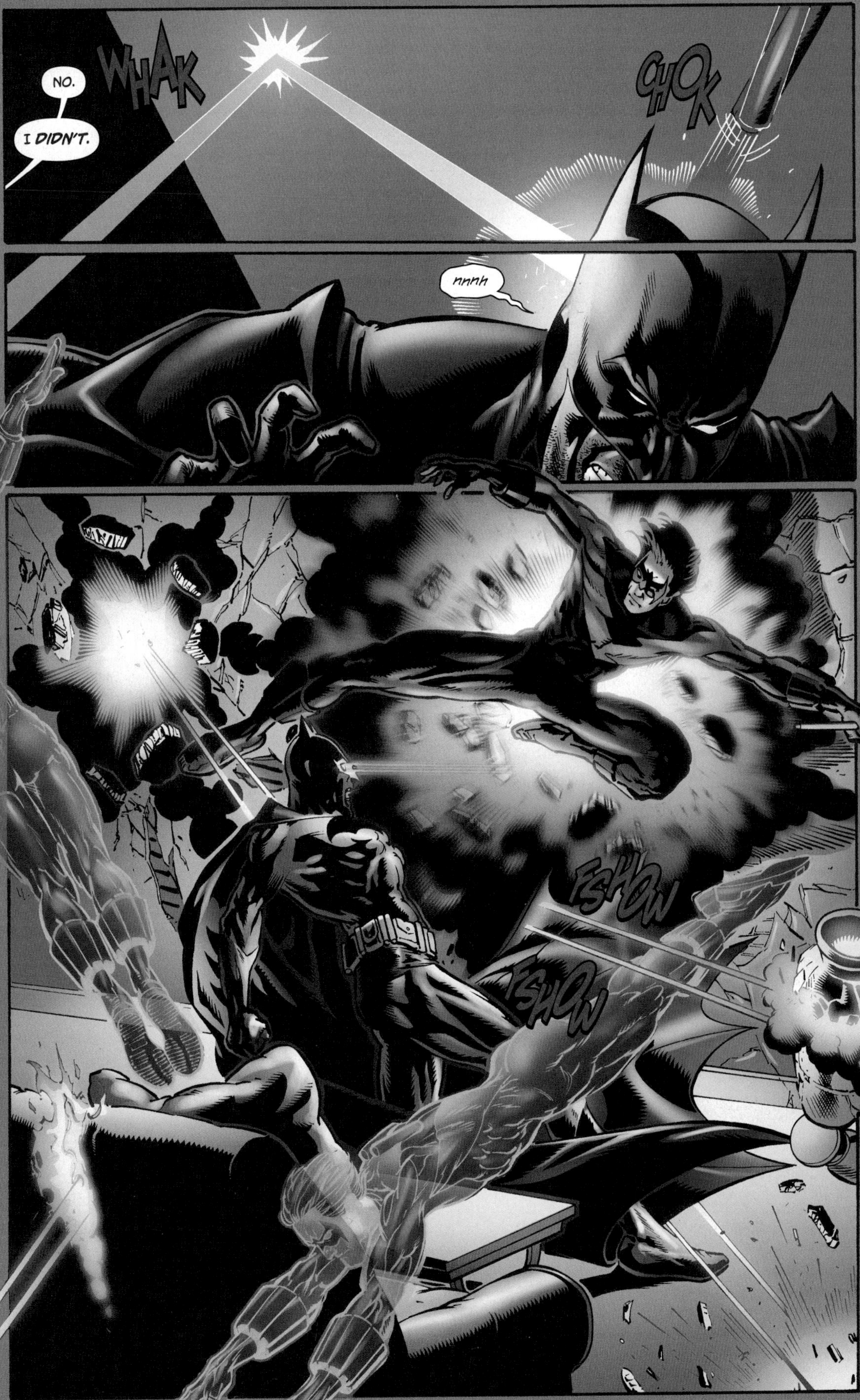

WHAK
NO.
I DIDN'T.
CHOK
nnnh
FSHOW
FSHOW

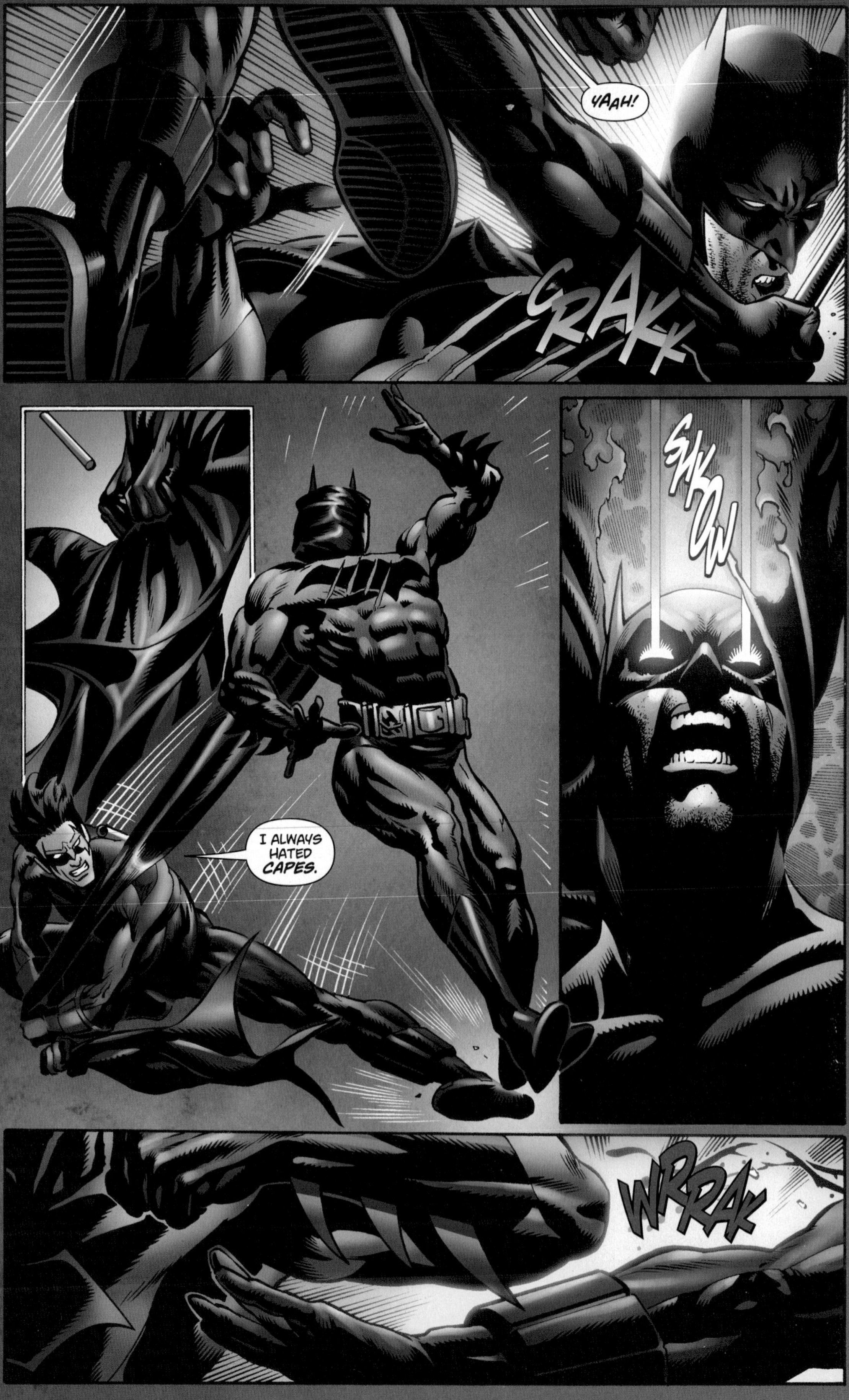
YAAH!
CRAKK
I ALWAYS HATED CAPES.
SKAKOW
WRRAK

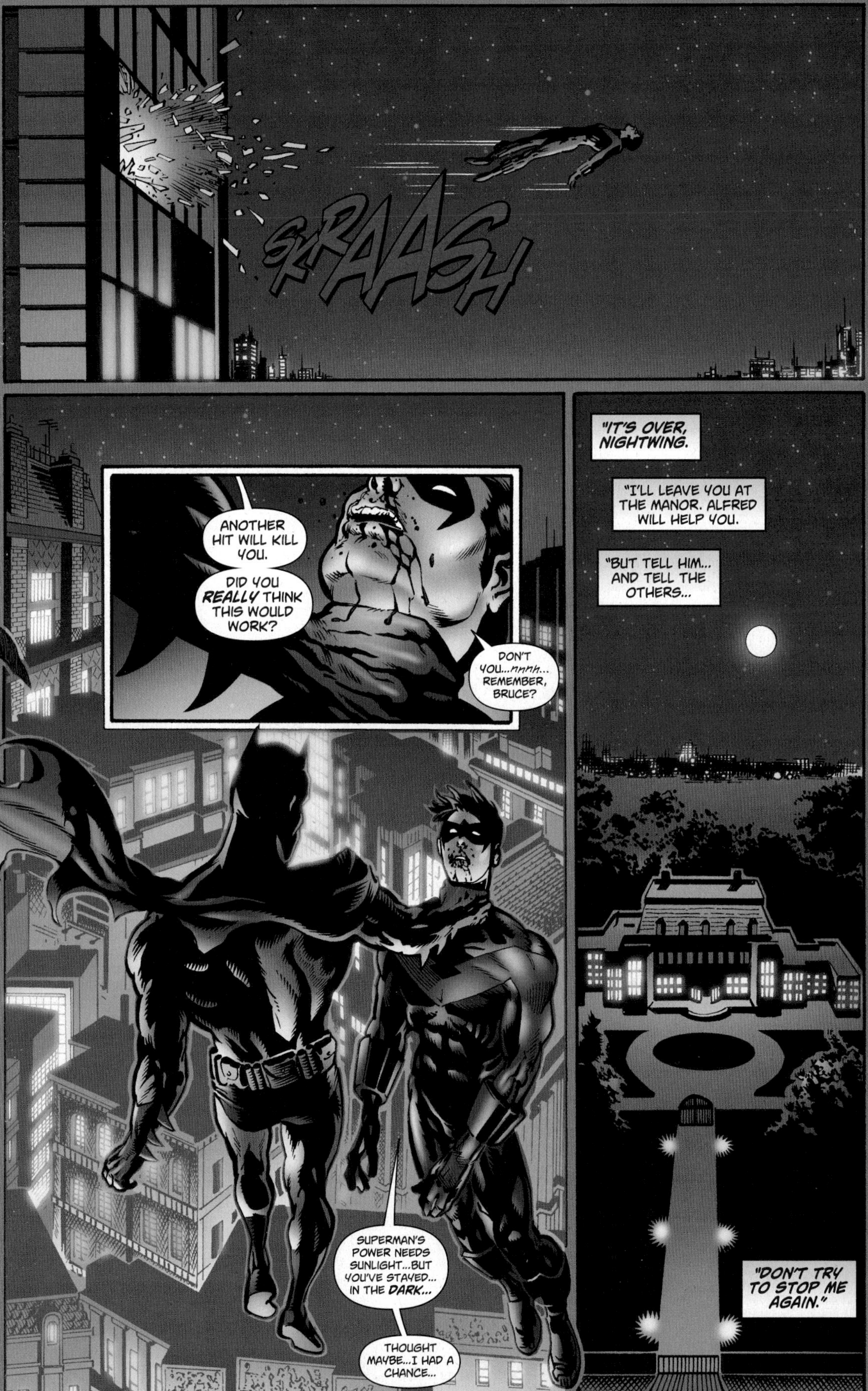
SKRAAASH
ANOTHER HIT WILL KILL YOU.
DID YOU *REALLY* THINK THIS WOULD WORK?
DON'T YOU...*nnnh*... REMEMBER, BRUCE?
SUPERMAN'S POWER NEEDS SUNLIGHT...BUT YOU'VE STAYED... IN THE *DARK*...
THOUGHT MAYBE...I HAD A CHANCE...
"IT'S OVER, NIGHTWING.
"I'LL LEAVE YOU AT THE MANOR. ALFRED WILL HELP YOU.
"BUT TELL HIM... AND TELL THE OTHERS...
"DON'T TRY TO STOP ME AGAIN."

MULTIPLE FRACTURES, LACERATIONS, MISSING TEETH...

EVEN UNDER THE CIRCUMSTANCES...

I'M NOT SURE I'LL *EVER FORGIVE* MASTER BRUCE FOR THIS.

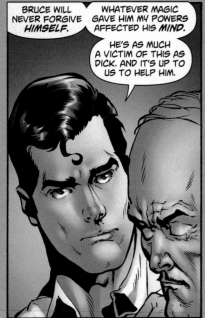

BRUCE WILL NEVER FORGIVE *HIMSELF.*

WHATEVER MAGIC GAVE HIM MY POWERS AFFECTED HIS *MIND.*

HE'S AS MUCH A VICTIM OF THIS AS DICK. AND IT'S UP TO US TO HELP HIM.

OKAY, HERE WE GO!

BRUCE WOULD FREAK OUT IF HE KNEW I WAS USING HIS COMPUTER FOR THIS KINDA THING, BUT I'VE CREATED A *MAGIC MAP.*

WITH ZATANNA'S HELP WE'VE PINPOINTED ALL OF THE MAGICAL ACTIVITY ON EARTH SINCE SILVER BANSHEE'S ATTACK.

NEVER THOUGHT I'D BE CROSS-REFERENCING INTERPOL WITH THE OBLIVION BAR, BUT THIS IS OUR BEST SHOT AT TRACKING DOWN BANSHEE.

*EXCELLENT* WORK, TIM. I'M NOT RESTING UNTIL WE FIND HER AND REVERSE HER SPELL.

LEAVE THAT TO ME AND ROBIN, SUPERMAN. YOU'RE IN NO SHAPE TO GO CHASING BANSHEE.

I'M FINE, ZATANNA. AND I CAN'T JUST SIT HERE WHILE BRUCE IS IN *TROUBLE*.

JUST BECAUSE MY POWERS ARE GONE DOESN'T MEAN I'M GIVING UP THE *FIGHT*.

I EXPECTED AS MUCH, MASTER CLARK. AND I PREPARED ACCORDINGLY.

WITH MASTER BRUCE GONE, I HAVE FOUND MYSELF WITH TIME TO SPARE. AND YOU KNOW WHAT THEY SAY ABOUT IDLE HANDS.

"I THOUGHT IT BEST TO PROVIDE YOU WITH APPROPRIATE PROTECTION SHOULD IT BECOME NECESSARY.

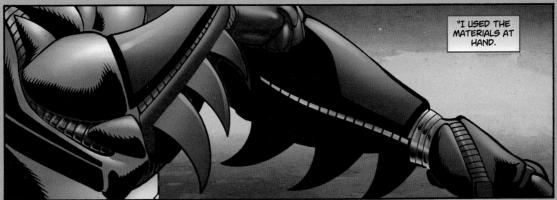

"I USED THE MATERIALS AT HAND.

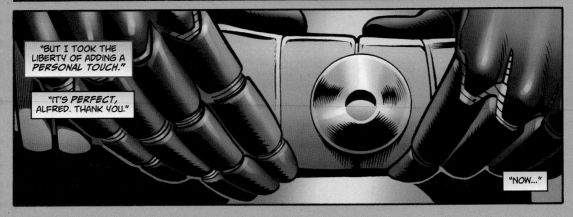

"BUT I TOOK THE LIBERTY OF ADDING A *PERSONAL TOUCH*."

"IT'S *PERFECT*, ALFRED. THANK YOU."

"NOW..."

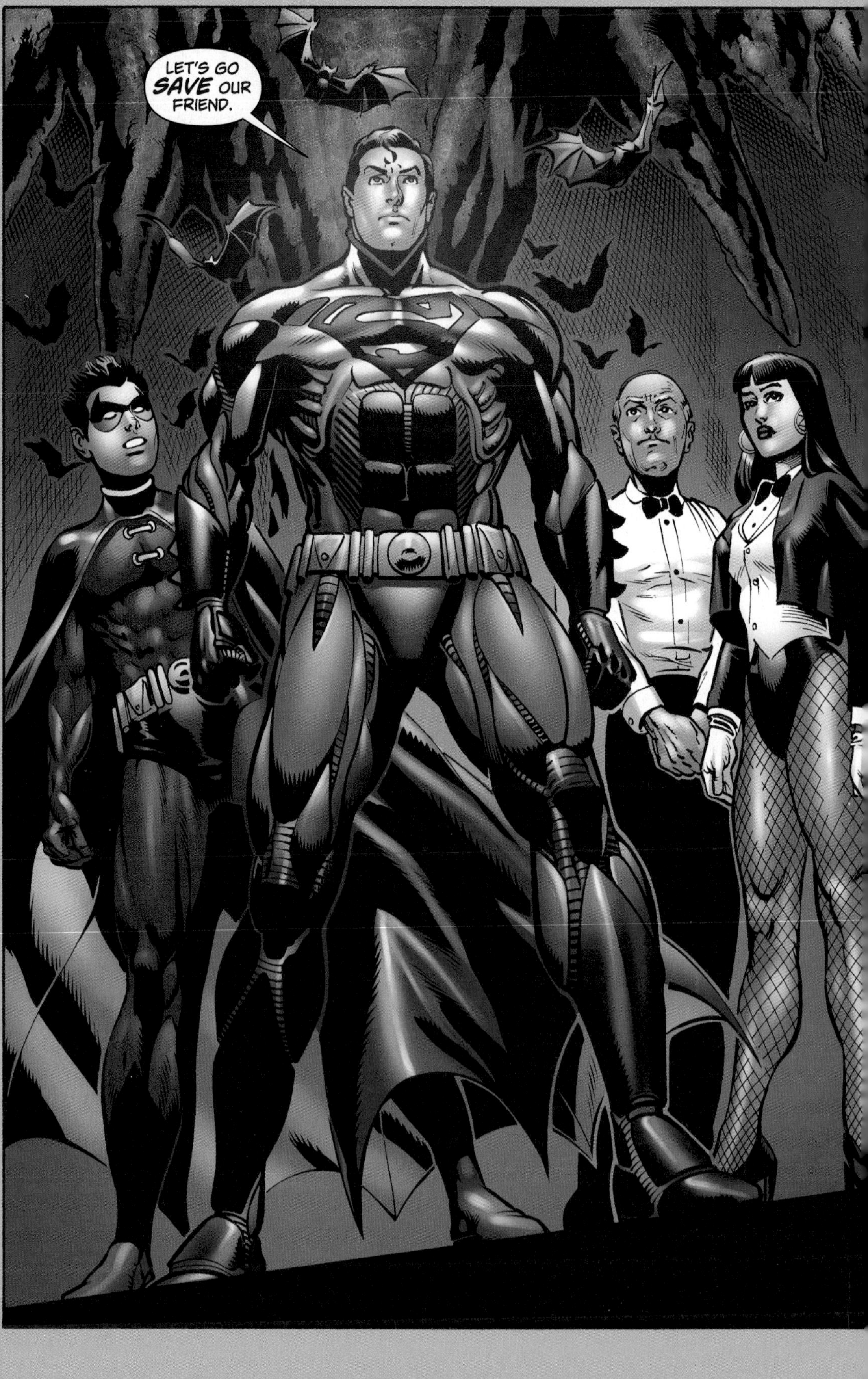
LET'S GO SAVE OUR FRIEND.

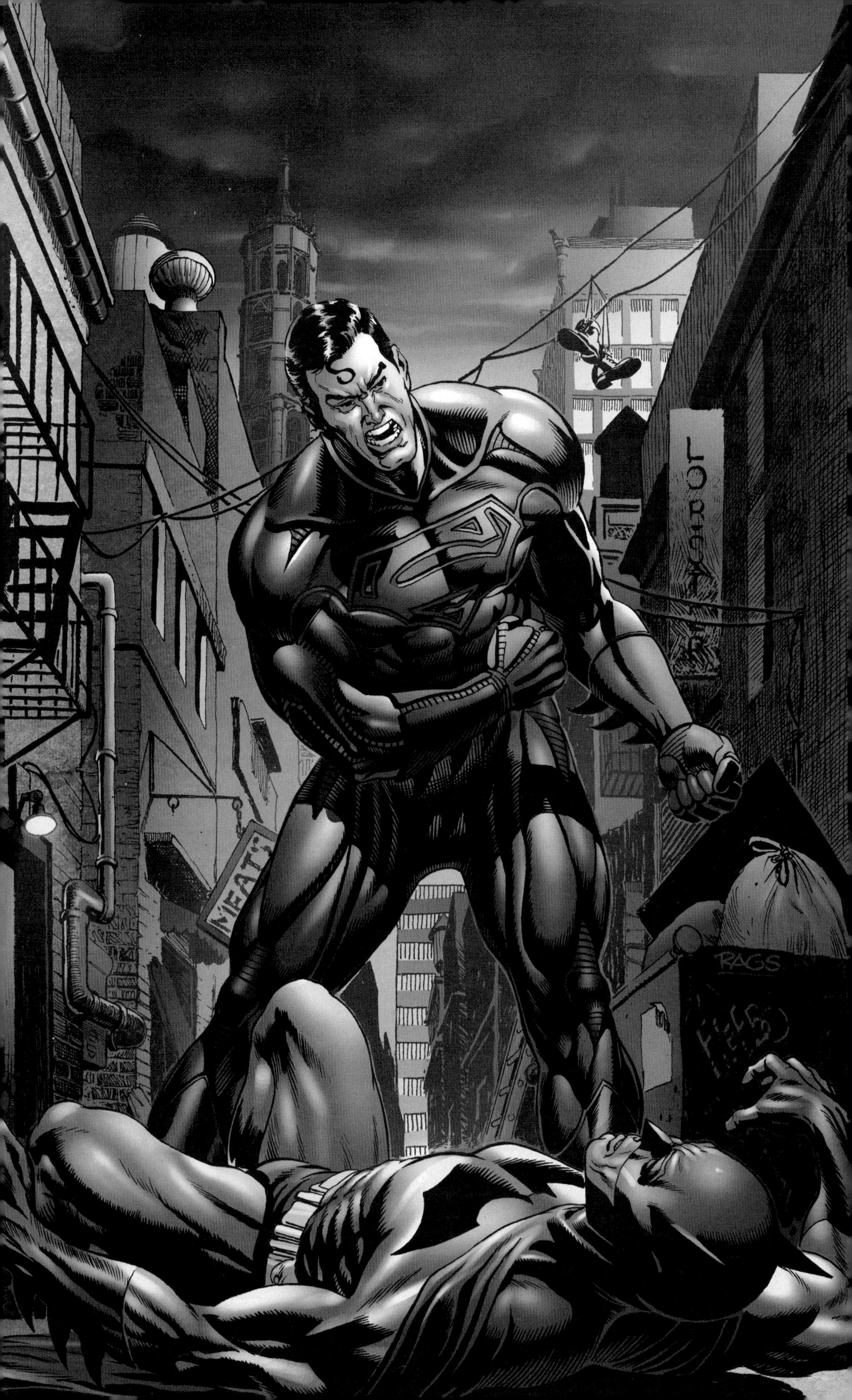
MEATS
RAGS

SUPERMAN/BATMAN 56

SUPERBAT
part four

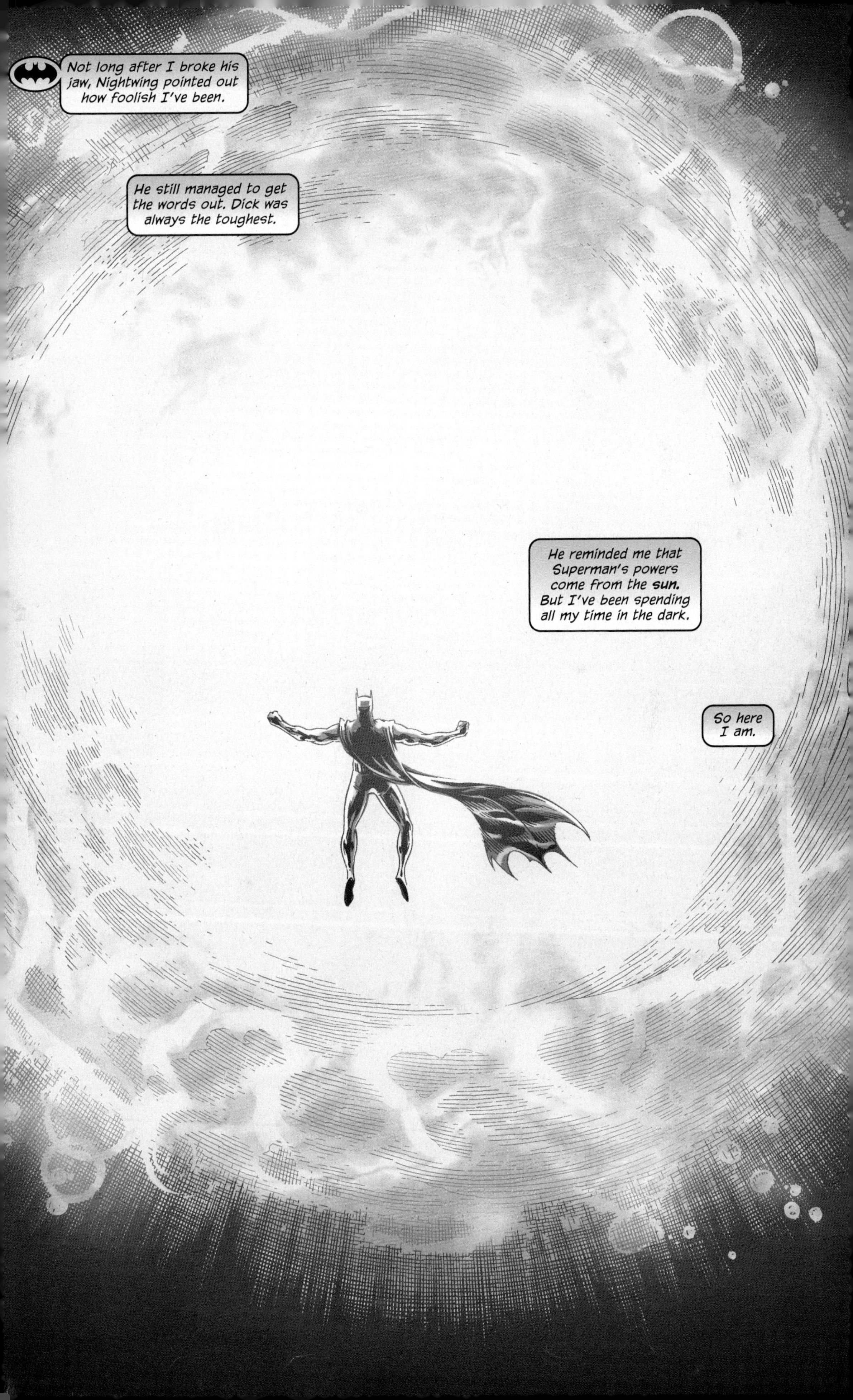
Not long after I broke his jaw, Nightwing pointed out how foolish I've been.
He still managed to get the words out. Dick was always the toughest.
He reminded me that Superman's powers come from the **sun.** But I've been spending all my time in the dark.
So here I am.

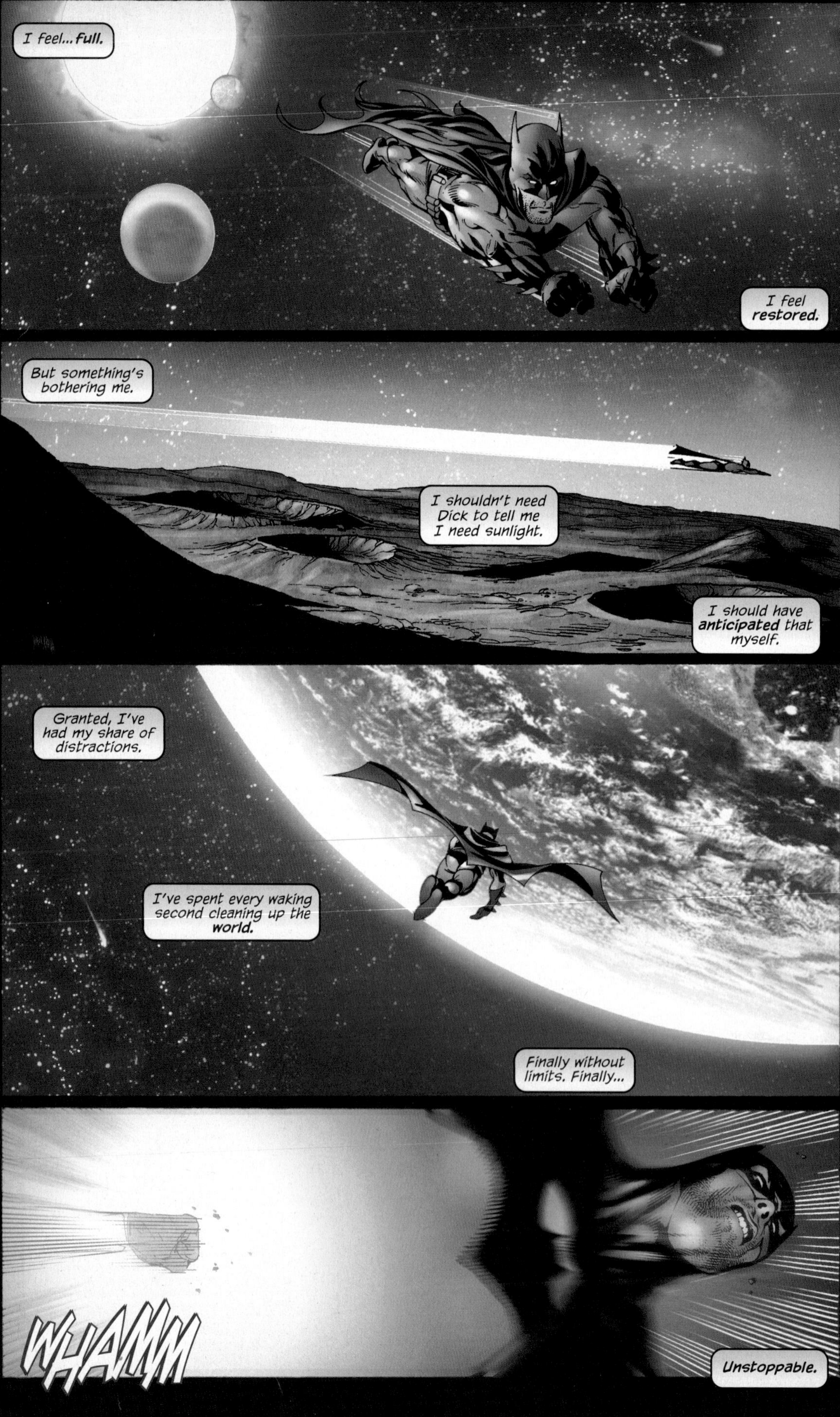
I feel... **full.**
I feel **restored.**
But something's bothering me.
I shouldn't need Dick to tell me I need sunlight.
I should have **anticipated** that myself.
Granted, I've had my share of distractions.
I've spent every waking second cleaning up the **world.**
Finally without limits. Finally...
WHAMM
Unstoppable.

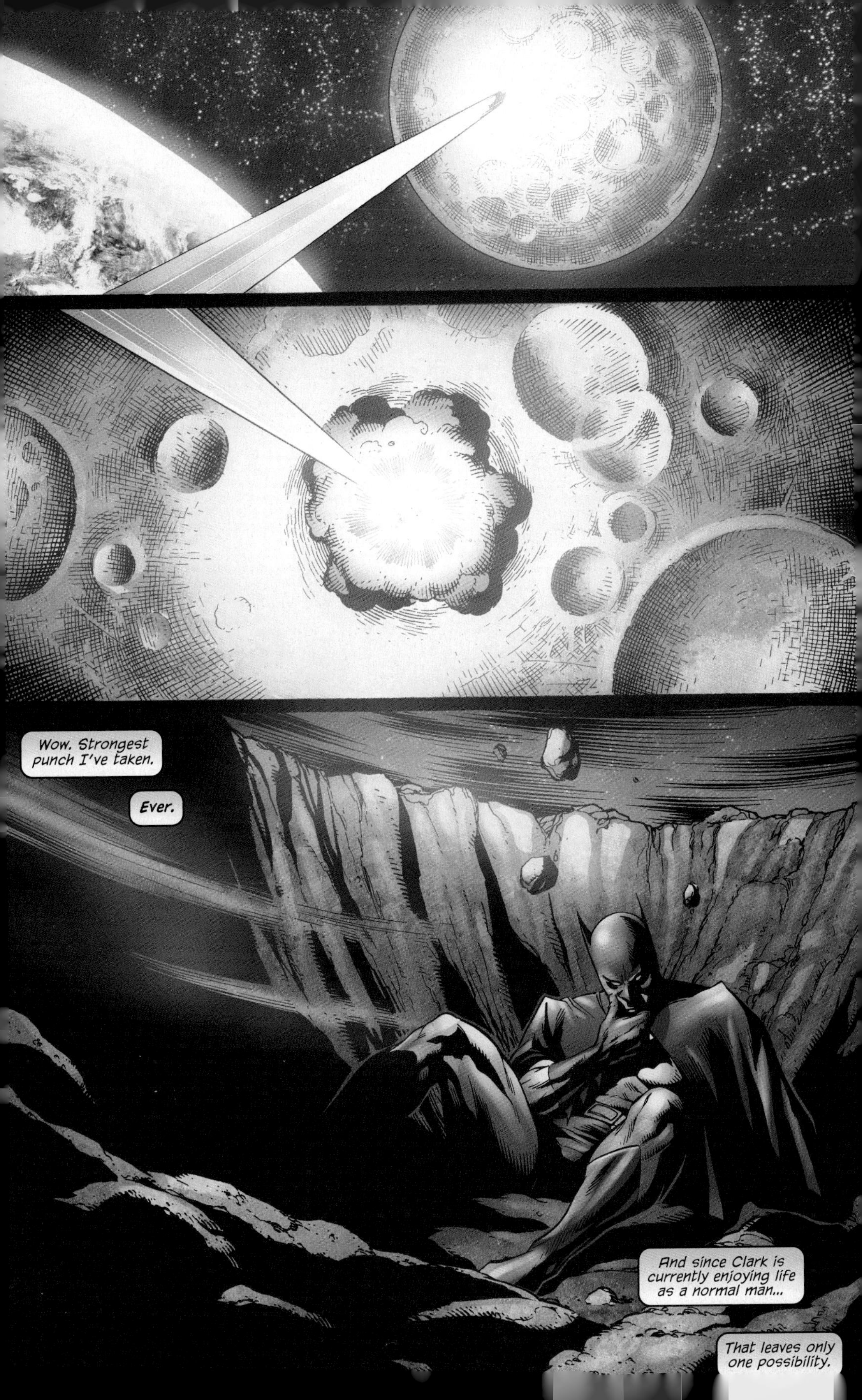
Wow. Strongest punch I've taken.
Ever.
And since Clark is currently enjoying life as a normal man...
That leaves only one possibility.

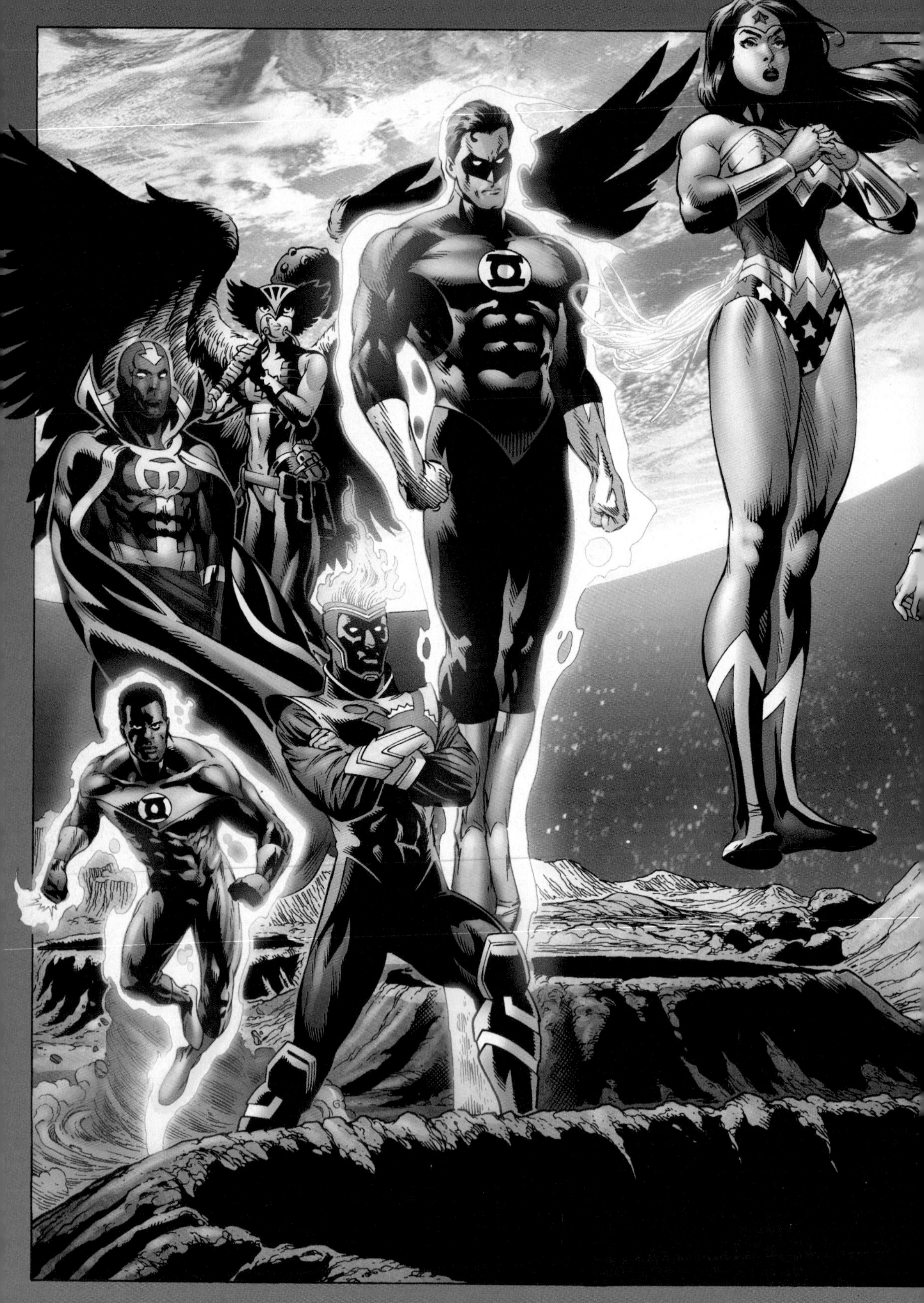

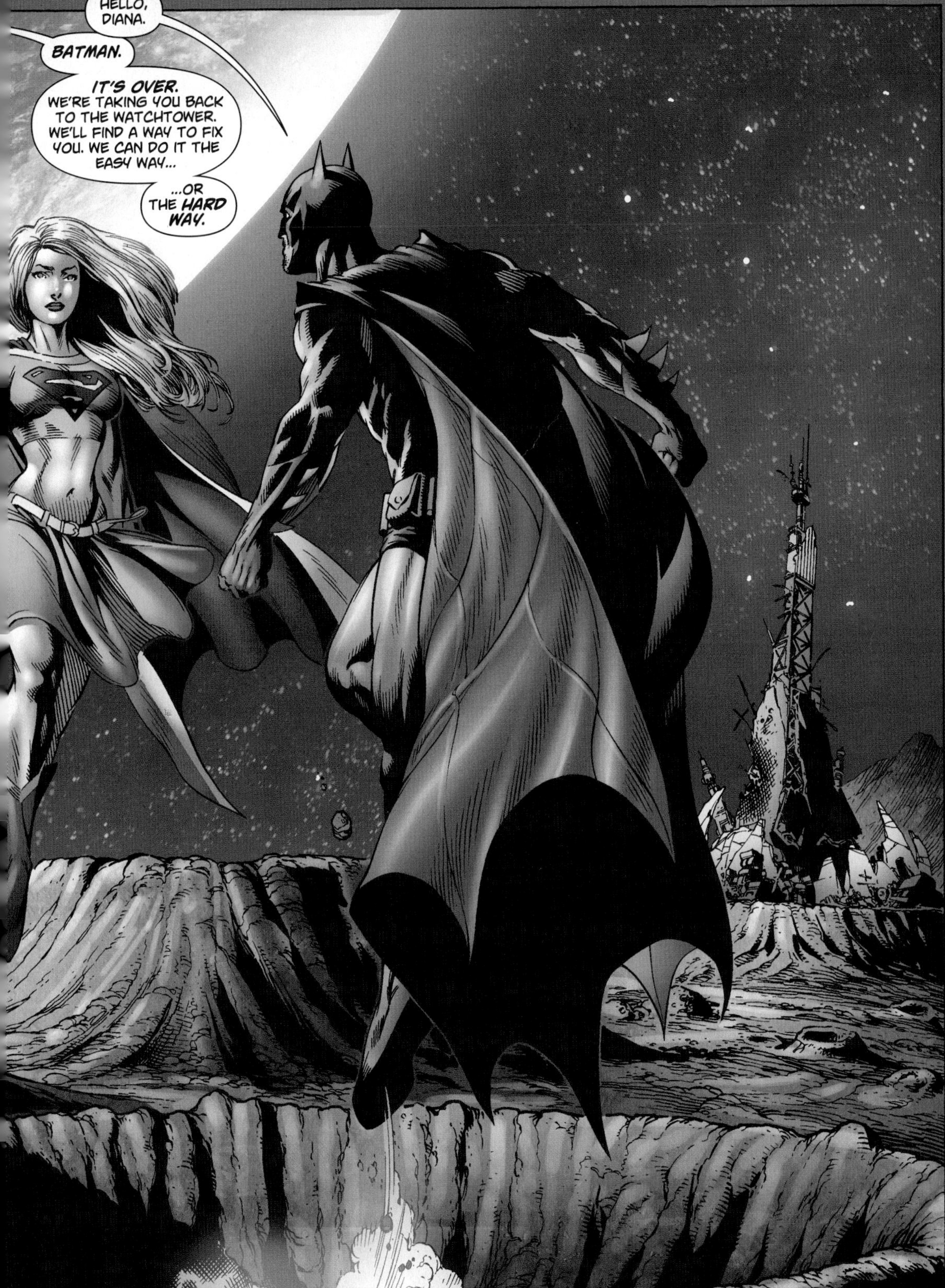
HELLO, DIANA.
BATMAN.
IT'S OVER. WE'RE TAKING YOU BACK TO THE WATCHTOWER. WE'LL FIND A WAY TO FIX YOU. WE CAN DO IT THE EASY WAY...
...OR THE HARD WAY.

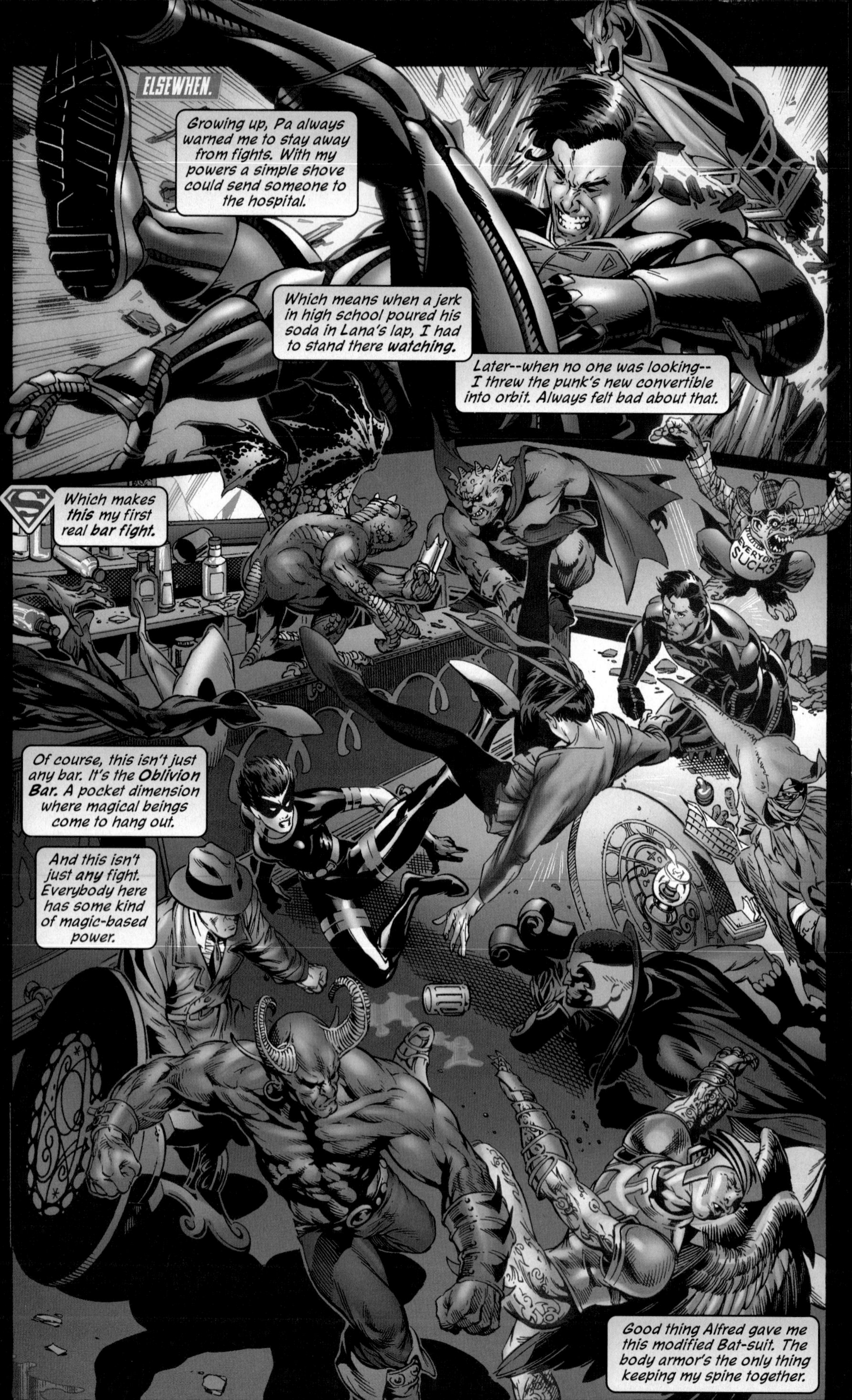
ELSEWHEN.
Growing up, Pa always warned me to stay away from fights. With my powers a simple shove could send someone to the hospital.
Which means when a jerk in high school poured his soda in Lana's lap, I had to stand there watching.
Later--when no one was looking--I threw the punk's new convertible into orbit. Always felt bad about that.
Which makes this my first real bar fight.
EVERYONE SUCKS
Of course, this isn't just any bar. It's the Oblivion Bar. A pocket dimension where magical beings come to hang out.
And this isn't just any fight. Everybody here has some kind of magic-based power.
Good thing Alfred gave me this modified Bat-suit. The body armor's the only thing keeping my spine together.

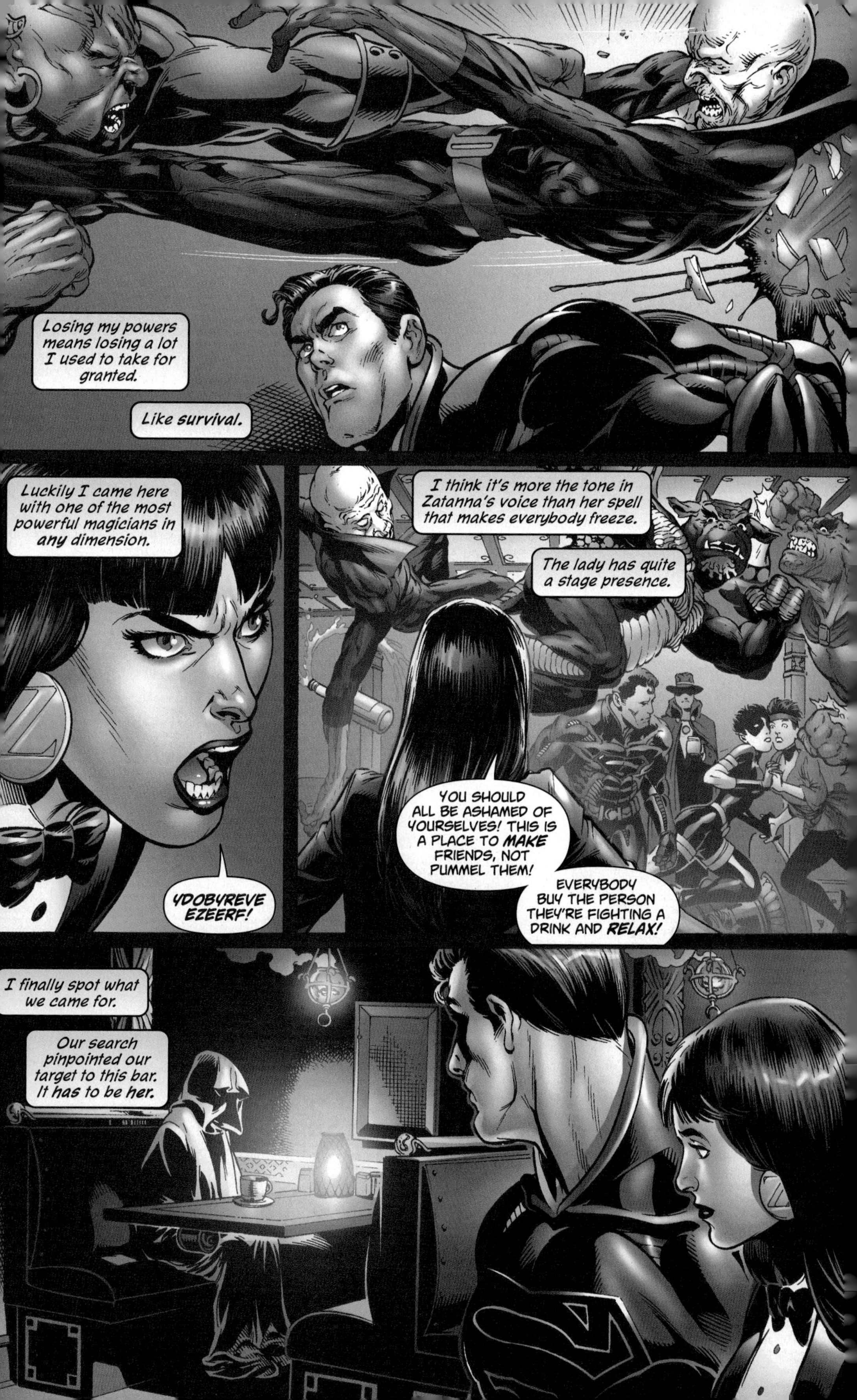
Losing my powers means losing a lot I used to take for granted.
Like survival.
Luckily I came here with one of the most powerful magicians in any dimension.
YDOBYREVE EZEERF!
I think it's more the tone in Zatanna's voice than her spell that makes everybody freeze.
The lady has quite a stage presence.
YOU SHOULD ALL BE ASHAMED OF YOURSELVES! THIS IS A PLACE TO MAKE FRIENDS, NOT PUMMEL THEM!
EVERYBODY BUY THE PERSON THEY'RE FIGHTING A DRINK AND RELAX!
I finally spot what we came for.
Our search pinpointed our target to this bar. It has to be her.

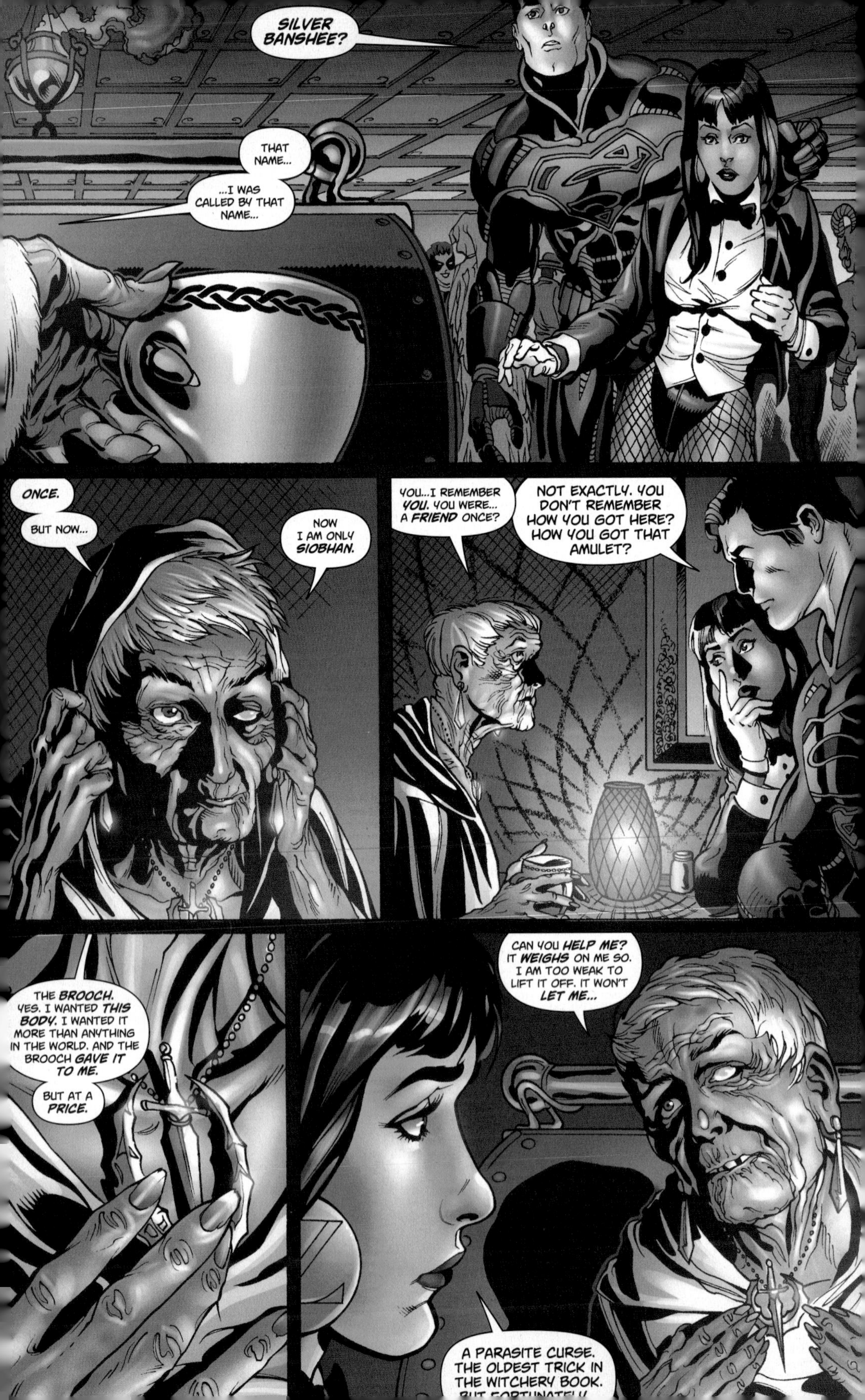
SILVER BANSHEE?
THAT NAME...
...I WAS CALLED BY THAT NAME...
ONCE.
BUT NOW...
NOW I AM ONLY SIOBHAN.
YOU...I REMEMBER YOU. YOU WERE... A FRIEND ONCE?
NOT EXACTLY. YOU DON'T REMEMBER HOW YOU GOT HERE? HOW YOU GOT THAT AMULET?
THE BROOCH. YES. I WANTED THIS BODY. I WANTED IT MORE THAN ANYTHING IN THE WORLD. AND THE BROOCH GAVE IT TO ME.
BUT AT A PRICE.
CAN YOU HELP ME? IT WEIGHS ON ME SO. I AM TOO WEAK TO LIFT IT OFF. IT WON'T LET ME...
A PARASITE CURSE. THE OLDEST TRICK IN THE WITCHERY BOOK.

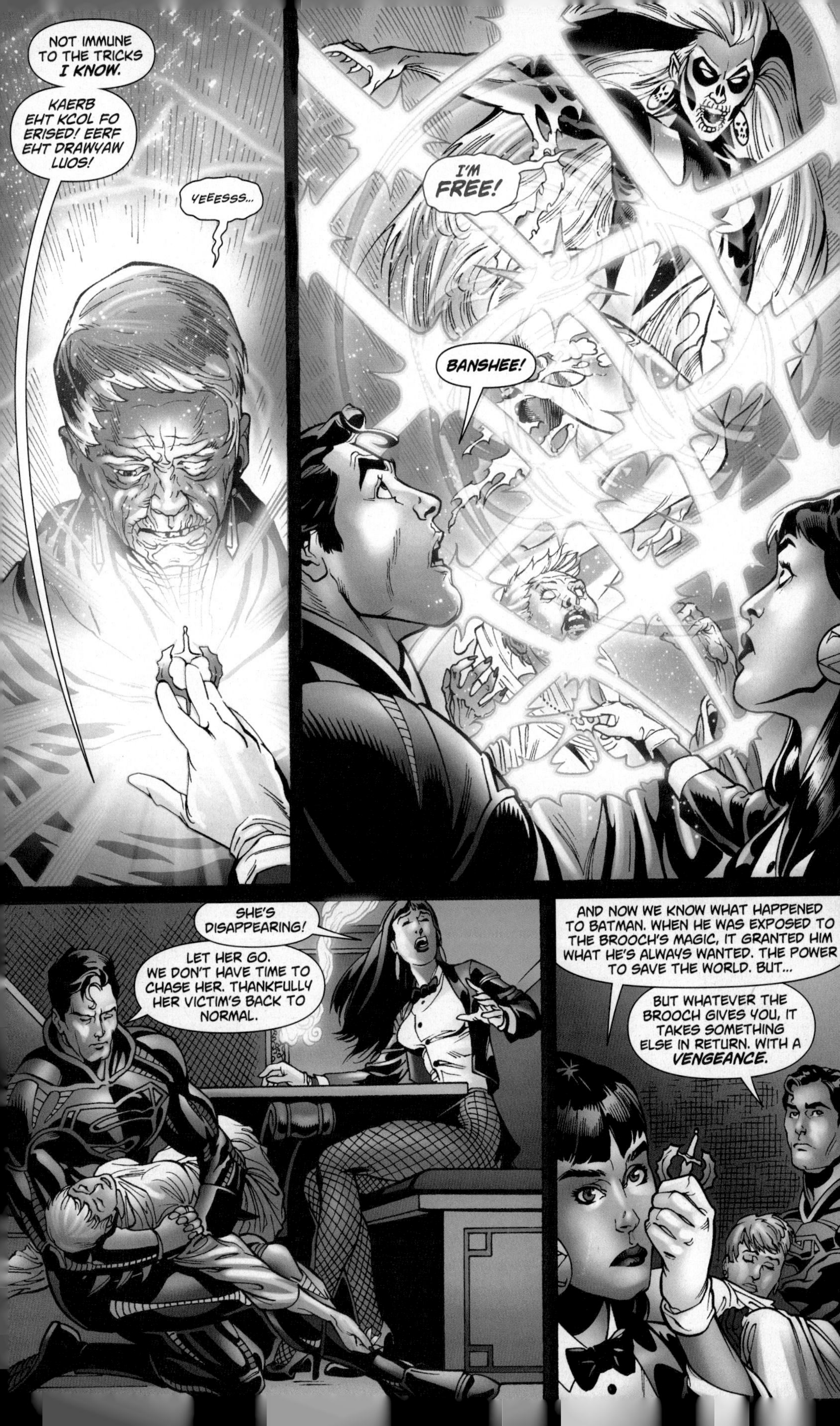
NOT IMMUNE TO THE TRICKS I KNOW.
KAERB EHT KCOL FO ERISED! EERF EHT DRAWYAW LUOS!
YEEESSS...
I'M FREE!
BANSHEE!
SHE'S DISAPPEARING!
LET HER GO. WE DON'T HAVE TIME TO CHASE HER. THANKFULLY HER VICTIM'S BACK TO NORMAL.
AND NOW WE KNOW WHAT HAPPENED TO BATMAN. WHEN HE WAS EXPOSED TO THE BROOCH'S MAGIC, IT GRANTED HIM WHAT HE'S ALWAYS WANTED. THE POWER TO SAVE THE WORLD. BUT...
BUT WHATEVER THE BROOCH GIVES YOU, IT TAKES SOMETHING ELSE IN RETURN. WITH A VENGEANCE.

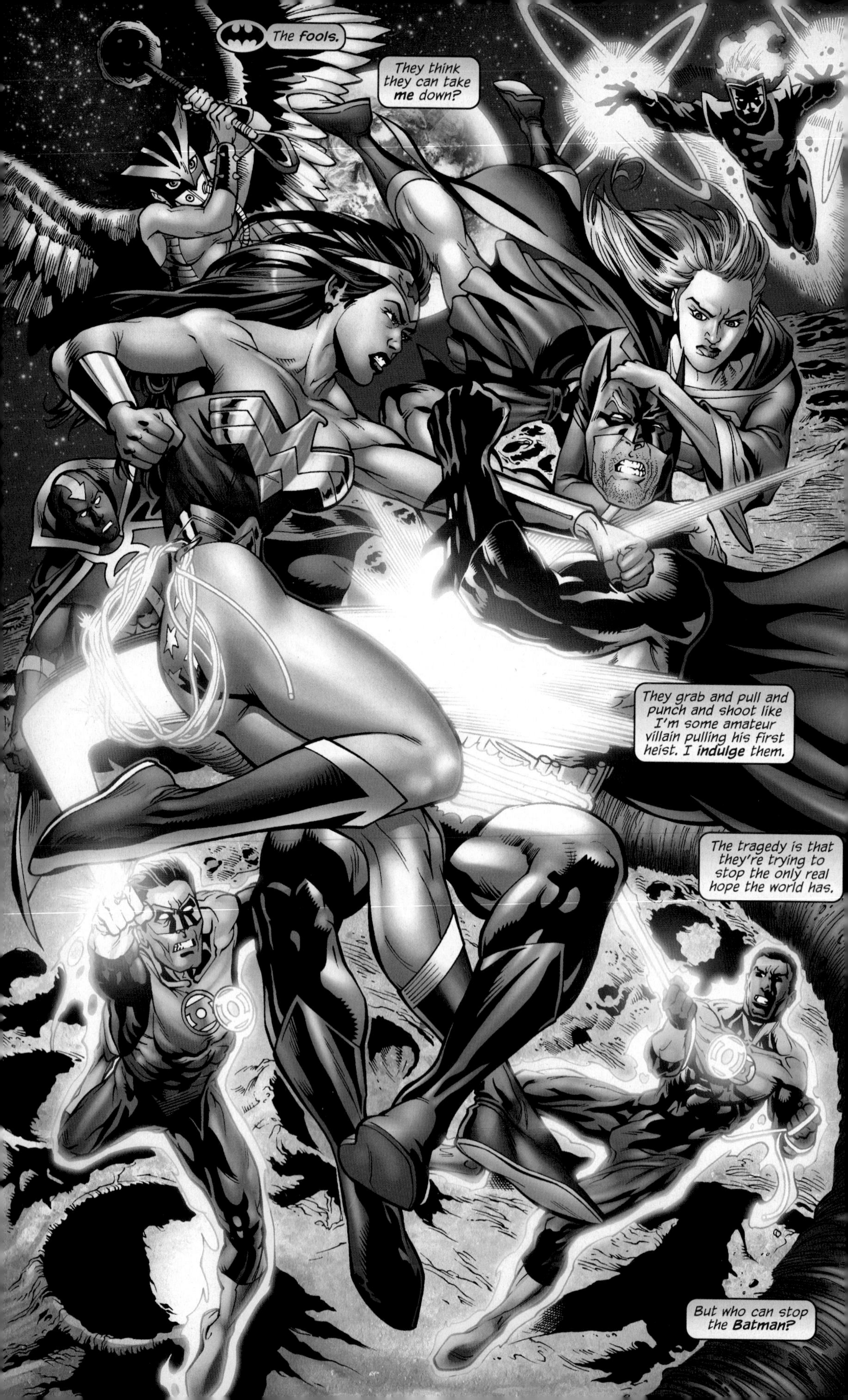
The fools.
They think they can take **me** down?
They grab and pull and punch and shoot like I'm some amateur villain pulling his first heist. I **indulge** them.
The tragedy is that they're trying to stop the only real hope the world has.
But who can stop the **Batman?**

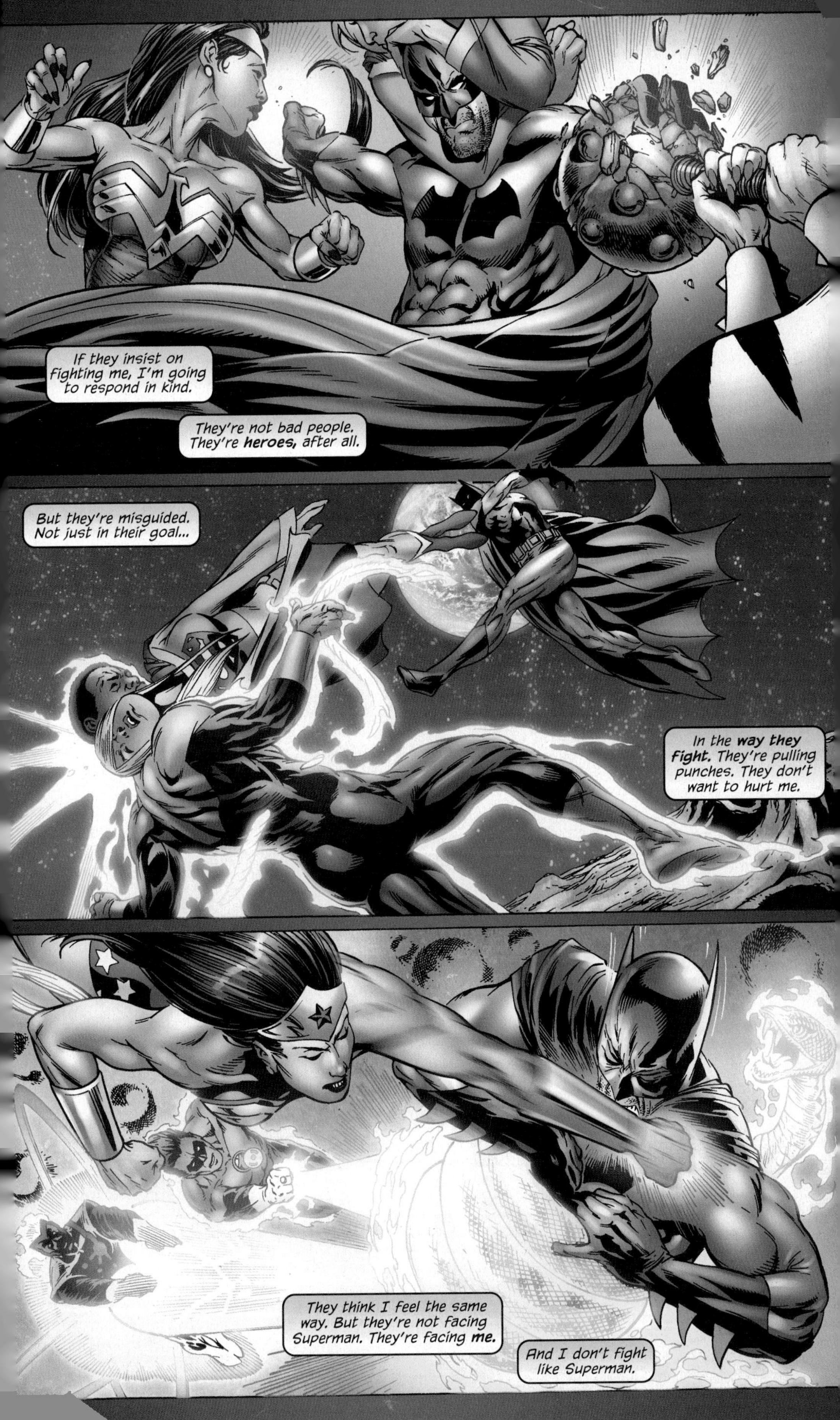

If they insist on fighting me, I'm going to respond in kind.
They're not bad people. They're **heroes,** after all.
But they're misguided. Not just in their goal...
In the **way they fight.** They're pulling punches. They don't want to hurt me.
They think I feel the same way. But they're not facing Superman. They're facing **me.**
And I don't fight like Superman.

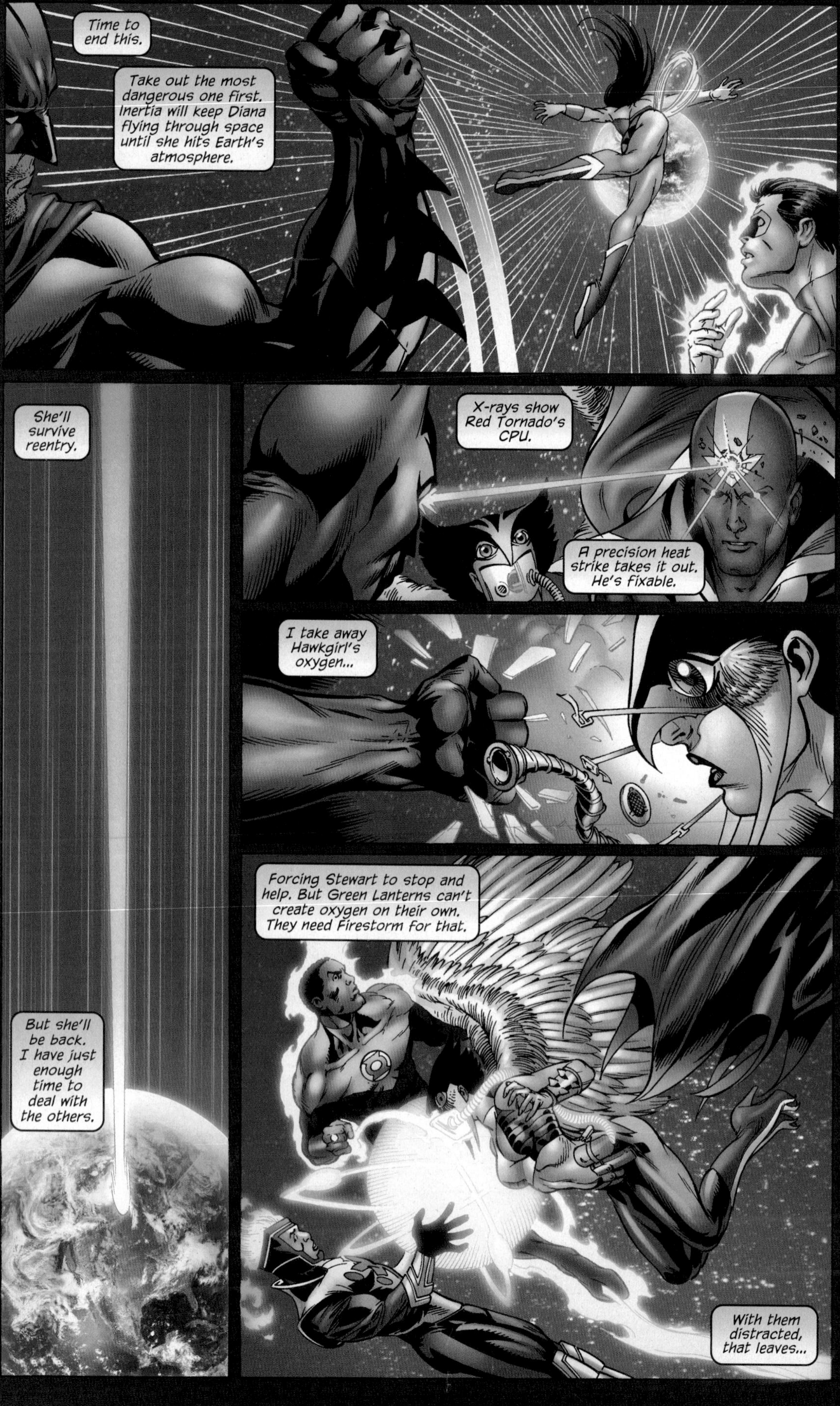
Time to end this.
Take out the most dangerous one first. Inertia will keep Diana flying through space until she hits Earth's atmosphere.
She'll survive reentry.
X-rays show Red Tornado's CPU.
A precision heat strike takes it out. He's fixable.
I take away Hawkgirl's oxygen...
Forcing Stewart to stop and help. But Green Lanterns can't create oxygen on their own. They need Firestorm for that.
But she'll be back. I have just enough time to deal with the others.
With them distracted, that leaves...

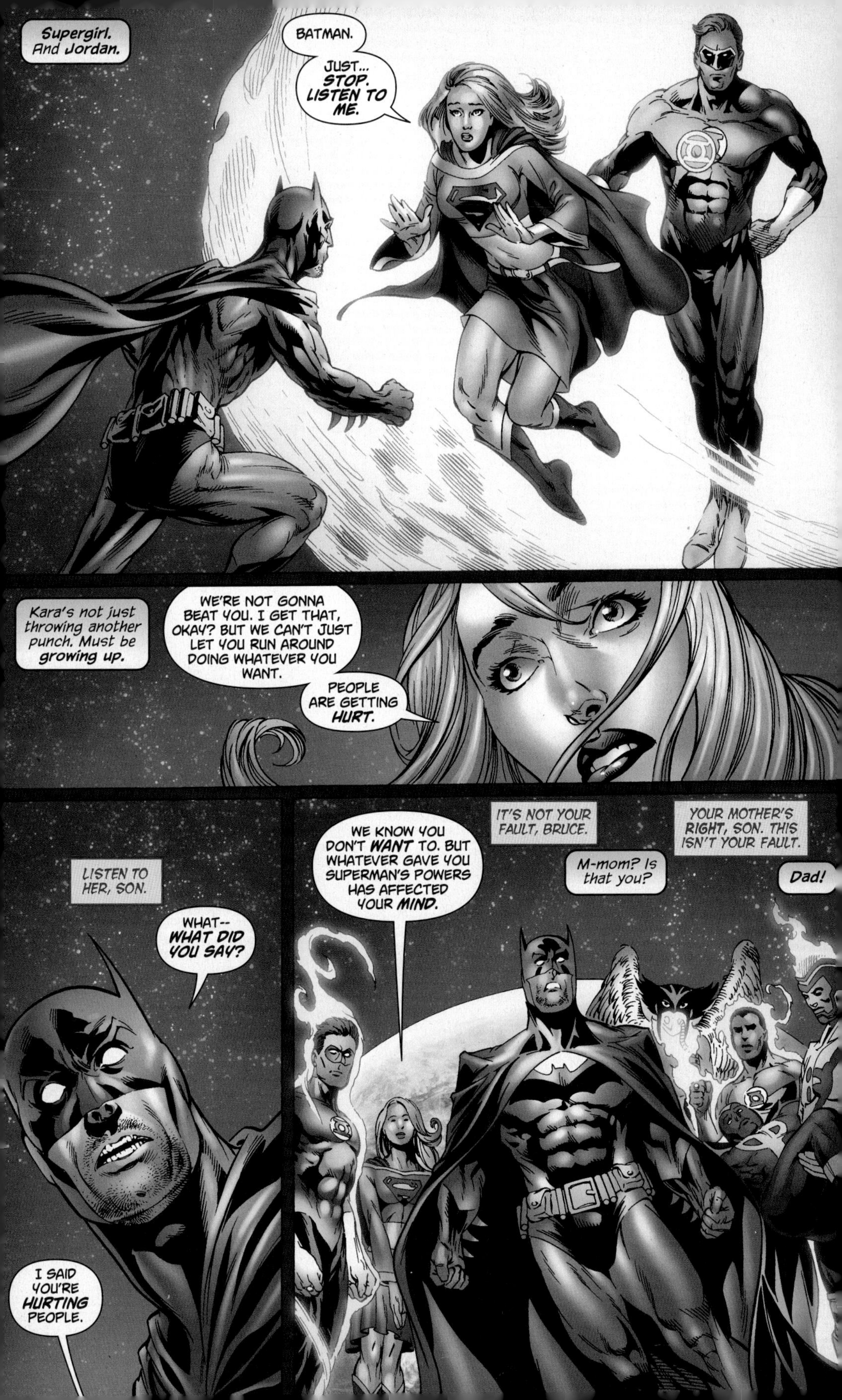
Supergirl. And Jordan.
BATMAN.
JUST... STOP. LISTEN TO ME.
Kara's not just throwing another punch. Must be growing up.
WE'RE NOT GONNA BEAT YOU. I GET THAT, OKAY? BUT WE CAN'T JUST LET YOU RUN AROUND DOING WHATEVER YOU WANT.
PEOPLE ARE GETTING HURT.
LISTEN TO HER, SON.
WHAT-- WHAT DID YOU SAY?
I SAID YOU'RE HURTING PEOPLE.
WE KNOW YOU DON'T WANT TO. BUT WHATEVER GAVE YOU SUPERMAN'S POWERS HAS AFFECTED YOUR MIND.
IT'S NOT YOUR FAULT, BRUCE.
M-mom? Is that you?
YOUR MOTHER'S RIGHT, SON. THIS ISN'T YOUR FAULT.
Dad!

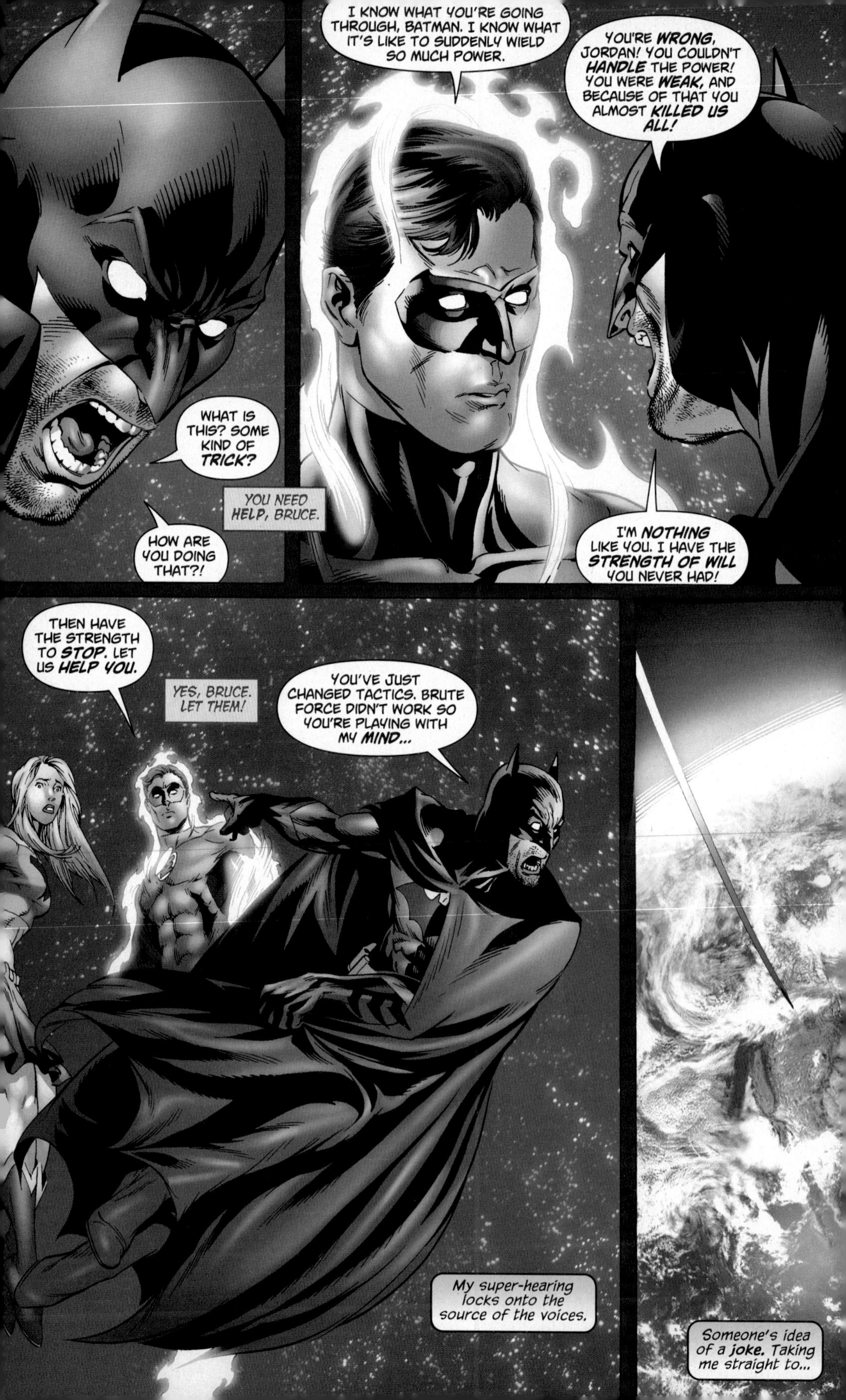
WHAT IS THIS? SOME KIND OF TRICK?
HOW ARE YOU DOING THAT?!
YOU NEED HELP, BRUCE.
I KNOW WHAT YOU'RE GOING THROUGH, BATMAN. I KNOW WHAT IT'S LIKE TO SUDDENLY WIELD SO MUCH POWER.
YOU'RE WRONG, JORDAN! YOU COULDN'T HANDLE THE POWER! YOU WERE WEAK, AND BECAUSE OF THAT YOU ALMOST KILLED US ALL!
I'M NOTHING LIKE YOU. I HAVE THE STRENGTH OF WILL YOU NEVER HAD!
THEN HAVE THE STRENGTH TO STOP. LET US HELP YOU.
YES, BRUCE. LET THEM!
YOU'VE JUST CHANGED TACTICS. BRUTE FORCE DIDN'T WORK SO YOU'RE PLAYING WITH MY MIND...
My super-hearing locks onto the source of the voices.
Someone's idea of a joke. Taking me straight to...

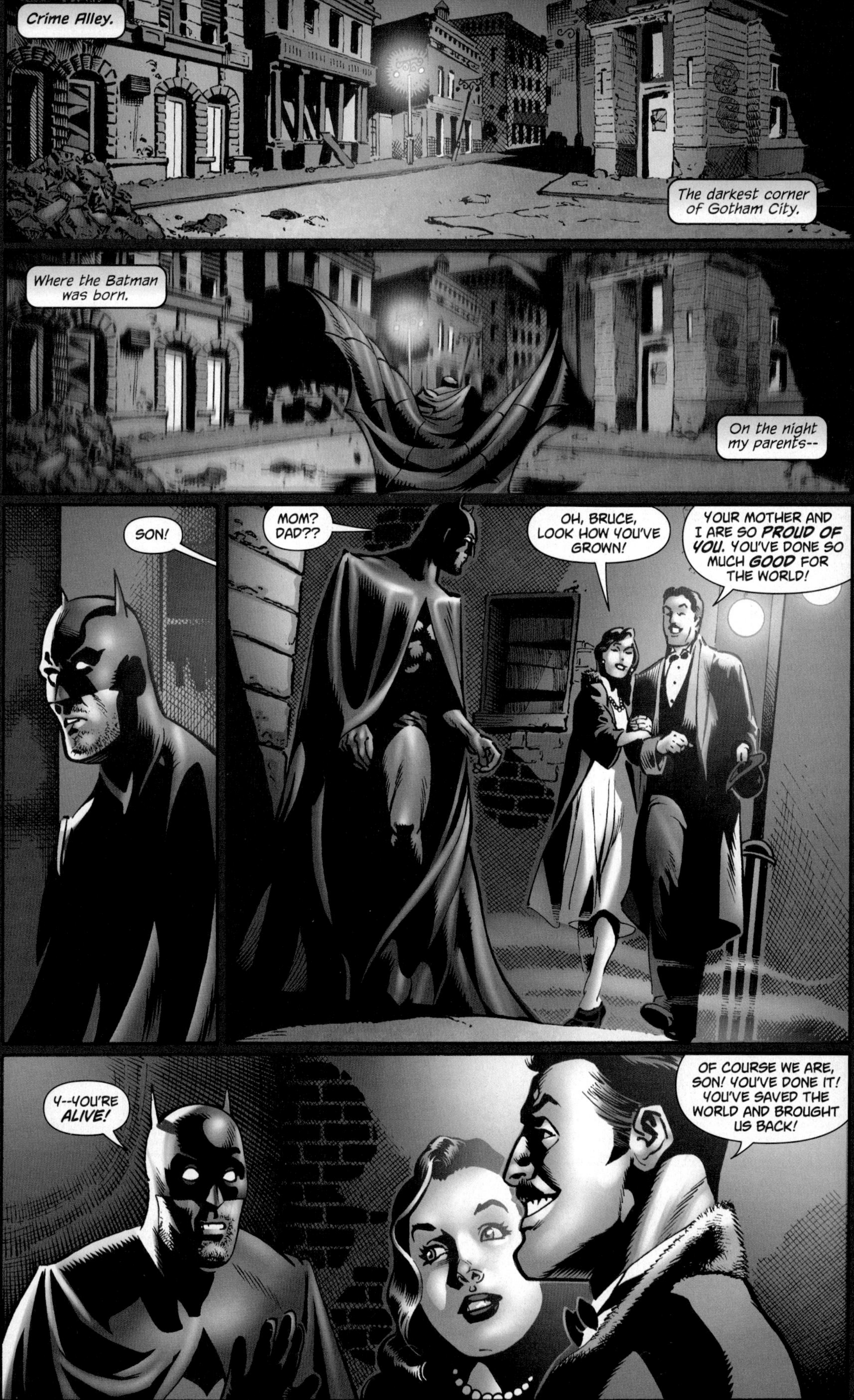
Crime Alley.
The darkest corner of Gotham City.
Where the Batman was born.
On the night my parents--
SON!
MOM? DAD??
OH, BRUCE, LOOK HOW YOU'VE GROWN!
YOUR MOTHER AND I ARE SO PROUD OF YOU. YOU'VE DONE SO MUCH GOOD FOR THE WORLD!
Y--YOU'RE ALIVE!
OF COURSE WE ARE, SON! YOU'VE DONE IT! YOU'VE SAVED THE WORLD AND BROUGHT US BACK!

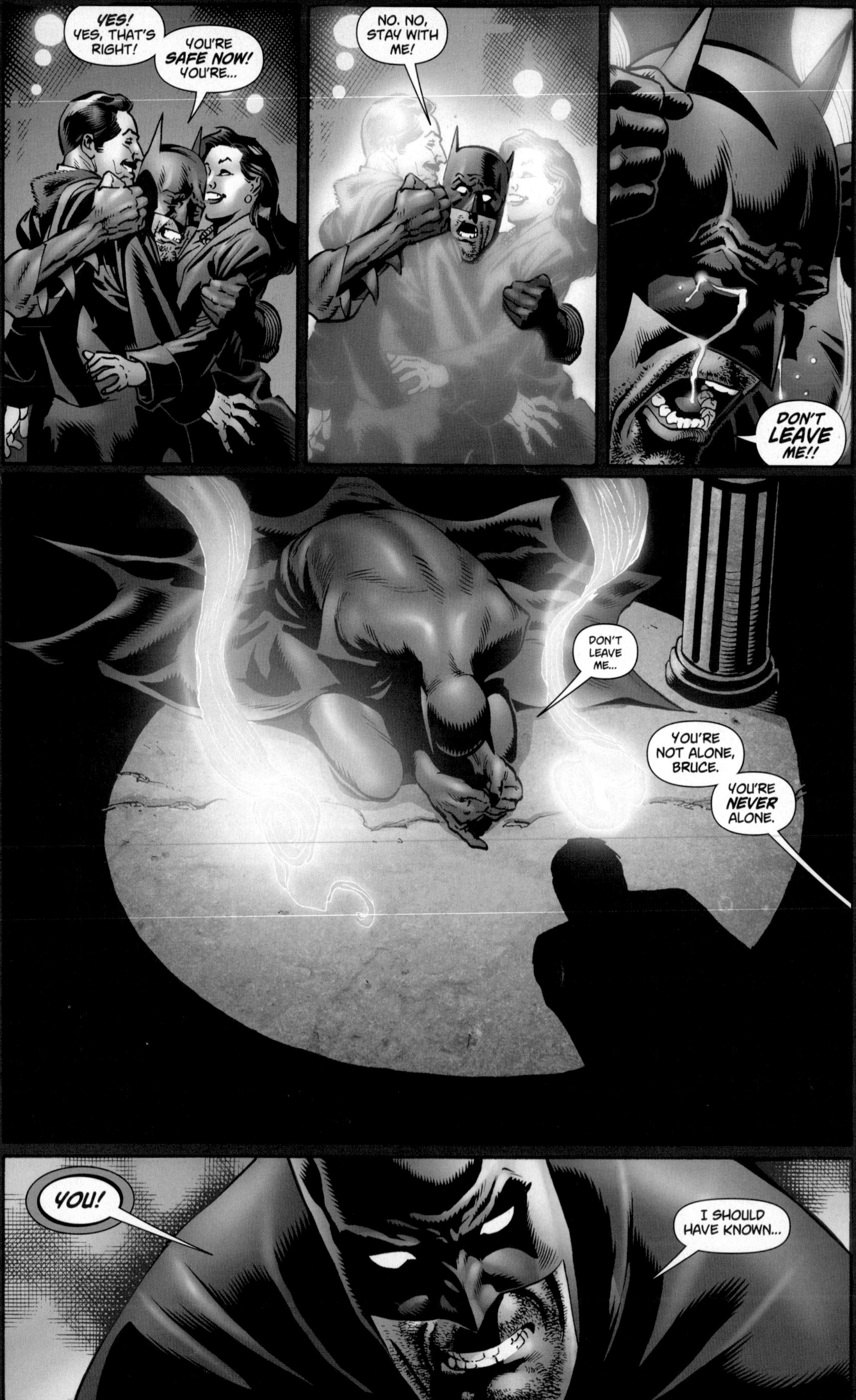
YES! YES, THAT'S RIGHT!
YOU'RE SAFE NOW! YOU'RE...
NO. NO, STAY WITH ME!
DON'T LEAVE ME!!
DON'T LEAVE ME...
YOU'RE NOT ALONE, BRUCE.
YOU'RE NEVER ALONE.
YOU!
I SHOULD HAVE KNOWN...

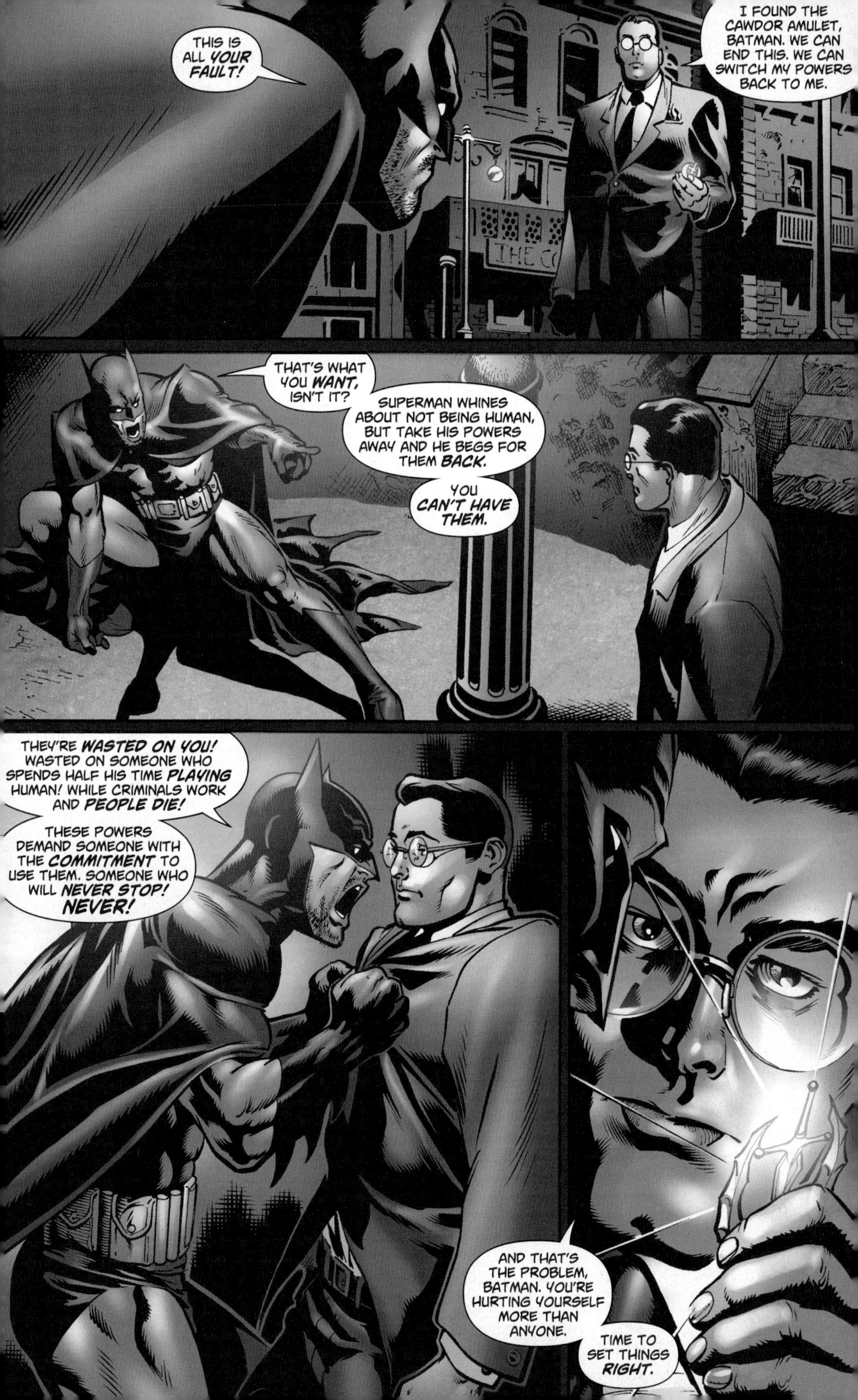
THIS IS ALL *YOUR FAULT!*
I FOUND THE CAWDOR AMULET, BATMAN. WE CAN END THIS. WE CAN SWITCH MY POWERS BACK TO ME.
THE C
THAT'S WHAT YOU *WANT,* ISN'T IT?
SUPERMAN WHINES ABOUT NOT BEING HUMAN, BUT TAKE HIS POWERS AWAY AND HE BEGS FOR THEM *BACK.*
YOU *CAN'T HAVE THEM.*
THEY'RE *WASTED ON YOU!* WASTED ON SOMEONE WHO SPENDS HALF HIS TIME *PLAYING* HUMAN! WHILE CRIMINALS WORK AND *PEOPLE DIE!*
THESE POWERS DEMAND SOMEONE WITH THE *COMMITMENT* TO USE THEM. SOMEONE WHO WILL *NEVER STOP! NEVER!*
AND THAT'S THE PROBLEM, BATMAN. YOU'RE HURTING YOURSELF MORE THAN ANYONE.
TIME TO SET THINGS *RIGHT.*

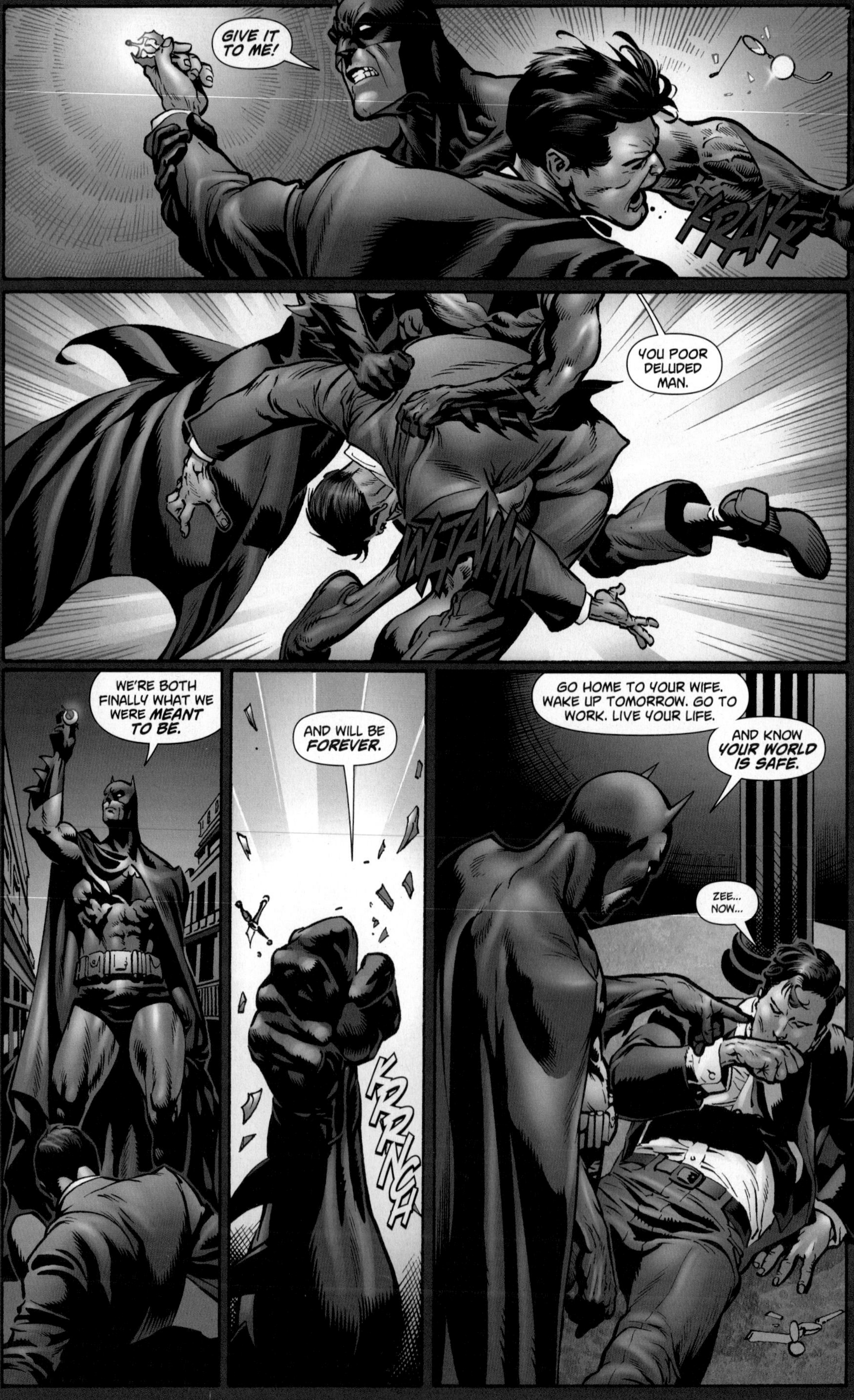
GIVE IT TO ME!
KRAK!
YOU POOR DELUDED MAN.
WHAMM
WE'RE BOTH FINALLY WHAT WE WERE MEANT TO BE.
AND WILL BE FOREVER.
KRRNCH
GO HOME TO YOUR WIFE. WAKE UP TOMORROW. GO TO WORK. LIVE YOUR LIFE.
AND KNOW YOUR WORLD IS SAFE.
ZEE... NOW...

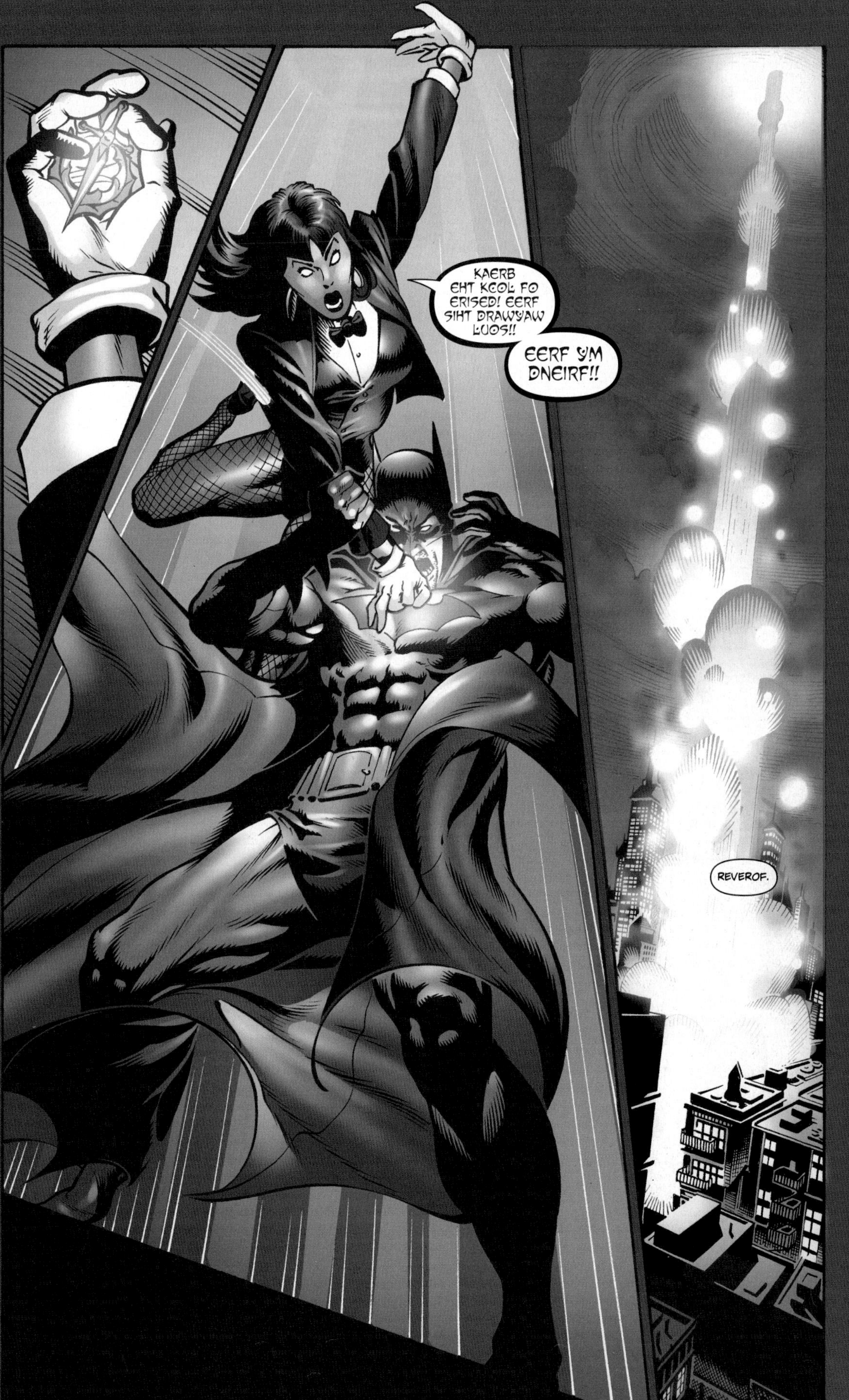
KAERB EHT KCOL FO ERISED! EERF SIHT DRAWYAW LUOS!!
EERF YM DNEIRF!!
REVEROF.

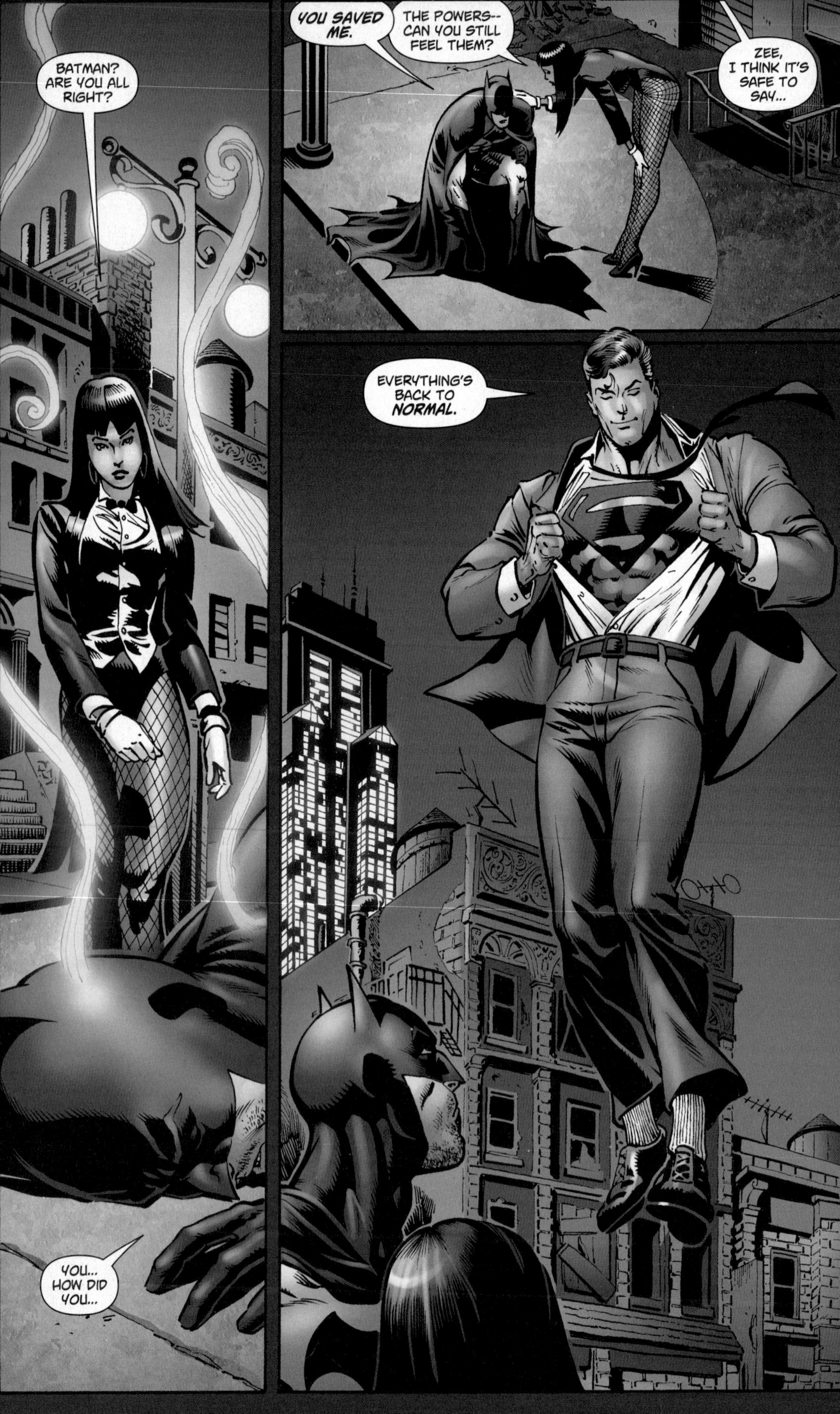
BATMAN? ARE YOU ALL RIGHT?
YOU... HOW DID YOU...
YOU SAVED ME.
THE POWERS-- CAN YOU STILL FEEL THEM?
ZEE, I THINK IT'S SAFE TO SAY...
EVERYTHING'S BACK TO NORMAL.

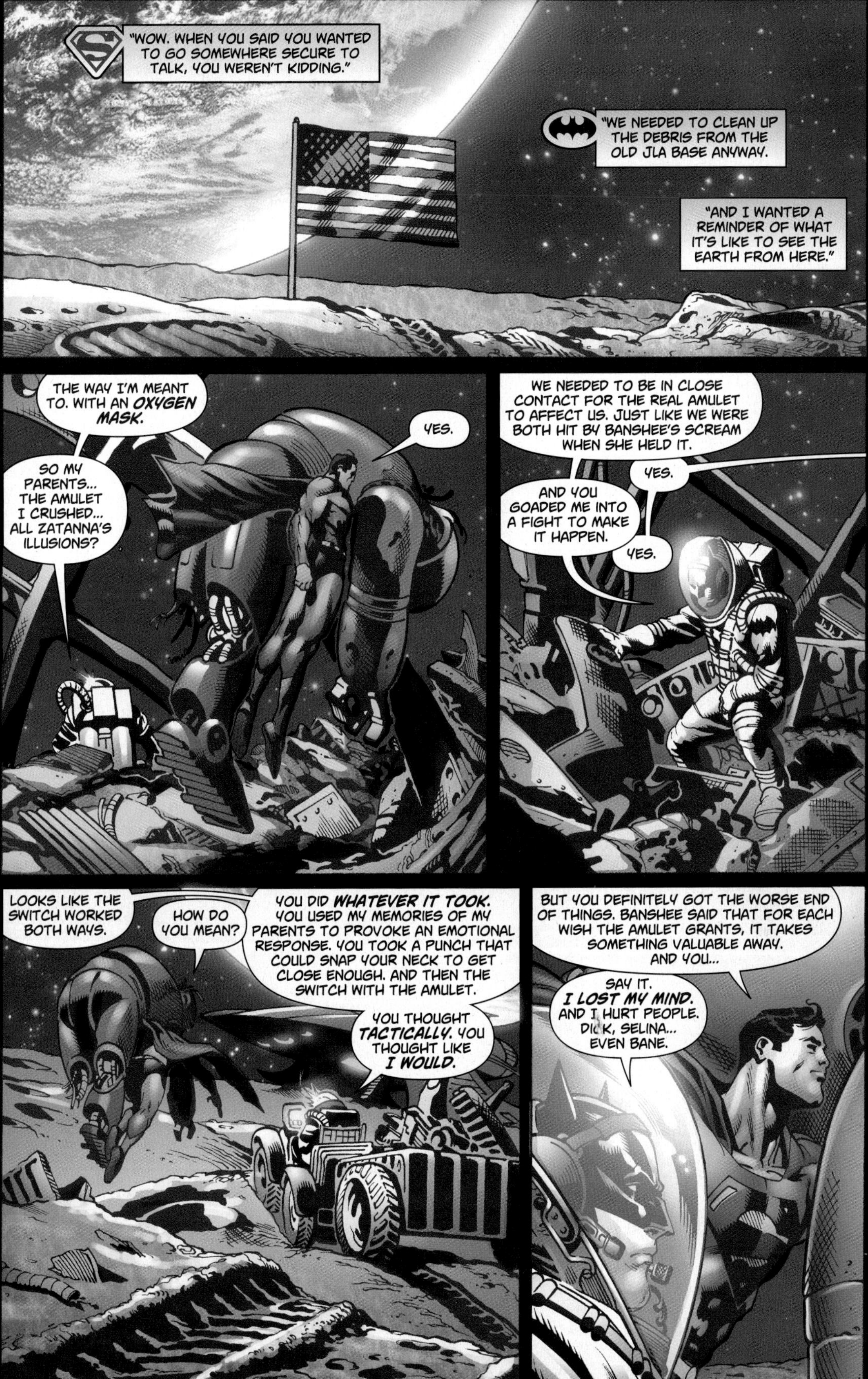
"WOW. WHEN YOU SAID YOU WANTED TO GO SOMEWHERE SECURE TO TALK, YOU WEREN'T KIDDING."
"WE NEEDED TO CLEAN UP THE DEBRIS FROM THE OLD JLA BASE ANYWAY.
"AND I WANTED A REMINDER OF WHAT IT'S LIKE TO SEE THE EARTH FROM HERE."
THE WAY I'M MEANT TO. WITH AN OXYGEN MASK.
YES.
SO MY PARENTS... THE AMULET I CRUSHED... ALL ZATANNA'S ILLUSIONS?
WE NEEDED TO BE IN CLOSE CONTACT FOR THE REAL AMULET TO AFFECT US. JUST LIKE WE WERE BOTH HIT BY BANSHEE'S SCREAM WHEN SHE HELD IT.
YES.
AND YOU GOADED ME INTO A FIGHT TO MAKE IT HAPPEN.
YES.
LOOKS LIKE THE SWITCH WORKED BOTH WAYS.
HOW DO YOU MEAN?
YOU DID WHATEVER IT TOOK. YOU USED MY MEMORIES OF MY PARENTS TO PROVOKE AN EMOTIONAL RESPONSE. YOU TOOK A PUNCH THAT COULD SNAP YOUR NECK TO GET CLOSE ENOUGH. AND THEN THE SWITCH WITH THE AMULET.
YOU THOUGHT TACTICALLY. YOU THOUGHT LIKE I WOULD.
BUT YOU DEFINITELY GOT THE WORSE END OF THINGS. BANSHEE SAID THAT FOR EACH WISH THE AMULET GRANTS, IT TAKES SOMETHING VALUABLE AWAY. AND YOU...
SAY IT. I LOST MY MIND. AND I HURT PEOPLE. DICK, SELINA... EVEN BANE.

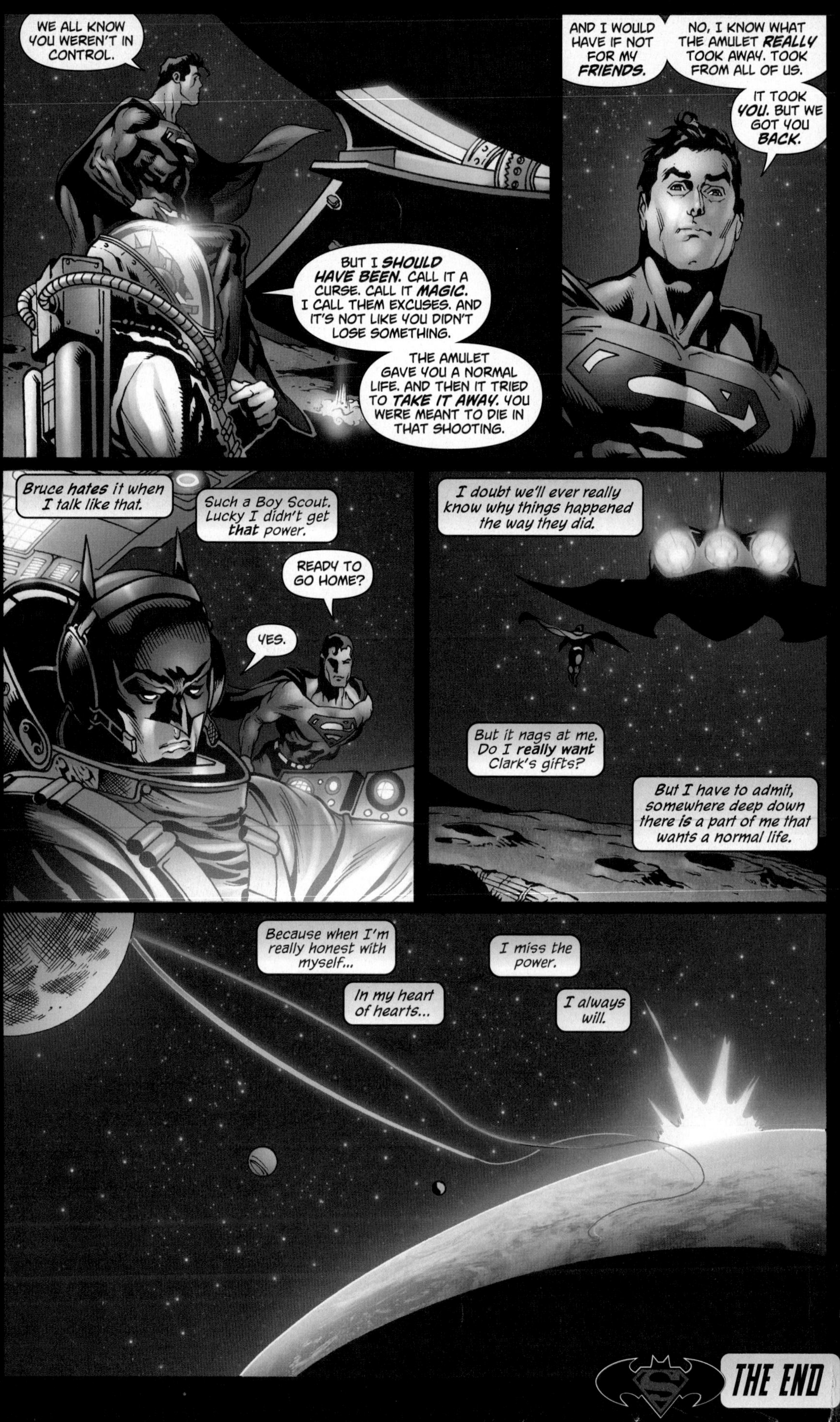
WE ALL KNOW YOU WEREN'T IN CONTROL.
BUT I SHOULD HAVE BEEN. CALL IT A CURSE. CALL IT MAGIC. I CALL THEM EXCUSES. AND IT'S NOT LIKE YOU DIDN'T LOSE SOMETHING.
THE AMULET GAVE YOU A NORMAL LIFE. AND THEN IT TRIED TO TAKE IT AWAY. YOU WERE MEANT TO DIE IN THAT SHOOTING.
AND I WOULD HAVE IF NOT FOR MY FRIENDS.
NO, I KNOW WHAT THE AMULET REALLY TOOK AWAY. TOOK FROM ALL OF US.
IT TOOK YOU. BUT WE GOT YOU BACK.
Bruce hates it when I talk like that.
Such a Boy Scout. Lucky I didn't get that power.
READY TO GO HOME?
YES.
I doubt we'll ever really know why things happened the way they did.
But it nags at me. Do I really want Clark's gifts?
But I have to admit, somewhere deep down there is a part of me that wants a normal life.
Because when I'm really honest with myself...
In my heart of hearts...
I miss the power.
I always will.
THE END

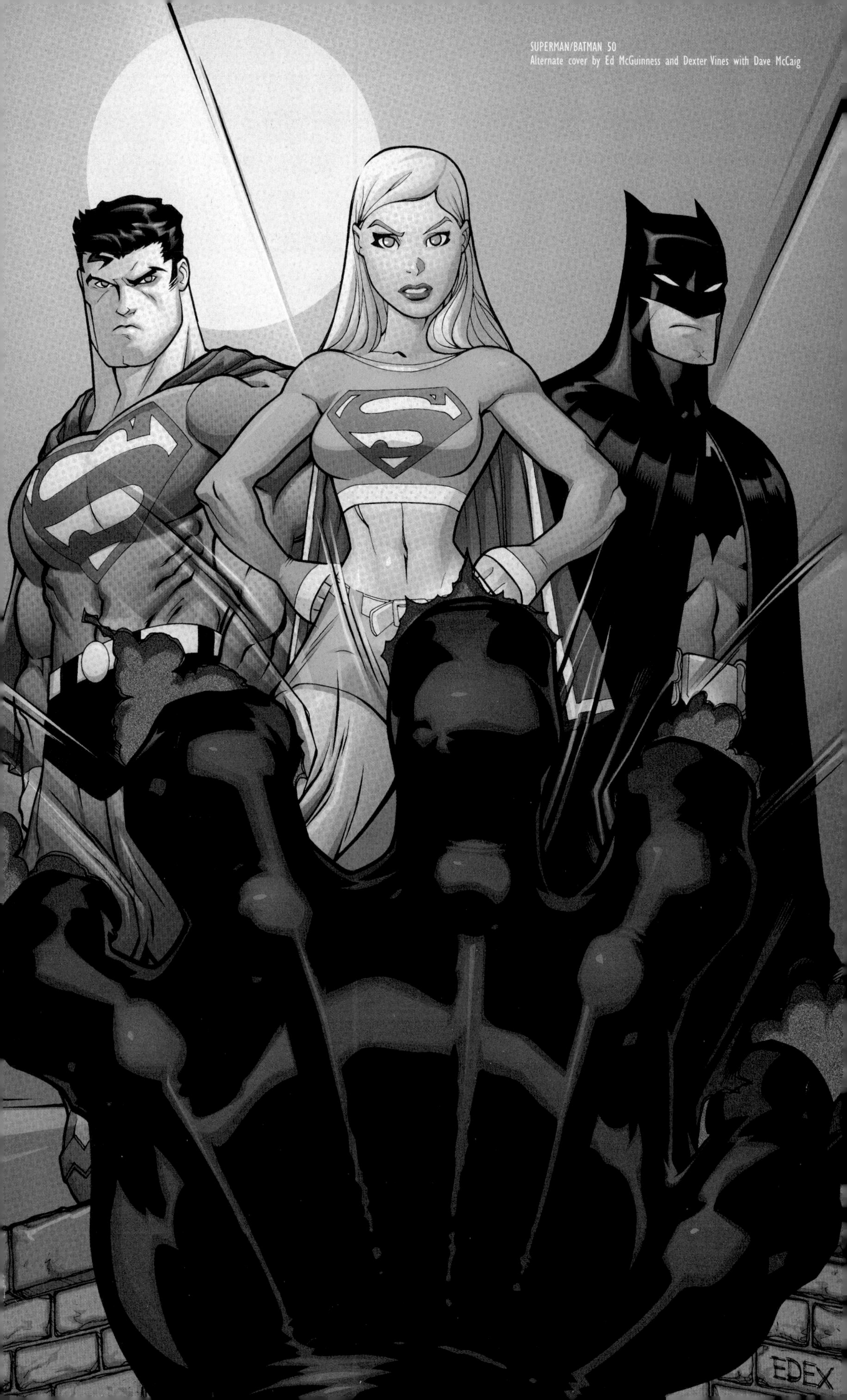
EDEX

SUPERMAN/BATMAN 50
Alternate cover by Ed McGuinness and Dexter Vines with Dave McCaig

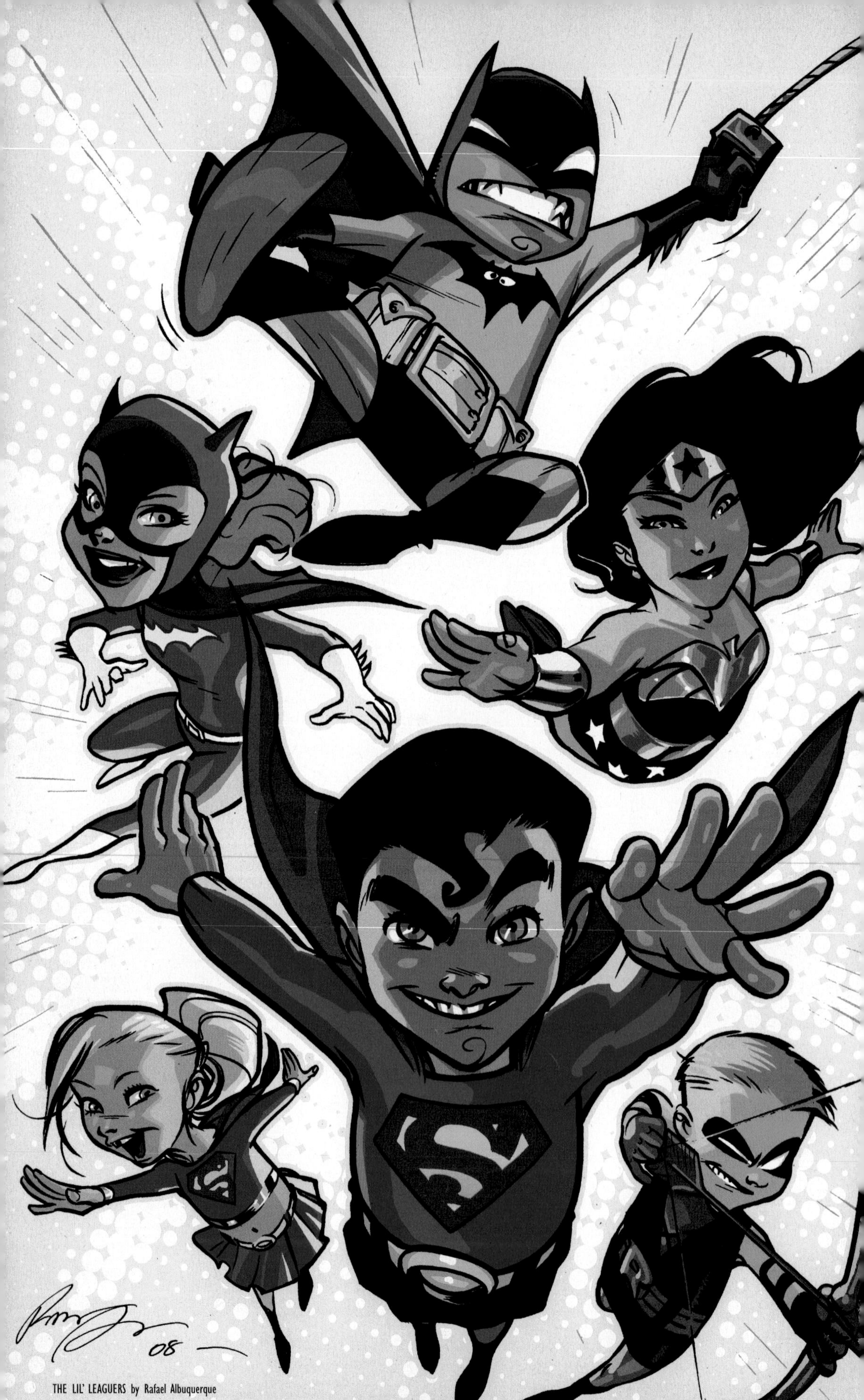

THE LIL' LEAGUERS by Rafael Albuquerque

# MORE CLASSIC TALES OF THE DARK KNIGHT

BATMAN: HUSH
VOLUME ONE

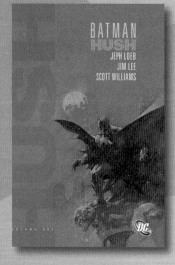

BATMAN
HUSH
JEPH LOEB
JIM LEE
SCOTT WILLIAMS

**JEPH LOEB**
**JIM LEE**

BATMAN: HUSH
VOLUME TWO

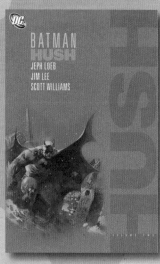

BATMAN
HUSH
JEPH LOEB
JIM LEE
SCOTT WILLIAMS

**JEPH LOEB**
**JIM LEE**

BATMAN:
THE LONG HALLOWEEN

JEPH LOEB TIM SALE
BATMAN
THE LONG HALLOWEEN

**JEPH LOEB**
**TIM SALE**

BATMAN:
DARK VICTORY

JEPH LOEB TIM SALE
BATMAN
Dark Victory

**JEPH LOEB**
**TIM SALE**

BATMAN:
HAUNTED KNIGHT

From the Eisner Award-winning creators
JEPH LOEB TIM SALE
BATMAN
HAUNTED KNIGHT

**JEPH LOEB**
**TIM SALE**

BATMAN:
YEAR 100

Batman
Year 100
by PAUL POPE
with JOSE VILLARRUBIA

**PAUL POPE**

SEARCH THE GRAPHIC NOVELS SECTION OF
**DCCOMICS.COM**
FOR ART AND INFORMATION ON ALL OF OUR BOOKS!

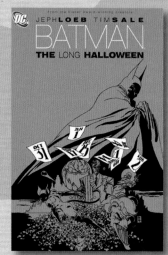

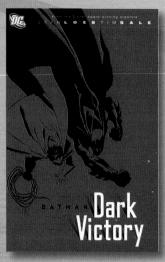

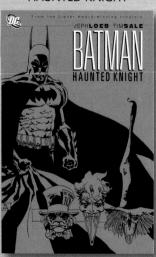

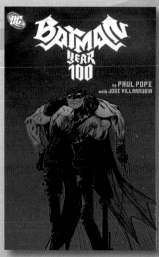